Season with Solti

SEASON WITH SOLTI

A Year in the Life
of the Chicago Symphony

William Barry Furlong

Macmillan Publishing Co., Inc.
NEW YORK
Collier Macmillan Publishers
LONDON

Macmillan Publishing Co., Inc.
866 Third Avenue, New York, N.Y. 10022
Collier-Macmillan Canada Ltd.

Library of Congress Cataloging in Publication Data

Furlong, William Barry.
  Season with Solti.

  1. Solti, Sir Georg, 1912–   2. Chicago Symphony
Orchestra.   I. Title.
ML220.8.C52S96   785'.06'277311   74-17446
ISBN 0-02-542000-3

First Printing 1974

Printed in the United States of America

Photographs by Arthur Shay

CONTENTS

To the men and women of
the Chicago Symphony Orchestra

OVERTURE

Just before eight o'clock in the evening, the long black limousine swings off the boulevard, down a side street, and into an alley near Chicago's Loop. It glides to a stop at a shadowed back door to a seventy-year-old building. The man who emerges moves a trifle awkwardly. He has a neck problem, developed through years at his work, that prevents him from moving his head easily from side to side. His formal wear—white tie and tails—appears to fit poorly and his complexion is a little gray: he's been fighting a cold and he's been sleeping poorly. ("My little girl got us up at four o'clock the other morning and we did not sleep the day.") Georg Solti is not a young man; he was sixty-two in the autumn of 1973 and he is eternally apprehensive about his energy level meeting the demands of his work. "At eight o'clock," he told me later, "I was *daid*. I was not sure I could do it. I did not think I could go on."

He steps into a tiny two-man elevator and is lowered, with a security guard, to the basement. The area, brightly lighted, has bland, cream-colored walls and one strikingly garish note: the huge pillar adjacent to his dressing room is painted a bright red—"to keep people from bumping into it." Some of his players are still in the green-carpeted locker room. Others are on the stage and a few are in the corridor, hoping to catch a glimpse of him, a glance of recognition from him. For the most part, all they are producing in these moments is the anarchic cacaphony of men preoccupied with interior things.

—The principal cellist is checking the strings on his instrument ("I break the A and D strings about once every four days, even though they're made of steel wire coated with chromium," says Frank Miller).

—The principal bassoonist has carefully selected which of his thirty reeds he'll need for this performance ("for a Beethoven symphony, I'll need a heavier-sounding reed than for a Haydn," says Willard Elliot).

—The principal oboist and the principal flutist will sit down next to each other onstage but they will not speak. They have not spoken to each other for five years and they do not expect to speak for the rest of their lifetimes. It is the legacy of an old and bitter dispute, one which once threatened the tight-knit fabric of the orchestra. Today they speak only with their music and it is enough. ("I think we play better together," says oboist Ray Still, "since we stopped talking to each other.")

For a taut, tense ten minutes, the discordance of individual tuning goes on. At one time, the Chicago Symphony Orchestra tuned up, individually and collectively, before anybody appeared onstage. "We took the A together in the basement," says James Hansen, a second violinist. That was in the days of an earlier conductor who insisted that the players never practice or tune onstage and that they file onstage and off in the order in which they were seated and ranked.

Now this conductor waits in his dressing room, sipping tea poured from a thermos. He expects that the players will find their seats and tune their instruments in the way they think best. With one minute to go he gets up and checks, almost reflexively, the pocket in the tails of his formal wear; he has two bonbons tucked in the pocket, so he can retrieve them and nibble them in case he feels the need for a surge of "energy" while on the podium. He marches to the elevator, rises to stage level, and pauses at the door to the left rear of the orchestra. He will be precisely forty seconds late.

The houselights are dimmed for a moment. He pushes open the door, strides onstage, and marches down the narrow aisle between the first and second violins, bald head down and slightly to the side, as if he's plowing the furrow of some unseen wave. The energy is coming back to him now, the years are falling away.

As he steps onto the podium, he radiates a sudden authority. The players are spread out before him, bright-eyed and alert as blackbirds at breakfast. He turns and responds to the applause of the audience with a quick, Teutonic, noncommittal bow. Then he turns back to the orchestra, raises his arms, and spreads his feet elaborately in his—as one player calls it—kung fu stance. There is a hush, a vestigial snapping to attention. This is the world's most renowned conductor about to lead the world's greatest orchestra, and it is a moment to be caught in history.

He gives a downbeat, the orchestra responds with an opening chord in the key of B-flat. And the season is on.

It appears so effortless—the rising magic of this magnificent instrument. It is not only a magic of the moment but one woven into the seminal past of symphonic music. Under its early conductors, Theodore Thomas and Frederick Stock and later Fritz Reiner, the Chicago Symphony Orchestra evoked the gray frown of gutted facades, the musty memories of a München that never was, the deep sonorous rumble of Wagner marching on to heaven to lay out his terms to God. The Chicago Symphony came to be known, in those days, as an excellent *American* orchestra; it was only rarely heard outside its own city and it was never heard outside the United States. Later, the sound was altered; it became glossier, perhaps subtler, and in the mid-to-late-1960s it was embroidered with an airy Gallic elegance and hard tonal sheen. The orchestra seemed to stumble for a while and the talk of the Chicago Symphony subsided, as did its accomplishments. Some thought, forever.

Then came Solti—bald, intense, filled with a machismo that only Wagner could understand. He mellowed the orchestra's hard-diamond glints, shaped and honed its sonorous rumble, and built on it a logical edifice of telling detail and perfect dramatic emphasis that could leave even the most indifferent of audiences spellbound. Thus in one long gush, like a city that survived a siege, the Chicago Symphony came to greatness. On a world scale.

What happens in this season is a reflection—and a continuation—of that greatness. It was not, in candor, built alone on a cascade of flashing arpeggios or the darkling glances of a single conductor. Rather it was built on a million tiny details, the minutiae of men and music, that affect and color every minute and hour, every day and week of their lives, onstage and off. "Behind every musician," wrote Deems Taylor, "lurks a man who is fully as interesting as the art he pursues."

All this detail has been, until now, invisible. For it is the essence of the great symphonic act that, as it happens, it remains a mystery in which hundreds or even thousands of people—in the orchestra, in the audience, on the staff—fit one fragment of a total secret together, none of them quite knowing in advance the shape of the whole.

What happens in the following pages is an attempt to explore part of that secret. No one man can tell it all, either now or much later. The transaction in creed and culture by which such an orchestra comes to greatness is so vastly complicated that even those most intimately involved in it can never know more than a fragment of it. But it was my belief that some segment of the secret might be unlocked by looking at the men as well as the music, by examining the fears, doubts, angers, and vaulting ambitions of the individuals who make up the orchestra, by searching the trials of hope, sorrow, scorn, and selflessness that go into their reach for greatness.

There are some qualities that all great orchestras have in common: they can, for example, save a charlatan and make him seem like a Toscanini on the podium. There are some qualities that they do not have in common: the Cleveland Orchestra, under George Szell, was a great ensemble made up of generally anonymous men who overcame their anonymity by playing with unparalleled unity. The Chicago Symphony, by way of contrast, is a virtuoso orchestra—it is made up of many "stars" in the musical world; it was harder for them—given the primal instincts of the musician—to sublimate their skills within the orchestra, but the manner and style with which they've done it have produced not only an incredibly unified sound but a personality of heightened exaltation.

It is the differences that we address in this text. For it is the force of the individual personality that gives the Chicago Symphony its special dimension. There are, to be sure, many who tend to regard all symphony players as middle-aged, intellectual longhairs—the operative put-down of an earlier age—who are locked in a monklike cloister where they devote themselves to esoteric sounds and determined irrelevancies. It is easy to understand the seed of this thought: since symphony musicians all look alike, in their tails and concert-hall posture, it is concluded by many that they must *be* alike, different only in whether they spend their time blowing, bowing, or banging their instruments.

Quite—as we shall see—the contrary. Far from being the same in mien and appearance, the members of the Chicago Symphony are spirited, independent thinkers who are likely to disagree not only with themselves—perhaps no more than 90 percent of the time—but with their conductors. ("We still have a story that goes around the orchestra," says Sam Denov, a percussionist, "when there's something less than a great conductor on the podium—and it's always the lesser conductors, somehow, that give you the worst time—that 'If he doesn't watch himself, we'll play exactly the way he's conducting.' ") Nor are they weak and effete intellectuals. They have the intellectual vigor to speak out on their situation and their leaders, including Georg Solti, with a candor and fearlessness that is customarily absent from business, entertainment, sports, and other forms of the arts. That is not a passing muscularity: it was the members of the Chicago Symphony Orchestra who challenged the power of James Caesar Petrillo, for forty years the autocratic czar of the musicians' union, and ultimately helped break him, sweeping him from office and electing a more democratic administration to run the local.

Beyond all that, it can be said that the men and women of the Chicago Symphony live in a contemporary world filled with the everyday problems of commuting and paychecks and pension systems; of lockouts and love affairs and lost hopes from the past: Frank Miller, perhaps the greatest living orchestral cellist, dreamed—as a boy—only of going to Yale and playing baseball under T. A. D. Jones. He failed that ambition because his older brothers "persuaded" him to stick to playing the cello. ("They told me," he says, "that I would have nothing when I was forty." Today, past forty, he earns a salary of $35,456 a year playing the cello and enjoys a renown, a respect, and a satisfaction that very few baseball stars ever know, even at the peaks of their careers.)

They pursue their works despite the irritations, aggravations, illnesses, and handicaps that attack all workers. Willard Elliot, the principal bassoon player, is plagued by a herpes virus that leaves him with cold sores on his lips in much of the winter. Arnold Jacobs, the principal tuba player—who needs, of course, a huge air passage from lung to mouth—has suffered from bronchial asthma for the last three years and must spray his throat with a bronchodilator before going onstage. Adolph Herseth, the principal trumpet player, was in an automobile accident in 1952—"I broke the steering wheel off with my lower jaw"—that split his lower lip (he had fifteen stitches taken in it), killed the nerves leading to two of his lower teeth, and snapped off many of his other teeth at the gum line. His lip was left numb, two of his teeth—knocked flat in his mouth—are brown and dead now, and others are merely crowns pegged into the bone of his jaw. But he learned a slightly different placement of the trumpet on his mouth to compensate for all the injuries. And today he is recognized not merely as the best trumpeter in the world but—in the view of some members of the Chicago Symphony—as the best trumpeter who *ever* lived.

They are occupied by music but they are diverted by a variety of personal compulsions. They raise orchids, breed dachshunds, and sell grapefruit—one of the bass players has a ranch in Texas which sends out citrus fruit as Christmas packages wrapped in crinkly cellophane. They build electron microscopes, collect fossils, and speculate in real estate—one of the players owned four homes on Chicago's swank North Shore that he was renting out and would sell when real estate values in the area soared. On the whole, they tend to devote as much zeal to their avocations as to their art: "One time I got off a great three-iron shot in a motel room in Flint, Michigan," says Burl Lane, the contrabassoonist who doubles as a golfer. "I thought," he added with a beatific vision, "three people would be killed before that ball stopped bouncing off the walls."

There are other myths that come under question in a close examination of the symphony. By tradition, musicians are said to look like their instruments and the comparison is valid among some in the Chicago Symphony: clarinet players are supposed to be tall and thin, and Clark Brody, the principal clarinetist is—or was—certainly that. Trumpet players are supposed to be shorter and stocky, and Adolph Herseth, the principal trumpeter, is certainly that. But when it comes to temperament, the traditions fail. Reed instrument players are said to be touchy, oral, somewhat introverted people, the resident neurotics of the orchestra who are tormented by the knowledge that their careers hang on the reliability of tiny lengths of shaven bamboo, approximately the thickness of a thumbnail. Yet Burl Lane is an open, easy person with the taut strut of an athlete—"He's a *jock!*" says one of his colleagues—and Grover Schiltz, an oboe and English horn player, is a highly verbal man who can speak easily and authoritatively on everything from the whelping habits of the long-haired dachshund to the motifs and meanings of the Kazak prayer rug. Trumpeters have a reputation for being long on ego and short on subtlety, a notion nurtured by—or born in—the facts that (a) their playing posture is straight-ahead, even aggressive, sending sound straight out, instead of down as with the woodwinds; and (b) their position is to the rear and often raised so that they can look down on the orchestra, perhaps patronizingly. Yet Bud Herseth is anything but that. "You look at my career and you've got to think I'm a failure in life," he says cheerfully. He became first trumpet of the Chicago Symphony at the age of twenty-four—in itself a spectacular feat—and he's never had, or sought, another job. "That's why my son says, 'My dad's failure. He's never been able to get a promotion.' "

Another point: classical musicians do not necessarily come from a "hothouse" background, an eclectic, insulated background that is itself of classical music. Many members of the Chicago Symphony Orchestra had parents who possessed no contact with, much less insight about, classical music. The father of Grover Schiltz worked in metalworking factories in Aurora, Illinois. The father of Fred Spector, a first violinist, was a pharmacist in Kiev, then in Cuba, and finally in Chicago. The father of Roger Cline, a young bass player who joined the orchestra in 1973, was a cabinetmaker in Tacoma, Washington. The father of Radivoj Lah, another bass player who doubles as personnel manager for the symphony, operated a crane in a tanning plant in Waukegan, Illinois. The father of Donald Peck, the principal flutist, was a school maintenance man in Seattle, Washington. Even Music Director Georg Solti shares this distinction. For three hundred years his family baked bread for the villagers of Balatönfokájar in Hungary, and his father was distinctive in one way: he left the family business to go to Budapest and become a real estate salesman.

Nor did they all love music at the moment they first encountered it. Gordon Peters, the principal percussionist, hated the piano when he was forced to play and practice it as a youngster; a fortuitous attack of scarlet fever freed him from that and he turned eventually to the drums. Richard Graef, a flutist, hated the piano so much when he was a youth that—at the age of eight—he kicked a hole in the piano, and thus got his message across to his parents. (He wanted to play trumpet in the school band. However, his piano teacher intervened. She said Dick needed something terribly, terribly simple to play in the treble clef because "he's not very musical." Her recommendation as a "simple instrument"? The flute!)

The point is that these men and women are not lost in an aching anachronism but are celebrating a contemporary life. It is true that the Chicago Symphony does not indulge in the writhing, undulating, switched-on clamor of the "asylum," as the pop music industry likes to call itself. But neither are its members insulated from the thrust, drive, and impulse of pop music. Radivoj Lah almost left the Chicago Symphony to slap the bass in Stan Kenton's combo. Joseph Golan, the first-chair man among the second violins, leads a rock group called the Chicago Current that is made up entirely of players from the Chicago Symphony. Bud Herseth looks not to himself or to classical music but to the world of jazz and to Maynard Ferguson to identify the "greatest brass player of any kind in the last fifty years."

The fact is that the men and women of the Chicago Symphony are involved in exactly what Bob Dylan, or Blood, Sweat and Tears, or the Funky Highs are engaged in: emotion.

Symphonic music, like rock, acid, jazz, and swing, is simply emotion made audible. The emotion may be more delicate and disciplined—and certainly less sweaty—in classical music but it *is* human and it *is* as contemporary as yesterday's movie. It is, as a matter of fact, heard more often by more people in the movies than in the concert hall. A tone poem by Richard Strauss, *Also Sprach Zarathustra*, was used on the sound track of *2001: A Space Odyssey* (and more recently as background music for a TV commercial for an antacid tablet). Beethoven was used on the sound track of *Clockwork Orange*, Mozart was used on the sound track of *Elvira Madigan* and later on *Sunday, Bloody Sunday*, Mahler was used on *Death in Venice*, and Bach was used on the motion picture version of Kurt Vonnegut's *Slaughterhouse-Five*.

To be sure, there is a gap between the musical language of the man in the street and that of the creative artist. But there was a gap also in Bach's time. That the gap is greater in America than in Europe is because of the mixed nature and mixed antecedents of American music. In Europe, music developed from a religious tradition in which the organ was a primary instrument. In America, the national musical style is more closely related to the tom-tom than the organ. It is expressed through both a melancholy mood and a Dionysian impulse. There is also, of course, a streak of the prurient and erotic in modern pop music, as well as a current of masochism that is the melancholy accompaniment of teen-age life. This music has itself had an enormous vigor. Indeed, it might be said that America has exported the music of this generation to Europe with a great deal more success than Europe has exported the music of the past century to the United States.

And yet today there is a significant give-and-take between the pop music of America and the classical music that is the proud product of Europe. The opening program of the Chicago Symphony this season featured Bach's Suite no. 3 in D Major; it can be heard in a slightly different incarnation when played by the Swingle Singers (who not only play but sing the theme in wordless scat syllables—*ba ba da ba dee*). Onetime Beatle George Harrison admits that the soaring obbligato in *Penny Lane* was inspired by Bach's Second *Brandenburg* Concerto, and blues-rock singer Paul Butterfield has named Bach as his favorite composer. ("I don't always know what Bach is going to do," he has said, "but we seem to be friends.") Indeed—like many other classical composers—the beat of Bach has enjoyed unprecedented popularity in contemporary society. In 1949, there were fifteen Bach albums on the market; today there are more than five hundred, including twenty-four versions of the complete *Brandenburg* Concertos. It is, perhaps, the sense of order in Bach—and, indeed, in much classical music—that appeals to so many people who see around them a world in chaos.

There is one bromidic view of the symphony orchestra—in Chicago, as elsewhere—which has much truth in it. That is the charge of élitism. "A large segment of the public is convinced that symphony orchestras, like opera companies, are the toy of a few rich people in evening clothes who once a week go to hear an orchestra, similarly dressed, play incomprehensible music by dead composers," writes Philip Hart, who has been involved with the management of three symphony orchestras (including Chicago's). That feeling is, to a large extent, well founded; it *is* the rich—whether old-rich or new business-rich—that support most symphony orchestras, both in person and in purse. Normally, this has not been a matter of great concern to the general public, at least until symphony orchestras began receiving public funds through taxes. The Chicago Symphony was, until this moment in history, the exception in this respect: it was the only major orchestra in the nation, and in the world, that did not receive one penny in subsidy from its city government. (That tradition was broken only when the city of Chicago offered $100,000 to underwrite a portion of the costs of each of the two European tours of the Chicago Symphony.) This might be contrasted with the Berlin Philharmonic, one of the two European orchestras which might be said to stand beside the Chicago Symphony, which receives a subsidy of $1.5 million a year from the city of Berlin. The Chicago Symphony gets a $140,000 grant from the U.S. government—but the Vienna State Opera gets $6 million a year in subsidy from its national government.

The dimensions of the Chicago austerity are many. For one thing, ticket prices are high. They range from $6 to $12 a performance, which tends to take them beyond the reach of the general public. (Tickets to the Vienna State Opera cost $1 to $6 with a few standing room tickets available at 20¢ apiece.) Yet price has not hurt popularity in Chicago during the Solti era; virtually every ticket to every Solti performance in Chicago was sold out before the season began. There is, nevertheless, a deficit in running the orchestra. One reason: newcomers in the rank and file of the Chicago Symphony are paid seven times what a member of the rank and file of the Vienna State Opera gets and twice as much as the rank and file of the Berlin Philharmonic.

Still, it cannot be said that the Chicago Symphony does not suffer from the élitism that characterizes the symphony orchestra all over the country (though it is less a "plaything" than a "workthing" for the élitists in Chicago who have to raise money to support it). This is not the goal or desire of Music Director Solti. He prefers that it possess an earthy commonality that would make the orchestra "the property of all the people." Accordingly, the Chicago Symphony in this season not only presented ninety concerts in Orchestra Hall but:

—Presented twenty-four youth concerts for grade school children.

—Sent its members three hundred times to public schools in the Chicago area to perform and explain classical music to the students.

—Played four times on college campuses from Northern Illinois University to the University of Connecticut.

—Supported and nurtured the Civic Orchestra for young people who might one day develop into symphony musicians.

—Played ten concerts in nearby Milwaukee (albeit as part of a profit-making subscription series).

On the whole, it is a long season and an exhilarating one. This is how it began.

INTERLUDE: The Waning Summer

T he sun lay on the grass and warmed it. In the shade under the grass, the insects moved—ants and flies and gnats that nick and nibble the ankles. Later there would be drop craters in the dust where the rain had fallen and clean splashes on the corn in the fields far to the westward.

The summer season opened on a day limned in light and dark. In the evening, before the concert, there would be a heavy dense rain, followed by bright sunshine. The program featured Beethoven's mighty Missa Solemnis with the Chicago Symphony Orchestra and Chorus—in their less formal incarnation of the summer—under the direction of James Levine, music director of Ravinia Park, who also is principal conductor of the Metropolitan Opera in New York City. It would be heard again early in the fall under Solti. So would much of the Beethoven to be played here this summer.

But Ravinia, a verdant picnic-and-pavilion parkland setting some twenty-one miles north of Chicago, would not be of Beethoven alone. Or even of the classics. There would be a night of Norma and of Nero—Beverly Sills featured in the former, Peter Nero in the latter—as well as nights of Bach and Brubeck, Mozart and Mahler, Goodman and Gershwin. There would be nights of John Denver and Mischa Dichter, of Arthur Fiedler and José Feliciano, of Lotte Lenya and Alicia de Larrocha. There would be folk festivals and film festivals and art exhibits and the Joffrey Ballet. And now, as the summer waned, the members of the Chicago Symphony would be off in those pursuits that distinguish them as men as well as musicians.

Just before Labor Day, Frank Miller, the principal cellist, was preparing and producing his own version of the first Gilbert and Sullivan opera. "Gilbert and Sullivan is my great hobby in music," he says. "I've conducted more than three hundred performances of Gilbert and Sullivan." In 1871, Gilbert and Sullivan collaborated—for the first time—on a comic opera called Thespis. It took three *weeks to create and it ran eighty nights at London's Gaiety Theatre. (Gilbert called it a "crude and ineffective work." Sullivan wrote to his mother that he had "rarely seen anything so beautiful put upon the stage.") Later Sullivan's score was destroyed in a warehouse fire, and in 1949 Frank Miller, then Toscanini's principal cellist with the NBC Symphony, undertook to rewrite the Sullivan parts, using his own impressions of style, vocal contour, and orchestration to imitate—but not duplicate—Sir Arthur's musical language. He conducted it first in January 1953 with New York's Gilbert and Sullivan company ("The New York Times gave it a nice write-up") and later that spring on Long Island. Then the score lay dusty and dormant for twenty years.*

"Until we decided to do it this year," says Frank Miller. The "we" included the Savoy-Aires, a G&S opera company that Miller organized nine years ago from the chic North Shore of Chicago. It was to be accompanied by the Evanston Symphony Orchestra, which Miller also conducts.

The text of Thespis by Gilbert had survived but was "arranged and edited" by Miller to compensate for the "tipsy" balance in the original structure. Miller also did not use the fragment of two Sullivan songs that had escaped the fire; in his devotion to G&S, he felt he should do better than G&S.

His audiences agreed. For four nights as the Labor Day weekend approached, the Savoy-Aires and the Evanston Symphony presented the Gilbert and Sullivan and Miller version of Thespis to a packed-house crowd in a high school auditorium.

"Next year we'll do Pinafore," says Miller.

And maybe let Gilbert and Sullivan have their own way with it.

Burl Lane headed for the golf course. Best score he shot all year: "A seventy-three." . . . Donald Peck headed for Carmel, California. When he got home and found that the orchestra still was not ready to play—it hadn't settled its labor disputes—he turned right around and drove back to Carmel. . . .

Tom Howell, the twenty-five-year-old associate horn player, headed for a month of backpacking with his girl friend in Rocky Mountain National Park in Colorado and later in the national parks and forests of the West Coast. "We tried to go backpacking in Crater Lake, Oregon, but they have very bad facilities and the fire hazards were extremely bad so that you couldn't make campfires." That didn't bother him—"because if you backpack you usually like to carry a little stove." But the hot summer weather had dried up the little streams in the park "and you couldn't pack in enough water for those great distances." . . .

Joseph Guastafeste, the principal bass player, headed with his family for the island they'd "discovered" in the Caribbean. "No one seems to have heard about this island—very little has been said about it. But it was always talked about in the books as about the most 'lush, plush island in the whole West Indies.'" The airline schedules in and out of the island were so uncertain that "we spent a week trying to get out of the island instead of just sitting back and enjoying it." . . .

Louis Sudler, chairman of the board of trustees of the Orchestral Association, parent body of the Chicago Symphony, headed for his special refuge—a little town in Michigan, on a bay near Mackinac Island, where he has his boat docked. It is

called the Pagliacci *and it is a sixty-foot Chris-Craft with three master cabins and accommodations for nine people (including a crew of three). He has a Boston whaler mounted on its davit and he and his friends go cruising in the nooks and crannies of the Great Lakes shorelines, looking for places to swim and to fish and to spend a comfortable night. "It's a good way to get prepared for the storm—I don't mean literally the storms on the lake; I mean just for the things that come along in life.". . .*

Sam Denov, one of the percussionists, thought he was headed for law school. He'd gotten his college degree—a baccalaureate in labor education—in July, after two and one half years of extra-time study, and then, approaching fifty, he decided to seek a degree in law. "If I can work it out this semester," he said.

Willard Elliot, the principal bassoonist, headed for the greenhouse just off the sunporch of his suburban home. All around him was a wild burst of color—azaleas and hibiscuses and orchids. He loves the orchids best and grows them for his own pleasure. The azaleas and hibiscuses would grow through wintertime—the temperature in the greenhouse would be maintained at 55 to 65 degrees, even through the harsh winter that was approaching. He touched a small orchid with orange petals dappled by red dots. "This one starts blooming in August and stays in bloom through October," he said gently. The orchids that are in flower are his reminder of the joy of life and its transience.

Vicki Graef, the wife of flutist Dick Graef, came home from a summer workshop for her church group in Colorado—"there was an old, old organ, an 1887 organ, in the building where we held our meetings and I played that. And there were bats who'd made their nests in the pipes, so just turning on the organ would blow all this bat dust out. . . ." She didn't realize then that such dust might carry some very subtle, ominous organisms. Now, at home in Glencoe, she touched the left side of her face and noticed a hard little lump in front of her ear, near the hairline. "It felt like I chipped a bone or something. It was very small," she says.

INTERMEZZO

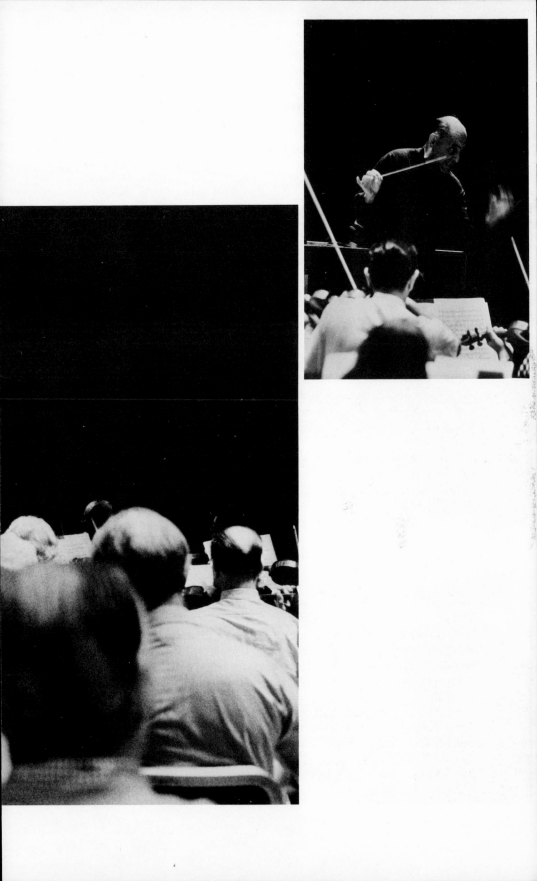

The Season in Conception

All through southern Europe, the heat of summer lingered into autumn. In early October, the sun rose like a hot ingot over the shadowed hills of Tuscany. In the cloistered white studio in Roccamare—"Rock on the sea"—the air was warm and the gentle wash of the Tyrrhenian Sea could be heard on the nearby beaches. "No pollution," said Georg Solti with great satisfaction. "No ship traffic—very few ships, so no pollution."

He was seated at a long wooden table in the studio of his retreat in Tuscany. "It is five hundred years old, this table!" he said. He pounded it with a hand. "A refectory table! Monks ate at this table five hundred years ago!" He swatted a mosquito.

On the table before him was a score of a violin concerto by Bohuslav Martinů that the Chicago Symphony would play early in the season. It had been discovered in the Hans Moldenhauer Archive at Northwestern University and a copy of the score had been sent to Solti. "I have the greatest headache," he said. "The notes are very, very little. Very hard to read. They write very nicely in the photographic manuscript; they write very nicely but it is just not real. It is too small. So I have a hell of a headache trying to read."

He came here to rest and study—to embrace the dying sun of summer and indulge the shade of the umbrella pines. London is his home. Hungary is his birthplace. Germany was his professional incubator. France is his twin podium —for opera and the concert hall. Chicago—or at least its symphony—is his love. But Italy is his refuge.

Even in rest and refuge, half of all his waking hours are given over to music. He was a late starter in conducting: he did not get his first job until he was almost thirty-four years old—"Today I would tell a person, 'No! It cannot be done. You are too late.' " Now, in his sixties, he is still pursued by the late-start syndrome; he feels he must work harder than others to make up for lost time. "Work does not hurt me." It exalts him. He comes early to his retreat by the sea—often starting just after dawn—and studies his music for five to seven hours. It does not drain him, it fulfills him; studying his scores renews him much as a steak renews a starving man.

He projects the strength of his labors. He is a sturdy man, not tall, not heavy, muscular without trying to be so. ("I get almost no exercise but what is in music," he says.) His expression is of a man in the full power of his years. He has a mobile mouth, and cheekbones that are strong and prominent—Magyar cheekbones —but his face is ruled by his eyes. Dark eyes and bold ones. They hold you in their grip when he is absorbed in your conversation; they dart—usually downward and away—when he is irritated or distressed. He cannot conceal what he feels. His face shows all of it.

In a sense, that is fortunate. For his facial, and body, language helps make up for the exotica of his verbal language. Solti is serenely confident that he speaks perfect English. His conviction is reinforced by occasional episodes of unlikely justification. Some years ago, when his wife called room service in a Chicago hotel, she could not, with her very British English, make herself understood to those accustomed to Chicago English. Solti picked up the phone and in his heavily accented Hungarian English—which lacks the high polish and "perfection" of, say, Zsa Zsa Gabor's Hungarian English—made his needs clear. He is not always so successful in reaching the more distant players in the Chicago Symphony Orchestra, at least by his English alone. "They think it's Chinese," says one member of the orchestra, "but they watch him and they know what he means."

There is something of the peasant in Georg Solti: the love of hard work, the impression of shrewd judgment, the disdain for flashy possession, the frank appreciation of a few elegances—notably the knighthood conferred on him by Queen Elizabeth II—and his comfort in spare, even sparse, surroundings for his work.

His studio has a bare, disciplined, unfinished look. There is one window high up in a wall, with no draperies. The wires of his stereo set snake nakedly across the floor. There are four pictures mounted on the white walls but a half dozen unused picture hooks scattered around the walls. There are one shag rug, one old upright cabinet, one table, and one fifteen-foot-long refectory table, now with a green velvet cloth thrown over his work space and cluttered with musical scores, with records, with a stereo tuner-amplifier. ("You see why I need such a long table?") The spareness seems to appeal to the spirit of Georg Solti; he may be Gothic—or romantic—in his preferences in music, but he has no taste for Gothic, or indulgent, pleasures. He grew up poor and he remained poor for much of his early adult life. "I think it wasn't until 1954"—when Solti was in his forties—"that he had enough extra money to buy his own piano," says his wife, Valerie. "Up to then, he had to borrow"—or borrow time on—"the pianos of friends."

Now he was earning a huge sum: one report was that he was paid $134,803 for this particular thirteen-week season with the Chicago Symphony and his total income from all positions, records, and guest appearances is said by some to run close to well over a quarter-million dollars annually.

Yet the stern lonely disciplines of his workroom are an authentic reflection of the Solti personality. He is a very disciplined man and a very private one. This is not to say that he is diffident or retiring. "He is humble," says a friend, "the way all Hungarians are humble." Rather it is to say that—though he enjoys performing musically in vast crowds—he does not like performing personally in them. He much prefers the company of a few friends where the taste and tempo of the conversation have the quality he seeks.

"What is *this* doing here?" he said one afternoon at tea in Roccamare. There was a bottle of a very expensive scotch—twelve-year-old Ballantine—on the table of his patio. He was ready to relax but not that way; he was put off that any of his friends, a mixture of British and Americans on this day, would be drinking scotch in broad daylight. "We do not need this here," he grumbled. Solti drinks liquor only rarely, usually a weak scotch late at night after a very taxing concert. His drink is tea, a pallid brew laced with plenty of honey. He does not move anywhere—in a car, plane, or concert hall—without a thermos of tea within easy reach. He even drinks it between bows after a concert. He never—but never!—has liquor in a situation of need or whimsy. Indeed, the rumor within the Chicago Symphony Orchestra is that one staff man, a nonmusician, lost his job when he too transparently needed a drink—or a bottle—while accompanying Solti to a concert one day.

On this day at Roccamare, his wife or his father-in-law indicated that the scotch had been put out on the table for the use of friends, that some of them might like scotch or tea, or some combination involving the two. That enlightened and mollified Solti. "Ah! yes," he said. "Very good scotch," he said, almost proudly. He was not quite sure the *women* should have a drink but with the men he was the extravagantly generous host after that, happy with the age, taste, and depth of the scotch. "A very good drink. A very strong drink," he said. "In tea."

In a sense, this is classic Solti. He takes direction as well as gives it. But there are situations in which he *must* be given it. Once given that direction, he bends over backward for his friends and his guests. Later that same evening, for example, he changed the menu several times in order to accommodate the taste and desires of his "anglo" guests. This did not sit well with his Italian cook, Carla, who'd been with him a long time and—in the manner of a long-cherished woman—had not yet decided to give in to his temperament. Their give-and-take over the changes was blunt and to the point, a fact which bothered neither of them so much as it bothered the other women around the table.

"You'd better be careful," warned Valerie, about his sharpened tongue. "You might wind up being cook in this house."

Clearly he did not feel endangered by this threat. Or much chastised by its expression. "Bah!" he said offhandedly. "I make very good pasta."

Solti is no lover of silences. Tough, taut, and topical, he uses words like a staccato sword thrust, keeping the conversation going with jabbing enthusiasm. On this day, he sat in the shade of a mimosa tree and talked of:

—The outrages of the Italian customs process. He'd been delayed for an hour or more at the Rome airport a few days earlier because somebody in customs thought that—with his strong, hard, bald features—he looked vaguely like a refugee from a mug shot.

—The chaos of the Italian telephone system. It is designed, he indicated, "to frustrate the best efforts of the English-speaking world." There was in this a sly, even bemused, suggestion that—as a member of the Italian-, German-, French-, and Hungarian-speaking worlds—he might be exempt from this problem. If only because he rarely uses the telephone, in any country, in any language, for any reason.

—The vastness of the English tax system: Solti is a British subject and he pays taxes there, much more than in the United States. He indisputably thinks it's all worth it—except when he's reminded of it. On this day, he compared the English system, which gives British subjects a priority on the passport examination, with the Italian system and—talking to an English friend—found it worthy. "But you pay for that privilege, my friend. You pay for that privilege."

Curiously, there was no talk of music. When it is time to relax, Solti—as a disciplined man—turns to things other than music. There is no musical instrument in his home in Roccamare, not even a piano. Yet Solti was a gifted pianist before he became a conductor. He won numerous international prizes for playing the piano in a long self-imposed exile in Switzerland during World War II and he still accompanies some of his singers, in rehearsals of operatic or choral works, with great expertise and enthusiasm. There are times when he feels pulled to the beguiling skills of yesteryear. "But it would take me six months to get my hands back into the shape for fine playing," he says. Now, he would not have a piano in Roccamare. Perhaps because it would distract him from the studying of music into the pleasure of playing. Perhaps because it would drive him berserk. For Solti has perfect pitch. He can discern, even in the densest orchestral fabric, the tiniest differences in a musical tone—an A sounded at 441 vibrations per second, for example, instead of the internationally accepted 440. It was this gift that, when it was discovered in his fourth or fifth year, prompted his family to give him piano lessons and later to send him to the Franz Liszt Academy in Budapest. But perfect pitch becomes a liability when a piano is mixed with the high and swift-changing humidity of Roccamare. For the strings would constantly change in tautness and pitch with the repeated changes in humidity, and the piano would seem—to the perfection of Sir Georg's ear—constantly out of tune. "So we have no piano," he says.

The mountains and the sea give Roccamare its humidity—and its allure. For Roccamare is located on a sun-swept spit of land on the west coast of Italy, about 220 kilometers (or 125 miles) north of Rome. To the west, the Tyrrhenian Sea spreads out, looking alternately like a sheet of pounded metal or a scattering of diamonds in the sun. To the east, the full green hills are round and soft as breasts and have personalities as variable as the weather: brush-covered slopes of mauve, gray, and purple in the cloud-filtered light, their heights broken here and there by falls of dark rock or dun-colored remains of old towns. There are miles of sandy beaches—fine, sable-colored sand—backed by steep cliffs along these shores, and nearby is a medieval fishing village between hill and sea. It is called Castiglione della Pescaia and it is the "urban" touch of the region. For Roccamare itself is not a village but a *place*, an enclave for the well-to-do (among its residents: film star

Claudia Cardinale). Behind its guarded gates are miles of narrow roads, winding and twisting among the umbrella pines and subtropical shrubbery, leading to discreet earth-colored homes made of the local rock or light brick. Their homes do not have addresses so much as names—German and French and American and English and even Hungarian-cum-Italian names: Casa Solti.

The Soltis' home is comfortable, not elaborate; he is not one to indulge the splash of great wealth. It has a sense of maturity—no trees were allowed to be destroyed in its construction—and a touch of the tropics: two lime trees are growing in terra-cotta pots in a corner of the entranceway. In the living room, gold-colored rugs are thrown on highly glazed turquoise tiles, and the "sitting cluster" is of contemporary, blue, deeply cushioned chairs and sofa. Nearby is a bookcase that tells something of the man that is Solti. There is a book on Miró: though Solti is aurally of the eighteenth and nineteenth centuries—"I will admit, I am a conductor of the romantic era"—he is visually of the twentieth century; he and his wife collect modern art in a quiet, unostentatious way. There are works on and by Thomas Mann: Solti reads best in German and this historic German figure of world literature is among his favorites. There is a book on the letters of Béla Bartók: Solti had studied under Bartók in Budapest and he played one of Bartók's works, *Bluebeard's Castle*, as a "big" number in Chicago and New York in May 1974. The truth is that their ties back in Budapest were not terribly intimate; Solti was a teen-ager at the time and Bartók—who had not yet won renown as a composer—was a remote figure who would review Solti's piano playing every six months or so. "He was an incredibly shy man," says Solti. "He would listen to us play and never say a word. Later we would get a written notice from him."

The Soltis' living room opens to a loggia, which is centered with a table where Solti likes to gather with the family and friends for afternoon tea. There are children's toys scattered about the lawn and a playpen in the corner of the living room. Solti's daughters are still small—Gabrielle was three and one-half years old as the season started and Claudia was barely five months old. ("Would you believe," said Valerie, as she tested diapers on drying frames in a corridor, "that we'll be packing thirty-two diapers when we go to Chicago?")

The studio is separate—a retreat within a retreat. Down a path leading seaward is another small structure—"the castle," as it is called. It is a walled, glowing building with small but very modern living quarters on one side and—separated by a garden—Solti's studio on the other. It was built to give Sir Georg a home away from home—about fifty feet away from home. "He gets terribly involved when things are going on around him," says Valerie. He cannot maintain his isolation within activity; he always yields to the temptation to become involved in the activity. And so "the castle," which has a walkway around the ten-foot-high wall, from which to peer out to sea—was built to give Sir Georg and Valerie some seclusion, particularly when friends or relatives are staying over at the house. He can get up rather early in the morning, slip out of the bedroom, usually before seven o'clock, make coffee in the kitchen, and then walk a few steps over to his studio to begin working, without disturbing anybody else. And without being tempted by the distractions of up-and-early friends and family. ("If he doesn't work in the morning," says Valerie, "he doesn't work.")

Normally, Sir Georg spends eight or nine weeks during the summer in his retreat. But this last summer had been a short one and a hard one. So, for that matter, had been the spring before it. In March, he'd rushed back from a tour of Germany with the Orchestre de Paris, for which he is also artistic director, to begin preparing the Paris Opéra for its "reawakening." The Théâtre National de l'Opéra had been dormant for a year or more, then brought back to life and vibrancy under the administration of Rolf Liebermann, an old friend of Solti's who recruited Solti as musical adviser. The preview performance, at the end of March, was Mozart's *Le Nozze di Figaro*, played—at $185 a ticket—at the precious little Théâtre Royal of the Palace of Versailles. ("This little theater is the most beautiful in the world," said Solti. "All made of wood, like a Stradivarius. The sound is marvelous.") The response of the critics was unanimously enthusiastic ("Solti's 'Figaro' wins Paris critics' raves," read a headline), and Solti then rushed off to prepare the Chicago Symphony for a concert hall rendition of act 3 of Wagner's *Götterdämmerung*. He played it in New York and Chicago to the acclaim of the critics and audience ("As the final D flat chord faded away, the audience responded with a roar of approval that was almost tangible in its physical intensity," wrote critic Peter Davis).

It was May now, and he had no time to relax. He was scheduled to record some Beethoven symphonies with the Chicago Symphony but he canceled the session: his wife was expecting their second baby and he did not want to be separated from her at that moment. He also had to be thinking ahead. In July, he would not go to Roccamare. Instead he would return to the Royal Opera at Covent Garden, in London, to conduct Bizet's *Carmen*. He'd been musical director at Covent Garden for ten years in the 1960s and had won knighthood for his achievements. He'd left only after he turned to Chicago and Paris; he was not leaving London so much as leaving the opera to turn to the concert hall. He'd been back to Covent Garden in 1972 as a guest conductor but felt a little uncomfortable in the role. "I had not been away long enough to be a real guest conductor," he said. "It was like coming back home when the divorce is still going through. Now I've had my time in Paris, and I am the full divorcé." He wanted *Carmen* to be exceptional but he knew that it would be trouble. For one thing, he hadn't conducted it in fifteen years, though in the period before that he'd conducted it often as musical director for the opera houses in Munich and Frankfurt. "I probably did fifty *Carmen*s. More *Carmen*s than any other opera. But always in German: Now I have to learn to think another way." This *Carmen* was to be in French. Solti had, in fact, been studying French under a tutor, to learn how to think as well as speak in the new language—to know how to communicate with his musicians in Paris as well as to interpret the *Carmen* in London. But it is one thing to learn French and another thing to teach French to Englishmen, with all the idioms and nuances of the language involved. Beyond that, French is a somewhat difficult language to sing, compared to English or German, because it demands so much of the closed-throat sound as compared with the open-throated sound of the Saxons.

The fact was that this opera was written in French and Solti had decided to adhere more closely than is customary to original score and libretto. He dropped the recitatives writen into *Carmen* by Guiraud and returned to the spoken dialogue of the original. He also restored some of the musical cuts that appeared in the original score. ("It must be a *Carmen* with as much Bizet and as little Guiraud as possible," said Solti.) On the face of it, the situation was a trifle chromatic: here was an opera written in French to a Spanish theme sung by an English chorus and conducted by a Hungarian with a German opera house background. But there were cares which paled that factor. Franco Zeffirelli had agreed to stage this *Carmen*, then asked to be released from the obligation some six months or so before the opening. The Royal Opera had gasped with pain, then complied. It also recruited Michael Geliot to take over with Solti still in the pit with the orchestra. Geliot had less than six months' time to prepare for the orchestra, months in which he would mount—almost simultaneously in the spring—the Scottish Opera's *Tristan und Isolde* and the Welsh National Opera's *Don Carlos*, all while preparing to direct Alban Berg's *Lulu* in Germany in the late spring. (In fact, he flew in from Germany and *Lulu* with just ninety minutes to spare before turning to *Carmen* and its first rehearsals.) There were, of course, technical problems of loudness and balance that had to be resolved between director and conductor. The spoken dialogues are more difficult to hear in a large opera house than are the sung recitatives (and Covent Garden *is* a large opera house). At the same time, the largeness of the opera house invites the brass and percussion to play *fortissimo*—an invitation which Solti, a very big man with the brass and percussion, has been accused of accepting all too often. In this production, he would have to keep the brass and percussion thoroughly under rein so that the strings and woodwinds could glitter and glow in the Spanish flavor of the dances, and so that the dialogue could be heard in the farthest reaches of the hall.

On the whole, it worked out well. The critics were restrained but the audiences weren't, and Solti was gratified as finally he was released to go back to Roccamare. He had much to think about in terms of the next season and not much time to think about it. For he'd be conducting three symphonies in three cities in three countries: the Chicago Symphony, the Orchestre de Paris, and the London Philharmonic. He'd be conducting at the Paris Opéra and as a guest at the Royal Opera at Covent Garden. He'd be touring with the Chicago and the Paris Symphony orchestras; the latter was planning a long tour to China in the spring. And he'd be recording—the Beethoven symphonies with the Chicago Symphony and *La Bohème* and *Così fan Tutte* with the Royal Opera. The *Bohème* presented a special challenge. He had never conducted it in the opera house. "Not so strange. As a young man, I am always working in Germany as musical conductor in the opera house and there the public always expects from the director big pieces —Mozart, Strauss, Wagner. In Germany, *Bohème* is not a big piece, so I do not do it." This was all in time past, of course; he has not been musical director in German opera houses for fifteen years. But he is still opening new pathways for satisfaction, as in daring to do *Bohème* for the first time while in his sixties. "It is so easy to get typecast," he says. "I go to an opera house and they expect Mozart and

Strauss only. In the concert hall, it is Mahler and Bruckner. This is one reason why I am doing *Carmen* and *Bohème* in London and why I have decided to conduct a lot of twentieth-century music with the Chicago Symphony."

He had, in fact, no time to escape music or its contemplation in this summer at Roccamare. He normally releases himself from music for a brief period every summer, then works himself back into it gradually, studying in the studio and gesturing as if leading an orchestra while walking in meditation along the pathways of the enclave of Roccamare. This summer, he had only four or five weeks to spend at Roccamare before returning to Paris to prepare the Orchestre de Paris for the Edinburgh festival. There in Scotland in early September the music was as mixed as the background. On the one hand there was the classically ordered and finely chiseled Craigleith stone that was responsible for Edinburgh's being dubbed the modern Athens; on the other hand, there were the severe facades of massive gray stone houses, standing shoulder to shoulder in a closely defensive formation that seems to speak of a class that has drawn itself apart and intends to perish that way. Similarly, the musical styles of Edinburgh ranged from the gentle lyricism of Carlo Giulini to the avant eclecticism of Pierre Boulez: "The sheer quantity of Edinburgh festival music is impressive and the roster of stars even more so," wrote Clive Barnes in *The New York Times.* For, besides Solti, Giulini, and Boulez, there were Leonard Bernstein, Daniel Barenboim, Zubin Mehta, and Riccardo Muti. Solti and his orchestra played two programs, one featuring Berlioz's *Symphonie Fantastique,* the other featuring Roussel's *Symphony* no. 3 and Stravinsky's *Le Sacre du Printemps.* ("It did very well," said Solti of his orchestra's performance. "It was a very good success.") But there was no time for Solti to relax and enjoy the association of his peers. He had to leave Edinburgh and return to Paris and prepare the Théâtre National de l'Opéra for one of the most venturesome and unlikely productions of the season: Arnold Schoenberg's *Moïse et Aaron* (Moses and Aaron).

"The opera may be a noble statement; it may even be a masterpiece," wrote Harold C. Schonberg in *The New York Times.* "But the economic facts of life all but prohibit its entrance into the repertory." He did not think it was likely to happen in the United States: "Certainly neither the Metropolitan Opera nor the New York City Opera has displayed any interest." Actually, Solti conducted a production of *Moses und Aron* at Covent Garden with Peter Hall as director. He even garnished it with a nude scene that shocked some Englishmen and had others speculating timorously on the value of putting it in the repertory. Later, in the autumn of 1971, Solti conducted a concert hall version of the opera—the music without the acting—with the Chicago Symphony, the Chicago Symphony Orchestra Chorus, and with a children's theater chorus from suburban Chicago that he had tutored for the occasion. ("Mr. Solti made 'Moses and Aaron' an engrossing experience," wrote Schonberg in *The New York Times.*)

One of the problems in presenting it to most operatic audiences is that *Moses und Aron* violates some of the familiar dimensions of classical opera. For one thing, it is not a beguiling comic or tragic story, with soaring arias and vast amour; it is an oratoriolike ecclesiastical/philosophical music expression devoted more to dialogue than to action. As it happens, the opera describes a common modern conflict; the inarticulate stumblings of a man with sublime ideas versus the slick huckstering by his brother, a peddler of false images. Moses is, of course, the possessor of an exalted vision of an invisible and indescribable God while Aaron is the smooth talker who has "gods" that his people could see and touch—false gods by the biblical definition. The twist, caustic in the most modern vein, is that the Lord chides Moses and decides to use Aaron as his spokesman. For his own purposes, of course. So—though it is Moses who has the true message, one which would save his people if only they would believe him—those people chase out Moses in favor of Aaron. At God's will. This is done despite objections from the young ("Tear down and smash this image of mortality!" cries out a youth, referring to the Golden Calf. "Keep pure your vision of eternity!") The style and thrust of the plot are uncomfortably close to every major modern cynicism. When Moses returns to his people, for example, Aaron tries to justify himself with the glibness of an ad salesman: "I could offer no image of your god, so I had to fashion an image that they could understand." And further: "No race will trust a god it does not feel." Moses is urged to "speak to all the people clearly, and in words they understand." But this Moses cannot do. ("Be false to the truth of my Vision?") People will have to come to terms with his Vision and the way he articulates it. "I'm bound to my Vision: as these Ten Commandments embody it." The opera ends, as Moses does, in despair. The curtain closes on a cry from the frustrated adman's heart: "Oh. Word, Word, Word, that I lack."

That he would turn and return to this opera tells us something of Georg Solti: that he is a modern man concerned not merely with the idiom of music but with the force and flow of the ideas that it expresses. He is fonder of older music and its classical dimensions: Schoenberg, after all, introduced the twelve-tone technique, using a single arrangement of all twelve tones within the normal octave and thus tending to do away with chords built in thirds and with major-minor scales. Moreover, he composed this opera more in the contrapuntal form favored in twelve-tone music than in the harmonies of the more familiar classical style. That is to say, the listener tends to be aware of separate strands of voices, giving and taking, then giving again, rather than progressions of chords. This did not bother Solti in his presentation of the opera; he could adjust to the modernity of the music in the interests of the ideas and the art it expressed.

He did more than adjust. He inspired the production with a theatricality that gave it movement on the stage when there was little movement in the libretto. ("He opted," said David Stevens in the *International Herald Tribune*, "in his staging for opera instead of oratorio, for a naturalistic theatre of illusion instead of a stylized theatre of ideas.") Thus he gave those ideas body and warmth and a sense of conclusion that Schoenberg did not. for the first two acts of this opera were written by 1932, and it was not until 1951 that Schoenberg turned to trying to write a third act. He failed. The opera, as presented, concludes with the end of the second act. But with Solti, it does *conclude*, not merely end.

It was not easily done. The opera was to be sung in French instead of the original German (hence *Moïse et Aaron*). That caused dissonances of spoken and musical accents: correct French pronunciation did not provide the accents in precisely the same places that Schoenberg's German did—and where Schoenberg's music demanded them. It was easier in Solti's Covent Garden and Chicago Symphony performances, if only because English, when forcefully spoken, is closer to German accents than is French. In any case, the members of the chorus under Jean LaForge had literally hundreds of rehearsals for the opera, and the orchestra, under Solti, gradually overcame its problems in differences of accent. The commitment to the opera was exceptional and it came right from the top: Rolf Liebermann chose to produce this opera in his first, and hence most critical, year as the administrative head of the Paris Opéra because he regards it as the greatest opera of this century, if not of all time. He was more confident of its reception than was Solti who was taken aback by Liebermann's proposal that the opera be presented to Parisians on a subscription-free basis. "All of these tickets were free to buy!" says Solti, still astounded. "Four performances of *Moses and Aaron* with no subscriptions. I was very pessimistic about it. But Liebermann was right."

Liebermann was spectacularly right. The opera received critical acclaim and an eruptive warming of the audience toward its unlikely posture. ("Word *must* have gotten round," said Ronald Crichton in the *Financial Times* of London, "that this was the thing to see.") On a night early in October, when I saw the production, the audience reacted with cries of "Maestro! Maestro!" When Solti responded with only one curtain call, the audience set up a rhythmic chanting and clapping that seemed to command: "Sol-*ti*! Sol-*ti*! Sol-*ti*!" It did not bring Solti back; he was content to have Liebermann and LaForge and Raymond Gerome, who did the staging and performed as Moses, share the credit.

On that particular day, Solti had undertaken a most hazardous and uncharacteristic project. He'd flown to Italy and driven to Roccamare for the weekend, after the Friday performance of *Moïse et Aaron*. On Monday morning he flew back to Paris to conduct the Monday night performance. He had a cold at the time and the flights might have seriously complicated his problems: a very small change in inner-ear pressure—because of the impact of the cold on his ear passages—might have caused a rupture that would have ended forever his ability to hear precisely and thus to conduct. It was not that he was unfamiliar with the hazard. Only ten months earlier, his whole family had come down with a plaguey problem of colds, virus, and ear infections while returning to London from Chicago. Valerie had, in fact, been deafened by the experience for four and one-half months—from the time she fell ill until Claudia was born. Sir Georg was also deafened, but only briefly. He had to cancel performances in London, Paris, and Rome, and he was warned not even to try to use the telephone; he could not hear anyway. But he recovered for the spring season—and he forgot by the fall season. Now, he said of the flights-during-colds in the *Moïse et Aaron* span, "I will never do that again."

In the wake of *Moïse et Aaron*, he'd planned to stay in London for a while, then fly to the United States for the first of his three terms with the Chicago Symphony in this season. But there was a work stoppage in Chicago; the first and then the second and third and fourth weeks of the season had to be canceled. "I may be a conductor without an orchestra," he said moodily. But he took solace in an expected manner: he took the whole family and flew back to Italy for a few days until the labor dispute in Chicago was settled or the season was called off entirely. He studied in the morning when only the chirping of the birds and the wash of the sea could be heard in his studio. Then one day he relaxed enough to discuss a dimension of the Chicago Symphony that is not often revealed: how the season came to be.

This was to be the fourth season of Georg Solti with the Chicago Symphony. As such, the whole style and substance of the season were rooted in the years-long traditions and preferences of Solti and his orchestra—elements that cannot be changed or will not be changed in the effervescence of a moment. Out of this grows the planning for the single season with all its passions, joys, exuberance, suffering, its grace and fragility, its ecstasy and charm.

To understand the one season, one must first understand the roots that give it strength. For example:

What music does Solti prefer?

"I am very much of the romantic period—the classical period before it. The eighteenth-, the nineteenth-century music, yes, that is very much what I prefer." That means he leans to the music composed roughly between 1750 and, perhaps, the death of Gustav Mahler in 1911—Haydn and Mozart, Beethoven and Bach, Schumann and Schubert, Wagner and Weber, and their contemporaries. He also leans more to the heavy, dramatic German sounds—Wagner, Bruckner, Mahler—than to the French sounds or to the operatic sounds of southern Europe. That is why it was no trouble for him to drop *Carmen* by Bizet, a Frenchman, out of his repertory for fifteen years and why he'd never conducted Puccini's *La Bohème* in an opera house. ("Puccini wrote two and one-half great operas: *Turandot*, *Gianni Schicchi*, and *Bohème*," he has said. "Perhaps three and one-half if we add in *Tosca*. But his most complete work is *Bohème*.")

This brings up the question of modern music versus Solti's preference for the romantic era composers. Though he'd had an "antimodern" reputation, Solti loves and programs much twentieth-century music, some of it by composers still living. To be sure, he finds some of the music of the French impressionists a trifle uncongenial, because of its lack of strong rhythm, and he does not care for ultramodern, experimental music, especially electronic music. ("I do not like very much this tinkly-tinkly bonkly-bonkly music.") He makes clear, however, the difference between "experimental" and "modern" music, citing the works of Gunther Schuller as examples of music that is modern but by no means experimental. In general, his position might be best defined by these statements of a few years ago in *High Fidelity* magazine (October 1969):

"For me as a conductor [modern] music stops around 1950, with late Stravinsky, Schoenberg, Bartók. I don't go much further. Such people made the musical revolution of my lifetime. What a revolution that was in 1925! When Alban Berg came, what a new experience it was for us to hear for the first time *Wozzeck*, *Lulu*, the Violin Concerto. So equally, I stop. I stop. I leave to the next generation to explore after 1950.

The Season in Conception

"But this is the essential point: me, and a few other talented conduct¢
generation have a duty to preserve the classical masterpieces, and give the
next generation. That's my job. I concentrate on that. That's what we
Toscanini, Furtwängler, Walter, Kleiber. If we don't do it, there will be a gap and
nobody will know in fifty years' time how a Beethoven, a Brahms should be played;
or a Bruckner."

What sound does Solti prefer—or hear—in the Chicago Symphony?

"The Chicago Symphony has a very particular sound which I would call the
'German' sound. A heavy German sound in combination with American virtuosity. That sound which no other American orchestra has, which maybe you can
compare with Vienna or Berlin. Having more virtuosity than a European
orchestra—a combination of a solid European base with American virtuosity. It is
like the IBM would be made in Germany, something like that. Excellent. A very
fortunate combination."

It is all the more fortunate because it coincides with the sound that Solti
responds to reflexively. In effect, it is strongest in playing the sounds that Solti
wants to hear; it seems weakest when it was asked to play the more Gallic sounds
demanded by French conductor Jean Martinon in the mid-1960s. The members
of the orchestra tend to disagree; it is part of the persona of any orchestra that it can
play any music with equal facility—"There is no nationality in sound," says
Grover Schiltz, the oboe and English horn player. But the players will concede
that the Chicago Symphony emphasizes and stylizes the brass more than the high
strings and the woodwinds, and it is the sound of that brass—the depth and
sonority that rise from it and from the cellos and violas—that gives the Chicago
Symphony a more Teutonic depth than Gallic sheen. Thus the Chicago Symphony is inclined by tradition and temperament to play precisely the sound that
Solti is trying to draw from it.

One of Solti's close friends, Terry McEwen, head of London/Decca's classical
division in the United States, has commented that there are only three orchestras
that Solti could have fallen in love with over, say, the period of the last ten to
fifteen years: the London Symphony, the Amsterdam Concertgebouw, and the
Chicago Symphony. "The New York Philharmonic is too brash for him, the
Cleveland too refined and intellectual, the Vienna Philharmonic too
schlamperei-oriented," said McEwen. "This gutsy sound of Chicago, it has something to do with the middle sound of the cellos and the viols. That had to be the
orchestra for Solti."

The gratifying fact is that Solti is not so plugged in to one sound that he does not
recognize the value of other sounds and other orchestras. He believes the Chicago
Symphony is the finest orchestra in the world today. "But you know, I must—I am
not unbiased in this matter." The Vienna Philharmonic, with all its *schlamperei*,
is one of the orchestras he would rank with it. "I would mention in Europe, yes,
Berlin and Vienna. In the United States, the Philadelphia. Yes, these are our
major rivals." His nomination of "the Philadelphia" is perhaps surprising because
the Philadelphian sound—the lush, rich brilliance of the strings—is so different
from the profound sonorities of the Chicago. There are some who insist that

anything so lush cannot have value, particularly when it is employed on splashy records so deeply in contrast with those of the Chicago Symphony (the Philadelphia: "The Glorious Sound of Christmas," "The World's Favorite Tchaikovsky"; the Chicago: Mahler's Eighth, Beethoven's Ninth Symphony). Philadelphia conductor Eugene Ormandy has defended the Philadelphia sound in these terms: "My conducting is what it is because I was a violinist. Toscanini was always playing the cello when he conducted; Koussevitzky, the double bass; Stokowski, the organ. The conductors who were pianists nearly always have a sharper, more percussive beat, and it can be heard in their orchestras." Solti, a pianist, obviously prefers the percussive sound. But he sees no need to criticize the Philadelphia Orchestra for its sound. He considers the Philadelphia Orchestra a well-balanced organization that must be considered to rank with Chicago and Berlin and Vienna in effectiveness. "It is a matter of taste," he says. "What sort of sound, what sort of sonority, what sort of technical precision you look for, what sort of color you prefer. I can say the four orchestras I mention are well balanced in all sections. Probably the Chicago and Philadelphia are better balanced in all sections, as I think it, than Berlin and Vienna."

There is a factor of temperament and technical precision that is involved not only in the orchestra but in the planning for the season. For Solti, and all musical directors, must ask themselves: can the orchestra play this piece of music to my satisfaction in the time allowed for rehearsals?

There are, obviously, two qualifying factors in this question: of time and of temperament.

—Time. Can it be done in the time allowed? The increasing strictness of union rules in America makes this an important question. If the orchestra cannot master the piece in the time allowed for rehearsals, then it cannot master the piece. In Chicago, the union contract is, as we shall see, somewhat complicated. But in reality, it provides for three rehearsals of two and one-half hours for each of Solti's programs—seven and one-half hours of rehearsal time in which to perfect three, and possibly four, numbers, consuming one and one-half hours of playing time. It is part of the genius of the Chicago Symphony that it can take almost any piece of music and master it in a remarkably short time—so little time, in fact, that Solti frequently ends rehearsals a half hour or so early. ("My dears, you play beautifully. I know you are tired. Why not take this next half hour for yourselves?") He has enormous confidence in the members of the Chicago to read the music, at sight if necessary, and then play it with extreme virtuosity. It is not always the same elsewhere. "I believe every American orchestra—I prefer to say 'Anglo-Saxon,' because the English have it also—has this tremendous ability to read the music, to concentrate very well," he says. "Because this is what many European orchestras do not have." There is a tendency on the Continent for musicians to gossip, dream, and even read the newspapers—when they have a long rest—during rehearsals. The lack of concentration and cohesion makes for a lack of coherence. The conductor must often start and stop and summon the players back to concentration. This can cost twenty or thirty minutes of every rehearsal time. "That isn't so in America," says Solti. "In Chicago, I do not lose two minutes in a rehearsal with that 'Please, would you be quiet' and so on." He is terribly disciplined with his time on the podium. "He's the best-organized conductor I've seen—he doesn't lose a second," says Grover Schlitz. Thus it is sometimes difficult for him to accept the dawdling of the continental orchestras during rehearsals. "Therefore it is much easier to work with an Anglo-Saxon orchestra. An English or American, it doesn't matter. Both are excellent. As with a Latin orchestra, the Latins are very difficult. The Latins have to be persuaded. They are looking at the conductor as an enemy and you have to get nearer to them. You have to break down the barrier at first. But not the Anglo-Saxon. They are ready to play when you are." It is that fact—the knowledge that he can get the most out of rehearsals with the Chicago Symphony—that frees Solti from being concerned with the difficulty of the scores he selects: whatever he picks, they can play—and within the time given.

—Temperament. Can the music be learned to the satisfaction of the conductor? That satisfaction is variable. Some conductors can accept pretty much what the players give them. Toward the end of his career as a conductor, Richard Strauss would explain a passage and try it out once or twice. If it went well, fine; if it went poorly, he would shrug his shoulders and do nothing more about it. ("When I was young, I had to take the blame if others made a mistake. Nowadays, if I make a mistake, it is all *their* fault," he is quoted having said.) Solti, on the other hand, is a driving perfectionist. His ability to detect a flaw—and his insistence on correcting it—borders on the incredible. While recording a Beethoven symphony in the autumn of 1973, he heard something wrong in one passage and he had the tapes played over and over again until he identified it. The flaw turned out to be one of the violins—out of thirty-two in the section—who had reversed a particular two-note sequence while the others were playing it correctly. Solti then listened to all the other takes of that sequence to determine whether it was a one-time error or whether the particular violinist—he did not say who it was, but one suspects that he knew—was playing it wrong all the time. Then he went back to the podium and asked the orchestra to rerecord that segment, merely warning the violins in general—he is too much of a gentleman to excoriate a particular individual—to watch the sequence in question. On the next take, he got exactly what he wanted. The point, of course, is that out of the hundreds of thousands of notes—perhaps millions—in all the parts of that symphony, he heard two that were out of order and he had to make them correct.

There is another reflexive consideration in building programs for an entire season: can the audience accept it?

The style of music presented in the concert hall must appeal to the audience or the audience will disappear. The audience of the New York Philharmonic became, in the early 1970s, an example. It has one of the most renowned and cerebral conductors in the world in Pierre Boulez. But Boulez is an open and ardent advocate of very avant-garde music and the New York audiences were not accepting it. Hence an increasing number of empty seats at the performances of the New York Philharmonic—and packed and enthusiastic houses when the Chicago Symphony visits New York.

"Playing in Carnegie Hall is a unique experience, a unique experience." Solti likes to repeat, as in a coda, for emphasis. "We have created a special audience in Carnegie Hall," says Solti. "I think it is absolutely fabulous. Absolutely marvelous. It is my favorite audience today in the world." He pays it the ultimate compliment: "It is as good as any London audience ever." He has definite feelings about the audiences in the cities in which he performs. "Paris is developing to be very much in musical taste now," he says. "Paris is mainly a visually oriented city. It is not by chance that it has the most wonderful painters of our time. But not as many first-class musicians"—which is a reflection on the population which contributes the musicians and makes up the audiences at his performances.

"There are some German audiences that are very good, very knowledgeable. In Munich, in Hamburg, very knowledgeable, very good audiences.

"London is the most musical audience imaginable. They are not going to listen to people. They are going to listen to the work; the performers are second. This isn't so in America. This isn't so in Paris yet."

He makes one exception about the New York audiences, at least as he knew them in the early 1960s. "I don't find the New York opera audience as knowledgeable. They are looking for different followers. They are unfortunately trained by Mr. Bing in the wrong direction, looking for who can hold the note higher and higher. I think this is childish. This is absolutely not music!" Solti was guest conductor at the Metropolitan Opera on several memorable occasions during the 1960s. He then had a difference of opinion with the Met's general manager, Sir Rudolf Bing, and Bing's view prevailed—to the extent that Solti stopped conducting there. ("Solti runs Covent Garden," Bing said, "but he is not running the Metropolitan Opera.") As the years passed, Solti has not hesitated to express his disapproval of much of Bing's way, Bing's ear, Bing's music. Thus his feelings on an audience, tutored, as Solti insists, to listen to the long notes—that is, the wrong style—by Bing. "This is very much Italian, particularly the southern Italian way of life," says Solti. "They love that in southern Italy." He is not, as we have seen, much enraptured by Italian opera. "If you hold a long note, whatever else you do, success is surely there," says Solti on the southern Italian operatic tradition. "In New York opera, very much the same—the Italian tradition—and nobody has tried very hard to work against it."

All this is a moot matter in Chicago. The people of that city are so delighted by their symphony—Chicago is so glad to be first in something, first in *anything*—that it could play almost any music and they'd respond with full houses. But of course that is not necessarily an enduring condition. The international celebrity of the orchestra came swiftly: "I would not have believed it would happen in three, four years," says Solti. "I believed it would happen, but in ten years perhaps, not in three."

Given all these specifications, Sir Georg is free to go about building the season's program. The planning starts more than three years before the season starts and it involves not only Sir Georg but John Edwards, the rotund, acute general manager of the Chicago Symphony, and some members of his staff. They gather in Solti's Chicago hotel suite overlooking Lake Michigan. "Mostly we do it on Sunday morning, because that is my only free day in Chicago," says Solti. "Early Friday evening and Sunday morning, those are our days. Usually I do a certain amount of prethinking. But it takes hours. Hours. Not even the symphony orchestra members know how many hours we put in on planning."

There are certain personal and professional specifications that Solti imposes on the planning.

One is that he will conduct in Chicago for no more than thirteen weeks a year. He knows that this is not in the tradition of the American symphony orchestra. In the old days, Theodore Thomas conducted almost every session of the Chicago Symphony. In the 1903–1904 season, when he was not far from death, Thomas conducted twenty-three out of twenty-four programs. (The one relief week was conducted by Richard Strauss.) His successor was Frederick Stock: in 1927–28, Stock conducted twenty-seven out of twenty-eight weeks of the Chicago Symphony (an assistant conductor worked the remaining week). Even in the Fritz Reiner era, the musical director shouldered much of the load: in 1955–56, Reiner conducted twenty weeks out of the twenty-eight-week season of the symphony.

Solti responds: "I find that thirteen weeks is most satisfactory for everybody—for the orchestra, for the public, for the conductor. Because there is no man that can do that much right all the time." It also allows him to keep one foot in Europe and the other in the United States, one arm in opera, the other in symphonic conducting. And it makes him, at an estimated $10,000 a week, one of the highest paid wage earners in the United States.

Solti has always been candid about his thirteen-week limit. At the very outset of his association with the Chicago Symphony he laid out a limit—and agreed to a way to ameliorate it. "Ideally, I would like somebody to share it with me that I liked, whom I knew, and who is so different from me. Like Giulini. I would like to make two co-conductors, really. That is what I told the board when I took the job. I said, 'Why don't we ask Giulini? Giulini and me together.' That is what I told them." Carlo Maria Giulini is as different from Solti as possible. He is Italian and had spent many years as a conductor at La Scala. He is tall, slim, impeccably dressed, elegant, somewhat retiring—whereas Solti is shorter, bald, casually dressed, earthy, and very aggressive. Their music is as different as their looks. Solti's is very muscular, dramatic, played to the moment; Giulini's is gentle, lyrical, more fully rounded, and deeply *musical*. Since the two draw two entirely different kinds of music out of the same symphonic instrument, it makes for an even more glorious moment of music in Chicago.

But Giulini has no taste for the burdens of administration, the intrigues of concert-hall politics that so involve a music director. Solti, on the other hand, thrives on them. "I like it because I have been doing it all my life," he says. "So they said to Giulini, 'All right, if you do not want to do that, at least give us a good block of time and you will be principal guest conductor.' " Giulini agreed to that. He devoted eight weeks to Chicago in the first years of the Solti reign and became, officially, principal guest conductor. But now he would cut back; he would spend only four weeks in Chicago and he'd given up his official title. That was, in the view of a great many Chicagoans, a loss to the city and its symphony. But Solti tried to make the most of it. He would give Giulini, even now, first choice of music and dates. "I always let him have the priority in his program. I am not even making my own programs until he makes his." There is a chance of conflict in timing but not in aesthetics. "Perhaps he does not know that a piece was played with somebody else last year. But I go to him and say, 'Look, can you do something else?' And he understands." There are a knowledge and integrity between the two men that one will not—in the long, loving history of classical music—seek an advantage over the other. "He is entirely different," says Solti. "His program is entirely different. His way of life is different. We are very, very different creatures. There is no way we have collisions except, of course, if we do the same work. But if he does a work and I do a work, it is a very, very different sound. Which is very interesting, of course. And very good."

This is where the tact and the planning of John Edwards come in. To avoid any possibility of conflict between Solti and Giulini, Edwards took steps years ago to establish their private priorities. "I worked out a list of major works that Solti and Giulini want to do," he says. "These are major pieces. I do not mean long symphonies but ones that involve soloists, that involve a lot of planning to get the people of the stature they want for the piece." On occasion, the same piece has turned up on both lists. "*Missa Solemnis*—both of them want to do it," says Edwards. "It was long a neglected work here. It was not really done until 1960 and now it's been done three times since I've been here"—that is, three times in seven seasons. "Not necessarily because *I* like it, though I think it is one of the most formidable and marvelous works in the whole repertoire; I'm crazy about it. But Giulini had mentioned doing it some time ago—that was back in the 1960s. Solti mentioned it at about the same time, but Giulini and I had already talked about it. Solti is immensely generous about such things to his colleagues and especially to Giulini. So he said, 'All right, let him do it first and then I will do it the next time around.' So that is what happened. Giulini did it, I think it was in February 1970, and now it is 1973 and Solti will do it." (Martinon had led the *Missa Solemnis* in May 1968.)

The give-and-take in such matters springs readily to mind and tongue in the planning sessions. But they are part of the discipline of planning, for the major vocal works conducted by Solti and Giulini must be laid out very early—perhaps three years in advance of the playing—in order to line up the singers. "The choral works, and the concert versions that Solti does, are planned further in advance than anything because the availability of the cast is very difficult," says Edwards. "I mean, to get all the people he wants at the same time is not easy." And then things do not always work out. Solti first put *Missa Solemnis* on his schedule not long after Giulini performed it, knowing there would be a three-year gap before it came into being under his baton. He got commitments from all the vocalists vital to the performance and everything went well—until the week of the performance. Then three of the long-contracted singers came down with colds and other ailments and even their substitutes ran into problems. "We had eight changes in three perform-ances in one week," says Edwards. Solti could not, of course, know that ahead of time. He simply went ahead and scheduled *Missa Solemnis* for the autumn of the 1973 season and then slated Bach's monumental St. *Matthew Passion* for spring of

1974, and he and Edwards then began scouting for the singers they wanted to see if they were available for the three weeks involved. For *Missa Solemnis*, they got commitments from Karl Ridderbusch, bass; Wendy Fine, soprano; Peter Schreier, tenor; and Julia Hamari, mezzo-soprano. Then, for *St. Matthew Passion* they enlisted Gwynne Howell, bass; Heather Harper, soprano; Jerry Jennings, tenor; and Helen Watts, contralto. This is one area in which Solti is particularly strong—"his opera background put him in touch with all the fine voices of the world," says Edwards, "and his reputation inspires them to want to work with him." There are, to be sure, factors which sometimes frustrate the planning —such as singers who prefer opera in an operatic setting rather than in a concert version. The most frustrating thing is when all the factors seem right and the talent is still too busy. "We've been trying to get something arranged with Birgit Nilsson for five years," says Edwards. She'd worked with Solti on his magnificent records of Wagner's *Ring* cycle and their mutual regard is high. Edwards and Solti even mapped certain works that she'd be likely to accept in a performance with the Chicago Symphony—"*Salome*, for example, which she does not do on the stage anymore but will do in concert version." So far, it just hasn't worked out. "But maybe next year," says Edwards. No maybe. The next season in 1974–75, Birgit Nilsson would appear in a concert version of *Salome* under the baton of Georg Solti.

Even as all this is being talked out, the discussion of the guest conductors intrudes. For they, too, must be booked two or three years in advance, and for the same reason as the singers. "With a conductor or a singer, you have to have at least a full week of his time—to rehearse and play the three concerts," says John Edwards. This is not the case with instrumental soloists—violinists, pianists, and so forth. The reason is that the program for instrumental soloists is usually built around something they already know, something they're expert and even re-nowned in. So they don't need as many or as demanding rehearsals. A run-through with the orchestra, the three performances, and they're gone—three or four days in Chicago and they're on to their next performance. But a conductor usually has to be present the entire week, to review and mark scores and run rehearsals as well as to play the performances. And the symphony usually likes to have the same conductor for two to four weeks, to give greater continuity to the sound of the season—"just to avoid the feeling of spottiness," says Edwards. That means they must ask the conductor to set aside a much larger block of time than the instrumental soloist must offer; and that means signing of guest conductors three years in advance.

The guest conductor schedule rests, of course, on the commitment of Solti and Giulini. In this season, the Chicago Symphony would play a thirty-week subscription season in Orchestra Hall, starting September 27 and concluding the following June 1—"from before Labor Day to past Decoration Day," says Edwards. Solti was committed to thirteen weeks; Giulini was committed to four weeks. That took care of seventeen of the thirty subscription weeks. They would have to fill the other weeks with guest conductors, not to mention seven nonsubscription weeks of mis-cellaneous concerts and tours.

And this is where the inexorable calculus of modern life takes place. For there are fewer renowned conductors than in the past, and there are more orchestras with more gaps in schedule seeking them out. So the supply is decreasing while the demand is increasing. "What we do is make a list," says Edwards. It is an informal list, scribbled on a large yellow legal-sized pad or around the margins of papers already marked up during the planning session. "I just horse around with my list until I see where it ends," says Edwards. That means he puts the "impossibles" on it. These are conductors that he's sure will not or cannot take on a commitment in Chicago. He lists them on the chance that Solti knows something that he doesn't.

On the list for this season, the "impossibles" included Leonard Bernstein; Pierre Boulez, conductor of the New York Philharmonic; Eugene Ormandy, conductor of the Philadelphia Orchestra; James Levine, principal conductor of the Metropolitan Opera, and Seiji Ozawa, chief conductor of both the Boston and the San Francisco symphonies.

"Bernstein? Bernstein just tells everybody no," says Edwards. "When he accepts something, it's so highly personal"—he once performed with the Cincinnati May Festival Symphony on the intercession of a special friend, one with whom he liked to go skiing, says Edwards. Even this was a violation of his policy. "He always feels if he does it for one, he has to do it for everybody," Edwards explains. "Solti has written directly to him and I've known him for years. But I've given up asking because I think it's embarrassing for him to say no, and it's embarrassing for me to have him say no."

Boulez? "Same thing with Boulez. He was a guest conductor here before he took the New York Philharmonic and the BBC. After that he begged off. He and Solti are close friends"—but there are things that even close friends won't do for, or to, each other. So Boulez's name was not a "possible."

Ormandy? "Ormandy has taken the position that his wife doesn't want him to do any guest conducting," says Edwards. He'd performed many times with the Chicago Symphony and, indeed, there was even a time—when the 1940s turned into the 1950s—when he was the unseen *meister-direktor* of the Chicago Symphony—a period when he gave it behind-the-scenes guidance and continuity when there was no similar continuity from its out-front conductors. But he's now well up in years—he'd be seventy-three before the first downbeat of this season of 1973–74—and it is not as easy for him to travel as in the past. "He's even reduced his work in Philadelphia a great deal," says Edwards. So Ormandy's name was also not a "possible."

Ozawa? "We invited him for the last season—he came and conducted for two weeks." He already had considerable renown and respect around Chicago from his past: he'd been music director for the Summer Festival at Ravinia. But now he's conducting two major orchestras: "He's made a deal with San Francisco and Boston that he won't do anything besides them. And so he said, 'I can't get out of that,' " reports Edwards. This is not unusual: Solti won't make any concert-hall appearances in the United States without the prior permission of the Chicago Symphony—and both sides understand that such permission is very unlikely to come. (Indeed, it was that clause in his contract which blocked a tour of the eastern

United States by the Orchestre de Paris under the direction of Solti.) So Ozawa was not free to guest-conduct in Chicago.

James Levine? He also is enjoying a rising popularity in Chicago, because of his conducting at Ravinia. "The guy is working like hell with the Metropolitan," says Edwards. That is merely a reflection of a rising regard for him in New York and, indeed, around the world. ("They overbook Levine. As frequently happens," states Edwards, "they push them too hard"—the rising young conductors. "They don't have time to study. They don't reflect on anything. They just run around, wham-wham, until they get to the point—well, like Ozawa." The latter has the reputation of being so fast-moving that he studies his scores on the plane to the next performance. But he also is an incredibly quick study—and he absorbs with stunning rapidity—and "he does it with such charm that most orchestras just go along," says Edwards.) Yet none of these factors would block an appearance by Levine in Orchestra Hall. It's his commitment to Ravinia that blocks it. There is nothing formal in this objection; it is just a feeling that the Chicago Symphony doesn't want to be in the position of making off with the bright young talent turned up by Ravinia. For Ravinia is no prep school for the Chicago Symphony; it is a separate and highly individualistic enterprise with its own aesthetic imperatives. "We have a nice cooperation there," reports Edwards, "so we try to avoid the same soloists, the same conductors." That eliminated Levine from this year's guest schedule.

There is one "impossible" who doesn't even appear on the list. Edwards is too discreet to put his name there. It is that of Zubin Mehta, the music director of the Los Angeles Philharmonic. "Outside of the Met he doesn't guest-conduct at all in the United States," says John Edwards. "He doesn't even have 'management' "—that is, an agent—"in America." But the real reason, admits Edwards, is that such a suggestion "involves Solti's life." Mehta was the "party of the third part" in what was, as we shall see, one of the bitterest disputes and disappointments of Solti's life: his abortive career as music director in Los Angeles. The dispute was not with Mehta; it was with the directors of the Los Angeles orchestra. There is no animosity between Mehta and Solti; even the anger at the old dispute has pretty much died in Solti. Nevertheless, the matter was so delicate—and difficult—that the niceties are still observed: Mehta does not guest-conduct the Chicago Symphony, and Solti does not guest-conduct the Los Angeles Philharmonic.

The list of "possibles" is, of course, much longer. "Kubelik, Barenboim, Davis, Abbado, Previn, Schippers, Haitink, Foss, von Dohnányi, Dorati, Maazel, Foster, Dixon, Muti . . ." It goes on and on.

Solti and Edwards and sometimes one or two others discuss them all. The discussion, and the deal, may range over one or two seasons—"Somebody can come next season, not this season."

Rafael Kubelik, for example. He's been music director in Chicago in 1950–53 and he'd left thoroughly bloodied by the comments of Claudia Cassidy, the critic for the *Chicago Tribune*. But he'd come back, under Edwards, as a guest conductor in 1969 and he'd enjoyed a warm and enthusiastic reception. He'd come back again, but not this season. He was music director at the Metropolitan—he'd resign during the 1973–74 season—as well as his work with the Bavarian State Radio and he had no spare time right now. But in other years—yes. "Kubelik," said Edwards speculatively. "Last season and next season. Not this season."

Similarly with André Previn—"he's coming next season." Or Lorin Maazel, music director of the Cleveland Symphony—"last season." Bernard Haitink, music director of the Amsterdam Concertgebouw Orchestra—"next season, not now." Colin Davis, successor to Solti as music director of Covent Garden who conducts in the United States as a guest in Boston—"Solti tries like the devil to get him to come here," says Edwards. "Davis says no, not this season. He's committed to Boston until the spring of 1976."

There are always further extenuating circumstances: Lawrence Foster, conductor of the Houston Symphony—"he's pretty much Ravinia." Another conductor—he'd gotten into a pretty harsh give-and-take with a principal in the Chicago Symphony on his last appearance: "We'd rather think that over for a while." Antal Dorati, music director of the National Symphony of Washington who also conducts the Stockholm Philharmonic—"Dorati's one of those guys that's sort of pending all the time. He has a fairly elaborate schedule in Washington and Stockholm. And you know, there's the money."

Gennady Rozhdestvensky, the co-conductor of the Leningrad Philharmonic Orchestra—he'd be on tour with the Leningrad Philharmonic for much of the U.S. season, so he could not appear with the Chicago Symphony this year. But he seems a conductor of enormous confidence—he sometimes switches the baton to the left hand to get the phrasing he wants—and great potential. So "not this season but next." The Chicago Symphony scheduled an all-Russian program under his direction to open that next season at home. ("The prospect of a first meeting between Rozhdestvensky and the Chicago Symphony," wrote Thomas Willis in the *Chicago Tribune*, "is more interesting than anything else scheduled in Orchestra Hall for the rest of the season.")

The arrival of Rozhdestvensky reflects a special circumstance of an extenuating nature—that is, the philosophy that there's no harm in a "little something extra." For Rozhdestvensky would not only come to conduct three weeks of all-Russian programs but he'd have his wife, Victoria Postnikova, as piano soloist. This "something extra" is not unusual in modern symphony scheduling. When Lorin Maazel was guest conductor in Chicago in the 1972–73 season, his wife, Israela Margalit, came to Chicago as a pianist the week before his appearance. And when Sir Michael Tippett accepted a one-week guest appearance in Chicago in this season, it was to offer a program made up entirely of his own compositions—with the world's finest orchestra as his showcase.

Through hours of such give-and-take—and volumes of correspondence—Solti and Edwards were not only able to schedule guest conductors to fill the balance of the season but to fit them into the time slots that were acceptable all around. Some of the high spots of the coming season would include performances under the direction of:

Daniel Barenboim, like Solti, is a superb pianist who is winning heightened renown for his conducting skill. He agreed to come to Chicago twice in this season, preceding Solti's appearances both times. The first would be in September, just after the Edinburgh Festival where Barenboim would conduct five performances—which drew raves—of Peter Ustinov's new version of *Don Giovanni*, then for two weeks in April, just before Solti returned to Chicago to conduct *The St. Matthew Passion*. There was, to be sure, a little something extra in all this: on his first trip, Barenboim would have the chance to record certain of his preferences with the Chicago Symphony on the Deutsche Grammophon label—not inconsiderable achievement for a thirty-one-year-old conductor. Unfortunately, both circumstances and tragedy tracked Barenboim in these weeks. His first two weeks had to be canceled because of the work stoppage of the symphony. And in that period, it was made known to the world that his lovely wife, Jacqueline du Pré, an immensely gifted cellist, was suffering from multiple sclerosis.

Claudio Abbado, who has had one of the most spectacular careers in conducting. In 1958, he won the Koussevitzky award for conducting at the Berkshire Music Festival and ten years later was permanent conductor of La Scala in his native Milan (the first individual in almost a decade to win that appointment). By the time he came to Chicago, he was not only conductor at La Scala but also permanent conductor of the Vienna Philharmonic, one of the very few orchestras in the world that—in view of Georg Solti—can, as we've seen, compare with the Chicago Symphony.

Christoph von Dohnányi, grandson of Ernst von Dohnányi, the composer who was one of Solti's tutors in his early days in Budapest. Solti returned the favor: he hired young von Dohnányi to conduct opera when Solti was music director of the Frankfurt Opera. Now von Dohnányi was himself general music director of the Frankfurt Opera and Symphony Orchestra. This would be his first appearance with the Chicago Symphony Orchestra.

And Thomas Schippers, often a conductor at La Scala, Bayreuth, and in Venice, who is also conductor of the Cincinnati Symphony Orchestra (he would fall ill before he could make this appearance in Chicago); Lukas Foss, who "triples"—as did Leonard Bernstein—as conductor, composer, and commentator (he was once a fellow student of Bernstein's in the classes of Fritz Reiner and Serge Koussevitzky) and who is now chief conductor of the Jerusalem Symphony in Israel and conductor and music adviser for the Brooklyn Philharmonia; Dean Dixon, musical director of the Sydney Symphony in the mid-1960s; and Henry Mazer, the associate director of the Chicago Symphony, who would conduct two subscription concerts this season (plus all of the Youth Concerts).

It is not just a generalized knowledge but a specific knowledge that is applied to the selection of a guest conductor. Through his work in Paris, with the Orchestre de Paris, Solti became acquainted with the conducting of Zdenek Macal, conductor of the German Radio Orchestra in Cologne. He invited him to conduct the Chicago Symphony, but his work in this season was wiped out by the work stoppage. ("We hoped to have him do one of the makeup weeks," says Edwards, "but he didn't have any time available for the rest of the season.") In the previous season, Solti had also conducted a competition for young American conductors, awarding $2,500 to the winner. He was so impressed by the talents of twenty-seven-year-old Guido Ajmone-Marsan—who was born in Turin but became a U.S. citizen—that he asked the winner to become guest conductor of the Chicago Symphony just after the Chrstmas holidays in this season.

These men did not all have the great celebrity of a Bernstein or an Ormandy —but they had the mark of quality. Says Solti: "Look, I know my colleagues—the good ones and the bad ones. And I try to get the good ones. The principle is that I should engage the best possible guest conductors as it is very wrong to be afraid of the competition. You must play a good season; this is important even if the guest conductor is better than you are. You should not be afraid—you should not feel that anyone 'is better than I am.' You should not feel any inhibitions and therefore you must try to get the best possible conductor. You must not think of avoiding anybody who is better than I am. Which I do not do, I do not feel. I have not many inhibitions; therefore I try to get the best possible conductor. But it is difficult to get them because there are few—a few, only a handful, and they are incredibly busy. So you have to work a long time ahead."

The next step is even more difficult. It involves working out programs for each of the guest conductors. This step, combined with the conductor-selection process, demands not only a diplomatic skill but a determined energy. "This is peck and peck and peck," says Solti. "Endless. With correspondence going on all the year. I would imagine that, for this year alone, I would have at least one hundred cables."

The basic structure, of course, is made of the programs laid out by Solti and Giulini for their own seventeen weeks of work. After that, the guest conductors are given the initiative. "A guest conductor who is asked to work two, three, four, five weeks, whatever it is, he is making his own program. And it will be shown to me," says Solti. "Now this must fit into the general program. We cannot repeat the same pieces"—not even the same piece that's been played by the orchestra in the preceding two years or so. Most—not all—guest conductors have two things in mind when selecting a program: (1) they prefer the music that most expresses their inner feeling and outer image—even as Solti does—and (2) they are not much interested in learning new scores. "There are certain repertoire pieces that they want to conduct all the time," says Solti. "The Beethoven symphonies. The four Brahms symphonies. The Schubert C Major Symphony. Tchaikovsky five and six, Mahler eight and seven, Ravel, that sort of thing. There are about twenty-five pieces that everyone would like to do." Is it because they are easy to perform? "No," says Solti. "It is because they are important. It is because this is what the public likes and they are a success."

There are some problems of duplication or multiplication that simply cannot be overcome. And yet, they are quite provocative to the more sophisticated audiences that hear several orchestras a year. In the 1970–71 season, for example, three different orchestras—the Chicago, the Philadelphia, and the New York Philharmonic—built major programs around Bruckner's Eighth Symphony. This did not disturb every listener: "The interpretations varied from intense excitement to lyrical non-excitement, each quite individual, so that a listener marveled at the flexibility of the work," wrote Miles Kastendieck in *The Christian Science Monitor*. But in the 1969–70 season, Solti with one orchestra and Claudio Abbado with another arrived in New York and offered near-simultaneous performances of Brahms's First Symphony, a coincidence which touched off in *The New York Times* Harold C. Schonberg's "annual threnody about stereotyped programs, intellectual laziness, and the easy if not cynical way of doing things."

It is Solti himself who must tell his fellow conductors that they must change their programs. "This is a very difficult, tricky situation," he says. "I must tell them, 'This work cannot go on next year. You have to do something else. Listen, *this* piece is possible.' " It is all the more difficult because Solti wants to get the best of all possible guest conductors, and he knows—in a decent respect to their own aesthetic drives—that he cannot dictate to them what they can play and cannot play with the Chicago Symphony. "So it is very difficult. It is a puzzle, fitting pieces in here, pieces in there."

The pieces must be fit together with purpose and a philosophy. For Solti believes that a great symphony orchestra in a city such as Chicago, one whose audience tends to be conservative, must function on what might be called a "modified museum philosophy." In this framework, the great works of the old masters are continually available as the central exhibit, while in the surrounding galleries there are periodic displays of selected examples from the moderns. Solti is so successful at this that, though he has a reputation for favoring the old Germanic masters, he gets enough diversity out of the orchestra's season-long program that in 1972 the Chicago Symphony won the ASCAP award for programming the greatest number of pieces written since 1940.

"All sorts of leitmotifs are going through," says Solti. "You must have a certain amount out of the classical repertoire, a certain amount of modern music, preferably a certain amount of American music because it is an American orchestra, and it must keep the American composer and his music prominent because European orchestras won't do it." This must be woven in with the selection of pieces for singers; these choices cannot be changed later because "to get the vocalists, you have to 'fix' the work you are doing." All this is intertwined with the imperatives that can be thrust upon the guest conductors—and those that can't. "It is very difficult because often guest conductors do not want to learn a new piece so I have to leave it to myself and to younger people to struggle with." It is a matter of hard planning for the five "guest conducting" months of every season— "sometimes you are a year putting the whole program together."

It is illuminating to see how Solti builds the programs for his own appearances. For this is the foundation of the "museum" and its attractions.

There were two notable aspects about the Solti programs in 1973–74.

One was that he did not schedule any Wagner into his weeks on the podium in Chicago, though he is perhaps the world's most renowned interpreter of Wagner. Nor did he schedule any Bruckner for himself, though this, too, is supposed to be one of his compulsions. The other is that his weeks were loaded or overloaded with Beethoven. Not only would he play Beethoven's *Missa Solemnis* but he would play the first eight of Beethoven's nine symphonies. He was not too obvious about it. In his first three weeks in Chicago—his "autumn season"—Solti would play only one Beethoven symphony plus the *Missa Solemnis*. But he would schedule other Beethoven works for out-of-town appearances of the symphony—in Milwaukee, where the Chicago Symphony makes ten appearances a year, for example; and in college towns—De Kalb, Illinois, and Storrs, Connecticut; and even in major tour towns, such as New York and Washington. He would not play any of the Beethoven at all in his winter season, in January. Then, in his last trip to Chicago, the "spring season," he would concentrate four Beethoven symphonies, a Beethoven piano concerto (the *Emperor*), and a Beethoven overture *(Coriolanus)* into two weeks of programming in May.

Why so much Beethoven? Because Solti was planning to record the eight Beethoven symphonies for London/Decca records. And he would do it during this season. (He and the Chicago Symphony, with the Chicago Symphony Orchestra Chorus, had already recorded Beethoven's Ninth Symphony and it had become a best-seller among classical records.) It has become a common tactic for conductors to prepare and rehearse their orchestras for a recording session by playing the numbers to be recorded in the concert hall shortly before the record session. In this season, Solti would be recording in the autumn and again in the spring but not at all during January; thus he had not scheduled any Beethoven for his appearances in January.

Why is this done?

Because of the high costs of recording with an American orchestra in the United States. The recording company—in this case, London/Decca—must pay the same high rates for rehearsal time as for recording time ($101.00 per man for a three-hour session, $134.67 per man for a four-hour session). Those hours are "forty-minute" fours; the agreement between players and recording companies dictates that the players be given twenty minutes off for every hour of recording time. So Solti, like a great many other conductors, prepares the orchestra in the concert hall for the recording sessions; he has it rehearse and play "in season" in the concert hall the numbers that will be recorded because the recording company then is saved the time and cost of rehearsal in the recording room. It is, perhaps, the only way to persuade recording companies to work with American orchestras instead of working with the less well-paid European orchestras. Says Solti: "To record an American orchestra is still three times as much as a European orchestra. You must work at least three times faster than in Europe in order to compensate for that extra cost." And one way to do this is to shift preparation time from the recording room to the concert hall.

If this sounds as though Solti was exploiting the orchestra, then consider these factors: (1) the Chicago Symphony had been paying RCA about half the costs of making the orchestra's records in the mid-1960s; (2) the players each received a fee for recording the Beethoven symphonies—as much as $1,000 apiece. Not to mention the renown and ego rewards which accrue from worldwide—as opposed to citywide—recognition of their work. Great symphonies greatly recorded are simply another way for the orchestra to break out of the strictures of time and place—to belong to the world as well as to the city—and earn an enduring stature in other lands.

So the recording contract dictated the concert-hall scheduling of the eight Beethoven symphonies.

Now there was another "hard" factor: what to play in New York?

The Chicago Symphony had scheduled four appearances in Carnegie Hall this season, two in the autumn and two more in the spring. They'd all be under Solti's direction and they'd all be sold in subscription series, which means that the audience bought its tickets in advance expecting to hear a certain kind of sound from Solti and the Chicago Symphony. They want no surprises but they do want something special.

In turn, Solti wants to give them something special, because of the special rapport that exists between the Carnegie Hall audience and the Chicago Symphony. "Four different programs—of *course*, we must supply something interesting. Four different programs—for there is a special interest to the orchestra and to me. This is very difficult because certain composers come to my mind. This is a puzzle game which one must fit." In the past, he'd been superbly successful in fitting the puzzle together. In 1970, he'd done the Mahler Fifth Symphony and the response had been astounding: the cheering and shouting had gone on for twenty minutes after the concert ended. "It probably would have gone on all night," wrote Winthrop Sargeant in *The New Yorker*, "but for the fact that Mr. Solti led his concertmaster off the stage, signifying that enough is enough."

In the season preceding this, Solti and the Chicago Symphony had achieved some sort of apogee by scheduling Berlioz's *La Damnation de Faust* in one New York visit and Wagner's *Götterdämmerung* (act 3) in the other. "But, of course, you cannot play that every year," he says. For this season he settled for a less overheated appearance in the autumn, in New York. He would make Beethoven's Third Symphony *(Eroica)* the capstone of the first appearance. Then, as if to demonstrate that he was not locked into the "old masters," he preceded it by Henze's *Heliogabalus Imperator*, a modern piece that had been commissioned by the Chicago Symphony a year or so earlier. A nice contrast. To them he would add the overture to the opera *Oberon* by Weber (which, not too surprisingly, Solti was planning to record and release in another Chicago Symphony orchestra album). For the Saturday night show, he'd made a climax of Mahler's Sixth Symphony—"Mahler because, of course, in New York they love Mahler. The orchestra plays it marvelously. So it is logical." Then he decided to pair it with the Bach Suite no. 3, a very exact piece for a small ensemble within the orchestra. It would show off the precision and virtuosity of the players more than their muscularity. Again, a neat—and calculated—contrast.

"Now in the spring, it was more difficult," says Solti. He was always in the position of topping himself without appearing to try to do so. Ultimately, for the first of the two spring appearances, he selected *Bluebeard's Castle* by Béla Bartók—"which I like, which is very near to me, which I think will be very good. The orchestra played, with Reiner, Bartók very much—the whole Bartók repertoire they know." He would flesh out that program with Schumann's Symphony no. 4 in D Minor. For the other program he would select a "non-Teutonic" work that would again establish the orchestra's broad capability. "We must play Stravinsky's *Le Sacre du Printemps*. We are going to do it again for two reasons: (a) I think they do it well. (b) I think I do it well." There was a third reason—or two: (a) he was very inclined to play the Stravinsky when the orchestra toured Europe the next season, and (b) the thought that the orchestra might record it in the not too distant future. Thus he would have prepared it and tested it against a very tough, if receptive, Carnegie Hall audience. He would augment it with Elgar's *Enigma* Variations and with Mozart's *Haffner* Symphony (Symphony no. 35), "which we didn't play before this year." On the whole it would be a test of the audience in New York as well as the orchestra: he would give the audience quite the sound it was expecting, but not in the quantity it anticipated. And he would give it a demonstration of the variety of the orchestra, whether the audience much wanted it or not.

The detailing of the New York schedule helped fill the Chicago schedule, because everything that's played in New York is played first in Chicago. So two weeks of New York appearances assured Solti of enough material for four concerts in Chicago. The Beethoven provided several more weeks of material. To this, Solti added some composers familiar in the "old masters" group—Mozart, Schubert, Schumann, Strauss, Verdi, Haydn, Bach. For music by American composers, he selected Charles Ruggles's *Men and Mountains*, though he'd never read the score or heard it played. He bowed to "modern" music, as well as "American" music, by insisting on Henze's *Heliogabalus Imperator*, but he also had additional pieces—from the preelectronic era, of course—by Bartók, Britten and Hindemith. He recognized the parochial interests of Chicago-and-its-neighbors by agreeing to play the obscure violin concerto by Martinů discovered in the music library at Northwestern University. He returned to the particular sound of the symphony by choosing an overture by Berlioz, *Les Francs-Juges*. It, too, would be recorded and released in another album by the Chicago Symphony.

Then there were the choral works. They are fascinating on many levels. Theoretically, any conductor can choose to do them by enlisting the aid of the Chicago Symphony Orchestra Chorus. "But there's a limitation: on account of costs, we give Solti and Giulini first chance at the choral works. And then Barenboim. And then it's an open field, depending on what somebody wants to do," says John Edwards. The cost factor is an ominous one, since the chorus is so large (175 to 200 members, depending on the work). Sometimes it can be justified in other terms—such as the presentation of modern music. In 1971, Solti conducted the orchestra and the chorus in a concert version of *Moses und Aron* and cheerfully demolished the budget for the year. "I mean *Moses und Aron* is nothing to take lightly," says Edwards, with only a mild sense of desperation. "That's a whole orchestra's budget, in some cases, for ten years."

For Solti in particular—perhaps because of his long background in opera—the choral works are particularly significant. He chose, as we've seen, *Missa Solemnis* and *The St. Matthew Passion* as his choral works for this season but his placement of the latter was significant. He chose to conduct it on April 12 and 13— Good Friday and Holy Saturday—for obvious reasons: Bach composed it as a Holy Week anthem, and it was first played in public on Easter Sunday, April 15, 1729. But perhaps the most significant thing is that Solti chose to present it to a nonsubscription audience, in two special concerts for which anybody who had the money could buy tickets, whether or not they had season-long subscriptions. The plan had to be changed, and one of these became a subscription concert, because of the work stoppage. But the point of preference remains the same: Solti has a special enthusiasm for nonsubscription audiences, and a wariness of subscription audiences.

"If you *have* to go to something, you don't like it," he says. "You may say, 'Oh, I have to go to the symphony, and I would rather stay home than go to the symphony or the opera.' But if you buy a ticket when you like to, you say, 'Oh, I am going to the symphony.' You are looking forward to it. So the audiences in those cities where there are no subscription audiences are very much better than subscription audiences. They are warm. They are very generous in their applause. They are better. They want to be there and they look forward to be there. It is very human. It is of nature. So having said that . . ."

He acknowledges the absolute necessity of having subscription audiences. It is the way of achieving some security in the concert hall in the United States (as opposed to Europe, where public funds pay for so much of the musical activity). "Look, they know clearly how much income they will have at the end of June," he points out of the orchestras playing to subscription audiences. "They will know it because they have sold their tickets. They are gone so that they have that money, that income. But if you have single concerts, selling each by one, the result will be different, very different."

Solti subdivides the point neatly. "Having said that the subscription audiences are never as warm as nonsubscription audiences, I must add that Saturday evening subscription audiences are the best audience," he says. "For the simple reason that the people did not work Saturday. They are free to enjoy themselves. The problem of symphony concerts or music in general in America is this: they are living more and more outside themselves." By this he means that the demands on the population are becoming less internal and less cerebral, they are becoming more external and more demanding physically—one has to invest a major physical effort simply to enjoy a cerebral or emotional one. "Now if you live in the city and you leave work at five o'clock, whether you go home and change and you come back—which is a terrible thing because of the distances involved in Chicago—or you stay down and keep your time open and come to the concert. Practically coming from your office or your bureau or whatever it is to the concert. This is not easy. This is not right for listening to a concert. Now in Europe it is still different, because in Europe the people going home, the distances are not as big. By Europe, I do not mean London. London is a different case. London is a lot like America in that sense. A great deal of people living in the suburbs, a great deal."

The Saturday night audience does not have to make this huge investment of energy; it invests only one round trip between home and downtown instead of two, as on work days. "So in Chicago and probably the rest of the country, the Saturday evening and maybe the Sunday afternoon audiences are the best audiences at the concerts." He thinks the Thursday night audiences are the poorest, if only because they are most densely attended by patrons. For one thing, they've had the full workday and perhaps a round trip home before the concert; for another, their interest in music is dutiful rather than passionate. "Look, I know there are very many people on the Thursday night who do not want to be there," he says. "Psychological—I am probably unfair; I don't want to sound unfair but they have the psychological: (a) 'I paid in advance for my ticket.' (b) 'I gave some extra money for the symphony, so why should I have to like it?" That is changing—changing very much. Ever since this orchestra in Chicago began having such incredible successes."

He sees the change most conspicuously in the Friday afternoon audiences. These are, historically, the "rich, little old lady" audiences—the women who feel that culture is a Friday afternoon concert. Traditionally these audiences drive conductors crazy, because the applause with daintily gloved hands is so smothered and measured—like the muffled fall of snow, says Pierre Boulez—and because the ladies get up and leave when it's time for tea or time to catch a train, not simply when the concert is over. ("Besides," said Solti, "I do not like one-sex audiences.") Solti is more optimistic about the Friday afternoon audiences than most conductors. ("Friday afternoons are now excellent, no?") The reason is that he sees more and more young people coming to the Friday afternoon concerts. "There are still old ladies—young ladies as well—but a great number of young people so that has very much changed the atmosphere." He recalls that when he first was guest conductor in Chicago "there was a great deal of circulation, coming and going on Friday afternoon." He had, in fact, expressed a wish that the whole Friday afternoon audience would go away. "This is very much better now. It still appears that, whatever happens, there are still certain ladies who at four o'clock they are going away. But it is not as bad as it was. It is very little now. And through the mixture now with the young people, we have a very good audience."

This is not to say that the Friday afternoon concerts still might not disappear. In this season, the Chicago Symphony was starting a series of Sunday afternoon concerts, and there were many who felt that Sunday afternoons might one day replace Friday afternoons in the concert hall—at least until the gasoline shortage threatened attendance at these Sunday concerts.

Solti is not, however, willing to indict the Friday afternoon audiences as the cause of that possible change. Instead, he says, it is the strain of playing on Friday afternoon. He is a man very aware of the strain that his work places on him and on the orchestra; he points out that the customary schedule in Chicago has the orchestra playing the complete program four times in three days and—with the Friday afternoon concert included—three times in a matter of thirty hours. "You have on Thursday morning a dress rehearsal when you play the whole program, nearly always." That is at 10 A.M. and the rehearsal lasts until 12:30. The players then have just under eight hours off; the Thursday evening concert starts at 8:15 P.M. and concludes between 10 and 10:15 P.M. Many of the players go home in that afternoon break—even to the distant suburbs. So they make two round trips from home to concert hall that day. That means that for some of them there are three to four hours spent in commuting and four and a half hours spent in playing on Thursday.

"You play twice the program on Thursday and then you go home after the concert and eat, and it is always one or two o'clock in the morning when you go to bed and I never sleep well after a performance."

Yet there is no chance to rest on Friday; he and the players must be dressed and ready to start the concert at 2 P.M. The concert ends around 4 P.M. and then everybody can relax until the next concert at 8:30 P.M. Saturday.

"This is terrible timing," says Solti. "If you have a big work, let us say we have *Missa Solemnis*, on Thursday morning, Thursday evening, Friday afternoon, and then Saturday evening. Now this is very hard. This is terrifically hard. For the orchestra, for the chorus, for the soloists, for everybody."

With a Sunday afternoon performance substituted for Friday afternoon—"It is a trial, five Sunday afternoons, for five Friday afternoons"—everybody will get a forty-six-hour rest period between Thursday night's performance and Saturday night's performance. ("I have Friday off," says Solti, who does like to recuperate from the exertion of his work.) And then there is a little extra break on Sunday afternoon because the concerts start at three o'clock: "from Saturday evening to Sunday afternoon at three, instead of two, that is also longer." So, "this is the only objection I have to Friday afternoon. It is a physical objection."

The Season in Heritage

The members of the orchestra themselves had no voice in all this planning —though they'd like to. Indeed, the Chicago Symphony players, like symphony musicians all over the world, are becoming more and more demanding about taking part in the aesthetic planning of the season. This is a dramatic change in attitude—a firming of purpose—compared with only a very few years ago. And it reflects a growing confidence and sense of identity within the orchestra.

These changes are not singularly of this season. Indeed, they are not even rooted in the Solti years. Instead they began evolving because of the pressures and events that took place ten and twenty years ago. These were years of great turmoil, for players, for conductors, and for managements of the symphony. It is, perhaps, the most significant achievement of Georg Solti that he calmed the turmoil while bringing the orchestra to greatness.

To understand this accomplishment, it is necessary to know something of what the Chicago Symphony has experienced, or endured, in its years of glory and of turmoil.

The Chicago Symphony Orchestra was organized in 1891, the conception and instrument of Theodore Thomas. He was a strong-willed, strong-minded man who'd had as much failure as success in symphony work in New York, and in keeping a symphony orchestra alive while on tour.

In his New York years, he was approached to conduct the New York Philharmonic as an alternative to the Damrosches—père et fils (Leopold and Walter). When the yearly receipts fell from a high of $15,480 under Carl Bergmann to $841 under Leopold Damrosch, Thomas was asked to take over the New York Philharmonic. He appeared reluctant to do so: "All they wish," he said in a letter of that time, "is that I should give up my symphony concerts, gain theirs, and step down to their comfortable muddy ways." Nevertheless, he took the job and conducted the New York Philharmonic for thirteen of the next fourteen seasons, sextupling the receipts in his first year and ultimately raising them to peak of $17,914. Then, in 1891, he made what Chicagoans like to consider a step up in life: he abandoned New York forever and launched the Chicago Symphony Orchestra. He was not afraid of work—his touring orchestra sometimes played as many as six concerts in six different cities in a week—or damnation, if only he had full continuing control of a symphony ("I would go to hell if they gave me a permanent orchestra," he said in the days before he was able to bring the Chicago Symphony to reality). But he was not so single-minded as to place his orchestra and its music above all other considerations. In 1899, he turned down an invitation to take the Chicago Symphony to France—an invitation he wanted achingly to accept, if only to show off his new toy. The reason he rejected the invitation: he was personally scandalized by the actions of the French government and the French military in the Dreyfus affair and he would not accept an invitation from a French government-connected agency because of it.

Thomas died early in 1905 and was succeeded by his associate conductor, Frederick Stock, who brought the orchestra both consistency and a rising sense of acclaim. Stock, in turn, died in 1942, after having been conductor for thirty-eight years. That meant that the orchestra had just two conductors for the first fifty-one years of its existence. In the next ten years, it had three music directors—Désiré Defauw, Artur Rodzinski, and Rafael Kubelik—not to mention two full seasons when it had only guest conductors. These were not peaceful years or pleasant ones, for either the orchestra or the conductors. Some conductors felt hounded by "outsiders"—often the critiques of Claudia Cassidy of the *Chicago Tribune*—and some players felt uncomfortable with the professional habits of others. It was not until 1953, and the arrival of Fritz Reiner as musical director, that a purposeful new era was started.

Reiner was out of the Hungarian school of music. The conductors produced by it have included, among others, Eugene Ormandy, Antal Dorati, and George Szell, as well as Georg Solti. The Hungarian school was German-dominated in sound, and so Reiner's handling of the Chicago Symphony resurrected the deep sonorities of the past and gave it a richer, more substantial tone. But he kept the warm Magyar blood well under control, perhaps more so than does Solti. His music had bigness and dignity; his melodic material was sculpted with confidence, elegance, and style. But he did not lean into the melody as some more sentimental conductors have been known to do. He could take wild, thrashing phrases and—while building surges of sound—limn them with a beautifully articulated clarity of texture and balance. To many of his colleagues, he was a conductor's conductor—a precisionist, a perfectionist, whose iron technical and mechanical control never relaxed, whose rhythm never broke ranks. His aim, like Toscanini's, was not to interpret the music, not to add frills or lush sounds, but merely to take it off the page as the composer wrote it and present it with the composer's purpose—more than the conductor's flair—always in mind. Igor Stravinsky once said that the Chicago Symphony under Reiner was the most precise and flexible orchestra in the world.

His sense of control—his refusal to yield to emotion—was displayed most obviously in his baton technique. He is said by some to have been the greatest of all baton technicians. The notable thing is that he waved the baton so little; he once explained that he sought to achieve the maximum musical result with the minimum physical effort. He attributed this technique to the influence of yet another great Hungarian conductor, Artur Nikisch, who died in 1922. "It was he who told me that I should never wave my arms in conducting, and that I should use my eyes to give cues." He liked to use a big baton but he barely moved it; the tip would cut—as Regina Resnik used to say—"little chocolate squares" in the air. It was not always easy to follow him because the musicians could not pick up his beat and his motion through peripheral vision; his beat was so small as to be indiscernible, unless the musician was looking directly at him. "And even then, you couldn't see it from the stands in the rear," says one player in the Chicago Symphony. And yet he held the orchestra in full and undeviating control, cuing the players in and out, shaping phrases, holding the rhythm perfectly, creating an effect of infinite nuance. He was literally able to cure orchestras of their own private tantrums through his tiny tip-movement. He antagonized the New York Philharmonic on one particular occasion by his cutting remarks about its quality, and the orchestra—as it has so often been known to do—decided to "break" him by responding too slowly to his beat, by trying to force him to a bigger movement and thus force him into something he was not—a very calisthenic conductor. "Our rhythm hung back until it started to collapse," one player remember later. "Reiner knew what was happening all right." He just compressed his lips and his beat, which had been tiny to begin with. "Now it got absolutely minuscule." The musicians could do only two things: ignore Reiner altogether or, as professionals, respond to the inner drives of their duties. They responded: "We *had* to follow him." And Reiner gave it to *them* by making the baton movement even smaller. "It was a sort of bawling out, in reverse."

The music that the Chicago Symphony made under Reiner was glorious. Some of the players believe that it was better then than today; many believe that the records made for RCA during Reiner's regime—notably one of Strauss's *Also Sprach Zarathustra*—were the finest ever made, including those of the Solti era.

"Reiner always had a very clean sound," says Donald Peck, principal flutist in the Chicago Symphony. "He also favored the brass and percussion; he didn't particularly care about the woodwinds. Yet he was a brilliant conductor. Just as Solti is a brilliant conductor. I find that they're very much alike in many ways. Maybe Reiner had a more sensitive side to him than Solti. Now Solti is aware of this. It's a lacking in his nature. Every conductor has a lacking somewhere—every human being does, not just Solti. And Solti realizes this; he just doesn't conduct the music he doesn't do well. When have you seen Solti conduct a French composer, except something bombastic, like a Berlioz? Solti knows his forte and he does it better than anybody—I mean Mahler and Bruckner, wow! Reiner was a bit more—well, he tried to do French things. Some were very good, some were not."

The impression that Reiner made on the members of the Chicago Symphony endures today. In one respect, this is natural: eleven of the fifteen principal players in the Chicago Symphony when Solti arrived had been seasoned under Reiner. But another respect was the depth he gave to the music he shaped. "Whenever we play a piece that we worked on under Reiner," recalls Sam Denov, the percussionist-soon-to-turn-law-student, "it's still his conceptions and his ideas that are in our minds."

The tributes offered to Reiner from the members of the orchestra are remarkable—because most of them loathed and feared him.

The reason: he ran the orchestra in the Toscanini tradition, which is to say that he was autocratic and tyrannical, cutting of tongue and unsparing in his criticism. He did not draw music out of his players; he frightened it out of them. He was impatient, irascible, sarcastic. He would attack a player during rehearsal and flay him verbally until he almost drove men crying from the stage. "He was a sadist," one player of that era told me. And another and another and another. If he could not drive a man from the orchestra, he would fire him. "He always had a list of people to be fired," recalls one player. "There was always a lot of insecurity in the orchestra then."

One of Reiner's greatest weapons was a corrosive wit. For a long time the targets tended to remember the acidity more than the wit, for Reiner had a way of using it to explain everything he thought about you. For years he labored in Pittsburgh with a general manager whom he disdained. They had many long, wrangling fights and Reiner did not emerge from them with an exalted view of his antagonist's skills. One day the manager came to Reiner about some issue and, in the course of the conversation, began complaining about his various ills. "On top of all that," he said finally, "I somehow seem to have sprained my back." Reiner looked at him impassively, then uttered the one comment that totally summed up his attitude: "From trying to make far-reaching decisions, no doubt."

Now that time has stilled the tongue, the wit tends to surface as much as the acidity. Some folks around Orchestra Hall still remember when Reiner, as was his custom, arrived at Orchestral Hall about forty-five or fifty minutes before the concert. He paused in the doorway to the box office and said to the ticket sellers: "Good evening, gentlemen. Are we sold out *again?*"

"Yes, sir," was the reply. "We certainly are, Dr. Reiner."

"You see," said Reiner, "I have always had to take the good with the good."

Ray Still recalls the time he was playing a prominent oboe part on Beethoven's Symphony no. 6 *(Pastoral)* not long after coming to the Chicago Symphony from the Baltimore Symphony. He played a few bars when Reiner interrupted him and said, "No! Wrong. Play it again!"

"I started again," says Still. "He stopped, slammed the stick down, and said, 'Say, have you ever played this piece before?' I was indignant—to think that he'd believe I hadn't played that part before."

"Of course I've played it before," snapped Still.

Reiner tilted his head and looked at him over the rim of his glasses. "Where did you play this? It must have been in Baltimore." He looked slyly around at the orchestra. "Mit the Orioles."

As a perfectionist, Reiner demanded perfection all the time. And there is no musician who does not miss notes or play wrong ones from time to time. Reiner was unmoving about mistakes during a concert. "For Fritz Reiner, you didn't spoil concerts," says Sam Denov, "because if you did, you weren't around for the second time." He was a trifle more lenient in rehearsals, if only because he could express himself verbally at the moment of error. "Fritz Reiner was a man that wanted to have things work—function—and he didn't want always to go through it a second time," says Denov. "You did it right the first time and if he did give you a chance to do it again and you failed the second time—'good-bye.' He was the kind of guy that if the machine didn't function well, he didn't try to find out what's wrong, he'd just give it a kick and expect that it's going to work this time."

Even the most secure men in the orchestra, such as trumpeter Adolph Herseth, were a little tentative around Reiner when they made a mistake. "I recall one week when he was doing Mendelssohn's *Italian* Symphony," Herseth recalled recently. "In the first movement, there's a place in the trumpet part where you sort of anticipate a modulation. It's not a solo entrance or anything like that but you have to come in right. Well, there are two lines of music in the part. One line has about twenty-nine bars of rest. The line below, there's thirty-one bars of rest. And after each one of these, you come in with the same note. Well, I picked the wrong line and so I was two bars early. So I figured I had destroyed that concert rather adequately."

He also figured he'd better not wait for Reiner to react; he'd better take the initiative. "So the next morning I went to his dressing room and said, 'Dr. Reiner, I want to apologize for conduct unbecoming a first trumpet player.' He looked at me and said, 'Yes. You knew it and I knew it, but I don't *think* anybody else knew it.' Then he looked at me over the tops of his glasses and said, '*Don't* let it happen again.'"

The principals have the assurance of their own skills but not always the equable personal security that Herseth possesses. "Reiner was the kind of guy—if he found you were not functioning the way he wanted you to, he had no use for you," Sam Denov asserts. "If you were, you could apparently do no wrong—he would excuse all kinds of errors made trying to achieve something in an honest way. But if you were just incompetent and trying to cover up, well, he could spot a phony in just a minute and he had no use for that kind of people. He had no time for them; he would not accept excuses. He wanted performance. He wanted a function. He had no use for you if you couldn't function." Reiner would test everybody who was new to his regime to see if he was strong or weak—personally as well as musically. It was often rougher on the back-stand players than on first-chair players, perhaps because there were more of them, perhaps because he felt their insecurities had to be excised if the orchestra was to be made stronger. Whatever his reason, he made life hell for these men and women. "He was constantly probing and testing the people in the orchestra," says Denov. "He didn't want to waste time with individuals—if you couldn't produce, you'd better leave. If he found the kind of guy in his orchestra who had a thin veneer, who wasn't sure of himself or not confident of his own capabilities, he would drive a crack into that veneer, and he would exploit that crack, and drive a stake through it. And that guy would be gone

Fred Spector, violinist.

within a matter of a year or two. It had happened to every orchestra he had been with. But the people that were able to pass the test always got along well with him. He respected them and you were part of the family."

An illustration of how all these factors came together in the Reiner regime is in the experience of Fred Spector, who joined the orchestra in the 1950s on the last stand of the second violins. "He brought me into the orchestra," says Spector, "which doesn't necessarily mean he liked me. I had to prove myself." Just a few months after Spector had joined the symphony, he was summoned from the last stand of the second violins to replace a man in the first stand who'd fallen ill. "The first day that I sat up there, Reiner made a point of stopping the orchestra a number of times and saying to me, 'Spector, you're doing it wrong, you are playing it wrong.' He never tells me what I was doing that was wrong. But just, 'It's not right.'" Spector was not about to become flustered; he'd come from a background that included everything from low-level strafing in World War II to conducting the pit orchestra for touring Broadway musicals (*Brigadoon, Top Banana*) to playing lead violin in the Chez Paree in the heyday of Chicago's turbulent nightclub life. So he didn't even blink an eye at the maestro's ranting. "My only attitude was, 'I only have one way of playing this piece, I only know of one way to play in the orchestra. If you don't intend to tell me what I'm doing that's wrong, I'll go on doing it the way I'm doing it.' " So he didn't change and neither did Reiner: the conductor kept stopping the orchestra and heaping abuse on Spector, still without telling him what he should be doing. "I figured that, 'If I'm sitting here for a long time and he's going to keep on stopping the orchestra and telling me that I'm doing it wrong, without telling me what it is I'm doing wrong, eventually I'm going to have to go up to him and ask him what it is that I'm doing wrong.' "

The confrontation never came to pass. The abuse stopped as suddenly as it started. "The following day and every day after that, there wasn't a word said to me," says Spector. The newcomer sat in the first stand for four to six weeks without another comment from Reiner; then when the player who was ill returned, Spector went back to the last stand of the second violins. "Reiner made a point of stopping the orchestra and telling me I'd done a very fine job," making one of his rare, warm little comments.

That was fine. But Spector didn't forget. "Subsequently we became good friends, but not because of my violin playing. Because of my interest in cameras. Reiner was a Leica nut and loved collecting various lenses for the Leica. And I was able to get some of these lenses for him at a very low price." It took years before Spector dared venture the question, but finally he asked Reiner why the conductor had stopped the orchestra on that one day and given Spector such a hard time.

"I said, 'What did I do wrong?' "

"Nothing," said Reiner. "I just wanted to see if you would get nervous."

That was the key to dealing with Reiner. "Obviously I didn't get nervous. It bothered me but it didn't show in my playing. Once he knew I wasn't going to get upset about something like that—well, that's the kind of player he wanted in the orchestra. Somebody who was able to keep his cool, no matter what."

The difficulty is that most players don't like to be tested in this way. Whether they kept their cool was not as important as whether they cherished their resentment. They did.

Reiner spent ten years with the Chicago Symphony. In those years, the reputation of the orchestra grew enormously. So did the resentment within it. The players assigned demonic qualities to Reiner; they could not believe he'd do anything to avoid hounding and harassing them. When the Chicago Symphony's first European tour was canceled in 1959, many of the players felt it was just another of Reiner's devices to bedevil them. They made their displeasure evident in a demonstration in the players' locker room at Orchestra Hall. "We all but hung him in effigy," says Sam Denov. The reason for the cancellation was not Reiner's temperament but Reiner's health; he was beginning to be seriously affected by the cardiovascular problems that were eventually to take his life. Yet he would not allow this fact to be made public. Nevertheless, he slowed down perceptibly in the next few seasons, and in 1962–63 he became musical "adviser," not—as he'd been in the past—musical "director." The search was already on to find a successor as music director.

A number of guest conductors were examined in performances with the symphony, and candidates from outside that realm were also considered. In fact, Solti got a bid to come to Chicago in this period. The offer was blunt and to the point: Dr. Eric Oldberg, then head of the Orchestral Association, flew to Texas—where Solti was conducting the Dallas Symphony—with a contract in his pocket for Solti to take over the Chicago Symphony. Solti turned him down. He was then music director of the Royal Opera in London; he was attracting considerable acclaim as a guest conductor of the Metropolitan Opera; and he had a commitment to carry out in Dallas. So the Orchestral Association turned instead to Jean Martinon, who had made a profoundly favorable impression in several appearances as a guest conductor for the Chicago Symphony. Martinon became musical director in October 1963; Reiner died on November 15, 1963, just prior to beginning a five-week engagement as a guest conductor of the Chicago Symphony, an engagement that was to celebrate his seventy-fifth birthday.

Martinon was, at the time, fifty-three years old, a spare, wiry man with a thick shock of white hair, like a crew-cut that had half grown out. He had style and a certain substance—he belonged to that generation which, as adults, had to fight and endure World War II as the experience of their thirties. An infantryman in the French army, he was captured when the German forces swept over northern France. He escaped. He was recaptured. He escaped again. He was recaptured and sent to a prison camp in Germany. Then he realized he could gain freedom only through an ersatz legalism. There were certain French prisoners the Germans were willing to release—those with large families, those who were farmers, those who were clergymen, those who handled garbage or worked in the sanitary systems of the nation, those who were, mysteriously, from Brittany. "I tried everything," Martinon once explained. "I 'became' a priest. I 'became' a farmer. I suddenly 'became' the head of a very large family." These transformations were accomplished by forging the identification papers carried by all members of the erstwhile French army. The tool of his forgery was primitive: a potato. Martinon became a master at cutting a potato so that it had a flat face, then applying that flat face to a genuine set of papers so that it picked up the ink on the documents. He would then reapply the flat face to a blank set of papers so that the ink impression was left on the new papers. "Lighter than the original but good enough," he said.

When finally he "became" a member of the sanitary service, Martinon was released and shipped back to Paris. From there he made his way to *France libre*—"which was not free"—and he settled in Clermont-Ferrand, a city in a "wild, savage" section of central France not far from his native Lyon. There he composed music by day and worked with the French Resistance by night. "I was what was called a 'transmission agent,' " he recounted. After dark, he would slip into the Loire River—some miles west of his home—with messages that "sometimes were written down, sometimes were only in my head." He would swim for miles up and down the river until he encountered another agent to whom he passed on the message. Then he would swim home. "The river was much better than the road," he said. "I never met a German in the river."

Not long after the war ended, Martinon had ready for presentation one of his compositions. It was called *Psalm 136—Song of the Captives* and it won the Grand Prix of the City of Paris. Indeed, it attracted so much attention that, at the age of thirty-six—and with no previous experience as a conductor—he made a triumphant debut as conductor of Paris's Concerts Pasdeloup. Within ten performances he was asked to conduct the London Philharmonic Orchestra, the orchestra that Solti now guest-conducts in London, through a ten-concert series. "I knew nothing about conducting," he said. "I had to learn backward the rules." Indeed, he was—like Solti—a late starter. Yet Martinon did not feel in the least bit retarded for suffering a late start. Nor should he. He became associate conductor of the London Philharmonic, headed the Concerts Lamoureux and the Israel Philharmonic in the 1950s, and made his American debut with the Boston Symphony in 1957. At the same time, he continued his labor as a composer, and he was sometimes able to combine the two efforts: at a 1962 guest appearance with the Chicago Symphony he received both an ovation from the audience and acclaim from the critics for the performance of his Symphony no. 3 (*Hymne à la Vie*).

His early days with the Chicago Symphony were happy and rewarding ones for all sides. He took a look at the basement quarters of the players—then dark, cluttered, crowded—and declared that they would have to be enlarged, better lighted, and made more comfortable. ("We do owe the rebuilding of the hall, which was a success—the basement part of it—to Martinon," says Fred Spector.) He took a look at the future schedule of the orchestra and began planning trips to both the East and West coasts of the United States to enlarge the audience and the reputation of the Chicago Symphony. His performances were, for many, stunning in their effectiveness; everybody from tart-tongued Claudia Cassidy of the *Chicago Tribune* to eastern music critics gave him hosannas:

"The Chicago Symphony is still one of the world's great orchestras. And Mr. Martinon is a conductor with decided ideas," wrote Harold C. Schonberg in *The New York Times*.

"The orchestra is a beautiful instrument, sonorous, balanced, and clean," wrote Alan Rich in the *New York Herald Tribune*.

"Of all the orchestras appearing in Carnegie Hall's international festival of visiting orchestras this season, the Chicago Symphony aroused the most interest," wrote Miles Kastendieck in *The Christian Science Monitor*.

"The overall ensemble is often breathtakingly accurate, and the average sound produced is of a mellow, relaxed, and well-integrated sort that we often associate with European ensembles," wrote Winthrop Sargeant in *The New Yorker*.

"It embodies the flexibility as well as the strength of a master technician's ideal of orchestral culture," wrote Irving Kolodin in *Saturday Review*.

Then bit by bit, almost imperceptibly, it all began coming apart. The autocratic head of the Orchestral Association retired and a newer, less decisive man came in. The general manager of the orchestra was fired and a younger, less experienced man was brought in. The attitude of Miss Cassidy, certainly the most influential critic in the history of Chicago, became less enthusiastic and considerably more acerbic, finally deeply bitter. The revamping of Orchestra Hall did well by the basement but poorly by the concert hall; in the view of many, the singular sound of the hall had been destroyed. Union-management problems began to gnaw at the interior fabric of the orchestra, and the players divided into pro- and antilabor camps of unusual bitterness. The enthusiasm for Martinon's programs waned as the traditional Germanic sound gave way to a French sound and a contemporary one. Attendance began falling and so did gifts to the orchestra; the deficit began growing. Even the Internal Revenue Service got into the act: it began to hound Martinon for back taxes, claiming that he had not cleared his special tax status as a foreign citizen visiting these shores—as Solti has done—and thus owed more than a hundred thousand dollars in back taxes. Under all these pressures, Martinon seemed to withdraw and take refuge with the few close friends he had within the orchestra. Within a few years, in short, the situation degenerated so deeply that it seemed catastrophe was inevitable.

It is baffling to understand from the outside how the situation got away from Martinon. He did not appear to be a fear-ridden man, nor one lacking in awareness or imagination; his wartime existence reflects all this as well as an ability to cope with difficult problems. Just why he could not conquer the problems within the Chicago Symphony remains a matter of problematical discussion, in the orchestra and out of it.

Through the years, Martinon, who left Chicago to become head of the French Radio and TV Orchestra—certainly a prestigious group—maintained a dignified silence on Chicago and his successor there. Finally in the spring of 1973, more than five years after the Chicago situation achieved its final, tormenting climax, he said: "The Chicago Orchestra is the best that I have ever had as musical director, both for the quality of the orchestra, which is marvelous, and for that fact that in five years I was there I repeated only four pieces. Yet many persons [i.e., in the orchestra] seemed insecure and some wanted to make others insecure. There was a little game of destruction and too many people played it."

There *was* a game of destruction. But not all the players realized how broad and how deep it was to become. Even today, they tend to measure Martinon in terms that are more enlightening for the general response of an orchestra to a conductor—responses that suggest what Solti and other conductors had to meet in this and other seasons. Here, for example, are some of the views on Martinon offered by the men who played under him in Chicago:

"He was not a big enough man for this job musically or intellectually," says Sam Denov.

"He had to find people who loved him," says Ray Still.

"He wasn't a secure man, inwardly," says one player who was hired by Martinon. "And if you don't have that inner security, that comes across to the orchestra in three minutes. And sooner or later they will find out why you're not secure."

"He tended to be very rigid," says Grover Schiltz, an oboe and English horn player. "He also tended to be very much the professor. The men resented him from that standpoint—that no matter how you played a solo for the first time through, he always found something to complain about. Always he had to interject his own idea as to what would make the solo better. It was always a game of one-upmanship with him—he was always trying to create the feeling that he was really the musical master and you were the disciple, the tool that he used to project his own musical idea. Whether it was valid or not valid was not as important as the fact that it was his idea and it was superimposed on yours. Some of his ideas may have had validity, but by the time you got through his kind of—uh—egotistical French personality, you weren't ready to accept much of anything he said. He just had a way of putting people's teeth on edge."

"I felt that Martinon himself was his own worst enemy," says Joseph Golan, now leader of the second violins. "Here was a man of many talents—first of all a charming man, he made a good appearance, he had a way of dealing with people to make them smile, he was robust—he was a mountain climber. He was a pretty good stock man. His problems were mostly of tension—he was a little tight when he conducted. He championed modern music, doing it very well. I thought he was a pretty good composer. He had a few flaws in his handling of the orchestra, which I think contributed to his downfall more than any of the outside intrigue. Among other things, he played musical chairs. He had, for example, a violin audition where he offered the opportunity for all the violinists to play for the purpose of reseating. On the basis of the audition, regardless if one played at the audition or not, he changed every violinist's position except those sitting on the first stand. He pushed one up, he pushed one back, he pushed one across from first to second. Everything was changed and this was not at all constructive for orchestra morale." Golan was one of those who moved from second violin to first under the changes. "But even those who were promoted realized that a shake-up like that was just devastating towards the morale."

"The orchestra needed someone with a deeper insight into the total picture of music making than Martinon had," says Fred Spector. "There were many things he did very well. But there were many things he did poorly. He did very well with contemporary things. Where it took a deep insight into the music, for some reason it never came off. Maybe with another orchestra he could do it. But not with this one. He had some conducting idiosyncrasies which got in the way of this orchestra. For instance, he tried to give the orchestra too many subdivisions of the beat, to the point where it restricts the playing ability of the orchestra. That is where the greatness of a Solti and a Giulini—and a Barenboim—comes out. They are always in control but they never get in your way. They allow you to express yourself within their realm of music making. When you start subdividing and breaking down the various components of the beat, and try to give too many cues and intimations, there are times when you get into the way of the music making of the orchestra. This kind of conducting works very well with an orchestra that isn't as well trained as the Chicago Symphony, with a small, minor orchestra where you have to lay it on the line for them. But with this orchestra, it got into the way of the expressive qualities that it had. It made for very static performances many times.

"But he had a good stick technique and was able to give all the indications. And for contemporary things where the melodic line is not required or expressiveness is not required, he'd just lay it on the line—give you every beat and every subdivision so you knew exactly where you were in the most complicated rhythms—that he could do."

Gordon Peters, the section leader among the percussionists, admits that he liked Martinon, even if he did not always agree with the conductor. "I thought he was particularly at home in the French repertory and I have great respect for him for that," he says. "There were other situations where I thought he perhaps overtaught the orchestra. He was really too conscientious for his taste and didn't realize that this orchestra didn't really need quite that much teaching." He had respect for Martinon in other ways. "What I learned from Martinon was respect for the art. I respected him as a composer, I respect his absolute conscientiousness towards preparing his scores. Being a composer, he had a great structural awareness. You could see the way he studied. One of the pitfalls he fell into now and then was being a composer—he would change orchestrations and make little adjustments and things, which I felt were contrary to the composer's intentions. There are those times, of course, when you feel—and every individual feels—they can help the score along. So you change something. It's ultimately a conscious thing and an artistic decision. You either have the right to do it honestly in your own mind or you don't. He did some rather serious altering, some of which I didn't agree with. He had a good sense of balance; he had a good technique. I respected him for honesty in working with symphonic music—I had some very fine associations with him. He was a very honest man."

Yet another principal says of Martinon: "He was out of his element. He was at best an average, even mediocre conductor. And he was conducting a great orchestra. Occasionally he would rise to the occasion with a piece that we didn't necessarily know, one that he knew pretty well—certain pieces he did quite well." The problem was that he couldn't command the respect of the orchestra; he tended more to request it. And in Chicago you get nowhere by a nice request. "It didn't matter what he did with his hands, what he did offstage, or how he talked, or how many parties he threw. Nothing helped and he thought he was greater than he is. That's a very sad state of affairs. That's the case with most conductors: they think they're much better than they are."

In the end, the most destructive matters were not professional so much as personal. Some members of the orchestra today recall with some heat that Martinon would sometimes use, or satirize, Americanisms in what they thought were purposefully maladroit ways. "It was a cute little joke which we chose to ignore, as the French think they can choose to ignore the Americans," says Grover Schiltz. Others accuse Martinon today for playing the Frenchman in more human ways: "The thing that hurt him was the favoritism he showed toward pretty women in the orchestra, bringing them in in the first place—suddenly the members thought they were being threatened by women who were simply good-looking, and that helped fan the flames of resentment against him." Still others recall deep insults that, they say, Martinon hurled at the orchestra. "We did the Tchaikovsky Fifth with him and after rehearsal he was heard to say, coming off the stage, 'They sound like pigs; they don't know this music,' " says one eminent player. "Now when this gets around an orchestra, the guy who is saying this is not going to be liked by too many people. People ended up not liking him purely from that end of the matter—personally."

The climax came in a confrontation between Martinon and his principal oboist, Ray Still. It was not a fortuitous clash for Martinon. For Still is not only a superbly skilled player but a very strong personality, and an independent one. He has no inclination to sublimate his dislikes. In the season chronicled here, he expressed his disdain over the conduct of one conductor by taking the third oboe chair, instead of the first, in one program. Still is simply not a "go along to get along" kind of man; when he feels disgust or disdain, he takes no pain to conceal that fact. And he felt a great deal of disgust and disdain for Jean Martinon.

The result was a rising friction that put more and more pressure on the orchestra and on Martinon. He was faced with the problem of all overseers: if he let one member get away with certain kinds of give-and-take, he might soon find all the players indulging the same kind of give-and-take. So ultimately he resolved to fire Still. In any orchestra, this had to be a traumatic move, if only because Ray Still is among the most distinguished men of his instrument in the world. It was obvious that he could not be fired for reasons of incompetence; he is simply beyond challenge in his skills. And so the basis for the dismissal was "discipline." This demanded interpretation. Still is a man devoted to music and the disciplines of excelling at his playing. "They were talking of another kind of discipline," says Still, "where you're supposed to toady to the conductor, and you're supposed to say 'Yes, maestro' when you don't feel like calling him 'maestro,' because Martinon was no 'maestro' as far as I was concerned. Only a few brownies in the orchestra would call him 'maestro.' "

In any case, Still decided to fight the firing. He went to the union and it joined the fight—heartily at first, reluctantly (he feels) later on. In any case, the struggle became a long, drawn-out fight that totally divided the orchestra. There were many members who lined up behind Still and his prerogatives as a player. There were others who lined up behind Martinon and his prerogatives as a conductor. There were reports and feelings that some players would be rewarded by management if they testified against Still in the appeal procedures; others would be punished in subtle ways if they supported him. Still feels that insinuations were made that he find a position in another city, if only to avoid embarrassing the Orchestral Association. But Still was not about to give in to that kind of suggestion. He stayed in Chicago, he fought it out, and he won. It cost him, by his estimates, $10,000 that he might have earned otherwise. It also cost the orchestra the seamless garment of unity. For Still felt there was a cabal within the orchestra working against him, one which threatened mass resignations if he returned to his first chair. No such resignations came but Still will not talk, to this day, to some of the people who were, in his view, involved in the testimony against him ("It is very unusual, one union member testifying against another union member") or in the alleged agitation to prevent his return. One of them is Donald Peck, the principal flutist who sits beside him. Another is Victor Aitay, the co-concertmaster, who signals to Still to tune the orchestra to A just before a concert begins. Still another is Milton Preves, principal violist, who sits closer to the conductor than Still but who is close enough to be tapped sternly on the shoulder by Still—or his oboe.

Thus the Chicago Symphony Orchestra—one of the world's greatest ensembles—was a riven group: the conductor besieged, the members barely speaking to each other, the management distracted by deficits. It was clearly time for a change and three changes took place: the conductor was changed, the general manager was changed, and the head of the Orchestral Association was changed. Out of these changes arose the orchestra that Sir Georg Solti was to conduct this season.

Influence of the Executives

The first change, chronologically, was the most critical and remarkable one. For it brought in Louis Sudler as president of the Orchestral Association, the parent body of the Chicago Symphony. Sudler is one of those implausible characters who seems to operate smoothly and efficiently in a dozen worlds at once: on the one hand, he seems no more contemporary than an old-fashioned Sunday sermon, no closer to the imperatives of the modern symphony orchestra than Machault; on the other hand, he's the multimillionaire boss of the very modern John Hancock Building in Chicago—for a brief time the tallest building in the world—and the real estate genius of a dozen or more key locations in the development of Chicago's Loop and Near North Side. His most notable specifications are also his most improbable ones: he knows music not as a hobby but as a vocation—he's a working baritone who made his operatic debut with the Chicago Civic Opera in *I Pagliacci* (as Silvio, amidst the Canio of Giovanni Martinelli and the Tonio of Leonard Warren) and who today makes campus tours, chamber music appearances, and TV shows. "I've been a student ever since I was seven years old until five o'clock this afternoon, when I take my next lesson," he said one day in Chicago. His discipline for that day: the *Mystical Songs* of Vaughan Williams (for a performance with the Chicago Symphony String Quartet) and *Dover Beach* of Samuel Barber.

Sudler is an immaculately dressed, impeccably mannered man with pink skin, white hair, and a carefully modulated voice of deep organ tones. His family was in real estate before him but he can remember his compulsion for music from his earliest years. "I always had some kind of a voice," he says, "but what I wanted to do was take piano lessons. My mother very wisely would not let me take piano lessons until I was seven. On the morning of my seventh birthday I woke up with the wonderful feeling that today was the day." On that day he received two of the most memorable gifts of his life: "I took my first piano lesson and I went to my first Chicago Symphony concert. *Both.*" Subsequently he went through Chicago

Latin School, Hotchkiss, and Yale (cum laude), all the time knowing he was destined for business, all the time yearning to develop further in music. He practices hour upon hour a day—he still practices at least an hour a day. ("I don't let any time get by. And I always have somebody listening. I think it's important that all performers have somebody to listen.") He studied music at Yale, studied further under Giuseppe de Luca and Robert Weede, sang at Ravinia, with the Grant Park Symphony, and at several Republican national conventions and under numerous symphony conductors: Erich Leinsdorf, Pierre Monteux, Rafael Kubelik, Antal Dorati, and Seiji Ozawa among them. When he made his debut with the Chicago Civic Opera on October 26, 1945, the *Chicago Tribune* recognized the multiple nature of the event by sending both its society editor and its top critic. ("Opera House Is Filled for Sudler Debut," reported the society editor. The critic, Miss Cassidy, said, "I don't believe in the history of the opera, Silvio ever before attracted so much attention and there was exactly nothing Mr. Sudler could do about it, and so he did just that. He sang the small role designed for no other purpose but to inflame Canio to the high pitch of lament and he sang it well in a lyric baritone of good quality, simply correctly, and in admirable Italian. His nervousness will wear off with experience, and I hope next time he musses up that all too neat suit and store window makeup, and remembers Silvio is no gentleman.")

When the Chicago Civic Opera died in 1947, not to be replaced until some years later by the Lyric Opera, "my opera work quit," says Sudler. He had a choice of uprooting himself and trying to make it as an operatic baritone in New York or staying in Chicago in a thriving real estate business. He did a little of both: he stayed in Chicago in real estate and he signed on as an available baritone with the National Concert and Artists Corporation, then one of the biggest booking agents in music, to take whatever singing opportunity developed.

"That must have been a very glum day in your life," said a friend of the day the opera died.

"There are no glum days in my life, really," replied Sudler. "I felt terribly fortunate just to have a chance to sing. People were very kind to me really. And there were other fields." He plunged into them—radio, TV, college appearances. He not only sang but eventually he produced. His "Artist's Showcase," once televised weekly, now televised monthly, offered a showcase for young, relatively unknown professional musical talent and won not only a number of Emmys but a Peabody Award.

The only flaw in all this is that his real estate business was becoming enormously successful. One day early in the 1960s, an investment man walked into his office in the antique, historic Rookery in Chicago and asked his views of the best site on Chicago's Near North Side for a big building—a big site for a big building. "It looked like one of those things where you don't know if you're wasting your time or not," he says. "So I said, 'All right, I think I know. Let me work on it.' " He found the site on Michigan Avenue between Delaware and Chestnut streets and he put together a land package for the developers. The developers invited him to take a look at a model of the building they planned to build there, a vast black pyramidal structure that was two to three times as tall as the white buildings around it. "My brother took one look at it and said all the rest looked like sheep grazing under a tree," says Sudler.

The site now contains, of course, the John Hancock Building, and Sudler's firm became the management and rental agent for the building.

As a positive thinker, he undertook to tackle one of the building's most conspicuous features—the huge X-shaped girders that crisscross the window areas of the building all the way up. He moved his office into the thirty-second floor, where one set of girders crossed, and he placed the conference and display room right at the very intersection of two of these girders. His idea was to show that the presence of the girders might be regarded as unique from the interior—"We wanted people to believe that to have one of these things in your office was a status symbol," he says. The designs in most offices were modern; in his own office, Sudler prefers a very traditional decor. That was a little more difficult to deal with, since the sides of the building slope inward as they rise upward. But he simply disguised the upward slope by building walls and columns within the office so that their straight sides enclose the sloping sides of the building. "You work in the mind with real estate a great deal," he says. "We sell concepts. And with an imaginative mind we can paint you a picture, and you say, 'Yes, I can relate to that. I've seen something just like that. That's exactly what I want.' "

He was so active and successful in his various fields that he didn't have time to go the normal route of the rich society type—onto the board of the symphony and upward through it. In fact, it was not until 1964 that he joined the board. "I kept myself away from Orchestra Hall and Ravinia or from the opera company for a long time as far as a direct relationship is concerned," he says. The main reason was that he was so active as a performer. But he finally consented to join the board of the Orchestral Association in 1964 and two years later he was elected president of the board. It was not the propitious time. Not only was the orchestra in trouble—soon it had to start invading $1,850,000 in unrestricted endowments just to pay the bills—but so was the John Hancock project: there was trouble involving the caissons for the building, trouble so drastic that the original developer went broke before the problem could be solved. Yet Sudler never quavered over the Chicago Symphony assignment: "I thought it was a tremendous opportunity, one that I was prepared to give up a lot to take on," he says.

It was a decision that was to astound the world and gratify the members of the orchestra. For Louis Sudler is regarded by most of the players as anything but an antagonist, the way most top management is regarded. "He is an amateur in the true sense of the word," says Mary Koss, whose husband, Donald, helped carry out the negotiations for a new contract for the members in this season. "Which means that he acts from love."

The love that Sudler has for the symphony, and for music, was expressed in very simple, hardheaded terms. He did "just what any good businessman would do. First you get the best possible product. Then you let the world know you have the best possible product." It wasn't hard to lay out a program for improving the product: he sought first to get the best possible general manager in the business, then to get the world's best conductor, and through them to get the world's greatest orchestra.

It was less public and more imperative to determine who the best general manager was. "I made inquiries as to who was dean of the managers and all the answers came back 'John Edwards.' No other name." The choice of Edwards was a critical one, not only because he was the central figure in choosing the new conductor—Martinon knew his contract would not be renewed after 1968—but because Edwards was to become the most important figure, after Solti, in shaping the style, tone, and amplitude of this season.

In a sense, Edwards was the most unlikely match for Louis Sudler. Where Sudler is straight, neat, and urbane, Edwards is short, fat, and rumpled. His clothes look as though they were tailored for an oversized beach ball—Edwards was five feet seven and weighed 228 pounds when he took the job. (He lost thirty of those pounds but later, through sheer dedication, gained twenty of them back.) Sartorially, Edwards looks like a refugee from a fire sale, but he has a profound knowledge of music and the people in it. "He's the only manager, probably the only person in the world, who would dare argue with Fritz Reiner about some sequence of music . . . and the next day I heard Reiner say, 'John, you were right.' For Reiner to admit he was wrong and anybody else was right! Edwards is a fantastic musician. He knows all music and all levels of performance," says Henry Mazer, associate conductor of the Chicago Symphony.

He also knows the people in music—where they are, what they can do, what they *will* do, when is the best time to talk to them. And how much to talk to them about. He is not expert in playing music—though he played both piano and violin as a child—but he has the cerebral insight about music and its people that makes him unparalleled, at least since Rudolf Bing retired from the Metropolitan Opera, as a general manager.

He did not grow up aspiring to his job: a Louis Sudler may grow up dreaming of being a singer and Georg Solti may grow up dreaming of being a conductor, but nobody grows up dreaming of being general manager of a symphony orchestra. "I wanted to be a playwright," says Edwards. "That's what I studied in college."

He'd grown up in St. Louis. His father was an electrical engineer. "But he had a very serious accident which incapacitated him in 1929 and in those days there was not much in the way of pensions, you know. Damn little that a company did for anybody that got injured." His mother went to work for the Missouri Manufacturers Association—"she was a sort of a lobbyist and organized grass-roots support of legislation and so on. All in the interest of the big boss, which was not my cup of tea." His was, nevertheless, a happy German-American household where there was lots of singing and music and where going to the symphony in St. Louis "was part of one's life," he says. "When I was a kid, I was dragged, you might say. But later on I was a perennial goer-outer, and so I found myself enjoying it, just sitting there and listening." He was a terribly precocious kid who was ready for college by the time he was fifteen years old. Since he wanted to be a playwright, he was given the choice of two colleges by his parents—Carnegie Tech and the University of North Carolina, both of which had superb schools of the drama. He chose North

Carolina. "In those days, to get there from St. Louis you had to take the train to Cincinnati, change stations, take a train to Lynchburg, change trains to get to Durham, and then get on a Greyhound bus that went to Chapel Hill. And that was my idea of a great trip." He studied the theater, majored in English, and got an offer of a teaching post at North Carolina if he could get his master's degree in English literature at Harvard. So he got a fellowship at Harvard and it was there, in the early 1930s, that he fell in love with music. And with the idea of running a symphony orchestra.

It started with a decision to go to listen to the Boston Symphony, first tentatively and then compulsively. He bought a Saturday night subscription for twenty-four concerts—"this was in the heyday of Koussevitzky"—then he bought the series of twelve concerts run by the symphony at Sanders Theatre at Harvard, and then he bought a series of six Tuesday night concerts, and then he found he could get away from campus to attend the Friday afternoon concerts. "I had just three three-hour seminars a week—that was all I had to do in the way of formal classroom work. All the rest of the time was in my stall in the Widener Library. So I'd be there during the day and I had a helluva good time, all on Elizabethan and Old English literature, some eighteenth- and nineteenth-century literature, and then off to Boston Symphony Hall. It was a glorious two years."

When it ended he didn't go back to North Carolina. Instead he went back to St. Louis—"the Depression was reaching out for my family"—and got a job as a reporter on the *St. Louis Globe-Democrat*. He covered assignments from the city desk by day and the opera and symphony by night. "You had to dress up, sort of, to cover the opera and if you had a dinner jacket, that made you a critic as far as the *Globe* was concerned. I had a dinner jacket and so I became the music critic." That took him backstage and to some rehearsals, and "I decided that this is what I really wanted to do, to be in on the inside of all this." Finally he was offered a part-time job by the St. Louis Symphony—"I think there was a little blackmail in this; I was beginning to get by-lines"—and he leaped at it. The work was in the front office, not backstage with the musicians, but he managed to fit it in with his newspaper duties: he'd work at the paper from four o'clock until past one o'clock the next morning every day—"whenever the last edition closed"—then go home and grab a few hours' sleep before reporting to the symphony offices at nine o'clock in the morning.

He started out selling tickets. When he asked for a full-time job, one which would allow him to leave the newspaper, he was turned down. "But I can put you on fund-raising," said Arthur Gaines, then manager of the St. Louis Symphony. "In those days, fund-raising was not the big deal that it is now," says Edwards, "because you usually had an angel for the symphony—we had one like everybody else did. A marvelous old gentleman named Alex Primm. All the fund-raising was done in clubs—nothing vulgar—and so I would engineer little meetings, set up little luncheons, and have very little pledge cards for very large amounts at every table setting. Then Mr. Primm would come in and sort of shoot down the game, you see." Edwards still remembers the time with great affection and an expansive feeling—mostly about the waistline. "It was marvelous: I had lots of rich lunches—that was my undoing, in a way—and I got in on a lot of the work and understanding of how the symphony was run."

Edwards was making $25 a week from the symphony and $45 a week from the newspaper—$70 a week, almost $300 a month. "That was not so bad in those days. I mean you could live on it. In fact, three of us did live on it." But he was still seeking a full-time job in symphony and he still couldn't get one. He finally got his chance when he was asked by Gaines to go with him to a meeting of symphony orchestra managers "and sort of do a few things." The *Globe-Democrat* agreed because he could send back stories on the meeting and there'd be no cost to the paper; expenses were being paid by the symphony. He shared an office with the publicity man, William Zalken, now general director of the Municipal Opera in St. Louis. And one day Zalken asked Edwards to do him a favor and talk with a visitor that he, Willie, was too busy to see. Edwards did. The visitor turned out to be Walter Bruce Howe, then secretary of the Washington National Symphony, and he was so impressed with Edwards and the fund-raising program he'd laid out in St. Louis that, some days later, he offered Edwards a job.

"Full-time?" asked Edwards.

"Yes," said Howe.

And that ended Edward's newspaper career then and there.

In the ensuing years, he was to be restlessly on the move: Washington twice, St. Louis, Los Angeles, Pittsburgh twice, Baltimore. His experiences ranged over the full spectrum of symphonic torments. Once he was fired from Washington when a conductor noticed that he was not applauding after a particular number and reported to the board that he was not "loyal." On another occasion, he turned up as the reluctant "heavy" in the Marian Anderson imbroglio with the Daughters of the American Revolution. In those days, the National Symphony in Washington held regular Sunday afternoon concerts in the DAR-run Constitution Hall, including one on Easter Sunday, 1939. "So we had a reluctant orchestra and a reluctant management going down to Constitution Hall on Easter Sunday for a reluctant audience"—an audience that would prove its reluctance by staying away. So when the chance to let Marian Anderson have the Easter Sunday date in Constitution Hall came along, Edwards seized on it. But the DAR prevented him from doing it: they insisted that the original contract be upheld and that contract called for the National Symphony to occupy the hall, not Marian Anderson. Of course, the DAR was concerned over the color of Miss Anderson's skin, not the quality of her voice. And so Eleanor Roosevelt stepped in and arranged for Miss Anderson to make her appearance at the Lincoln Memorial. "I remember standing on the south terrace at Constitution Hall and hearing how beautiful her voice was as it came over the trees from the Lincoln Memorial," says Edwards. But he and the symphony were the "heavies," though it was the DAR that blocked the appearance of Miss Anderson. "I must say that Mrs. Roosevelt, who was very interested in the symphony, never held that against us. She held it very properly against the DAR," says Edwards.

He spent a bit of time as business manager of the Los Angeles Philharmonic and of the Hollywood Bowl—"back in the preamplification days." He had to fill

20,000 seats in the Bowl by booking performers whose musical capabilities could reach to the farthest bounds. "And with stunts," he says. He had Judy Garland and Mickey Rooney and Elizabeth Taylor—"she had just made *National Velvet*." ("What could Elizabeth Taylor do in such a setting?" "Nothing.") It was very glamorous. "Looking back, it was very interesting but at the time it wasn't. It was a pain in the ass." Edwards finally was glad to leave because (a) he doesn't drive a car ("and I could see what was coming in the way of driving out there") and (b) "there was an awful lot of backbiting, much more than is necessary to do in any job."

Overall, his memories are not only of the great men of music ("I had a marvelous time with Fritz Reiner when we were both at Pittsburgh") but of the renowned men of politics. "Washington in the FDR era was marvelous, exciting, beautiful. In the Eisenhower era, it was an uncomfortably dull city." During the latter administration, the presidential box—No. 13—was invariably empty at all the performances. One time Edwards and Howard Mitchell, then the conductor of the National Symphony, went to the White House to enlist the president's aid in getting the season off to a smashing start by giving him a specially embossed subscription.

"Well, Mr. Mitchell, what time do these concerts of yours end?" asked President Eisenhower.

"Well," said Mitchell, "we begin around 8:30 and the concert usually lasts an hour and half—maybe 10, 10:15."

"Oh," said the president with finality. "Well, that is past my bedtime."

Actually, Eisenhower did show up for one concert—but only one—in Edwards's reign. Richard M. Nixon, then vice president, proved much more amenable. "We always asked him to give speeches for us at luncheons and he came to all of them—he was quite nice about it," says Edwards. "He was an intelligent guy who knew something about the subject and who spoke quite well on it." But the most notable events were in the days when Harry Truman was president. "Truman came quite often"—even announcing he'd be there a few weeks after some Puerto Ricans had shot and killed several White House guards during an attempt to assassinate the president. ("The Secret Service advised him not to go out. And never to announce that he *was* going out. He paid them no attention—he came and he announced in advance that he was coming. That meant an automatic sellout crowd for us. . . . We never had so much security as that night.") Truman had one quirk that might have elevated him in the minds of the concert-going public, had it been known in his electoral days. "He insisted on having the score of the principal pieces," says Edwards. "He wasn't faking—he could read the score as the orchestra was playing it."

In any event, Edwards spent thirty years in various aspects of symphony management, the last twelve of them as manager of the Pittsburgh Symphony. Actually, he was offered the job in Chicago twice, three or four years apart—as Solti was—and he turned it down the first time, as Solti did. The first offer was in 1964 just after Seymour Raven, who'd been on the critics' staff of the *Chicago Tribune* before taking over as general manager of the symphony, left the Orchestral Association. But Edwards had just negotiated a twelve-week tour of Europe and the Iron Curtain countries for the Pittsburgh Symphony. The U.S. State Department was involved in the project and Edwards didn't think he could drop his responsibility for the tour. "Because with the State Department tours there are so many verbal amendments to the contracts that it would be totally unfair to the Pittsburgh Symphony. You could not even brief anybody on the details, even with all the note-taking." He proposed a plan by which he'd appoint an assistant who could start immediately in Chicago until Edwards was free of the obligations of the Pittsburgh Symphony's tour. But the Orchestral Association preferred a top man on the job right from the start. It rejected Edwards's plan. "I'm glad that it didn't work out," says Edwards. More because of his proposed assistant than anything else. "By the time I got back, he would have been deviled ham. It was lethal here then. The bitterness is still here although I must say the success of the thing—and Solti in his own particular way of handling things—is so good and so honest that we're overcoming it."

He thought that his refusal was the end of his chances to come to Chicago. But more than two years later, when the leadership of the Orchestral Association passed on to Louis Sudler, he was asked again. He wasn't much inclined to consider it again. "I'd been in Pittsburgh twelve years and was very comfortable." He'd just finished raising $6 million—"this was before the Ford Foundation endowment"—and plans were under way for a new symphony hall in Pittsburgh. "I'm not sure I want to go over there," he said in response to the first feeler from Chicago. But he was curious about Sudler. "I'd really like to meet a man that's brave enough to be president of the Chicago Symphony," he said. Once he met him, he took the next step: he said "yes" to the invitation to shift.

Edwards took over in the spring of 1967 and began to learn what it was like to have problems. For within a very few weeks, a donor withdrew a million-plus offer to help pay for the renovation of Orchestra Hall when the brouhaha of the new sound—or lack of sound—in the hall developed. And $1,850,000 in unrestricted endowments was quickly to be eaten up by deficits. The "game of destruction" within the orchestra, still under the leadership of Martinon, was becoming more bitter. He got a telephone call from George Szell, conductor of the Cleveland—"we've been friends for quite a while"—in which Szell sounded horrified. "It is impossible, that situation is impossible," Szell told Edwards. "It is an Augean stable."

"Then we'll have to find out if I'm Hercules," said Edwards.

A year or so later, Szell visited Chicago as a guest conductor, "and the first thing he said to me is 'Are you Hercules?' And I said, 'I don't know yet.' "

He's found out since then. Hercules cleaned the Augean stables in a day. It took John Edwards a little longer in Chicago.

With the situation in Chicago, there was no one thing to be done. Everything had to be done. But the most important thing was to find a conductor to succeed Martinon after his contract ran out in 1968. Edwards started his search by continuing his old patterns. "Whenever I go to a new city, I do two things. I start walking and riding around it, bus lines, subways, and so forth, to find out what it's like," he says. "And the other thing is that I read its newspapers." The newspapers had plenty of suggestions for Edwards—"they had new lists of conductors almost every week." The players also had some ideas: Sudler invited a committee of the players to sit down with him and offer their thoughts for a new conductor. The names mentioned at that meeting included Seiji Ozawa, then conducting the orchestra in its summer season at Ravinia; Rafael Kubelik, who'd conducted the Chicago Symphony from 1950 to 1953 before leaving under determined attack from the critics—he would conduct the Metropolitan Opera in the 1973–74 season—as well as István Kertész, who'd given many members of the Chicago Symphony stirring moments in his guest appearances, and Carlo Maria Giulini, who'd been conductor at La Scala and had a vast operatic reputation in Europe. "Then, of course, there was von Karajan," says one of the men at the meeting, "but I don't remember that Solti's name ever came up at the discussion." There was, of course, no commitment that Sudler would hire the man named by the members. But they were astounded, and gratified, that he asked them for their view; no other management in the symphony's history had done anything like that. "I remember that Mr. Sudler asked me what I thought if they'd have three conductors," says Jim Hansen, a violinist who was then on the members' committee. "He said that maybe one of them could be music director, but that they might have three conductors of equal merit to handle all the concerts."

That was a hint of what was to come, a general rather than a specific view. For there were three men at the top of the priority list that Edwards and Sudler shaped up. Two of them eventually came to Chicago—and in precisely the way that Sudler suggested in that meeting with the committee: one as music director and the other as "principal guest conductor."

Edwards had the job of finding the right man—or men. He went chasing all over Europe, so much so that he remained virtually unknown to the players in his own orchestra for a year or more after becoming general manager. "They called me the 'Invisible Man,' I was gone so much," he says. (They now call him "The Little King," in tribute to a profile that duplicates that of the comic strip character.) He talked with a number of conductors all over Europe, but only three were aware of all the subtleties of the negotiations. They were Herbert von Karajan, Georg Solti, and Carlo Maria Giulini.

Edwards had to start somewhere and so he started with von Karajan. ("There'd been contact made before I got there between his management and our board.") At the time, the lean, high-boned von Karajan was perhaps the most glamorous and coveted conductor in the world. From 1956 to 1964, he'd held major appointments in four countries—as music director at La Scala in Italy, as principal conductor of the Philharmonia in England, as lifetime music director of the Berlin Philharmonic in Germany, as general director of the Vienna State Opera and the Salzburg Festival in Austria. Indeed, he was busy and he rushed about so tirelessly that the story is told of him—as it was told of Richard Strauss before him—of a cabbie's asking him one day where he wanted to go. "No matter. Any direction. I'm in demand everywhere."

At the time Edwards was seeking him out, he was going to be in demand not only in Chicago but in New York: in the autumn of 1967 he appeared in Carnegie

Hall with the Berlin Philharmonic and also with Milan's Teatro alla Scala in addition to mounting a production of Wagner's *Die Walküre* at the Metropolitan Opera House. So von Karajan would have been an enormously satisfying catch —if he could have been caught at all.

He was the one name on the list that Edwards barely knew. But he knew some of von Karajan's idiosyncrasies. The maestro did not like to play before subscription audiences, of which Chicago offered thirty-seven weeks. He preferred recording and television to go along with his concerts, and both these efforts had been enormously successful in Europe; but there was then limited recording in Chicago—particularly since Orchestra Hall had been renovated out of acoustical existence—and virtually no market for television. (Indeed, the members of the Chicago Symphony are still against the taping for television of their performances, apparently because when the orchestra was signed for television appearances many years ago, the players got virtually nothing out of it.) "One thing I was quite anxious about was that he know the working conditions of American orchestras, which are quite different from European orchestras," says Edwards. "I was assured [by his managers] that he knew all about it because he was a guest conductor at the New York Philharmonic in the fifties. I said the fifties and sixties are two different worlds in terms of orchestra problems, and the relationship of orchestra personnel to management and to the artistic direction. So I insisted that he really had to be brought up to date on the current things. In fact, our trustees had one very definite thing that they wanted me to mention to everybody I talked to, and this is that the conductor will have to read the current contract with the union and agree to the artistic provisions."

Edwards flew to Paris, where von Karajan was performing, and met him at the Hotel Plaza-Athénée. "I was told that he had only a very brief time," says Edwards. As a matter of fact the conversation ranged over many subjects for more than two hours before von Karajan asked that it be resumed later. The second conference was thrown over into a third conference, and then von Karajan asked for time to think over the offer. When the deadline arrived with no response, Edwards went to von Karajan's management and asked "if that meant he was no longer interested. Could we assume that? I just didn't want to be jumping to conclusions." The rejoinder was that von Karajan was just mounting a spring festival at Salzburg —Easter in Salzburg—which involved recording and television. And that he was involved with planning and production, as well as conducting, and could he have a little more time to think it over? Edwards gave him more time.

"However, I made it clear to von Karajan the first time I met him that I was going to see some other people and I mentioned several names," he says. "Then I went to see Solti and Giulini. I said that I had talked to Karajan and that there was some consideration given to his being music director." He also told them that he knew how little time von Karajan had to devote to the broad responsibilities as music director. And would either of them be interested in sharing the responsibility with him? "Their answers were guarded," says Edwards. That was only natural. For the question had another side: would von Karajan be interested in sharing those responsibilities with either Solti or Giulini? That in itself did not seem likely; von Karajan's whole history suggested an expansion of his involvement, not a sharing of it.

In any case, the second extension passed without acquiescence from von Karajan. "So we said, 'Well, we can't wait any longer, because we've got to do something now.'"

Now there was no way that Edwards was going to find a replacement for Martinon by the time Martinon's contract ran out. Fortunately, the Orchestral Association had developed a year of guest conductors to follow the last year of Martinon's contract. Martinon himself was one of the guests signed up for that season. So also were Giulini and Solti, both of whom were good friends of Edwards, so that he could tell them of the status of the von Karajan conversations. He could also measure their long-term interest in the grinding responsibilities of the music director, over and above that of conducting. It happened in this period that Edwards saw Giulini first simply because Solti was working on the Continent when Edwards was in London.

The pairing of Giulini and Solti among the most coveted quarry of the Chicago Symphony was itself fascinating—chiefly in the contrasts they offered. For though there are superficial similarities in their careers, the substance of their being—and of their music—is dramatically different.

The similarities: Like Solti, Giulini was in his mid-to-late fifties; he is one and one-half years younger than Solti. Like Solti, Giulini was known more in Europe at that time than in the United States. He was known more for his work in opera than in the concert hall. Like Solti, he got his big chance in conducting in the wake of World War II because there was a need for conductors free of the dictator's taint. ("I did my first concert right after the liberation of Rome. I was the only conductor they asked because I had big trouble with the Nazis and Fascists," he says.) Like Solti, he was befriended by Toscanini and came to regard him as a warm, wise mentor.

But there was a vast difference in substance between the two men—even though there were superficial similarities—and this led to differences in the ways and means of the conductors. Solti, for example, is a very determined, ambitious, even aggressive man who radiates intensity and energy. Giulini is a retiring, gentle, elegant man who radiates warmth and dignity. Solti, for example, pursued Toscanini; he went where Toscanini worked in the summer months of the pre-World War II years and he hung around the environment of the maestro until he was received onto the staff of assistants. Giulini did just the opposite. He was afraid to approach Toscanini; he waited for Toscanini to approach him. "I did not have the courage to meet him," he says. This was in the days when Giulini was already established as a conductor and as one of the rising stars of Italy—at a time when Toscanini was spending much of his time in Milan. "I never went to him and never asked of him nothing," says Giulini in an Italian accent. Solti was in his early twenties when he first caught the eye and ear of Toscanini; Giulini was in his early forties. One day Giulini was performing an opera by Haydn with the Milan radio orchestra when he received a phone call from Toscanini's daughter, Wally, who was unofficial hostess, recruiter, and mother to La Scala. The maestro had heard the Haydn opera and very much wanted to meet Signor Giulini. The next day he went, at Toscanini's invitation, to the maestro's home at 20 Via Durini and began a relationship that lasted until Toscanini's death. "The first meeting was with just two persons, he and I, and we talked for three or four hours—oh, I don't know how much longer." In that meeting and later, Giulini acted and reacted typically: "I never talked one single word about myself to him. Sometimes he would ask, he would follow, and sometimes he would come to La Scala, but I would never ask of him nothing." He knows the reputation that Toscanini had for being terrible-tempered, but he never saw that side of the maestro's life. "He was so extremely friendly, more than friendly, we had between us the kind of affection of father and son, some of the sweetness . . ."

Giulini feels that in this, as in everything, he does not have the verbal powers to express his feelings. He fears the words in English appear more self-aggrandizing than the manner of the man. It was this inability to match his feelings precisely with his words that delayed and almost diverted his career in conducting. He was in his early twenties and he was studying music in Rome. But he was studying composing, not conducting. This was partially at his father's instigation; it was supported at his school. He mentioned his hopes sporadically, but every mention was rejected or hooted down. He did not have the right personality, the domineering determinism, to be a conductor; he was too gentle and retiring, he was told. This was no reflection on his musical genius—which was ample. "My teacher for composition said I should compose," he says. "My teacher of the violin and viola said I would have not to be conductor." Even his favorite teacher tried to steer him gently away from the podium. So he got to the point where he preserved his ambition, but he did not try to verbalize his feelings. "I wanted to conduct. But I said nothing to nobody," he says. Even when he got a chance to conduct some students in a youth concert in Rome, he kept the upcoming performance secret from his professors, instead of making sure that they came to hear and see him so that they might be impelled to change their opinion of his destiny. None of his teachers was interested enough to search out this performance—except one. His favorite teacher came. Giulini did not know it beforehand. "I did the concert and after the playing I was looking for the conductor's part and so forth and suddenly I see my teacher there. And he said, 'Carlo, I did the mistake. I was wrong and you were right. You are a conductor.' And he wrote to my father and said, 'Carlo is right. Leave him go his way. This will be his way.' And from that moment on he was my best friend in this way." Even now, almost forty years later, he is visibly moved by the memory. "It was very touching. Very beautiful. You can imagine—because I am so grateful that I had such a good and marvelous teacher, and you know how this was that they did not answer at all my feeling for conducting."

The most profound difference in the substance of Giulini and Solti can be heard in the music of the two men. Solti is very muscular, powerful, machismo, moving from climax to climax, playing upon the drama inherent in the architecture of the music. Giulini is more gentle, relaxed, richer and unwavering, playing not to the climaxes so much as to the overall lyricism of the work.

One critic tried to define it by analyzing the records that each man made of Beethoven's Symphony no. 9, Solti with the Chicago Symphony Orchestra and Chorus (on the London/Decca label, and Giulini with the London Symphony Orchestra and Chorus (on the Angel label).

"Solti's performance," wrote Robert C. Marsh in the *Chicago Sun-Times*, "is Promethean in quality. It strives mightily to lift us up to the heavens, to sweep the clouds away and reveal (as Schiller's poem suggests) God enthroned behind a starred canopy. Giulini, on the other hand, is seeking the kingdom of heaven within us. His performance is essentially pure and noble song."

The difference is significant to those within the orchestra. For both Solti and Giulini had been guest conductors with the Chicago Symphony, and the men in the orchestra were already aware of the differences in their styles. Donald Peck, the principal flutist, details something of the impact of the separate individuals in this way:

Solti, he points out, tends to encourage "the brass very much. And he either ignores or subdues the woodwinds." There is a bit of hyperbole in this, but not much: Solti, coming from the German school—the Wagner/Mahler/Bruckner sound—tends to seek the substance of that sound more from the brass than from other sections. So within the orchestra, the sound is not totally balanced. "So we play with a thinner, probably more brilliant sound than with some other conductors," says Peck. "Giulini likes an equal balance in the orchestra of all the sections, and he also encourages the strings to play very beautifully and in a very soloistic manner. So we play a fuller, richer sound, more of a blend. Solti's sound is, as I say, thinner—so we hear a little more clarity."

The very history of the Chicago Symphony, with its decades of conducting by men of Germanic background, would seem to suggest it more as a natural vehicle for Solti than for Giulini. But it is a matter of pride within the orchestra that it belongs to no man and plays for all men. It will play the Giulini sound as gracefully as it plays the Solti sound. "It is something that you do unconsciously if you are really a fine player," says Donald Peck. "You don't think, 'Well, Solti is here and I am going to do this and Giulini comes and I am going to do that.' This is something that the conductor evokes. I have found that I can't play a Giulini sound with Solti on the podium or vice versa. Not everyone feels this way. They feel that a flute should always sound like a flute. But I feel like being very flexible and very adaptable. But as I say, I do not have to try because that is something that they evoke. They are victims of themselves. We are all victims of ourselves that way. They evoke the sound, whether they want to or not. If Solti says to us, 'No, it must be sweeter, it must be lovelier,' he can talk to us all day and it will still come out as he looks—as he evokes. Solti, I think, many times would love to have Giulini's sound. He talks about it. He does not say, 'I want a Giulini sound,' but when he talks to us we know that he wants that but he cannot get it. It is not him. He can only get his sound."

The difference in music and in personality between Giulini and Solti is heightened by a difference in ambition. Solti likes the idea of being music director—or shaping the organization as well as the music. Giulini does not. "I have no patience, no tolerance for the organization," says Giulini candidly. Even as the top man in an organization, he likes to focus on the music making, not the details of administration. John Edwards appreciated this when he approached Giulini about the opening with the Chicago Symphony Orchestra. Says Edwards, "I've known him long enough to have some very definite ideas about his preferences—that if he were to take this music directorship, he'd have to be sold on it. And he'd have to be supported by an artistic kind of staff support. Because we'd talked when he was guest conductor in Pittsburgh"—and Edwards was general manager—"about the different possibilities in America and he had expressed himself about his lack of interest in personnel work, for example—in picking people and getting rid of people." Giulini had, in fact, turned down other attractive posts because he had no taste for the administrative side of such work, or the politicking and backbiting that is so much part of it. "He wants to have the condition right for making music"—he considers making music, not shaping conditions, his main function. Giulini's assets were that he made beautiful music, deep, moving, elegant in its architecture and its subtleties, and that he was a "very lovable man—everybody liked him very much." But Giulini reacted much as Edwards anticipated: he didn't want the music directorship in Chicago or, really, anywhere else. "On the other hand, he said if Solti was music director, he'd be delighted to work with him." But just how was not defined.

All this time, Edwards was talking to other conductors to explore their interest and availability. But he didn't tell them everything he'd told von Karajan, Giulini, and Solti. "I didn't go into the number of people I was seeing or how I was arranging it or anything," he says. He was, in fact, waiting on Solti. He knew that the Hungarian-born conductor had both the vigor and temperament to tackle the music directorship.

Again he was right.

"When I got to see Solti, I found he was interested, very interested. But there were a lot of problems to be worked out." The most conspicuous were Solti's existing commitments. "He has this book that goes on for three years. And he was turning over page after page with engagement after engagement," says Edwards. Three years was longer than the Chicago Symphony could wait, even for Solti. "He said, 'If Giulini could do this and this and this, why maybe you could tie it together.' "

The idea of having more than one conductor—a music director relieved by a principal guest conductor—is not, as we've seen, new with Solti. Edwards traces some of the etiology of the concept to the years he'd spent in Pittsburgh when his music director, William Steinberg, was shared with the Philharmonia in London for two years in the late 1950s as "principal guest" conductor. "I worked on that then," he says. Later, Steinberg worked at the New York Philharmonic—while still music director in Pittsburgh—on the same idea, when Leonard Bernstein decided he wanted to give up some of his burden. "It was the predecessor of the idea, as far as I was concerned, that we brought here," says Edwards. The idea would have been stunning in its dimensions if it had involved three men: Solti as music director with Giulini and von Karajan as principal guest conductors. Even as it developed—with Solti as music director and Giulini as principal guest—it was a captivating solution. For the men complemented each other in temperament and in their music. The formula was simple: Solti would conduct ten weeks in Chicago in his first year and Giulini would conduct eight weeks. After that they would adjust their time commitments as needed.

As it happened, the development was slow. Both Solti and Giulini agreed to the plan. But both men had to clear their tenure and proposals through the U.S. Internal Revenue Service in order to keep their taxes in the United States from virtually confiscating their salaries. In the meantime, the Orchestre de Paris approached Solti to see if he would become music director there. The rumors of this availability reached their peak just as the Chicago negotiations were ending. He pleaded busyness to Paris and in the end, the Paris post went, instead, to von Karajan, though only briefly.

Finally, in December 1968—more than a year and a half and several hundred thousand miles of flight time after he took over the Chicago post—Edwards was able to announce that Georg Solti would become music director of the Chicago Symphony in the autumn of 1969, succeeding Jean Martinon.

"We have gone," said oboist Ray Still, "from the ridiculous to the sublime."

Confluence with the Conductor

The Georg Solti who came to Chicago in 1969—and who reigns in Chicago this season—did not fit the classic image of the conductor. He affected no great personal flash. He did not try to be a tyrant on the podium. And he went about a continuing change in his personal and professional life very quietly.

For Solti is a private person. His ascendance has not been aided by publicity gimmicks and image-making habits. There is nothing in him of Toscanini's tantrums, of Beecham's wit, of Stokowski's showmanship, of Koussevitzky's dilettantism.

Where a von Karajan tools about in roaring sports cars and private jets, Solti is an uneasy flight passenger and a driver of spectacularly indifferent skills. The fact is that he simply has not mastered the finer techniques of operating a motor car—such as parking it. One time he walked into his office at Covent Garden in London and dropped his car keys on the desk of his secretary, Enid Blech.

"Will you find a better parking place for the car?" he asked, somewhat diffidently. "The traffic will build up during rush hour and I want to know that it isn't going to get blocked by traffic."

Mrs. Blech dutifully went downstairs to the street and found the car where Solti had left it after struggling mightily with it for a number of minutes: parked askew in the street with only its rear end tentatively headed toward the parking place.

Solti wants to build his reputation solely on the quality of the music he makes. Whereas Leonard Bernstein might show up at a rehearsal in flowering cape and flowing hair, the bald Solti is likely to show up in a black coat thrown over a loose shirt and baggy pants. His only decoration as he goes to the podium is a towel wrapped around the back of his neck, much in the manner of a Turkish wrestler. ("I sweat. I sweat dreadfully a lot. Very much.") But it is when he goes into action on the podium that the change comes about—and the reason for sweat appears obvious.

For Solti is perhaps the most choreographic of modern conductors. His every movement, his very being seem to suggest a protean personality: intense, fierce, sometimes irascible, enormously gifted, a man so viscerally caught up in the music that he seems—in his movements—determined to keep pace with a volcano that is about to engulf him. "His art, his humanity, all his qualities and his faults come out in every pore—there is no hidden Solti," says Terry McEwen, a longtime friend of the maestro's and head of the London/Decca classical record operations in the United States.

The singularity of Solti's movement is part of the electricity and tension he feels about the music and that he wants to communicate to the orchestra and the audience. The communication is intense and highly stylized. Just before he gives the first downbeat, he shuffles his feet and then plants them firmly on the podium while taking a bent, cramped stance, vaguely like a boxer in the corner of a ring in the instant before the gong sounds. He then plunges into a paroxysm of large and angular gestures, beating staccato with furious up and down movements of both arms, indicating a sforzando with a furious backhand slash of the baton, cuing the trumpet with a riveting spread of arms and fingers, bringing in the violins with deep left-handed scoops that reach almost to the floor, signaling the climactic crash of cymbals with a starburst of outthrust fingers. In these moments he looks like nothing so much as a spastic stork, bending and rearing convulsively, elbows pumping, knees popping, torso laboring until it seems almost as if he is going to tear the music from himself in a Dionysian frenzy.

And then there are quieter moments when he switches from harshness to softness, from parodic vulgarity to paradisiacal delicacy. He signals a pianissimo by drawing his left hand across his mouth—"softer, softer"—or mounts a moment of lyrical romance by cradling his left hand under his heart. In these moments he is so intently introspective—with his heavy-lidded eyes seeming to look directly at his thoughts more than at the people to whom they are being conveyed—that there is almost a messianic effect when he bursts out of it and suddenly stabs one regal finger into the air, seeming in that moment to twist dozens of destinies around it.

And through it all, he is singing, mouthing, humming, whistling to himself, experiencing the music vocally as well as aurally. It is something he feels and something he learned: "There is no music," said Toscanini, "without singing."

There are, of course, limitations to all this. One of them is physical. Solti has, from years of holding his arms at the conductor's "ready" and then waving them gymnastically—sometimes for four and a half to six hours a day—developed muscle problems in the neck and shoulders. "It is something you get from conducting, there is nothing to do about it—I cannot change it now," he says. The problem is manifested in stiffness of rotation of his upper torso and head. "I cannot move my head more than a few inches to the left or right without turning my body," he says. Nor can he turn his upper torso easily. So when he wants to direct his attention to, say, the cellos, he must turn his whole body and plant his feet anew to conduct that section. And that is why, if he wants to shift his focus on the extremities—from the harps on the left to the principal bass on the right—he must make a violent turn that appears to be something out of Balanchine, not Bach or

Beethoven. "So it is one more thing to account for," he says.

Another limitation is the feeling his choreography gives the orchestra—both the sensory and interpretive feeling. Some critics who remember him from the Metropolitan Opera of the early 1960s feel that on occasion he got so caught up in the convulsion of the moment that the Metropolitan orchestra got lost and could no longer discern the authentic beat within all those gymnastics. Not so with the Chicago Symphony. Solti has no fear that the Chicago Symphony could ever get lost. "You could conduct it with an old shoe—but not too big a shoe," he's said. In any case, he thinks that motion is better than stagnation. "A wild tasteless conductor is better than one content merely to be exact," he's said, "because he can at least interest the orchestra and the audience. They hate him if he just wants to go swimming with the orchestra. Bah!" It is not the motion that captures and enraptures in the great conductor, he says. "One must have ideas. It is man's nature to follow ideas, not sticks. The baton matters hardly at all."

There are other critics who insinuate a flaw by comparing his style not with his music but with lesser conductors who use motion as a disguise for music. This is not the case with Solti. Dale Clevenger, the principal French horn player of the Chicago Symphony, observes that "Solti's energy manifests itself in certain gymnastics but, whereas in other conductors the arm-flinging and the body gyrations get in the way of the music, with Solti they don't, because he has a steady inner rhythm."

Nor does he use the movements to attract the attention of the audience to himself and away from the orchestra. "When everything is going fine, he doesn't interfere with the orchestra by going into a lot of acrobatics to make the audience think it's his struggling which is producing such fine music," says Ray Still.

To be sure, the vintage Solti demands, on first sight, some interpretive as well as musical skills.

"His gestures are very large," says principal bass player Joseph Guastafeste, "and that took a little getting used to at first"—particularly after having been trained by the tiny, almost imperceptible beat of Fritz Reiner. "Now I'm very comfortable"—because he can "read" Solti.

"He will be beating very big at a certain passage but he will tell us, 'I want it very relaxed,' " Still adds. "Some conductors when they want a pianissimo start will give you a tiny little beat, almost daring you to play. Solti always gives you a very firm beat which could be interpreted as mezzo forte to forte. But at the same time he will tell you that he wants it very pianissimo."

Still sees Solti's gyrations as easing not only his muscular tension but that of the orchestra. "When he starts out, he makes sure that he has good physical balance before he plays. He never gets muscularly tense—it's almost like he's preparing to return a tennis serve. Physically he is loose"—so loose, in fact, that he's been known to lose the baton in mid-gyration and send it winging across the stage. (The stagehands invariably put two or three batons on the podium before every performance.) "But he takes a lot of deep breaths and he can shift his weight back and forth a lot to stay loose. "When you first see him," Still goes on, "he looks unorthodox, and he seems to use a lot of motion that isn't very efficient. But that is how he stays so loose all the time. A lot of conductors are studies in isometrics —one muscle tensed against another. Not Solti. Musically, this makes a big difference because then you are muscularly free, then you can play in a freer, more relaxed fashion."

There is one more limitation on Solti's style: he must always be in position to read the score. He has not followed the vogue, made popular by Toscanini, of conducting without a score. The legend was that Toscanini could conduct 50 or 60, and then 150 and 160, operas from memory, without ever making a mistake. Solti studies his scores as intensely as did Toscanini and, in the course of years of study, has committed most of them to memory. But he still prefers to conduct with the score open in front of him. "I know them all by heart," he says, "but I want the safety. Everybody makes mistakes. Musicians, especially singers, want the security that the conductor always knows. I get nervous myself when I sit down, even in the audience, and there is a concerto and the conductor doesn't have a score. I am so angry—it is such a stupidity, to create a nervous atmosphere." Beyond all this, he studied under Toscanini for two summers at Salzburg in 1936 and 1937 and he knows that—beyond having a fabulous memory—the maestro had another motive for not bringing the score onstage with him: he was too nearsighted to be able to read it. "Of course, he had that fabulous memory but that wasn't really why he never used a score. Because he was nearsighted. So today we have an entire generation of young conductors who think they must conduct from memory, all because Toscanini was nearsighted. It is total lunacy."

There are critics who say that—memory or not—he did not learn much of his style from Toscanini. It is true that Toscanini's gestures were shaped and honed to a streamlined, almost machinelike smoothness. His baton was so filled with grace that it seemed almost as if he could take the orchestra in his hand and, as though it were a pen, write with it. But Solti did not simply study Toscanini's style; he also studied the antipodal skills of Wilhelm Furtwängler. Furtwängler disdained the perfect, and even the perceptible, beat. "Standardized technique in turn creates standardized art," he would say. He would wiggle the baton at, say, the opening of a passage, but he never seemed to be able to deliver the full and authoritative downbeat. "He always seemed to be holding back," says Solti. "He could never seem to complete the upbeat and get on with the downbeat." (Friedelind Wagner, granddaughter of Richard Wagner, once commented on the ambiguity of Furtwängler in nonmusical realms that "he never managed to make a decision and go through with it.") All this provided a technique that was a nightmare to the members of an orchestra. He would gesticulate, shout, sing, and stamp, and when something went wrong, Furtwängler would roar for the musician to follow his beat. A member of the London Philharmonic once said that Furtwängler never really brought his baton down until after the thirteenth preliminary waggle. The orchestra had to sense when the oscillations would stop and they could start playing. In the Berlin Philharmonic there was a standard joke:

Q. How do you know when to come in on the opening bars of the Beethoven Ninth?

A. We walk twice around our chairs, count ten and then start playing.

Or:

Q. How do you know when to come in with such a baffling downbeat?

A. When we lose patience.

Another anecdote, repeated by Solti, made the rounds in the Vienna Philharmonic. The question is how the Philharmonic ever managed to get started together on Beethoven's Fifth Symphony, when Furtwängler could not bring himself to deliver a clear beat on the crashing opening: "We count five," said one player, "and then look at the bassoonist. *He* gives the downbeat."

In short, Furtwängler derided beautiful technique as an end in itself. Anybody, he felt, could develop a clear up-and-down technique. Once he stopped an orchestra during a rehearsal and said, "You think I can't give you an orthodox beat?" He "went straight" for a few minutes, delivering a very normal, orthodox beat and took the orchestra along with him. Then he stopped abruptly. "It has no quality," he said.

Yet Furtwängler was indisputably one of the great conductors of this century. He had ability to mesmerize both orchestra and audience. He could lift an orchestra and make it play as it had never played before. The lesson learned by Solti in this matter is that the manner and technique of conducting are less important than what Toscanini and Furtwängler had in common: a sound idea of the music, however individualistic in nature. Toscanini's view was, generally speaking, absolute faithfulness to the composer's notes; Furtwängler's was a devotion to the expressive content of the music. Moreover, Solti perceived that both had a tensile strength and a texture of almost indefinable dimensions that are felt rather than seen. One builds that on the podium not by gesture but by presence.

The presence of Solti radiates intensity. This personal projection of vitality is the essence of what Solti is doing on the podium. He is creating an atmosphere electric with tension and propulsiveness. He is not playing notes but giving the music color and drama, a larger-than-life immensity that touches the soul as well as the mind. He is tracing the architecture of the music—its high points and its lows—as much as the details of its engineering.

To some, this is an antithesis: Solti is a terribly disciplined man, one in whom life is—and must be—formidably organized; yet his music is romantic and tempestuous. To others, it is as natural as breathing; for Solti is also a driven man —the late starter who must catch up—and there is in his music much of this driven quality. In the final analysis, the discipline is a technique laid over the driven nature of the man; the music is a release that expresses the romance within him; through it he can respond to the grand line of drama. It is his genius that he takes these sprawling, almost discursive motives—this divergence in personal and musical impetuses—and welds them into a single pulsating entity. "Something," says principal trombonist Jay Friedman, "metaphysical happens."

There is a discipline within this intensity. Solti has trained himself not to pause sentimentally over a favorite melody or chord. He keeps his mind, and ear, on the architectural line, using rhythm and dynamics to sculpt breathtaking new shapes. The thrust and form of the music preoccupy him as much as its romantic pull. "The things that intrigue me are how to make forms clear," he says. "How to hold a movement together. Or, if I am conducting an opera, how to build an act or a scene."

The interpretive sagacity of it all—and the technical brilliance—evokes a sound that is clear and lustrous and a phrasing that is so compelling that it seems to move faster than it does. Indeed, there are some who feel that his rhythms move too fast. "He does not believe in pea soup or mush," says Terry McEwen. "The rhythm must be there all the time. He feels strongly about the clarity of texture." It is a feeling—and extraordinary grasp of rhythm—says McEwen, that Solti has in common with Toscanini. "He has this belief that the essence of music is rhythm and that music is like water—it must keep flowing. It musn't be stopped. If it is against nature to build a dam, it is against music to chop it into little pieces"—thus he lets the music flow, as water flows in nature.

The idea of Solti's music is to build from climax to climax, yet always saving enough of its drama and impact so that it can unfold and enfold in the heightened climax of the end. Solti himself is hesitant to analyze it too closely, as if the analysis will—by its very intellectualism—destroy the aesthetic impact. "Is a *mysterium*, music," he is fond of saying. It is his way of asserting that some things are left best to the imagination. "A great part of our profession is inexplicable. One should not try to analyze it too carefully. If one should try to explain everything, you really become too simple about it. Or the words are slipping out of your hands."

What Solti is telling us is that he retreats from the discipline of articulate sound. He exults in the discipline of musical sound. And the sound itself has its own sense of articulation.

For though the drama derives from Solti's operatic background, the sound is that of the Chicago Symphony Orchestra. It is remarkably clear and lustrous, a forward surging rhythm burnished with the seamless sound of brass. Far more than most orchestras, the brass comes up strongly in the Chicago Symphony, giving the orchestra a rounded, radiant, warm-blooded sound. This is not an unrelieved pleasure for other instrumentalists. ("I wouldn't say definitely that we're the greatest orchestra in the world," says flutist Richard Graef with a bemused smile, "but we certainly are the loudest.") But there are, within all this, sounds of ethereal sweetness, built on the warm mellow tones of richly honed woodwinds and on strings polished to the intimate precision of chamber music ensembles. And it is all reined by Solti so that the orchestra not only illuminates the large sweeping line of a work but traces revealing detail. His is an uncommonly sophisticated statement of those pieces in which hearty is often misconstrued as heart.

For Solti and the Chicago Symphony are able to offer color without blatancy —albeit colors of the more primary hues—and deep variation in detail without losing the grand line. He is able to bring up an inner voice under the grand line that enriches and enhances it: in the recitative chorus portions of Beethoven's Ninth Symphony, one can hear—on Solti's record of it with the Chicago Symphony—an oboe coming up as a tiny subtle statement of an inner voice under the rich power of the baritone, a conductorial inspiration that intensifies the expressiveness of a very brief passage in a very long and monumental work.

The details also are a matter of discipline. "In his enthusiasm, he has a tendency to force the brass to a climax," John Culshaw, a longtime friend of Solti's, has said. Culshaw was producer of the supernal recording of Wagner's *Ring* cycle, which, over a period of years, Solti made for London/Decca, and he pointed to an example in *Die Götterdämmerung* in which the recording people labored for three days to mitigate the enthusiasm of Solti for the brass. "He had forced the trumpets and trombones," said Culshaw of this passage, "and it virtually obliterated everything else." The reason was that Solti had been caught up by the surging emotion of the music: "He was in an understandable state of excitement and elation." Instead of fighting him over it, Culshaw—who has a precise aesthetic instinct —simply "implanted an idea in his head." The idea was in the value of balance, and it made its way into Solti's brain and spirit. He is not the arrogant kind of conductor who can find no fault with his own work. He thought it over, "and three days later," said Culshaw, "we were back redoing the offending passage."

To be sure, there are critics who feel that "*Der Solti-Klang*"—the sound of Solti—lacks refinement and finesse and, above all, attention to detail. And yet his catching of detail, in rehearsals or in recording, borders on the spectacular. At the rehearsals of Beethoven's Symphony no. 3, the *Eroica*, he corrected details of bowing in some of the strings; in Bach's Suite no. 3, he corrected the woodwinds' sound of grace notes which didn't appear in his score. At recording sessions, he spares neither himself nor the orchestra in making sure that every small detail is correct. "Too loud, the second horn," he will say while listening to a quick rerun of a tape just after the orchestra has played it. "The woodwinds and brass, every first note is shorter. You are trying with the strings but you are hanging over." On one occasion while recording Beethoven in the autumn of 1973, he went back and retaped one long movement because he could hear a single G being sounded flat by one instrument—"just a touch," he said—and he'd rather do the movement than try to splice an accurate G into the tape at that point.

It is not his attention to detail that is different from the great conductors of the past; it is the manner in which he corrects the detailed error. He does not focus on the faults of individuals; he does not try to correct them by excoriating them. In this respect, he was different from, say, Reiner, who had no patience with a mistake made once, much less one that was repeated. "He was cruel to the men—he sacked them left and right," Solti has said. "When I came here, I found an orchestra still operated on the principle of fear."

Solti's style is often brusque but never harsh. "I am no tyrant," says Solti. "He's a gentleman," echoed David Greenbaum, a cellist in the Chicago Symphony, perhaps as much in amazement as in relief. For the reign of the tyrant was not exceptional in any of the great orchestras around the world. Toscanini didn't just conduct; he terrorized. He maintained an unwavering irritability that mounted into rages that included—according to Samuel Antek, one of the string players in his NBC Symphony—"among the most horrifying sounds I have ever heard." He would abuse players frightfully and hurl everything from invective to batons at them. When he conducted at the Metropolitan Opera, it was said, "by the end of the season half the company was in a state of nervous collapse." Nor was

Toscanini alone in all this. The display of temper, the arbitrary firing of musicians on the least pretext, the hurling of batons were common in conducting through the first half of the century. There is, within the more cynical perspectives of musicians, a feeling that the most notable achievement of Serge Koussevitzky was not in building a great sound in the Boston Symphony but in finding a more punishing substitute for the thrown baton. In rehearsal, he'd put aside the baton and use instead a long thin rod—a dowel perhaps ten or twelve inches long and three-eighths of an inch in diameter. "He had a couple of dozen of them in a box right by the podium," says a product of the Harvard University Chorus, which worked with the Boston Symphony in Koussevitzky's years. When he became enraged, Koussevitzky would smash the dowels on the podium—at less cost than smashing batons—or he'd hurl them at the musicians. "He was quite accurate with them up to ten or fifteen paces," says the Harvard man. All this, of course, had a terrorizing impact on the musicians—and the effect of keeping them more closely attuned to the conductor's wishes and his beat. "You learned to keep a very close eye on the conductor," reports the Harvard man, "if only to know when to duck."

Solti will have none of it; he would not even take advantage of the Chicago Symphony's conditioning to terror and to bullying. "I really never do that. I really think—not bullying . . . well, naturally you might call it gentle bullying because you have to get your own way," he says. "But I do not lose my temper. I do not throw batons. That is nineteenth-century stuff. I never do any of that old-fashioned nonsense, which today doesn't work anyway." He learned from the lesson of Toscanini but again he did not follow Toscanini's exact example. "Toscanini once threw a baton, it hit the eye of a second violinist in Milan, and Toscanini had to pay for the rest of his life to that violinist." The man could not play—earn a living—without seeing. "Toscanini! Yes, he lost his temper. He threw his baton. The man lost his eye. And Toscanini had to pay for the rest of his life for that bit of anger.

"That sort of thing doesn't work today. It is just not possible. The whole atmosphere has changed and I daresay that we are making better music.

"This is a different sort of era. There is much more of making camaraderie, of working together towards a goal. I am not speaking of Chicago only. There is no case, no case, whether it be English, French, American, Abyssinian, Russian, or Chinese, the musicians will always cooperate with you as long as he respects you."

This was not always the case with Solti. For years, he, too, was a dictator of the baton. In his early years at Covent Garden he was known as "the screaming skull." And when some of the men who'd played under him many years back encounter current members of the Chicago Symphony, they're likely to ask, "How is the old son-of-a-bitch now?" He would not abuse individuals but he had a somewhat crisp, imperative air, and in the view of a close and admiring friend he did not altogether understand the psychology of the orchestra. Some members of the Philadelphia Orchestra resented his condescending attitude in the past. The New York Philharmonic would play beautifully for him at rehearsals and then—in the long tradition of the New York orchestra—cut him up in subtle ways in perform-ance. For years, the Vienna Philharmonic played as well for Solti, or better, than for any other guest conductor with the possible exception of Leonard Bernstein. But they didn't *like* Solti. " 'We like to play better mit Karl Böhm,' " is the way one Solti friend satirizes the experience. " 'He does not make us vork so hard and vat is that Hungarian prizefighter doing jumping around, sweating so much? Ach! We make music better mit Böhm.' " But he won respect from the Vienna Philharmonic some years ago by eliciting from it—an orchestra whose players prefer reflexively the *schlamperei* of old Vienna—a magnificent perform- ance of a twentieth-century work once considered avant-garde: Stravinsky's *Le Sacre du Printemps*. Not only the audience but the orchestra gave him a standing ovation, and Solti considers this one of the notable triumphs of his career.

In all this, there is a lesson which Solti articulated this season as he relaxed at Roccamare: "Do not act foolish. As long as you do not ask the player to do anything that is not within his system, he will respect you. As long as he is believing in you. As long as he is believing that what you are asking is in order to get a better performance. There is no possibility that he will sabotage you. Under no condi- tions, as long as you know the material and as long as you ask something which is in the main interest of the performance. It could be that you would start with very grand antipathies. It could be that the orchestra doesn't like you. They don't like your notes, your hair, your voice, or the way you rehearse. If you know your business, you make it with them. You have to make it. There is no other way. If you have an open-mindedness, there is nothing the conductor can't do. There isn't. They are giving you a chance to prove your worth."

He has been just as candid on the interior attitudes that provided a block—and a tradition of temper—in his own past. "It is not too difficult to analyze my life. I was a late starter under the most hopeless conditions." He came to maturity, and to an ambition to conduct, in a Nazi-dominated Europe, when he had a father who was Jewish. Thus he had to flee that oppression—from Hungary to Switzerland during World War II—while other already renowned conductors, such as Furtwängler and von Karajan, prospered under Nazi patrimony. He did not have the blood or the supple spine to cultivate success in such an atmosphere. And so he had to fight every step of the way. "It is very natural, very human that you are not generous, that you envy people, that you fight for things," he said. "Now this is not my nature and I think I got over it. But I needed a certain security as a musician to be able to be more generous." He got it first when he saw that an old friend—Edward Kilényi, Jr.—had been placed in charge of the reconstruction of musical culture in the Munich area when World War II ended. Kilényi had gone to the same school in Budapest with Solti before the Nazis came to power. But Solti—as a fighter—did not wait to be asked: he wrote and asked for a job. The Americans were seeking everybody, *anybody* in music who did not represent the Nazi past to help in the culture of a renascent Germany. Solti was a natural and enthusiastic choice: he was invited to come to Munich to rebuild the Munich State Opera. He did so and with such gusto, brilliance, and precision, and under such conditions—some- times he produced operas with the musicians, as well as the audience, wearing their overcoats—that within fifteen years he was conducting opera at the two great theaters of the Anglo-Saxon world: as musical director of the Royal

Opera at Covent Garden in England, as guest conductor of the Metropolitan Opera in New York. In a sense, he still had to prove himself because he'd moved from the defeated Germanic culture—Munich and later Frankfurt—to the triumphant English-speaking one and this produced certain protective colorations. "When I arrived at Covent Garden, I was a narrow-minded little dictator," he said not long before he left his assignment with the Royal Opera in 1971. "I'm leaving much more broad-minded, much more tolerant. Because of that, I'm much more respected. Remember, I came from Germany, where even without the title"—his knighthood—"nobody dared speak to me without saying *Herr Generalmusikdirektor*." (It took some years, says one friend, for Solti to realize that when the English and Americans like you, "they call you 'George.' ") "And now I don't think that my respect at Covent Garden was any less than it was at Frankfurt. It is more." But he also became more secure in his music. For at one time he felt the buffets of a rising regard for very avant-garde music while his own preference was for the music of the romantic era, and he had to consider that the affection for the avant might mean the end of his career as a "romantic-era" conductor. Time has reduced that apprehension. "I'm not as tense as I once was. I love more and more romantic music. Which is my nature. But now it is open. Now I am not ashamed of it." The result, suggested Solti, is in the attitude he exchanges with the orchestra and the people he works with: "I think I've become a much more generous person. I'm much less jealous. I let the people around me have their successes."

All this is not to say that Solti has freed himself from the cultural separation between player and conductor. Indeed, he sometimes does not seem to appreciate just how profound this abyss is. The story is told of his first rehearsal of the London Philharmonic Orchestra just after he was dubbed a Knight Commander of the British Empire by Queen Elizabeth. He became, at that instant, Sir Georg, not "Mr. Solti." On his entry into the rehearsal, the players, of course, applauded him. He sat down on a high, bar-type chair and, as he is inclined to do, exchanged small talk with the orchestra for a moment. "I do hope," he told the players, "that you will not allow my new honors to make a difference in our relationship." He paused generously. "You shall continue to call me 'maestro.' "

Yet in his season with the Chicago Symphony, Solti has been more flexible and receptive to musicians' ideas than ever before. At one recording session a few years ago, oboist Ray Still suggested to Solti that he—Still—would do much better a prominent oboe solo in a final take of Strauss's *Don Juan* if Still's assistant oboe played some of the less prominent passages that came earlier, instead of Still's tackling them all. Solti, who would—in his "we must fight for everything we have" phase of a few years earlier—have been cuttingly scornful of a principal player who didn't play all the solos, listened and quickly gave his consent to the change. For he preceived that it was not the persona of the player which was in question but the quality of the music.

His sense of security and self-assurance today is such that it astounds the whole world of music. "I don't think there is another conductor in the world today who has the stature of Solti and would invite a guest conductor of the skills of Giulini to share the podium with him," says Henry Mazer, associate conductor of the

Chicago Symphony. Mazer sees it as a reflection of Solti's conviction that "I am sure of myself and I only want the best for my orchestra, I do not care how good the competition may be." Mazer has seen what he believes to be an even more generous dimension to Solti. He recalls a time when the Chicago Symphony was rehearsing a concert version of *Das Rheingold* and Solti asked Mazer to take over the baton for a few moments during the rehearsal. Mazer was stricken. Solti is the world's greatest interpreter of Wagner and he—well, as associate conductor he could not possibly have studied the scores to the degree that Solti had. "Oh, Christ," says Mazer, "I just had to say I couldn't do some of it as he knew it." He feared desperately what this might mean; he'd been an apprentice under Reiner and Reiner—he felt—would have demanded that he "know the entire score and conduct the orchestra without a mistake." The alternative was dismissal. There was a time when Solti himself would have demanded that his associate know—as he'd once known under other conductors—all the scores that the principal was to conduct. But not in this incarnation. "Do you know what Solti said to me?" asks Mazer. "He said, 'Oh, no, I don't expect that you will do it all. I just want you to do this passage so that I can move over there to check the altos.' That's Solti—he isn't interested in trying to nail you. He's interested in the music."

All this is not to say that Solti does not exert a dominant influence when and where he feels it should be. In a small, subtle way, he resolved a number of problems that were plaguing the first European tour of the Chicago Symphony scheduled for 1971. The players fell—as they often do—into wrangling with themselves and the management over whose planes they should ride in and what hotels they should stay in. Solti, as a European, offered very firm thoughts and the orchestra accepted them. Says one member: "There was a big hassle about whether we should have air-conditioned rooms in Helsinki, where it's 32 degrees. Solti was great. He told us: 'Gentlemen, if we do not go to Europe, we will be the laughingstock of the world, canceling over little things like a plane and a hotel.' "

On musical matters, there is no doubt concerning the origin of decisions. Solti radiates a decisive sense of authority. One example was the long-festering feud over pitch within the Chicago Symphony.

In the late 1960s, as Martinon was about to leave and a series of guest conductors was about to arrive, the definition of pitch within the orchestra degenerated. In general, the concertmaster comes onstage and calls to the oboe for an A. The oboe sounds an A and gives it to the woodwinds, then the brass, and ultimately the strings. Thus the "tuning" of the orchestra—any orchestra. But in the Chicago Symphony there was a breakdown in communication—verbally—between the concertmaster and the principal oboe. Ray Still simply did not speak to Victor Aitay, the co-concertmaster. However, he did respond musically to the disciplines of the orchestra: he did give the A. But the way it was received was not altogether uniform. Ideally, the normal A is, as we've seen, 440 cycles per second. But the woodwinds often like a low A—say 437 or 438 cycles—in order to get a better response out of the profound sonorities of their instruments. The violins tend to prefer a high A—say at 442 or 444—in order to serve better the lush high brilliance of their potential. Since these were the years before Solti when there was no music director to give direction to the situation (and Martinon had effectively been stripped of his authority), there was no discipline or consistency concerning how the A was given or accepted. Soon many players got the feeling that the A sounded different from performance to performance and sometimes from section to section. "There were times when I'd swear it was 437 or below, other times I got the feeling it was up at 444 or 445 or more," one member of the orchestra told me. (He did not have perfect pitch and he could not measure the precision of a sound unless he had a tuning fork or unless the sound got five or six or more vibrations per second off what he'd heard before.) All this tended to exacerbate the divisions, personal and professional, that had already gripped the orchestra. People were not only dividing up for or against Ray Still but for or against his A and whether it sounded like something to which they were going to be perfectly attuned.

When Solti came in as the musical director, he could not know anything of this subtle, savage internal dispute—a dispute fought without words. But he heard about it. From friends. From the orchestra—he could not listen to the orchestra without knowing of it. He investigated and interrogated. And one day when he went out to a recording session, he looked up and said simply, "Mr. Still, would you give us the A, please? At 442."

The A came through at 442. Everybody tuned precisely to 442. And there has never been any dispute or discussion since then about the pitch of the Chicago Symphony. It is 442. For the oboe, the woodwinds, the strings, the brass. Nobody need dispute the matter with the maestro.

It is a firm conviction with Solti that the musical director makes musical decisions. Nobody else. He does not accept the view that a symphony orchestra is a democracy in which the majority rules, with the conductor merely first among equals. He does not feel that critical aesthetic decisions can be made by committee and still reflect a greatness. For the committee is, by nature, a compromise and thus a compromise without great instincts; committees cannot reach for greatness because they must satisfy all the elements of their constituency, which do not invariably represent greatness. Thus, as an autocrat, Solti rejects the notion that the orchestra—any orchestra—can select its own music and its own conductors, as was being suggested this season by members within the Chicago Symphony. "An orchestra can never choose a conductor," he has said, "because inside, playing, you can never see the right man. You cannot judge as long as you are inside: your judgment is not right. Orchestra has always been choosing wrong conductor. Always."

It is not just the players that, Solti feels, must keep their hands off musical decisions. It is also management. So compelling is his sense of authority—that is properly vested in the musical director or the conductor—that he has waged, in his more short-fused days, several spectacular fights with management.

One of them was with Sir Rudolf Bing, for twenty-three years the general manager of the Metropolitan Opera. Early in the 1960s, Bing engaged Solti to conduct a number of operas at the Met and the effort produced generally satisfying, often acclaimed, performances of *Tristan* and *Tannhäuser*, *Aïda* and *Otello*, *Boris Godunov* and *Don Carlo*. But he did not appear at the Met after

1964. The reason, Solti has suggested, was a difference in musical style. Bing, he indicated, felt that "if you collect five or six big names, you get a good performance. You don't. You don't." He does not condemn Bing personally ("Bing likes me and I like him as a human being"), but he does not hold back on his professional judgment. "His musical standards are absolutely nonexistent," he has said. "He educated the public to believe that the high top notes are the greatest thing in opera. That is wrong. It was depressing. He and his staff always made me feel I was wasting money if I wanted to rehearse. There was no heritage, no legacy left from Bing's twenty years at the Met and it was his fault because opera is first and foremost music. Opera does not start with engaging five stars and then finding an opera for them." It was the problem of which came first that appears to have been at the core of his ultimate dispute with the Met. Bing, who catalogues his old enmities with the care of a Sicilian *don*, wrote to *The New York Times* in 1971 to indicate that there'd been an initial disagreement over scheduling, that the Met wanted to have Solti conduct a new production of Benjamin Britten's *Peter Grimes* while Solti preferred to conduct Britten's *Billy Budd*. They resolved that—Bing's way: Solti agree to do *Peter Grimes*. "What made his return eventually collapse was the disagreement about one or two of the leading singers in the *Peter Grimes* cast whom he did not wish to accept and whom I insisted on casting," Bing told the *Times*. Solti objected basically to the soprano Bing chose, and when Bing insisted that the Met felt committed to her, Solti wrote a letter of withdrawal rather than accept the musicial decisions of the general manager. At the time, the exchange was temperate enough; Solti even suggested that, through his withdrawal, the Met could then hire a tenor he detested. It was Jon Vickers, who once walked out on him during the recording of *Aïda*.

Bing went ahead without Solti; Colin Davis—later Solti's successor at Covent Garden—was the conductor and Tyrone Guthrie handled the stage direction. "I think we had a very good performance of *Peter Grimes*," wrote Bing, "and the singers in question were extremely successful." But the feeling has grown in Solti that his authority and decisions in the musical realm are as valid as Bing's, or more so.

Another of his celebrated fights over his musical prerogatives took place with Mrs. Dorothy "Buffy" Chandler, wife of the late Norman Chandler, publisher of the *Los Angeles Times* and *grande doyenne* of culture in that city. (She conceived the idea, raised the money, and gave the main impetus of the concept that became the striking Los Angeles Music Center.) Mrs. Chandler has much of the personality of Solti: she is terribly well organized and very authoritative; some might say dictatorial. ("When Buff Chandler walks into a room, the rest of us might as well go home," another Los Angeles committee lady has said of the way she takes over.) So as a director of the Los Angeles Philharmonic, she became *the* director of the Los Angeles Philharmonic. In April 1960, the Philharmonic hired Solti as music director to succeed the late Eduard van Beinum. He was to take up his duties as conductor at the beginning of the 1961–62 season. It was a three-year contract at a reported $40,000 a year, and it gave him, Solti has claimed, absolute authority in musical matters—programming and the engagement of soloists and guest conductors. Since his commitment was for thirteen weeks a year, it was apparent that an associate conductor would be needed. Solti suggested a private competition among several young conductors and, because he'd been impressed with a performance of Zubin Mehta at Vienna, then twenty-four and one of the youngest men ever to conduct both the Berlin and Vienna Philharmonic orchestras, Solti went to the trouble of raising the money to bring Mehta to Los Angeles for the competition. Solti was gratified by the result; he thought Mehta has proven himself in the competition. He was prepared to accept the Bombay-born conductor as his associate when he learned, to his astonishment, that Mehta had decided to become conductor of the Montreal Symphony. There was no possibility that the No. 1 man of such an orchestra in Canada could also be the No. 2 man of an orchestra in the United States. He felt that Mehta understood this also. So Solti—who'd gotten a complete list of programs and guest conductors approved by the board of the Los Angeles Philharmonic—flew back to Europe believing that the associate's job was still unfilled. Some months later, he learned from a newspaper clipping that Mrs. Chandler had hired Mehta and that she'd told the press he would be "sharing the podium" with Solti. Solti was infuriated. For one thing, it appeared that Mehta was to be a co-conductor, not associate—or No. 2—conductor. For another, Mrs. Chandler's action had, in his view, violated their agreement that he would have complete control of musical decisions. So he sent off a corrosive cable resigning the post in Los Angeles. He had nothing against Mehta. Solti just didn't want management invading his prerogatives as music director. "It was a matter of principle," he said later. "If I had given in on this point, it would never have been the same. I had to do it and I think I set a good example for my colleagues."

In retrospect, nobody suffered greatly from the incident. Mehta took over as conductor of the Los Angeles Philharmonic, thus becoming the first man ever to lead two major orchestras on the North American continent. (Seiji Ozawa later became conductor of both the San Francisco and Boston Symphony orchestras.) Solti himself found some philosophical solace in it all. "If I would have stayed on in Los Angeles," he has said, "I would never have gotten the Chicago Symphony."

The Los Angeles incident was the preamble for a dramatic change in the direction of his career—a change which was fulfilled a decade later when he shifted his career from conducting opera to conducting symphony orchestras: in three years he took over symphonic assignments with three of the leading cities of the world—Chicago, Paris, and London.

The prior commitment of Solti to opera was both cultural and personal. Culturally, opera has always had greater prestige and acceptance in Europe than in America. In the nineteenth century, it was a more popular medium in Europe than was the symphony orchestra; it shared the popularity of the theater in general and, like the theater, the opera kept in constant touch with current excitement and social themes. The orchestra was "in the pit"—physically lower than the action of the opera—and somehow the prestige was similarly lower. Opera scores circulated more easily than what we would now consider the symphonic classics. Even though symphony orchestras began to appear around the middle and end of the nineteenth century, they tended for a long time to concentrate on operatic overtures and excerpts. Young men who became conductors turned, almost reflexively, to opera as their most immediate choice—an opportunity—rather than to the concert hall. For opera had both the prestige and the opportunity.

Solti did so, though he also had personal impetus toward opera. His parents, who started him on the piano, also sent his sister for singing lessons. Invariably, Georg wound up playing the piano in accompaniment to his sister's operatic exercises. "So, early in my life I learned to follow a singer if she makes mistakes," he has said. "That is absolutely essential for an operatic career." At the time, Solti was considered solely a pianist, albeit a potentially brilliant one: he was giving recitals and winning raves at the age of twelve. But when he was thirteen, he watched Erich Kleiber, the celebrated Austrian-born conductor, lead a perform-ance of a Beethoven symphony and from that moment on, his ambitions were transformed: he wanted to become a conductor. After studying at the Franz Liszt Academy—under Bartók and Ernst von Dohnányi—he went to work, at the age of eighteen, doing all the dirty backstage jobs at the Budapest State Opera—for nothing. (The second year he was put on the payroll, at the equivalent of $20 a week.) Solti worked there for years, coaching and accompanying the singers as they prepared new parts, playing for the chorus rehearsals, setting up chairs and music stands, raising and lowering the curtain, doing everything but conducting.

In the summer, he and some friends would go over to Salzburg for the festival and seek to get into rehearsals at which Solti could study Toscanini's techniques. One summer day in 1936, some rehearsal coaches turned up ill and Solti was there, ready, willing, and able to take over. He was assigned to work under Toscanini who was, of course, preparing an opera: Mozart's *Die Zauberflöte*. At rehearsals, Solti played the piano accompaniment; at the performance, he played the glockenspiel in the orchestra. (There was a clandestine record made of the performance, and when Solti hears it now, on tape, he listens for the glockenspiel and says, "That's me. That's me." He has described the original experience of playing *Die Zauberflöte* as "fabulous," but the sound—in the perspective of later years—as "a great disappointment. I found everything highly exaggerated on the tape—too fast or too slow. I didn't find a single tempo with which I agreed.") Solti continued at Salzburg in 1937, albeit never as anything higher than a sort of third-line assistant to Toscanini. (The maestro's first assistant was Erich Leinsdorf, later conductor of the Boston Symphony and the Metropolitan Opera; his second assistant was William Steinberg, later conductor of the Pittsburgh Symphony.) But Solti's work gained some recognition back in Budapest. On January 16, 1938, he was given a chance to conduct the Hungarian Orchestra in—interestingly—a program of concert music, not opera (Bach's G-minor Suite, a *Brandenburg* concerto, Debussy's *La Petite Suite*, Mozart's G-minor Suite, the Schumann piano concerto, and the overture from Rossini's *La Gazza Ladra*). "Even if we think of this orchestra as being made up of beginners, we must admire the energy with which Georg Solti forced his musicians to play," wrote one of the critics at that performance. "He has great rhythm and lots of ambition. His conducting movements are both clear and determined, and one can see immediately how much he learned from Toscanini. . . . It was absolutely clear that during the performance he was enjoying conducting so much that he had not yet had time to show the depth of interpretation which is required in these great masterpieces. Nevertheless he started the overture to La Gazza Ladra with great gusto and had as much control over his orchestra as he had over his public, showing us that without a doubt he will make his way not only in the operatic field but also in the concert hall."

His next opportunity was in the opera house. Just under two months later, he made his conducting debut at the Budapest Opera with a daring effort—he conducted one of the most ambitious works of the operatic repertory, Mozart's Le Nozze di Figaro, after only one formal rehearsal and with singers in two of the major parts—the Countess and Bartolo—turning up ill at the last minute. Undeterred, he went ahead on the night of March 11, 1938, and again won critiques of commendation ("He conducted Mozart's masterpiece with great energy, keeping the overall form and style of the music. Here his natural conducting talent came to the surface and we can definitely count on him making his name in the future.")

The most notable reaction, though, was in the audience that night. During the second act, he noticed that the audience was becoming very restless and noisy; a constant buzz seemed to run through it. It was not because of Solti's conducting; it was because of Adolf Hitler's ambitions. At 8:45 that night, Hitler sent his armies marching over the border into Austria, and then into Vienna—only 120 miles or so from Budapest. There was some concern in the audience—indeed in the world—that this was the start of World War II and that Budapest would, like Vienna, be suddenly engulfed. Solti knew nothing of the invasion, of course, and so he was concerned that the reaction of the audience was indifference to the performance, not concern about the future.

As it happened, the Anschluss was to have a profound effect on Solti's career. For Toscanini resolved publicly never to return to Salzburg so long as Austria was under Nazi rule. (Hitler's first military elements had, in fact, marched through Salzburg on their way to seizing power in Austria.) So Toscanini began to spend his summers in Switzerland and Solti rejoined him there, in Lucerne, in the summer of 1939. It was a time when the war clouds were gathering once again, this time over the issue of Danzig and Poland, and when Hitler's minions were achieving undisputed power in Hungary. Solti's mother finally wrote to him in Switzerland and urged him not to come home. His Jewish blood might condemn him if he returned to Budapest. Toscanini offered an alternative: he invited Solti to come with him to New York. "Unfortunately," Solti has said, "I discovered that the Hungarian quota for the United States was filled up for the next fifty years. Or so they told me," he said.

So he seized on another alternative: he accepted an invitation from a tenor who lived in Switzerland to teach him the key parts in several Wagnerian operas, notably Tristan. Solti went to Zurich and moved into the tenor's house. He stayed there for a year and a half and, while he's not sure the tenor ever learned Wagner, "I did." In these years, he could not conduct; he could not get that kind of work permit from the Swiss. But he could play the piano and in 1942 he won first prize in the Concours International at Geneva. That gave his instrumental career a large boost, and he spent many of the war years giving piano recitals all over Switzerland. But his heart was still directed toward conducting. "People would always say that I was trying to orchestrate at the piano, trying to imitate the instruments of the orchestra," he has said. "No doubt it was true."

He entered Switzerland on a ten-day visa. He stayed there almost seven years. It was not until the spring of 1946 that he got a chance to leave and to conduct—and then it was opera again: the Munich State Opera was being reassembled by the American occupation authorities. It was not easy; his bid was accepted, then shuffled off—he was directed to Stuttgart instead and was so successful there in one performance that he was summoned back to Munich. He got married, he moved into a one-room apartment over a onetime fashion shop—its upper floors were bombed away—and he prepared to start his conducting career. Years later he was to say, "I can honestly say that in that little room, surrounded by all the rubble and horror, I started my life."

As a conductor, he had as many limitations as ambitions: he knew only two operas—*Le Nozze di Figaro* he'd performed in Budapest in 1938 and Beethoven's *Fidelio* that he'd conducted at Stuttgart. "I took great care to conceal my rather limited repertory," he was to say later. "It was not until several years that Munich began to discover that I was conducting everything for the first time."

Through study, cunning, and circumstances, he managed to pull it off. The circumstances involved the destruction during the war not only of the opera house but also of all its sets. So Solti was lucky: he was not confronted with a demand for an entire repertory at the instant he took over the Munich State Opera. "Every piece had to be built from scratch, and that gave me the chance to learn from the scratches, too." The cunning involved the selection of the works. The first piece that Solti conducted at Munich was Verdi's *Requiem*. It was a superbly fitting choice. On the one hand, it was ideal as an "occasion" piece—one which marked the end of a life and a way of life for Munich as well as for Solti. On the other hand, it was ideal for production: it required no sets. It became a hallmark: years later Solti conducted the *Requiem* in New York to mark a memorial for the death of President John F. Kennedy.

As a very determined late starter, he let nothing deter him in Munich. His second effort was an ambitious *Carmen*, produced in German. He then built his own repertory: the heavy Strauss works—*Salome, Rosenkavalier, Ariadne, Elektra*—and much of Wagner's *Ring*, most of Mozart, and Verdi's *Otello* and *La Forza del Destino*. Later he remembers that "in Germany, we gave forty-five operas a season, sometimes seven operas in seven nights." But his success was so notable that he began winning guest-conducting invitations in Italy and Vienna. In 1952, he left Munich to become music director of the Frankfurt Opera, then a most bountiful and prestigious opera house. He spent nine years in Frankfurt, adding forty-four new productions to the repertory of the company and generally giving it—in the estimate of some viewers and Solti himself—"nine of the best years the house had before or since."

There were, to be sure, moments in these years when he conducted symphonic music. He was guest conductor of the London Philharmonic first in 1950 and of the New York Philharmonic in 1957. But by far his greatest fame—and steady flame—was as a conductor of opera. He went to Edinburgh first in 1952 to conduct *Die Zauberflöte*. His debut in the United States in 1953 was at an opera house—the San Francisco Opera. His first steady assignment in Chicago was at the Lyric Opera. His recording in 1957 of excerpts from a Wagner opera, *Die Walküre* with Kirsten Flagstad, touched off a flurry of operatic recordings climaxed by a complete recording of the *Ring* cycle, finally finished in 1965.

Toward the end of the fifties, he seemed pulled toward concert hall music. His abortive commitment to Los Angeles was illustrative; later he made another commitment for a limited engagement with the Dallas Symphony. In general, he claims that it's time to seek new posts after nine or ten years—and he'd finished nine years with the Frankfurt Opera. It turned out he was a recidivist. He did leave the Frankfurt Opera but he signed on, starting in 1961, at Covent Garden and appeared as a guest at the Metropolitan Opera. The Metropolitan Opera appearances died of the fight with Bing, but he had promised to make Covent Garden —whose luster had dimmed through the years—one of the great opera companies of the world. He succeeded. He even turned down the offer of the Chicago Symphony in 1963 because he could not devote the time that the symphony fathers were then demanding. (He could not know that it would come his way again but later he was to say, "Somehow it seemed easier to follow Jean Martinon than to follow Fritz Reiner.")

His years in London became part of a profound and continuing change in his life. He got divorced and remarried. He became the father of a child, for the first time, at the age of fifty-seven. He became a British subject and decided to make London his home: he and his family live in the St. John's Wood section of London. It was time for a change in his professional career: by the time his last contract at Covent Garden was up, he'd have spent almost ten years with the Royal Opera. And so he decided at that time to make the significant shift away from opera and into conducting symphony orchestras. "I had to do it now or I would never do it," he says. Before he'd stopped, he'd made commitments to orchestras in three of the major cities of the world.

In the autumn of 1969, he started with the Chicago Symphony.

In the autumn of 1970, he started with L'Orchestre de Paris.

In the autumn of 1971, he started with the London Philharmonic, albeit as guest conductor.

And at the same time he ended his commitment to Covent Garden in the summer of 1971.

Not all of this was as methodical as it seems in retrospect. The reason is that most such commitments have to be made a year or more before they take effect. For example, his acceptance of the post in Chicago was announced in December 1968; it had been agreed to by Solti in the preceding spring or summer but there had been a delay until the U.S. Internal Revenue Service could clear his application for tax relief under the U.S. laws for a foreign citizen earning income for part-time work in the United States. As we've seen, there were rumors—at the very moment the appointment was announced—that he would take over L'Orchestre de Paris, which had been founded earlier under the leadership of the late Charles

Munch out of the seedlings of the old Paris Conservatory Orchestra. It is true that Solti had been approached. But he did not feel he could take the job because of his Covent Garden commitment and the upcoming acceptance of the post in Chicago. "At that time I told the Parisians I could not have three organizations," he said later. On their part, they could not wait two and one-half years, until Solti's contract with Covent Garden ran out. So Herbert von Karajan was named conductor of L'Orchestre de Paris instead, not as music director but as music "counselor." But, as it turned out, he could not devote a great deal of time to Paris either; he was heavily committed in other directions. So, after two years, von Karajan dropped the Paris post. The management in Paris promptly came back to Solti who found—on this occasion—the time to perform in Paris. "It wasn't that we played some kind of trick on von Karajan," he said.

Subsequently he took the London Philharmonic assignment, if only because it *was* London and would provide him a working respite near his home, a respite that—since it was a guest conductorship—would not demand the time and attention that running Covent Garden required.

Then with all those details tidied up, he promptly reversed himself: he took the post as music "adviser" to the Paris Opéra. ("He said to me, 'No more opera. No more opera,' " his U.S. manager, Ann Colbert, has said. "Then Liebermann comes along and he takes it.") He took it because of Liebermann and their longtime friendship. There could be no other explanation why he would leave a superb opera company that he'd built up—the Royal Opera at Covent Garden—to work with another opera company in Paris that was struggling to emerge from the shadows of a politics-ridden past. The acceptance gave him a rather bizarre stature: Solti—a foreigner—was leading the most prestigious opera company and symphony orchestra in France.

And yet neither of them had the substance of the orchestra he had in Chicago. His job was to build that substance into an international prestige. And he did it. "I did not know," he says, "it would happen so soon. Three years . . ."

The success—and the speed of his success—is a reflection of Solti's growth in understanding of the psychology of the orchestra and of the city that spawned it.

As a city, Chicago has long prided itself more on its muscle than its mind. It was not just Carl Sandburg who gave it an identity: "City of the Big Shoulders." It was also Theodore Dreiser: "This singing flame of a city, this all-America, this poet in chaps and buckskins, this rude, raw Titan, this Burns of a city!" It is a plainspoken city, without guile or subtlety, but immersed in its own conceits. This is not unusual: *every* city has its own conceit. New York's is that it is incurably romantic; Chicago's is that it is big-city. The roll-call of its "bigness" is trumpeted remorselessly; one can hear it almost any day and every day on radio and TV and see it in the newspapers: Chicago has the biggest and best of "anything"—the tallest building, the busiest airport, the largest underground garage, the most-used expressway . . . which translates into the world's worst traffic jams. It was always quantity—the materialistic—not quality that the city was eager to measure. Anything was acceptable as long as it was big and colorful. And so it had some of the biggest and most colorful thieves of modern civilization. One of the city's many such heroes was its traction magnate, Charles Yerkes, Jr., a man who—as a protagonist for some of Dreiser's novels—certainly had to rank among the biggest and the best in terms of an amoral, lustful desire for women, money, and power. He bled the people of the city for millions upon millions of dollars while flamboyantly buying up aldermen, state legislators, and anybody else who was for sale. "The secret of success," he once confided, "is to buy old junk, fix it up a little, and unload it upon other fellows."

The Chicago Symphony and Solti changed much of that. Solti's gift was that he had a high art, great integrity, and the cunning to know reflexively how to handle all this: he let Chicago know that *he* was the best and the city was lucky to have him.

Donald Peck, the principal flutist in the Chicago Symphony, put it aptly. "Solti approached the city of Chicago and this orchestra the only way a man could approach this city and this orchestra. Chicago is a brutal city. And the orchestra is a strong group of people. I mean, individually and as a whole. Jean Martinon, for example, came here wanting to be a nice man. He wanted to be liked by the men; he wanted the city to accept him. Whether he was a great conductor or not has nothing to do with it, in what I'm talking about. The fact remains that as soon as this brutal city and this strong orchestra saw this man asking for acceptance, they clobbered him. Absolutely *clobbered* him." And the contrast with his successor? "Solti came here with headlines which just as much as said, 'Chicago, you are lucky to have me. And everything I do is wonderful and right. The whole world thinks so and if you don't think so, you are wrong.' Well . . . this city was completely intimidated." In short, Solti—within his own personality—would never ask for acceptance; he commands respect. And says you're lucky to have the chance to give it. The result: Chicago fell completely and rapturously in love with him.

Solti also understood perfectly the dreams of Louis Sudler and the way they might be realized. The Chicago Symphony was in its seventy-eighth year when Solti took over and it had never made a European tour—not since Thomas turned down the Paris bid in the last century—and had not even made a U.S. tour. It had appeared in other cities in the United States—Milwaukee, New York, Iowa City, and so forth in regional towns—but it had never made a wide-flung tour of the continent. Solti made it a contractual matter that the orchestra would travel both nationally and internationally; he would not come unless he could make the orchestra's gifts clear to the nation and the world.

He was not so understanding about some sensitivities of the orchestra. For one thing, the orchestra was old in years. In 1970, the median age of the Chicago Symphony was fifty-five years. Of the fifteen section leaders, eleven had come to the orchestra under Fritz Reiner—that is, ten to twenty years earlier. At least twenty-eight of the thirty-two violins had been in the orchestra for ten years or more. Solti expressed his awareness of this age factor in public—and expressed a conviction that he was just the man to rejuvenate the group. The orchestra, proud to the utmost, resolved to make him change his mind. And to repent. When Solti arrived in Chicago, some of the principal players insisted on auditioning for him individually—before accepting his apology. Solti accepted the lesson and its import. He has not made a single change among the section leaders with the exception of the violins, when a co-concertmaster resigned to make a career of giving recitals.

On the whole, Solti was able to see assets in what others might consider a liability. There is a sense of cultural isolation about Chicago, real or imagined. The players feel this as a limiting factor, but Solti sees it as a factor that enlarges the skills of the orchestra. In cities such as New York, there are so many divertissements that the central thrust of the musician is threatened by dilution. "In Chicago," Solti has asked rhetorically, "what is there to do but to teach music or make music?"

Similarly with the age factor: Solti quickly came to appreciate that with age came experience—that the men of the Chicago Symphony had the cerebral as well as the mental skills to understand perfectly what he wants and give it to him when he wants it. He sees it in a capability beyond the basic, and historic, sound of the orchestra. "With the Chicago, you can achieve a smoothness of sound, like the Vienna Philharmonic," he says. "Or you can have a much harder sound. Or you can have French coloring. This orchestra is not only responsive but versatile." He was asked to compare it in responsiveness to the Vienna Philharmonic, which he has conducted on numerous records and in innumerable guest performances. "The Vienna Philharmonic is absolutely not responsive—well, if you make music the way they want to, they are responsive. But if you want to do something they are not accustomed to, then you have a fight. I don't envy anyony who has to fight the Vienna Philharmonic—including myself."

The degree of responsiveness in the Chicago Symphony is notable, even in Solti's view. For he does not have to work or overwork them in order to get the sound he wants. Indeed, often he needs only to outline his thoughts verbally to correct matters that he thinks need correcting. Early in the 1970s, Solti had taken the Chicago Symphony on a tour of the eastern United States. In a stop at Dartmouth in Hanover, New Hampshire, he was deeply dissatisfied with the orchestra's playing of the sunny, buoyant Symphony in B-flat by Schumann—the *Spring* Symphony. He said of the playing: "It was not my conception. It was not the usual conception. It was *nothing.*" The work was to be played again in New York one night later. Solti did not want a repetition of the Dartmouth performance. There was no time for rehearsal, even if Solti had been inclined to call for one. Instead, on the chartered plane from Dartmouth to New York, he wrote out a four-page list of details that he wanted to have corrected. Then he sent for the leaders of the five string sections—bass, cello, viola, first violin, second violin —plus his principals in the trumpet, clarinet, and oboe. He talked over the changes with them, urged them to play the changes where they thought necessary. Before the New York concert, the section leaders got the scores from the symphony librarians and made the necessary markings and changes to indicate Solti's views. They then met with their colleagues in each section and talked those changes through. That night in New York, the performance was precisely as Solti wanted it; the music rose contagiously in just the way that the vernal season rises. Only this time it was punctuated by the swift, darting pleased glances of the conductor who knows precisely what the Chicago Symphony can do—and will do.

Solti has likened the relationship built up in his early season with the orchestra to a marriage—"either it works or it doesn't." (Martinon was inclined to describe the relationship as one of horse and rider—with the conductor wielding the whip.) Quite obviously the marriage worked between Solti and the Chicago Symphony.

This is not to say that the marriage is not without its disagreements. For the orchestra is very much like a finicky woman—proud, temperamental, righteous, insistent. In the winter of 1974, Sir Georg gathered with reporters to talk of the orchestra's second European tour, which was scheduled for the following September. In the course of it, Solti—who is a competitive man—used certain analogies from games and sports ("it is a football game") to describe the goals and the competitive drive ("the boxing spirit") of the orchestra. One of the members of the orchestra promptly wrote to the *Chicago Tribune* to complain of this and other matters.

"The Chicago Symphony Orchestra is not an entry in a horse race, or, as the Maestro suggests, a football game or a boxing match. The competitive spirit has no place in serious art or music, as the aesthetic sense must go far beyond the barbaric concepts of winning or losing," said the letter. "Maestro Solti's attitude seems to express the unfortunate but prevailing motivation of American concertgoers who attend a concert to evaluate the performance rather than express the music. The result has led to the common and often valid criticism of American orchestras: 'real perfection but no soul.' It has compelled American orchestras to turn to the large bombastic late 19th century literature as the only hopes of crowd-pleasing. Only Mahler, Bruckner, or Wagner seem to really put points on the scoreboard. [*Ed. note: In this season, as we have seen, Solti would conduct no Wagner, no Bruckner, and only one Mahler symphony, albeit the latter was at the Big Scoreboard in New York.*]

"Very often any real refinement of the Chicago Symphony sound is gone. When our orchestra can bring down the house at Carnegie Hall with a program of Mozart or Haydn, we can then be convinced of our success. Instead, the Chicago Symphony Orchestra is sounding more and more like the brass band at the half-time show of Maestro Solti's football game."

It was pungent, sound, deeply rooted comment. It also gave a new dimension to a view Solti once expressed to define the relationship that developed when he came to Chicago:

"Something extraordinary happened in Chicago. I made no changes. We didn't have to adjust to each other. Our ways of making music were the same. Wine became champagne: we sparkle together. It's like Siegfried and Brünnhilde: the girl was beautiful and Siegfried turned out not to be impotent."

But Brünnhilde also turned out to have a mind—and muscle—of her own.

INTERLUDE: Idleness Enforced

It was opening night. The players in the Chicago Symphony Orchestra were dressed in their white ties and tails and they were heading toward the front doors. But they weren't carrying their instruments. They were carrying signs. For this was the opening of Lyric Opera in Chicago, not the Chicago Symphony, and the signs read:

"We, too, want to play for you"

and

"CSO members love the Lyric too."

At least the Lyric was working. The Chicago Symphony was not. There was a labor dispute, the first of many that were to sweep the arts in the season of 1973–74. The opening night of the Chicago Symphony—though not the Lyric Opera—had been called off. Every concert and recording session of the symphony for the next four weeks would be canceled. It was to be a test of the resolve of the members of the orchestra, of their employers, and of the individuals' chances of surviving on their own—without the Chicago Symphony.

The barking in his kennels was music to the ears of Grover Schiltz, the oboe and English horn player. He raised dogs and boarded them as an avocation, as something to do away from the symphony. In the months before this, he'd added on another room to his house. Then he and his wife had taken a brief vacation in Montreal where, after much agonizing, they bought an expensive bass for his wife. "It represented a fairly large chunk of change at a time when we didn't know whether we were going to have ready and steady income," he says. The kennels provided extra income but not enough to match the income from the symphony for a year, should the whole season be canceled. "Fortunately, the fellow from whom we bought the bass allowed us an extension."

The coughing of his banker was not music to the ears of Wally Horban. He's assistant librarian of the Chicago Symphony and he'd just bought a lot in Barrington Hills, a swank exurb of Chicago. Now he'd contracted to have a house built on it. One of those "invisible" men who keep the symphony going—in his case by finding, preparing, and upgrading the musical scores used by the orchestra—he was as closely attuned to the drives of the players as were the musicians themselves. Since he was working under the same contract they were, he was faced with a hard choice inspired by a high mortgage ("not one of your everyday kind of $30,000 mortgages," he says, "I mean a big mortgage"). Should he adopt a back-to-work stance or should he take the risks of trying to keep going—without work—with a high mortgage. "I decided that we had to hold together," he says, "and I'd take all the risks on the house by myself."

Just off Sheridan Road on the far North Shore of Chicago, threescore persons gathered in a rambling old Tudor house to hear the Contemporary Arts Quartet. There was no charge. It was a music lover's night. Nothing more than contributions—minimal contributions—were expected. But the members of the quartet—violinists Fred Spector and Otakar Sroubek, violist William Schoen, cellist Don Moline—were playing this in the first of a series of chamber music concerts to raise money for their fellow musicians in the Chicago Symphony. "I'd say that we got a contribution of well over a thousand dollars in four chamber music concerts," says Fred Spector.

At the signal, the conductor raised his arms and gave the downbeat, and the members of the Chicago Symphony swung into a stirring movement of Johann Strauss's Emperor Waltz. It was not at Orchestra Hall; it was at a recording studio in the suburbs. The conductor was not clean-shaven, bald Georg Solti; it was bearded, gray-flecked Dale Clevenger, the first horn player of the Chicago Symphony. And the occasion was not a concert of the Chicago Symphony; it was an industrial film for Sea World, the playland in the nation's "sunland." Each member of the Chicago Symphony who took part in this effort—fifty-five of them —would earn $26 an hour, about $74 in all. The date had been arranged by Clevenger, who arranged to have his fellow musicians hired, and he'd been selected as conductor. It was just one of many such dates he'd play during the work stoppage. "We found out," he said tentatively, "that it was possible I might make a living without the symphony schedule."

In a hall in New Haven the Chicago Symphony String Quartet gave a chamber music recital to a packed house. The violinists were Victor Aitay and Edgar Muenzer; the viola was Milton Preves; the cellist was Frank Miller—all members of the Chicago Symphony. They'd stay over at Yale University the next day, but the man who arranged the chamber music recital, Louis Sudler, would be on a plane on the way home. He had other engagements to arrange—for Dale Clevenger and his wife to appear as soloists for an Artists' Showcase production which was being taped now for production in February, for members of the Chicago Symphony and its

String Quartet to appear in a special Artists' Showcase production at Notre Dame. Thus he was in a position unlike any top management man who ever preceded him in orchestral affairs. On the one side, he was heading the Orchestral Association, which had maneuvered a lockout of the players in the Chicago Symphony. On the other hand, he was providing jobs for the members who'd been left out of work in this situation.

In his home in Skokie, Willard Elliot, the bassoonist, tended to the orchids in the hot autumn days in his greenhouse, and to the reeds of his instrument in the cool seclusion of his study. "I suppose I spend a minimum of two hours on each reed," he says quietly, "but not at the same time. But I'll do a whole batch—well, I will usually gouge maybe about fifty or sixty pieces at a time, which is good for the muscles of the hand—you get some calluses on your hand." A quiet man. He didn't care much for seeking after outside work. He'd take only two or three students this year. His wife, Gladys, played in the orchestra of the Lyric Opera and they would not be without money. As long as nothing serious happened.

On Michigan Avenue, flutist Dick Graef walked a picket line in front of Orchestra Hall. With him was his four-year-old daughter, Rachel, carrying a sign "My Daddy's Locked Out." Back home his wife, Vicki, went to a gynecologist and called his attention to the growth just below her left ear. "I know this is asking you to work on the wrong end . . ." But the hard little spur had been growing swiftly. "He felt it and said that he didn't know what it was but if it grew larger, I should see about getting help or advice from somebody who knew what it was," she says. It continued to grow larger.

FIRST
MOVEMENT

Dissonance in a Major Chord

I t began in the most beguiling of seasons, spring.

It began in the most beguiling of times—a period of great acclaim.

In Orchestra Hall, Georg Solti and the Chicago Symphony were bathed in applause for their performance of act 3 of Wagner's *Götterdämmerung*, so much applause that even Chicago's often blasé critics were impressed. "Usually, when Symphony audiences do not hurry for the exits," wrote Roger Dettmer in *Chicago Today*, "they incline to politeness rather than enthusiasm. But Solti's Wagner last night was the battering ram that broke through local constraint."

There was, at the moment, a small undertone, an inner voice of orchestra affairs, that was barely beginning to be heard beneath the crashing climaxes of *Götterdämmerung*. It could mean more than the acclaim of Wagner and Solti. It could mean disaster for the season. For on the seventh floor of Orchestra Hall—the management floor—and the nineteenth floor of a building two miles across the Loop on La Salle Street—the headquarters of the counsel for the Musicians Union—two sides of orchestral life were assembling their armor and their armaments for another climactic contract struggle.

The negotiations started in April and continued all through the months when summer lay its hot, smothering hand on the city. They were suspended during the post-Ravinia weeks—vacation time for the musicians—and then resumed in early September. Even then, there did not seem to be a sense of anxiousness or anxiety—certainly not on management's side. And then suddenly the simmering subterranean war of grievances on both sides broke out into open antagonism; the first five concerts, then the next three weeks of the symphony season were called off.

There is something dissonant, almost grotesque, in opening a symphonic season with a labor dispute. It is almost like opening a box of bonbons and catching a faint whiff of cyanide. Great Art and Union Militancy do not seem to go together—except to musicians, of course. But the labor troubles which inaugurated this season of the Chicago Symphony were notable in two ways.

For one thing, it was the hallmark, the test case, for similar disputes in New York, Cleveland, and other locations—not to mention other arts. And thus an added militancy was brought onto both sides, for they were symbols of a Greater Meaning.

For another, it seemed to pull the orchestra—which had been riven with enmities and dissension—together in an unprecedented way. Votes that the most optimistic of the union negotiators thought might win by a 2-to-1 or 3-to-1 margin were being passed by a 50-to-1 margin. Only 1 or 2 members, out of the 105 or so who vote on such issues, voted against the work of the negotiators. Thus the labor dispute may have had the effect of making this orchestra, made up of so many virtuosos, a more unified and cohesive unit than ever before.

Beyond all this, the work stoppage seemed to climax fifteen years of ferment within the orchestra—years in which members came to know and to hate each other, years in which they fought union as well as management . . . years in which their salaries tripled.

The turning point was in 1959. Before that, the Chicago Symphony Orchestra was run like orchestras from the birth of the symphony: on a paternal system. The musicians played at and for the pleasure of royalty and the aristocracy. They played for the rewards of their own art, which is to say that they got very little in the way of money for their efforts. That was the way of life in Chicago. It did not have royalty but it had an aristocracy of sorts and—until Louis Sudler came along—that aristocracy was far more dedicated to the production of steel, the killing of cattle, and the sale of dry goods than it was to the elevation of the arts. In the middle 1950s, the average musician was lucky to earn as much as $4,100 a year from the Chicago Symphony. ("The scale when I joined the symphony in 1954 was $145 a week for a twenty-eight-week year," says Sam Denov.) There was, of course, the Ravinia season but it was then a separate deal, lasting six weeks and usually at rates lower than the Orchestral Association paid. So between the two salary levels, the average player in the Chicago Symphony could figure to gross around $4,500 to $4,700 a year—and be completely without work for eighteen weeks a year.

It wasn't always easy to find work in the off-season: "You went to look for a job and you put down your work record and said you were a member of the Chicago Symphony and you make $145 a week, and they would say 'Gee, I don't think you would be happy here because we only pay $65 a week for temporary help,' " says Denov. Nevertheless, it was customary in those days for the members of the Chicago Symphony—virtuosos or not—to scrabble hard for work in the four months of the off-season. "I worked as a car-hike, as an office boy. I worked as a driving instructor. I worked in an electronics plant as an analyzer for tape recorders. I worked at God knows what," says Denov. His toughest job? "Working in a department store in the housewares department and dealing with housewives all day long."

They had a union, of course, but it was next to useless—at least for symphony musicians. James Caesar Petrillo had made himself a big man in both Local 10 of the American Federation of Musicians and later as head of the national organization. He fought everybody from the record companies to President Franklin D. Roosevelt and he invariably won. There was only one challenge to his authority in his forty years as head of Local 10, and the challenger was not only defeated but cunningly left without means of support for many years.

The source of Petrillo's power was, interestingly, not the full-time musician. It was the part-timer, the man who worked at another job in the daytime and moonlighted in music at night. For they were far greater in numbers than were the full-time professional musicians. In particular, the symphony musicians meant nothing to Petrillo. They numbered some 105 persons out of a membership of, perhaps, 10,000. So he could sacrifice these members in exchange for whatever power the Establishment in Chicago might offer him. There are many, many members of the Chicago Symphony—then and now—who are convinced that this is exactly what he did: he'd sit down with the head of the Orchestral Association—Dr. Eric Oldberg—and agree amiably to whatever the Orchestral Association suggested. He didn't know anything about the conditions of the working in a symphony orchestra; no union leader did. Nor did he know much about the workings of a nonprofit organization, such as the Orchestral Association. He was oriented totally toward telling hotels and record companies and nightclubs and anybody else who hired moonlighting musicians what they'd have to do on behalf of his part-time help. The full-time symphony musicians had to take care of themselves. "The only way we would know about what happened," says Sam Denov, "was that on the company bulletin board was a one-page notice saying that we had just entered into a new three-year contract—so many weeks, so many dollars a week. That was it. That was the whole contract—that single sheet of paper."

Two things happened in 1959 to start bringing about changes. One was the enactment of federal legislation trying to guarantee "democracy" within the various unions and their locals. The other was the canceling of the European tour of the Chicago Symphony, with a Russian tour as an offshoot, on what seemed to be arbitrary action of the management. The real reason, in retrospect, was the increasing infirmity of Fritz Reiner, but at the time the players got no such explanation. They wanted the tour and they wanted it badly: there were prestige implications and vacation implications as well as work implications involved. So when it was called off—after they'd made so many plans—they reacted in a fit of extreme pique. "We almost hung Reiner in effigy," says Denov. Failing that, they threw a dress suit—white tie and tails, complete with a baton—down on the floor of the changing room, and the members of the orchestra marched ritualistically and contemptuously across it.

"I think that was when Reiner first heard about it," says Denov. "He was incensed that the orchestra would protest anything he was doing. So the orchestra was assembled"—by the personnel manager—"and told that the tour was canceled and what right did we have to complain; after all, it was up to management to decide whether we go or don't go and we have no voice in that sort of thing. And on top of all that, Reiner demanded an apology from the orchestra.

"Well, up to that time, I'd been a very meek, quiet, go-along individual. But that got me up to here"—Denov gestured somewhat above the throat level. "And on the spur of the moment—I'd never done anything like this before—I made a very impassioned speech." He said that "Reiner was going to get no apology from this orchestra . . . and I said that it is he who should apologize to us, not we to him . . . and we absolutely refuse to apologize to him." He paused and a mote of dust reflected in the light of the lounge rolled down his bald pate. "The orchestra broke out in loud applause. I was absolutely amazed—I had never done anything like that before."

The cancellation of the tour gave the motive to the players to take advantage of the "democracy in labor" act: they organized a players' committee within the orchestra with the purpose of getting a greater and more vigorous voice in the negotiating position of the members of the orchestra.

The reaction was pretty much as expected. The management was against it. The union was against it. In 1961, five members of the Chicago Symphony—all players who'd worked to organize the committee—were on the list to be fired. Says Denov: "The committee ran down to Petrillo and said, 'What is this? These guys are being fired for their labor union activities, not for their musical abilities!" James Caesar Petrillo seemed to accept it all equably enough. "He said he'd have to go see his friend Goldberg," says Denov. Arthur J. Goldberg was then Secretary of Labor. But it would take time. The two men at the apex of union affairs in America just didn't get together overnight. But, as Denov remembers it, time passed . . . and passed . . . and passed with nothing happening. The trouble was that there is a deadline under the National Labor Relations Act to file such a protest, and five of the six monthly filing periods had passed before the members of the Chicago Symphony began to suspect what Petrillo was up to: if six months passed, they figured, no protest could be filed and thus Petrillo, and management, would be rid of these "malcontents." This, at least, was the view of the members of the orchestra and they promptly prepared their own filings for the National Labor Relations Board, without waiting for Petrillo's imprimatur. They also let management know that they were ready and willing to strike if necessary over this and other issues of the upcoming contract. The matter became so bitter that Mayor Richard Daley, a friend of both Petrillo's and Goldberg's, had to step in and arbitrate the matter, to preserve any hope of keeping the symphony going in Chicago. The result was that the players won enough points on the contract issue to gain a "new life" in their attitude toward union affairs. Moreover, the "firing list" was withdrawn and all players were reinstated without prejudice (although a sixth player was demoted—an action that the union and the players could not control).

All this gave focus to the militancy of the players: they had to get rid of Petrillo before they could begin to take on management successfully. Getting rid of Petrillo was like getting rid of psoriasis; you never knew when—or if—you were going to break out in a new rash. So the members of the Chicago Symphony decided to hit James Caesar where it would hurt: in the pocketbook. The idea was clear: if Petrillo lost money, then maybe he'd begin to get the message about the members' losing money.

And so they tackled Petrillo on his pension-seeking. In 1962, he asked for a guaranteed pension of $25,000 a year when he retired as president of Local 10. This would be added to a handsome pension that he'd already won as president of the American Federation of Musicians. To some in the symphony, it seemed as if he intended to earn more money for not working than he had earned for working —and certainly more money than the symphony players could ever hope to earn in a lifetime of membership in his union.

So the symphony members armed themselves in several ways. They prepared to go en masse—that is, with forty to sixty members—to an annual meeting of the local where Petrillo expected to get the pension passed. They armed themselves with a thorough knowledge of *Robert's Rules of Order* and the union bylaws. Each of the symphony members who attended the meeting was armed with slips of paper that outlined their reactions to any of a number of possible motions or points of order. When Petrillo, as presiding officer at the meeting, suggested a change of agenda in his favor, so many members of the symphony rose to their feet on a point of order that Petrillo couldn't find a friendly face. He finally had—in desperation—to recognize somebody he didn't know: it was a second trumpet player from the Chicago Symphony who was so nervous that he dropped the typewritten slip of paper that told him what to do under these circumstances. Petrillo pressed and harassed him, but the trumpeter—having seized the floor —made the proper procedural motion. The result: the second and the vote came in so fast and hard that Petrillo suddenly understood that he'd lost. He withdrew his request for a pension. Before it was all over, Petrillo began to sense the faint, distant import of the day's work: he and his management-bundling were at an end.

It took another fight. In 1962, the Chicago Symphony members put up twenty-two candidates against the twenty-two men Petrillo wanted selected as his officers and associates. The symphony members went out and developed a coalition with other full-time musicians working at radio stations, movie theaters, and elsewhere. The result: the full-time musicians won—Petrillo and his slate of officers were out. Some twenty of the twenty-two men backed by the Chicago Symphony swept into office. Among the losers: James Caesar Petrillo for president, Sam Denov for recording secretary. It was not quite a standoff. Petrillo would much rather have been president than Denov wanted to be recording secretary. "I was tickled to death later because . . . I would not have been very happy as recording secretary," says Denov.

That gave the symphony players a triumph over the union. Now they had to take on management.

For years, there was no crisis. That may have been because there was no consistent target at the top. The head of the Orchestral Association, Dr. Eric Oldberg, resigned to be replaced by another man who resigned after a few years, to be replaced by Louis Sudler. The general manager of the Orchestral Association was fired to be replaced by another man who resigned in lieu of being fired in favor—eventually—of John S. Edwards. The members of the orchestra could find no target except within themselves. There was a natural division between those players who made the "average" income and, on the other hand, the principal players who made considerably more than the average. Issues such as those involving the dismissal of Ray Still coalesced this division. It was not itself a classic union struggle, but it tended to exacerbate the division within the orchestra between the prounion and antiunion men. Still was himself prounion—"I'd been one of the people working undercover for the union as far back as my days in the Baltimore Orchestra," he says. He was one of the few principal players who was prounion. In general, the principals have greater access to and greater familiarity with management if only because they tend to negotiate individual salaries well above the average of the orchestra. It was not unusual for principal players in those days to earn twice as much as the base salary for the average player. And so they saw management in more friendly terms—or more fearful ones: there was always the chance that management might "remember" those principals who supported the union. As in most organizations, these men tended to see the union as something that couldn't do them much good and might do them some harm.

In the particular case of the Chicago Symphony, the promanagement players had a natural point of gravitation. He was John Weicher, a player whose impact on the orchestra was perhaps as great as that of some of its conductors. He was, for twenty-two years, concertmaster. He was also conductor of the Chicago Civic Orchestra, the training group which produced many members of the symphony. He became personnel manager of the orchestra, which means that he held considerable influence over hiring and firing—or at least who got auditions, even for promotion, and who didn't. He had considerable say in which players got the outside work that came the way of the orchestra. He sometimes decided who would play when something less than a full orchestra was required for certain numbers—as in a Bach suite—and thus overloaded some players while giving others time off. He handed out the paychecks on Friday, and he could annoy or harass certain players by the manner and timing in which he did this; it was within his power—real or assumed—to delay giving out checks to those "not in favor" so that they wouldn't have time to get to the bank before the Friday afternoon concert; and since the bank would be closed after the concert, and all weekend, he could decide which players would have cash in their pockets or money in their checking accounts over each weekend. In short, John Weicher profoundly affected the style of life within the orchestra and affected also some of its substance.

There are some players today who remember John Weicher with warmth and admiration. There are others who remember him as a gruff, bluff man who tended to intimidate players, perhaps personally more than professionally. He was always in a position to deny them something they wanted on nothing but his own whimsy. This deeply provoked some players and great traditions—mostly of aggravation —grew up around John Weicher. One was that—since it was his responsibility to signal when an intermission was at an end—the intermission was as long as he wanted it to be: if he was winning at cards or cribbage, so the legend goes, he'd let the intermission run on and on; if he was losing, he'd cut it short.

In any case, John Weicher was of the old German school of leadership and paternalism. Many players felt that his attitude seemed to be "You're lucky to have a job and I'm here to remind you of that." He tended to be promanagement, of course; the personnel manager is considered by the union to be a management position, even though he is a player, works among the players, and has his office just down the hall from the players' locker room. So, though he ran for offices in the union—and was defeated—he was regarded as a polar element in the antiunion sentiment.

More seriously for the fabric of the orchestra, he was considered—by Ray Still—to be a polar element in the move to get Still's dismissal upheld. Still felt that certain principal players formed around Weicher to deliver testimony damaging to Still's cause in the arbitration proceedings following his firing. (Not all the principals—some of them upheld Still and his behavior.) The significant thing is that this fight transferred the natural division over union matters to an issue involving a personal matter. It became a very bitter struggle, one that deeply affected the orchestra for years after John Weicher retired and then died.

Despite these corrosive internal struggles, the relations between management and players seemed to take on a more rational, if not placid, air. At the very outset of the union movement within the orchestra, the old-line management was so intransigent that it refused to let the musicians have a bulletin board that was not management-controlled. The players offered to put up their bulletin board at their own expense, but there was so much delay by management in identifying a location for the board that the players finally solved it in their own way: they inflated some balloons and suspended a bulletin board from them as they floated in the players' dressing room. By the end of the decade, management was agreeing to resolve such cankers as varying intermission times by putting an electric timer in the office of the personnel manager (by that time, Radivoj Lah). The timer is set so that a signal can be given—to the audience as well as the players—thirteen minutes after the intermission starts. Both players and audience then have two minutes to return to their seats in the concert hall. So there is now a constant fifteen-minute intermission, not a card- or cribbage-governed one.

There were, of course, always debates and give-and-take over salaries, but by the decade's end, the players had negotiated as salary based on a fifty-two-week year and an income of more than $15,000 a year—triple what they'd been making some ten or fifteen years earlier. Moreover, they had built-in pay raises that in the third year of the contract would pay them $320 a week for fifty-two weeks, or some $16,640 a year. That contract, which went into effect September 21, 1970, and was to be effective until September 17, 1973, had eighty-seven pages of text and seven and one-half pages of index. It is illuminating to examine some of the provisions of that contract, just to see how far the two sides had progressed since the "floating bulletin board" days:

—The members of the string sections would be rotated every two to three weeks so that some of them would not have to spend—as did many members of the current orchestra—five, six, or more years on the last stand. (The exception to the rotation: the players in the first two stands.)

—Every player, regardless of tenure, would be given seven weeks of paid vacation a year.

—The players could be asked to work six days a week.

—The number of "services"—concerts or rehearsals—was not to exceed eight in any given week (unless overtime was paid). And the average for the Orchestra Hall season was to be no more than seven and one-half. ("That means that if we had nine services one week, we could have no more than six the next week," says Don Koss, head of the players' committee.) Ravinia was made an exception, and so were the tours of the orchestra.

—A concert that had no intermission—such as the performance of act 3 of *Götterdämmerung*—would run no more than ninety minutes.

—A concert with an intermission could run no more than two and one-half hours.

—A rehearsal could run no more than two and one-half hours (with the provision that a fifteen-minute intermission be included).

With all that, and more, one might wonder what else the players could want.

There was a lot more they wanted. They wanted more of a pension system (it was raised to $8,000 a year for players who reach sixty and have thirty years' experience in the orchestra). They also wanted to have the pension fund administered in a slightly different way; a substantial portion of it now comes from a newly established, jointly administered trust. They wanted more in the way of health insurance; the major medical limit was doubled to $100,000. They wanted to take some of the concert pressure off by limiting the number of concerts to four per week. ("You could have one concert and seven rehearsals," says Don Koss, "but you could have no more than four concerts.") They wanted more of a say in some of the details of the tours—what hotels they would stay in, what airlines they might use, even when the buses would be scheduled to take them from hotel to airport. ("The way things were run, they'd have you getting on a bus at 9 o'clock in the morning—after a concert the night before in Carnegie Hall—to catch a noon plane out of JFK," says Don Koss. Some of the players thought such scheduling was a frivolous waste of their time. "With a little looking around, you might find an 11:45 A.M. plane out of La Guardia—which was much closer to the hotel than JFK—and you could schedule the bus to leave the hotel at 10:30.") The tour committee of the orchestra now has been given shared responsibilities with management to formulate details of tours and runouts (the short one-day runs to De Kalb for a college concert or to Milwaukee for a subscription concert).

What more could they want?

More money, of course.

The management offered a wage raise that would have given the players some $365 a week in step-by-step increases by the third year of the new contract. The players wanted $360 right away, with another $10 or $20 raise the next year—say to $380—and then with the right to negotiate their salaries for the third year. (One can speculate that the third-year level would have been more than $400 a week, which means that the players' demands would have been 10 percent higher than what management offered.)

To the players this was only logical; not only was it an effort to keep pace with inflation—which was increasing at an extravagant rate in this season—but it was an effort to draw even with professionals they envied. They feel, quite accurately, that their incomes have trailed dramatically behind the incomes of doctors and lawyers and other professionals who—like musicians in the Chicago Symphony—spend years in preparation for their careers. ("It takes sixteen years of playing for a violinist to become good enough to play in this orchestra," says Victor Aitay, a co-concertmaster of the Chicago Symphony.) They envision young doctors and lawyers and dentists starting out at incomes of $30,000 a year while they, as veteran musicians, struggle to get paid half that much. Their vision is not far wrong: at the age of twenty-nine, the average dentist in the United States grosses $42,156 a year, according to figures gathered by the American Dental Association. Out of this sum he must pay his work expenses; it's usually figured at around half the gross or, in the case of young dentists (whose payments on equipment and mortgage loans are higher at the outset), perhaps a little more. That means the dentist under thirty is making better than $20,000 a year. It's not all "easy success," of course: he sometimes has to wait a while to get into a $60,000-a-year gross —often until he's thirty to thirty-four years old.

Of course, the cases are not altogether comparable. The dentist, doctor, and lawyer offer their services as individuals; they can decide what individuals and income groups they want to serve and how much they can charge. In turn, each individual can decide whether he wants to pay that price—or forget about the service. The players in a symphony orchestra offer their talents as a group to groups—to an audience, even to the community at large—and they have no choice about who buys the talent or what they'll pay for it. One thing is certain: they won't pay enough. It's been estimated that box office revenue pays for only half the cost of a concert in Orchestra Hall, but John S. Edwards admits that any such figures are merely matters of how you interpret the accounting. One thing is certain: the Chicago Symphony Orchestra runs at a deficit, as do almost all such groups around the world. The deficit must be made up by gifts (as in America) or by government subsidy (as in Europe). For a long time, the loss in operating the Chicago orchestra was a mild one: during the first twenty years of the symphony's existence, the total loss was just over $1.5 million. In 1972–73 the operating loss was $2,499,097. (There were costs other than the operating cost, which deepened the loss.) The Orchestral Association went out and raised $2,669,718 in gifts and bequests, in an effort to offset that loss. And in the end, the symphony still wound up with a deficit of some $89,892. Even at that, the figure was an improvement: the year before the deficit had been $359,765.

In any case, one fact remains: one can measure an individual's ability and willingness to pay—to a doctor, lawyer, or dentist—but nobody knows what a community will pay for a great symphony orchestra. Or to support art in general. The players presume optimistically that this support is forever larger than it is and that the future will prove their case. The management dolorously describes the present as being the breaking point. The only way in which the real breaking point can be found is by trial and error—when the players demand that amount of money which the community can't, or won't, afford. That's the trial. The error, of course, is that the symphony season is then canceled. And it is too late to use this hard-gained insight wisely.

The test of insight is tougher on the players than on management. The reason:

there is a continual turnover in the negotiating team among the players but there is a continuity on management side. John Edwards, for example, was no newcomer to the labor-management negotiations of a symphony orchestra; he would have at his side attorneys and financial experts deepened in the tides of experience. But the players' side tends to have people who are freshly initiated to the skin-tingling experience of hard negotiations. They had, to be sure, some staff people from the union headquarters; but today, as yesterday, union staffers are not deeply involved in the problems or dimensions of the symphony experience. They would be there to provide "dress" and for the talks but not to offer overriding insights.

In the past, the players had turned, almost reflexively, to Sam Denov as the leader and savviest negotiator in the orchestra. He had the honor of being blooded early in his career: he was, after all, satisfactorily eminent on the list of players to be fired in the program of the early 1960s. But this time, Sam asked to be relieved of the negotiating burden. He wanted to go to law school, to study labor law, and he was having difficulty enough trying to fit night classes into the symphony schedule without trying to add a heavy burden of negotiations. And so the burden passed to Isadore Zverow, head of the players' committee in the season until September, and Don Koss, his successor as head of the players' committee. They were aided by three other players (though Denov was to relent and join the negotiations at a late stage), but Koss and Zverow present the metaphorical equivalent of the orchestra: Zverow as a career violist, a nonprincipal, who grew up in music and has played in the Chicago Symphony Orchestra for twenty-eight years; Koss as a principal player, young, aggressive, individualistic, with a career in mathematics and in teaching before joining the symphony, and who decided to go into the players' committee affairs because "many sections of the orchestra weren't represented on the committee—the woodwinds, the principals . . ." It was also his way of signaling management which—he felt—thought the labor militancy was the concern of a small group within the orchestra. The signal was that the matters of the contract and the players' working conditions were now concerns of the entire orchestra, not just a job group within it.

Izzy Zverow is a short, gray-thatched outgoing man whose eyes bespeak friendliness and cheer. He grew up in Chicago and learned to play the violin as part of the cultural impetus of the families of the times. He switched to the viola in high school. "The teacher said, 'Who wants to play the viola?' And I said, 'Why not?' So she dug up a viola for me somewhere." The viola is longer and larger than the violin but it is still tucked under the chin—though there have been experiments to place it on a peg, like the bass fiddle and the cello—and thus it is said to require a longer-armed man than the violin. You can't prove that by Isadore Zverow; his arms are as short as the next short man's arms. The viola is the alto of the string family whereas the violin is the soprano; thus it is different not only musically from the violin but also socially. Whereas the violin glows as a solo instrument, the viola speaks as a societal instrument; it was fashioned to fit in groups—say with violins, cello, and bass—and its function is to support, to augment, to enrich, to clarify. Thus it takes a different man psychologically than the violin; the viola does not seek the aggressive virtuoso so much—the Jascha Heifetz, the Isaac Stern—as the

Isadore Zverow, violist.

man who can fit in comfortably with the rest of the strings, the rest of the orchestra.

Isadore Zverow is the epitome of that drive. He can fit in. He demonstrated so by his skills in earning a living. He persisted in playing the violin on nonsymphonic jobs so that he could play the viola in a symphony. "For years I was with one of our dinner music combos at the Palmer House—I enjoyed it, it gave me kicks, and the responsibility was not that great." But he devoted his serious study to the viola: he went to New York to study for a year, played in the training orchestra of the New York Philharmonic, and later he moved to Kansas City to play in the symphony there. He'd come back to Chicago in the off-season to play at the Palmer House while his wife worked as a laboratory technician. One year she had an extraordinary patient: Frederick Stock, then music director of the Chicago Symphony. ("One of the things that a lab technician did was take blood samples and she had to take a sample from him." Right there in the hospital room, his wife set up a chance for Izzy to be heard by Frederick Stock. There was only one trouble: Frederick Stock never left the hospital room. "He died about two weeks later," says Izzy. Izzy's audition was not heard. Nor did he make it into the orchestra then—"it was almost five years later."

At the time that Zverow joined the orchestra, the principal violist was Milton

Preves. He'd been principal in the section for seven years at that time: he is still the principal violist, having played first viola under every conductor of the Chicago Symphony except the first one. So there was not what one would consider a great deal of opportunity for advancement in that era. The notable thing about Isadore Zverow, as one of the men who stood in the shadows of a Milton Preves, is that he never lost interest in being a better musician or producing a better sound. At the very moment that the negotiations were under way, he was going about a seminal change in the sound he sought from his instrument.

"All players have their own viewpoint as to what they are seeking out of the viola—sweetness, sonority, attractiveness, malleability," he said shortly after the negotiations had ended. So very often, a longer instrument will give a quality of sound. It will give decibels. It will give a sort of sonority, which is deeper, more profound. That is why it is three inches longer in the body than another viola. A smaller instrument might be a very intimate instrument, one that can be handled very easily. It might have a sweeter sound. The lowest string on the viola is the C-string and that is the one that, on small instruments, does not have quite the depth and loudness that a larger instrument might have on the same string. So violists make up their own minds concerning just exactly what they are seeking, particularly in an orchestra.

"For years I was playing the larger instrument and I was very satisfied. Then I think I decided that I wanted a smaller instrument which will give me the sweetness, the ease of execution. And I keep thinking I can get one which will project the sound but which will not necessarily have the profoundly deep tone."

Why did he decide to change now, after twenty-eight years in the Chicago Symphony?

"Well, part of it is my own outlook—my state of life, I suppose. Years ago I think I was very impressed with the need for the type of sonority in sound that does not seem quite that important to me now. I can say what I have to say on a smaller instrument as well as a larger instrument." He'd been experimenting on different instruments in an effort to find the one just right for himself. "I picked up an instrument which belonged to a colleague of mine, and after I played a few notes on it I said, 'You have my instrument. How do you own it and not me?' " The answer to that rhetorical question set him on the trail of finding the instrument that suited him better. It would have to be shorter than his present viola but it would have to be more than that. "I saw what I would call a good, practical, and acceptable instrument for about $5,000. It was what I would call acceptable, nothing more." He found, as have many other players, that the market in stringed instruments is booming; the cost of exceptional violins has more than tripled in the last ten years or so. "I did not feel that I should pay $5,000 for an instrument that would mean nothing more to me than that—'acceptable.' I would rather, well, go higher if I found an instrument which was very desirable. I think that I can find an instrument that is acceptable for less money than that." He did not know when he would find such an instrument. He did not know where he'd find one.

To all this, Don Koss was the perfect complement, if only because he is the polar opposite. Izzy Zverow, by personal and musical disposition, fits in authentically and represents and reflects—temperamentally and culturally—a broad spectrum of the orchestra. Don Koss is very much an individualist. He was the last one—the only one—in the orchestra to keep his hair crew-cut when society's whimsies turned to long hair (though he had lately let it grow out). He is also something of a jock. A golf nut—like Burl Lane and Bud Herseth—he's been known to tote portable TV sets around with him on playing dates to keep abreast of the professional golf tour. One Easter afternoon a few years ago, when the orchestra and chorus were performing Handel's *Messiah* in the mood-inspiring Rockefeller Chapel at the University of Chicago—a magnificent representation of the finest in Gothic architecture—one of the women in the chorus noticed that Koss, playing his kettledrums in the loft, would disappear altogether during some of the long rests. She peeked around a corner during one rest and discovered what he was doing. "He had this television set hooked up—it was on a landing—and he was there in front of it, watching Arnold Palmer make one of his shots."

Perhaps it is in the matching of temperament and timpani. For the timpanist always stands out; he is, perhaps, second to the conductor in a sense of display. They face each other across the breadth of the orchestra, each standing up, the conductor waving his little stick and drawing sound out of the orchestra, the timpanist waving his little sticks—in perfect response—and pounding sound out of the kettledrums.

The drums are, of course, a very masculine, very aggressive-sounding instrument. Percussive instruments, in general, serve to bring the senses to focus, to startle, to arouse, to incite. And yet they demand; the kettledrum, for example, is the one drum that plays to a definite pitch. Berlioz once described the percussionist as "an excellent musician endowed with an ear of extreme delicacy." The great percussionist lives in a world of sound values and total shadings that the average person can scarcely appreciate. The kettledrums, or timpani, are quite capable of musical sounds that few outside the orchestra can comprehend. Beethoven startled audiences by using them in octaves in his Eighth and Ninth symphonies, and Berlioz tuned them in thirds and fifths, thus making chordal effects possible.

Perhaps another reason that Koss is so much of an individualist is that he is principal—and sole individual—in his own section. For the Chicago Symphony has two men who are "principals" in the percussive instruments: Koss on the timpani and Gordon Peters as leader of the group that plays the other percussive instruments—the snare drum, the bass drums, the triangle, the cymbals, the gong, the xylophone, the chimes, even at times the gourds, the cowbells, and the thunder sheet.

Dos Koss certainly fits the masculine, aggressive image of the individualist as timpanist. Of middle height, he is in his middle thirties, has snapping black eyes and jet-black hair, and a faint bristling quality even when he is in repose. He is an individualist musically as well as temperamentally: for he is one of those extraordinarily few men of the symphony who mastered their instruments without having had any formal education in music.

"Oh, I took a couple of lessons along the way," he says. "But mostly I just read all the books on the subject I could get my hands on. And I played every chance I got." At one time in high school, he was playing in five different orchestras, most of them neighborhood and suburban symphonies all around Chicago. "I played just because I loved it. No money—nobody got paid in those days. I simply loved doing it."

"Those days" were spawned by the Depression. Koss grew up in Chicago, living with his parents in a two-room apartment on the North Side while his father sought work—"in hotels, as a bookkeeper, whatever was available." Economics tended to dictate the choice of musical instruments in a household where there was a long tradition of musical culture. As Koss was to say about his choice of the percussive instruments, "It's a lot easier to get started in music with an eighty-cent pair of drumsticks than with a $3,000 harp."

He began tapping on snare drums in grade school. Later in high school some of his advisers urged him to give it all up—"they told me that percussionists were a bunch of nobodies." To the contrary, percussionists—and timpanists in particular—are very much somebodies. He was in his second year at Senn High School when the school's orchestra leader suggested that he might want to try the timpani. "I said I did not want to play timpani. I was a snare drummer and I was good and that was a big deal in high school." But he finally agreed to give it a try and he found the experience exhilarating. For the timpani are a great deal more complex than snare drums. Usually Koss will have three or four of them spread around him onstage, huge copper kettles covered with a calfskin drawn taut, each kettle with a different pitch, each capable of being changed ever so delicately in pitch. They are far more flexible than the other drums; in many modern composi-tions they actually carry the melody: Hindemith's Concerto for Violin and Or-chestra even has a significant solo passage for timpani. "In an instrument like this, you either have an aptitude or not," says Koss. "It is not like a string instrument where you need years and years and years. If you apply yourself and in a year's time you've got enough technique to really be satisfied, then you can just get better."

It never dawned on him to study the timpani in a serious, formal way. For one thing, there was no money for such studies. For another thing, "in that day and age, nobody really paid much attention to it. I was one of those who *did*—I *wanted* to learn." But he had to do it on his own. He played in the North Side Symphony Orchestra, then in the Oak Park Symphony and the Evanston Symphony. He played in his high school band and orchestra and also in the Roosevelt University orchestra "because they didn't have enough people to go around." He played in two bands in the Chicago School of Music for the same reason—he didn't go to school there—and later on, when he went into the service, he played in the Fifth Army band at Fort Sheridan, Illinois. When he got out, he resumed playing in any and every orchestra available and, in addition, he tried out and won a post in the Civic Orchestra, the training group for the Chicago Symphony. Even then, he was doing it all for free, for the fun of doing it, and not because he intended to become a professional musician, much less a symphonic one. "But I was good at it—that is why I liked music. It is a corny philosophy but people say that you like what you are good at," he says. "At least that is the way I used to teach."

For his career wasn't in music. It was in math and, in particular, the teaching of math. He got both his undergraduate and graduate degrees in mathematics. Math also came easy to him; it is difficult now for him to think of any areas of math that he found difficult or undesirable. "I would think that statistical analysis is pretty easy but when you get into the theory and applications of probability—well, it's great but it gets very complicated very fast."

He made his living teaching math at Evanston High School, one of the best high schools in the land. "I was teaching advanced math and, the last two years I was there, teaching calculus and analytic geometry to some of the brighter kids," he says. For him, as for others, math and music went together; the composition and impulses of Johann Sebastian Bach are perhaps the greatest demonstration of that affinity in all musical literature. "I found the two work well together," says Koss, "but one"—the mathematics—"was my bread and butter and the other was the enjoyment. Now it is reversed."

The way it got reversed was through a series of successions. Through the Civic Orchestra, he met a musician who helped line up talent for the symphony orchestra that plays during the summer in Grant Park, on Chicago's Lake Front. That man asked Koss if he'd like to succeed a timpanist who was retiring after twenty-five years in the Grant Park Symphony. Koss leaped at the chance; he'd never before been paid for making music. In addition, his teaching gave him the summers off; this way he had paying jobs in the two fields he loved best. "So I played there for a couple of years and my wife and I bought a home in Evanston." The day after he bought the home, he went to a rehearsal of the Civic Orchestra and the conductor, John Weicher, approached him and asked: "Are you interested in playing timpani in the Chicago Symphony Orchestra? If you are, the man who has the job is retiring after something like forty years in the orchestra."

"The strange thing," says Koss, "was that I did not know whether I wanted the job or not. Because I really enjoyed teaching." He passed the auditions and he was the pick of the symphony. "After much soul-searching and talking with my wife, I knew I had to give it a try for a year or two." He paused, in thought. "So now I'm in my eleventh year."

Does he think he's better off than if he had continued teaching? "The only thing I regret is that I can't do both," he says. But if "better off" means economically better off, this is how he analyzes it: the teacher gets long vacations and works 185 days a year. "I would imagine that at the tops teacher salaries are around $14,000 or $15,000"—on the high school level—"with more for credits and a certain number of years of experience and all these things that they have built into the system." In this season, he'd have a longer work year, not more than seven weeks of vacation, and the base salary would be $18,200 a year. "And I get more than scale, which is no secret," he says. "I would hate to do it on an absolute dollar amount, but you would have to figure this job is worth about 50 percent more economically than teaching is."

He finds the life of the symphony and its demands match his temperament. "Some of the hardest music for other instruments to play is the simplest music to play for the timpani—Mozart, Haydn, Bach," he says. But there is no room for error: the other instruments can play wrong notes or miss notes and few persons other than expert musicians would ever know it. When the percussionist does something wrong, everybody knows it. "So you have to be letter-perfect. In Mozart, Haydn, Bach, and so forth. Not that you don't have to be in everything else, but there is some margin for error in some of the other pieces. If you've got a big thick orchestration, and you pride yourself in your inclinations, and it's a hair off in a big Mahler chord—maybe you sock the drum so hard that you knock it flat, which happens sometimes—you make an adjustment at once and it is not discernible. Boy, if you play one note out of tune in a Mozart symphony . . ."

Each timpanist has a different way of soliciting the sound from the instrument. Koss knows of one timpanist who religiously outflanks what the conductor demands. "If the conductor called for a drier sound, a drier pair of sticks," says Koss, "he'd set the sticks down on the table. He'd wait for a moment or two, then he'd pick up the same pair of sticks—he'd try to vary the sound with his touch." Koss himself varies the sound with the sticks. "I have twenty or twenty-five different pairs of sticks, and I have four or five pairs that are my favorites. And I tend to play with three or four of those." He doesn't plunge into arcane theories of what kind of sticks and drumhead provide a soft sound or a lean one or a dry one. "All I know is the sound I want to produce at a given time, and I have a pretty good idea what stick is going to make that sound."

Koss is different from other members of the orchestra in that he does not spend his preparation time in hours of solitude at home, working over reeds by the hour—as do the woodwinds—or exercising on finger scales, as do the strings. In fact, much of his preparation takes place not at home—"though I've got drums all over the place in my basement"—but in the concert hall. He putters around the kettledrums onstage in Orchestra Hall by the hour. "One of my problems is that I have to be like a good car mechanic—I probably spend two or three hours every week just doing routine maintenance on my drums. And then I get in long sieges where I try to rebuild something. This is in Orchestra Hall—I come down and mess around with my equipment, setting heads, testing the skin, and so forth. I am not like a trumpet player, who has to practice three hours a day. If I have a part coming up that's very hard, I might work on it for half an hour or so before a rehearsal, or after." But he must make sure that the kettledrums always possess the precise pitch and tone that he and Solti expect of them. "A string player can put on a new string in a few minutes, but it takes me hours to adjust the settings and the skins if they have to be changed."

He senses, as a product of mathematics, a lack of scientific backstopping for the timpani. "I would like to apply what I know in mathematics and physics to designing drums, but it is very time-consuming and the cost is prohibitive." This means that he couldn't possibly undertake setting up the ideal laboratory conditions in his home on his income; it's more a project for an expert working with a drum-producing corporation. "There is a drum manufacturer in town and he expresses interest, but we never quite get together, and I do not like to push myself on anybody."

One of the ironies in his career is that, though he loves teaching, he teaches very little in the percussion. Part of it is professional: his academic background is in mathematics, not music, and so there is no great clamor for him on the staff of Northwestern or De Paul universities, where a great many members of the symphony have faculty posts. Part of it is temperament: he'd rather be using his mind in pursuits other than music alone. That's what the contract negotiations gave him: a chance to use mind and research drive in a field that was clearly useful but not exclusively musical. He and Izzy Zverow spent months researching the contract and organizing their thinking, looking for things that could be improved. The idea was to appeal to the reason of the men across the table, not to arouse their emotions. "I think John Edwards"—who has a combustible inclination—"got upset because our negotiations were not what they'd been previously because John had said guys banged tables and yelled at each other," says Koss. "I'm not that way"—which is not to say that he can't communicate aggressively without table-banging—"and Izzy Zverow is definitely not that way. You know, this is the age of enlightenment, supposedly. Reasonable people should be able to sit down and talk to each other in a sensible sort of way."

His thinking and research developed notions which many a management man might bridle over. Here are some examples:

—"They claim," says Koss of orchestra management in general, "that there is all sorts of waste because this guy doesn't play and that guy doesn't play." That is true. There are many musical compositions which demand only a fraction of the orchestra: the Bach suite with which Solti decided to open the season is an example. There are whole segments of the repertoire which do not include certain instruments: Mozart, Bach, Beethoven, Haydn, all of the music of that genre has no part for the tuba simply because it was composed before the tuba was invented. The question then becomes whether such a player—and in the Chicago Symphony the tuba player is Arnold Jacobs, one of the great virtuosos of the instrument—should be paid only for the time he'd be performing. Or should he be paid on a fifty-two-week basis, just as the constantly working string players are? Obviously Koss's instincts are on the full-pay side. He uses an example from pro football and the Minnesota Vikings' placekicker as an example of why. "What about Fred Cox? What does he do? He comes out and he kicks the ball for a fraction of a second per game. Two or three times a game. But he wins the game for them. Or at least he keeps them in the game. And he doesn't get paid solely for the fraction of a second that he's kicking. You have to pay people for their talent and their availability, not just for time in action. And the most efficiently run symphony, like the most efficiently run football team, is going to have to pay men for those moments. So they'll have to pay them for their talent even if they play for only a few minutes out of every hour."

—On paying pensions and how to avoid it: prior to 1965, the pension payment was $1,800 a year. Imagine trying to live today, as an elderly person, on $1,800 a year! And it was not mandatory. Now, as we've seen, it's been more than quadrupled and comes under joint administration. But what galls Koss is that the pensions were long used by many symphony orchestras across the nation as a system for "tipping" the players for twenty or thirty or forty years' service. "If they liked you, they'd give you a pension at the end of your service," he says. "If they didn't, they wouldn't. It wasn't mandatory." Even when pensions became mandatory there were ways to get around paying a pension, ways that were used in many areas other than classical music. "If you had a pension after twenty years of service," says Koss, "and they didn't like you, they'd fire you after the nineteenth season." And of course hire somebody else who might last precisely nineteen years before *he* was fired. That's why job-protection clauses and arbitration procedures had to be built into the contract along with pension systems.

—On the abstractions of the peculiar problems of the Chicago Symphony Orchestra players: "We are the producers and we are, at the same time, the products," he says. His point is that the link in music between product and producers is different from most other fields in which businessmen—who are involved with the symphony—are aware. A businessman who produces a car, for example, must produce it with a set of workers. But if all those workers leave, the businessman can hire another set of workers and they'll produce the same car with no discernible difference in quality. And people would buy the car, knowing that fact. But with the Chicago Symphony, that system does not pertain. The Chicago Symphony produces a sound—the product—which has a singular quality. If all the members of the Chicago Symphony left and were replaced by other players, the sound—the product—would not be the same. It would decline drastically in quality. And people would stop buying the product, knowing that fact. So the Orchestral Association must "sell" both the sound of the symphony and the set of players who produce that sound. That product and the producers are, in fact, inseparable, in the view of Don Koss.

That bond changes some of the rules of the normal labor-management game. For management must have *these* players in order to produce the sound that they're selling. If these players don't show up, there is no alternative: the sound is shut down—management cannot come up with another set of players and pretend to produce the same sound.

There is another factor: the production of great sound involves no cost of materials. There is merely a payroll cost. "And you need a hall and some soloists," he says, "and a man to wave a stick in front of the orchestra." He does not consider these to be overwhelmingly burdensome costs. So he figures it is the payroll of the Chicago Symphony which is the main cost of the symphony, and it is that payroll which must be met by gifts and ticket sales. He figures the total payroll of the musicians in the Chicago Symphony Orchestra is something under $2½ million this year. Yet the budget for the entire orchestra for the entire season was around $5½ million. "Where does that extra $3 million go?" he asks, particularly since there is no cost of materials produced. He does not pretend to know the answer, though he suspects that it's in the building of a staff for the Orchestral Association. The question: are staff costs becoming greater than the costs of getting the musicians to produce the music? He does not know; he merely suspects. "We look at the figures they publish—I'm pretty good with figures myself—and we can't quite work them all out so that they seem meaningful," he says. "Particularly when you figure they're tyring to hide some things."

These dark suspicions, endemic in labor-management relations, became more pronounced in the year or so before the contract ended. The symphony, for example, had been selected to play at the grand opening of the stunning new $140 million Opera House in Sydney, Australia, in the autumn of 1973. Then in the summer of 1972, more than a year before the tour to Australia, the whole project was called off. The reasons offered and suspected were various. One was that the Australian and New Zealand Broadcasting commissions backed out of promises to pay the travel costs of the orchestra; a complementary one was that the members of the orchestra refused to waive their fees for appearing on radio or television Down Under. This, of course, would have meant that *they* were paying their way, by playing for nothing for the companies that were footing the bill. It also reflected the historic suspicion of the players in the Chicago Symphony toward those persons in radio and TV who figure out all kinds of exotic ways for the members to work for very little income.

Most of all, though, the cancellation of the tour reflected a conviction among the negotiators that management was simply trying to avoid a labor crisis while the orchestra was committed to an overseas tour. The suspicion was that if management expected a work stoppage it would be easier to handle the problem at home. Whether or not that was true, the labor negotiators immediately began clamoring in 1973 for a one-year contract, not another three-year contract as had been the custom since 1959. The reason: in early 1974, just one year after this contract would be negotiated, the Chicago Symphony was scheduled to take a second tour of Europe. If the contract ran out during that tour, the labor negotiators could have the duty, joy, opportunity, or responsibility of lousing up all the efforts that had gone into that tour if something extra could be achieved for the members of the orchestra. Management immediately resisted the move to a one-year contract. And so the length of the contract tended to become almost as important an issue as the economic issues.

The negotiations were carried out in an utterly civilized way. There was, by mutual agreement, no discussion in the press about the offers and counteroffers and thus none of the acrimony that accompanied previous contract negotiations. Indeed, there was none of the abrasive resentment of labor for management. One of the reasons is that, though the members suspected motives, they did not suspect personalities. Solti was removed from all this; he plunges only into artistic decisions. So the personality of the conductor was not involved. The personality of the board chairman—Louis Sudler—was an asset. "Without people like Louis Sudler, God bless him, you wouldn't have orchestras, you wouldn't have museums, you wouldn't have art in this country," says Don Koss. "Let's face it: culture would go smack right down the drain fast without the Louis Sudlers of this world." But management did not use this asset: Sudler did not take a personal part in the negotiations, though he was to play a decisive role in ending them. It turned out that John Edwards and attorney Stuart Bernstein, along with financial man Ralph Guthrie, sat in on management's side through most of the negotiations. Guthrie had no visible planes to the players; they barely knew him. Bernstein had a sympathetic side: "I think he's been a lawyer for the ACLU"—the American Civil

Liberties Union—"or at least he's been associated with them," says Koss. Surprisingly, Edwards's image also was largely favorable. "I think he's genuinely a compassionate person," says Koss. "I'm not saying anything about his business skill; I don't want to get into that. But the orchestra is running and he's got us some good conductors, and he seemed to do big things the way a manager should." He should conceive of some limitations to Edwards's skills. "The little things he doesn't like to bother with; that's why he hires a bunch of subordinates to do it."

All of this would seem to forfend a work stoppage. And none of it did. The players presented their wage demands early in September. Management did not make a counteroffer. Instead it began examining, debating, and attacking the position of the players. The heat of summer drifted off, the leaves turned from green to gold and then to a sere and lonely crisp.

There was the Minuet of the Wary and Anxious as the opening of the season approached. The players offered to continue working without a contract on a day-to-day basis, as long as they could call a work stoppage anytime on two weeks' notice. Management refused the offer. The players showed up for the first scheduled rehearsal—despite telegrams from management that it had been called off—and then were dismissed by Stuart S. Ball, president of the Orchestral Association, after they'd taken their places onstage. The players then used this sequence of events to describe the work stoppage as a "lockout," not a "strike": they were being prevented from working—in their view—by management, though they'd made every serious effort to work.

There the matter got stuck. One special concert at the outset of the season, to be conducted by Henry Mazer, was called off. Five rehearsals were called off. There was no progress. Then the guest appearances of Daniel Barenboim were called off, and with them the plans to record Mozart's Symphony no. 36 (*Linz*) and Saint-Saëns's Symphony no. 3 for Deutsche Grammophon. Also canceled were a runout to the University of Illinois at Urbana and Illinois State University at Bloomington. Next, the concerts of Zdenek Macal were canceled and this has a special season-strangling significance: the next concerts to go would be those of Solti.

All this time, the players were marching dutifully on picket lines in front of Orchestra Hall—in the morning and evening hours, and at lunch time. On opening night at Lyric Opera, they marched in very elegant fashion in front of the elegant operagoers. ("We handed out around two thousand leaflets that night," says Don Koss.) And all the while the various ensembles within the orchestra—the Chicago Symphony String Quartet, the Contemporary Arts Quartet, the various trios, and other groups—held small recitals in churches and homes all over the city and suburbs. The idea was not only to raise money for the musicians but to get across the idea that the music of the Chicago Symphony went on, despite the work stoppage—that the players were more than willing to continue bringing music to the people of Chicago. "It's the ideal way to play," says Fred Spector of the Contemporary Arts Quartet. "The quartet in a home, in a small room—the chamber. Of course, these homes were quite beautiful and some of them —between the living room and the vestibule—easily sat 100 people. One home in

South Shore—I believe we had 140 people in it." Those people gave of their own free will: what they wanted, when they wanted. In the first month, the total contributions came to more than $4,000. "We put that in the reserve fund," says Don Koss, "and by the time the next contract comes up, it will have grown to $5,000."

Nevertheless, there were many players who could anticipate, if not feel, the pinch. Wally Horban was one: the construction crews were waiting the go-ahead on his new home in Barrington Hills. Dick Graef was another: he took twenty students in the flute for the fall term—"too many," he admits freely. But many a player had done that: they took the risk of overloading themselves even if the contract were to be settled rather than risk being completely without income in case it were not.

Grover Schiltz couldn't step up the breeding or the boarding of dachshunds quite so quickly, but he could think about the implications of the work stoppage. "Coming from a laboring family, my dad being a factory worker, we thought that any work stoppage had to be extended in its possibilities," he says. "I remember my last year in college, my dad was out for twelve weeks and that was a very critical time." He feels that some men in the orchestra did not know the deep, acrid feeling of hopelessness that goes on with a continued work stoppage. "I think that the idea of the work stoppage impressed some people more as a novelty than as a hardship. It would be sort of like a mock war, one of the little weekend spats between minor principalities or something. Everybody marches up the hill and down again. But if you get right down to it, and get into the long term, it can mean hardship for a lot of people."

Among the people were those far outside Chicago. For the Chicago situation was being examined closely in many other cities, not the least of which was New York. It had been hit by a contagious series of strikes and work stoppages—the New York City Opera, the New York Philharmonic, and the New York City Ballet among them. And their strikes affected, in turn, the appearances of other orchestras in New York. The pickets of the New York Philharmonic closed Philharmonic Hall in Lincoln Center. That forced the Philadelphia Orchestra to postpone an eight-concert series there and forced the Boston Symphony to seek other halls for its concerts. (The Chicago Symphony was unaffected by the picketing of Philharmonic Hall because it plays its concerts at Carnegie Hall.) The relationships between the wage levels in New York and Chicago were clear: New York's symphony musicians had to have, as a matter of pride as well as cost of living, $10 more a week than Chicago's symphony musicians. Thus the New York Philharmonic was not inclined to settle until it found out what the Chicago Symphony would get; and then they'd negotiate, and perhaps strike, for $10 a week more. At the same time, it was a matter of faith on all sides that management in New York was also watching Chicago, hoping—and perhaps expecting—that the Orchestral Association in Chicago would draw so austere a line that the New Yorkers could use this as an example for denying increases to their own players.

In Chicago, a federal mediator had been brought in. He called for a cooling-off period. And there was hope in that period, for some progress had been made.

Management's offer of a $6,750 pension had been upped and accepted at $8,000. The exploratory efforts to change the number of services had been killed. The "extra pay" aspects—an economic issue in a minor key—had pretty much been settled. There is bonus pay for seniority now: the player who's been in the orchestra ten years gets an extra $5 a week, the fifteen-year veteran gets an extra $10 a week, the twenty-year veteran gets an extra $15 a week. The overtime pay was hiked a little. Previously it had been $4 for the first half hour of overtime. Players figure to be onstage and playing between eighteen and twenty hours a week—not counting their own practice time, their standby time, their travel time to places like Milwaukee and De Kalb. It was easy for them to figure out that overtime meant less pay instead of more pay: their old base rate of $320 divided by 20 comes out to $16 an hour, and they were getting overtime at the rate of $8 an hour, only half of their regular hourly rate. "We're the only business where you work overtime and get less money for doing it," says Don Koss. But he and his fellow negotiators settled at a half-hour rate double that of the past—$8 for the first half hour (which is $16 an hour, still less than the regular hourly rate they were seeking). "That's a small part of it," says Koss. "Overtime is insignificant. If we work ten extra half hours a year"—not counting Ravinia, where overtime tends to pile up—"that's amazing." But these little extra things do pile up.

The estimate by John Edwards is that only 15 or 20 percent of the musicians earn only the base income. Almost everybody else gets extra income of some kind. The estimate of Don Koss is that the real average income of the players in the orchestra is $60 a person over the base price—that is, that the average income this season will be around $410 a week for each player. That does not mean that all the "extras" in the contract come to an extra $60 a week. It means that the players, such as the principals who negotiate salaries over the base pay, get so much money over the base pay that they pull the average income up $60 a week. (And this does not include the "extras" that the players, principal or otherwise, might earn on the outside, from recording, from teaching, from consulting, from making jingles or commercials or sound tracks.) But the base pay is, for everybody, the starting point, the income on which everything—including the highest expectation—is made.

And this very basic money issue still stalled the negotiations.

Management had not come up from its first offer of $340 a week base pay; the negotiators had not come down from their demand of $360 a week. But the federal mediator, Douglas Brown, worked out a plan with management that he thought would get things rolling again—or at least get the music flowing. Under this plan, the orchestra would go back and work without a contract, as it had offered to do before the work stoppage. But there would be a difference: it would not work on a two-week notice basis but would guarantee to continue playing for thirteen weeks. Management, on its side, would guarantee not to lock out the players in that time. It would also guarantee to make retroactive any pay raises eventually negotiated. After that, talks and playing might continue indefinitely unless called off on thirty days' notice.

Management immediately accepted the proposal. The union negotiators said they'd think it over and submit it to a vote of the players. But they had spotted some holes in the plan. "Those thirteen weeks included Solti's first visit this season, Solti's eastern tour, Solti's recording session," points out Koss. That meant—to Koss and Zverow and their fellow negotiators—that the Orchestral Association would reap full-house money, plus income from the recording contracts, in the first thirteen weeks. After that, there's to be a succession of guest conductors, little known to Chicago audiences and thus not the hot box office that Solti is. "So they could actually put on a thirteen-week season and lock us out for the next thirty-nine weeks, and they could say they had a season"—and a profit. At the same time, the players' bargaining power was greatest in those first thirteen weeks; it would decline as the orchestra became more of a cost factor than an income factor.

The offer demanded quick action; there could be no long and leisurely consideration of the compromise or more concerts—including Solti's—would have to be canceled. So each of the five players in the negotiating session went home and called twenty other players in the orchestra. They also called a meeting at which the matter could be debated and voted on. "We asked for an exact copy of the proposal," says Koss—to ensure that there'd be no later claims of misunderstanding about the offer. The committee itself would have rejected the offer but the members felt it had to be put to a secret ballot. "Remember, these guys had been out of work for three or four weeks and when you've lost a thousand dollars and you don't know when you're going to go back to work—there's always a chance that they'd begin cracking," says Koss.

The matter went to a vote of all the players on a secret ballot. ("None of this raising hands and having everybody talking and haranguing everybody else.") One of the members of the negotiating committee was against using the secret ballot. "Look," he said, "the issues are too complicated. We've got to tell them what to do." No, the others decided on the secret ballot so there'd be no social pressure on the members to go along. "Look," says Koss, "when you're hungry, I can't blame a guy for wanting to cave in. Sometimes principles have to be set aside in a case like that." So the vote was strict and secret.

And the vote turned out at 101 to 2 to reject the compromise offer.

Then the negotiators put another question to the orchestra: how did the members feel about reiterating and supporting the previous offer of working on a day-to-day basis and walking out only on two weeks' notice? (This, of course, would give the edge to the union, not management; it could call a walkout at the worst possible time for management.)

The vote was 103 to 2 in favor of this offer.

Thus the orchestra, wrenched and riven for so many years over union and union-related issues—an organization with members who had strong ties to and deep respect for management—was united again.

But this time against management.

Ironically, the contract dispute had had an annealing effect on the orchestra that only music could match.

All this time, Solti had been keeping track of the negotiations via long-distance phone calls. On the Tuesday that the vote was taken in Chicago, he packed his bags and family and left Roccamare. He flew from Italy to London so he and the family could pause and refresh themselves for a few days before flying to Chicago. ("It is too long, the flight from Rome to Chicago," he said. "Too tiring. The children should not have to fly for so long.") In London, he postponed the flight to Chicago from day to day as the negotiations remained stalled. Now there was less than a week left before his first rehearsal. He'd need a day or so to recuperate from the flight and jet lag after he got here; he'd need another to make the trip. He'd not be able to move with less than three days' notice before the first rehearsal. That meant that Saturday was the decision day for Georg Solti; he could start the trip as late as Sunday but only at the risk of utter fatigue—and he was still suffering from his cold.

Back in Chicago, there were very small, almost imperceptible signs of a change. One of the members, who'd been in touch with a member of the board of trustees earlier in the year, reported he'd been approached again to see if the members wanted to talk directly to the trustees. This is a goal favored by Koss: he believes there should be dialogue between players and trustees in which management is not the middleman—"we never know what they're screening out from the trustees." (One characteristic complaint: "Maybe management tells them, 'These guys want chartered planes. They're greedy.' What they don't tell them is that the alternative to taking chartered planes is to fly to a big town, lay over for four hours, and then take another plane to a smaller town where you've got a concert that night. And then play the concert and reverse the procedure the next day. So it looks wrong to be asking for chartered planes, but maybe the alternative doesn't get through—I don't know.") In any case, he couldn't agree to such a dialogue now; there is some indication that any contract eventually achieved might be jeopardized—under federal regulations—by such a dialogue. Another sign was the sympathetic response of Louis Sudler when he encountered some members of the orchestra on the picket line. He thought it was degrading that great artists had to walk a picket line. "We're going to settle this thing," he assured them. He didn't say how or when—and the men involved forgot to pass on this bit of dialogue to Don Koss. At least not until after he'd left for a critical negotiating session on Friday night.

Now, for the first time—only hours before Solti had to leave for the airport —the talks began moving.

It was just after six o'clock in the evening when all sides gathered in the offices of counsel to the union on the nineteenth floor of the Board of Education Building in Chicago. Management came armed with certain figures—and found they led to other figures. The difference between demand and offer of union and management was $20 a week in the first year of the contract. That amounted to a cost of $109,200 extra to the Orchestral Association in that year. If they could find a compromise—say $5 a week—then the extra cost would be only around $27,300. The union knew this; they'd been working on the $10 compromise. "We're talking about $50,000 on a $5 or $6 million budget," says Don Koss. "That's 1 percent—1 stinky, smelly little percent."

There was a lot of talk about figures and escalation and cost-of-living increases.

The way inflation was going, the raises would be wiped out in one month of the inflation that was even then running rampant. There was also a lot of talk about a one-year contract and a three-year contract. There was more figuring and management had a hard offer: a three-year contract at $345 the first year, $360 the second year, $385 the third year. Thus everybody would get a $25-a-week raise the first year and the third year; in between they get a $15-a-week raise. The players' negotiating committee looked it over and asked for a revision: kick the first year up $5 and knock the third year down $5. "We'd settle for a last year of $380," says Koss. Why? "Look, we'd like to have that money right now. This year. Because all our guys are getting hurt this year." Agreed. The terms were set: $350 the first year, $360 the second year, $380 the third year.

And that left one more issue to be resolved: would the players help make up the concert lost to the subscription buyers? Would the management reimburse the players for the weeks they'd been idle?

That was another knotty problem. But a system for playing the lost concerts was worked out, albeit not with the conductors or soloists previously scheduled. (One of the *St. Matthew Passion* concerts of the Holy Week was moved from a non-subscription to a subscription status; an extra week was added to the end of the season; a missed trip to Milwaukee was scheduled for a certain Tuesday, not just Monday.) In turn management agreed to pay the players their four weeks' lost salary, and to do it in the first four weeks of the resumed season. But one of those four weeks would be regarded as paid vacation. Nevertheless, it was a concession that cost the Orchestral Association an extra $8,100. "I think it showed they really wanted to get us back. They lost productivity. There'd be no way they're going to get all those lost services back in the schedule. They're not going to get their money's worth out of what we're doing for that," says Koss. On the other hand, he feels it showed other cities around the country that the trustees of the Orchestral Association were enlightened, that they were not locked in the Mesozoic Age. "We all have a responsibility to get a good contract," says Koss, "because we're the leader among other orchestras in setting a pattern."

It was past 1:30 on a Saturday morning when finally the agreement was sealed.

Somebody found a bottle of brandy and everybody had a drink to the weeks of travail. And to its end.

"Be careful driving home," somebody warned. Not because of the drink but because of the emotional letdown following the hard, draining give-and-take of seven hours of negotiations—and a month of complete frustration.

Don Koss drove home carefully that night and, like his fellow negotiators, began phoning his roster of twenty to tell them the news. ("It was three o'clock in the morning, but we figured most of them would want to hear.")

The next day he went out riding—and had the first automobile accident of his life.

INTERLUDE: Autumn

In London, it was midmorning when Sir Georg Solti got the news. The day was brisk, the wind biting. The sun had given up its feeble attempts to sweep Regent's Park, near his St. John's Wood home. The next day would be colder, dull, overcast, cheerless—weather in which even Englishmen catch cold. By that time, Georg Solti would be on his way to Chicago—with a cold of his own.

They were all coming back now—physically and mentally.

Donald Peck was back from Carmel. . . . Tom Howell came back from Canada. He and his girl friend had taken the Algoma Central Railroad north from Saulte Ste. Marie along the east coast of Lake Superior, past Batchawana and Agawa Bay, through Eton and Perry and Hawk Junction, beyond Goudreau and Oba, into some of the most rugged and beautiful and magnificently undisturbed country on the North American continent. Of course, they went backpacking again.

Sam Magad, the violinist, came back from Aspen. During the lockout he'd had an offer to become concertmaster of the Dallas Symphony. He'd turned it down and risked a vacation instead. He'd gambled on the lockout—that it would last about as long as it took Solti to get to Chicago—and so he'd used some of the time to take a delayed trip to Aspen. Originally, he'd planned to go there during the Ravinia season but his co-concertmaster, Victor Aitay, had suffered a cardiovascular "incident" and could not play at Ravinia through the summer. So Sam canceled his vacation plans to take Victor's place. Now both he and Victor were back, the latter from the hospital. Victor was a little slimmer—"four or five pounds"—but just as casually impenetrable. "It was just a warning—I didn't even know it had happened," he says of the coronary incident. "I just had to stay in the hospital for about ten days or so."

Edward Druzinsky, the principal harp player, put aside his books. He'd gone through Loren Eiseley's The Immense Journey, through many of the letters and

James Vrhel, associate principal bass player.

papers of Sigmund Freud, through a volume on the Russian spy system against Germany in World War II (titled The Red Orchestra). Norman Schweikert, a French horn player, also put aside his book. It was not a book he was reading, it was a book he was researching. "I'm writing a book which is to be a history of professional horn players in the United States from colonial times to the present," he says. Jimmy Vrhel, No. 2 man in the bass section, also put aside his plaything: it is a thirty-foot sloop called the Lieutenant Kije after a laugh-provoking piece by

Prokofiev in which Vrhel played a magnificent solo on a Reiner recording, and he was putting it in drydock for the winter. Now, as ever, it was the stock market that grabbed his attention. It was in a long slump then, it would have a brief rally, and then the slump would worsen. But Jimmy Vrhel, a happy, talkative man who is considered the best stock analyst in the orchestra, was undeterred. "The stock market is the place to be," he said cheerfully.

Joe Guastafeste, back from the "hidden island" in the Caribbean, put aside his files and saws. He'd spent some of the out-of-work time laboring over bleached-gray pieces of driftwood at home. He does it entirely by hand and muscle—"no electric tools," he says. The reason: "One of our other bass players used to work with electric tools and he had an accident one day and took off part of a finger." Without fingers, one cannot play the strings. "So that man no longer plays in the Chicago Symphony." . . . Jim Gilbertsen, one of the trombone players, had to put aside one of his many projects until he could fit it into his schedule: he was grinding a lens for a telescope at the Adler Planetarium. "A ten-inch mirror," he says. "I received a book on how to make your own telescope, and I thought it would be interesting in my spare time to grind a lens." So he went to the Adler Planetarium: "They have a marvelous instructor over there . . . his first mirror he ground into one-twentieth of a wave length. That is within millionths and millionths of an inch." Gilbertsen didn't expect his first effort to match it. "I'll get up only to the thirteenth magnitude in space." Not good enough for far-out work. "But it should be really good for planetary work." . . . Sam Denov came back to the hard part of reality. He couldn't fit law school into his schedule—not this season anyway. The courses he wanted to take conflicted in time with some of the concerts of the Chicago Symphony. It bothered him; it frustrated him. "There is something about playing in the section of an orchestra that is so anonymous and so unrewarding, from an individual's point of view, that I'd have to say the bloom is off the rose for me," he says. "It does not thrill me like it used to. It does not give me the satisfaction that it used to. I just feel I would like to do more with my life as an individual than be caught in a big machine." But he would be in that machine for a while yet. Now he planned to enter law school in the following semester.

Willard Elliot, the bassoonist, put aside his gouging and shaving of reeds. There was always the chance that he wouldn't need them. Or that the weather would change and make obsolete the reeds that he had. He turned again to another preoccupation: the genealogy of his family. "I was going through some of my father's notes—he died about four years ago—and he'd been doing some research on the Elliot line . . ."

Vicki Graef felt the growth below her left temple growing larger and larger. She'd gone from her gynecologist to a dentist who'd sent her to an oral surgeon who sent her to a neurosurgeon. "They seemed to think it was a parotid tumor"—though they did not tell her. This is a tumor of the parotid gland and it is usually fatal. This also they did not tell her. They urged her to go to surgery right away. But she demurred. She had too much to do, playing the organ in her church work . . .

SECOND
MOVEMENT

The Rehearsal

The melancholy was gone now. Suddenly the knife edge of autumn cut across Chicago behind a biting wind. It was October 16 and inside Orchestra Hall, where the first rehearsal of the season would be held, there was an almost tangible feeling of expectation. "Ready?" said Radivoj Lah, the personnel manager, as he took a last look at the orchestra and went down to summon the conductor. The orchestra was more than ready: it was alive with a sense of being.

There was one exception: Georg Solti. He'd arrived for his first meeting with the orchestra still suffering from a cold and jet-lag. The latter is not just a superficial, one-day experience. It involves more than a loss of sleep or changed sleeping patterns. For there are changes in body temperature, in metabolic pace, in hormonal concentration, even in the pattern of nerve conduction. Some body systems take two or three days to adjust; others take up to six or seven days. Solti appears to be one who is not quick to recover.

Except when he is on the podium. In these moments, he undergoes an almost visible rejuvenescence. His color comes surging back into his face, his motion becomes more animated, his whole persona seems filled with a new energy. The change, even in rehearsal, is very swift in coming.

"I am glad to see you," he said with a small smile, almost as if he didn't expect to see them. It was a few moments after two o'clock in the afternoon. Solti was seated in a high-backed stool on the podium, wearing a loose red shirt and baggy blue pants. Already the regenesis of being with the orchestra, of being *in* music, was apparent. He started off with a few minutes of small talk—how happy he was that they could make music together again, what he'd been doing and why: he normally starts the first rehearsal with every orchestra by chatting for a few minutes. It is as if to reassert his intimacy and oneness with the players.

There was a patter of applause, of bows clicking on music stands, when he finished. Then—all business again—he said quickly, "Let us take the Beethoven first." It was Beethoven's Symphony no. 3, *Eroica*. The symphony has no introduction. It opens only with two crashing staccato E-flat major chords—like stabs to the mind, or in the heart—and then flows immediately into the first movement. Solti flowed just as smoothly and swiftly into his conductorial role. Soon he was humming, singing, whistling, commenting, in the particular manner that is Solti:

—In the first movement: "Much nice. Is a beautiful phrase."

—At an F-sharp: "I want a little non F-sharp. I will not mind it if you play a little shorter."

—After a pause: "Will you be so kind as to give me that a little more pianissimo. I *love* that pianissimo."

The first stop in this rehearsal came after twenty minutes. He rarely stops the orchestra. He is more interested in hearing the total flow of the music—to shape and hone it to the sound of his inner ear—than in tackling the details of every imperfection. On occasion, he will pause if he hears something stunningly gross, but he will not pause for long. "If it is done wrong again, I will mention it later on but I will not come always back to it," he says. "I will not force them to play it over and over again until it is done perfectly." Why not? "Because this exhausts the orchestra. And because this is a very intelligent orchestra. If we play it once or twice and it is not right, I know it will be right in the performance. These men are too intelligent. They do not let error persist." This is something for which most members of the orchestra are grateful. They, too, want to play and they tend to get annoyed when a conductor stops every few bars to tell them something they already know: that somebody made a mistake. *That* somebody not only knows it but knows how to correct it. So the players in the Chicago Symphony feel—with Solti—that the orchestra does not have to be stopped to be told the obvious. "It takes minutes to stop an orchestra and start it again," says Victor Aitay, a co-concertmaster. "Do it ten or fifteen times in every piece and you've wasted more than half an hour."

Solti was not always so smooth and long-suffering. In his more tense and short-fused days, he had a tendency to overrehearse and overcorrect an orchestra. Indeed, at Covent Garden, some of the singers can recall his moods and even what might be described as his tantrums. The first time he rehearsed Verdi's *Otello* at Covent Garden, he spent twenty-five minutes with the chorus working on just the first two words of the whole opera—"*Una vela*," which means, literally, "a sail"—in order to get the sequential accent exactly right. The members of the chorus never quite forgot it. Nor did they let Solti forget it. For the phrase "*una vela*" became a sort of password, a salutation, a word of affection or good luck when they passed each other—or sometimes passed Solti—backstage. "*Una vela*"—"a sail."

He had, in those days, what one friend has called "a necessary intensity: you could never get close to him." He himself recalls that he was often foolishly impatient at rehearsals. "I did not understand then that you cannot get everything right in a first rehearsal. I remember when Furtwängler came to Zurich, I snuck in through the roof of the Tonhalle to hear him rehearse. I was astonished that they made so many mistakes that *I* could hear. And yet he let them go on. It took me a long time to learn that first you have to let them play."

Normally in such first-rehearsal efforts as this one, he is likely to "beat one," in musicians' lingo. That is to say that at certain places he does not beat rhythm so much as he beats the bar lines and accented notes while he concentrates on listening to the inner movement of the music. When he does change styles, he is likely to say—as if alerting those who may not be watching—"Now I am beating two . . . now I am beating three." His communication with the orchestra is kinetic as well as verbal. He may pound his fist in his baton-hand lightly to demonstrate a beat or he'll tap out the tempo vigorously on his left arm with the baton. Often he augments it with whistling or a chant that sounds almost like Morse code—"ta ta *ta*" or "pom-pom-pom pomm" to demonstrate the length of the notes that he thinks are important and the value that he places on their length or shortness. He also loves to sing along with the orchestra, as if to lead it by his voice as well as his body language. His singing is not very good. One member of the London Philharmonic recalls the orchestra's reaction when it first heard Solti's sing-along: he had this "terrible falsetto sound, screaming away in his high-pitched register. We burst out laughing. But he didn't notice it most of the time. When he did, he said something like, 'Well, you must excuse me, this is the way I sing.' "

There is a sense of great tolerance of Solti's mannerisms in all his orchestras. "He has a very happy upbeat," says one string player in the Chicago Symphony. "It is very abrupt, jerky almost, compared to his downbeat, which is mild. After a while it becomes perfectly clear that you are not supposed to play any differently. You train yourself not to overreact."

Ray Still makes this point: "Some conductors, when they want a pianissimo start, will give you a tiny little beat—almost daring you to play. Solti always gives you a very firm beat, which could be interpreted as mezzo forte to forte. But at the same time, he tells you that he wants it very pianissimo. It works out especially well when you have a piece that is difficult rhythmically."

In the past, Solti talked a bit much to the orchestras he conducted. Now he does not. He is much more pointed and far better organized. "I don't think I've ever seen anybody who is so well organized in his rehearsals," says Grover Schiltz. But he is wary lest his verbal instruction, combined with his strenuous calisthenics with the baton, lead to overenthusiasm among the players. "One of the funniest things that Solti does," says Willard Elliot, "is that when we play something a little loosely, he will say, 'Don't play it like a super-Hungarian!' "

Ray Still adds: "He has his little jokes. He will ask us to do something a little faster or a little slower, louder, or softer. And sometimes we will do it a little more so. Solti always says, 'But, oh no, my dears! That is too good! Too good!' "

There is within the Chicago Symphony, and presumably in the other orchestras that Solti conducts, a sort of free-form interpretation of the maestro. "Solti does a lot of funny things," says Jay Friedman, the bearded young principal trombonist of the Chicago Symphony. "When he wants to tell you to attack something, for instance, he uses some very crazy syllables like 'Eh ta ta ta' with his hand on his chest—for a heart attack. Or if he means he really wants you to go at it, he yells something that sounds like 'Foo-ey yak!' "

To be sure, there are times when even the most veteran members of the Solti rehearsals are baffled by his intent. "We can hear 50 percent of what he says and understand half of what we hear," says one back-stand player in the Chicago Symphony. Partly it is because Solti has an inclination to speak in a mixture of languages. Indeed, his multilingual quality is a great asset in operatic or record production in Europe. He can speak to the orchestra in French, to the vocalists in Italian, to the director in English—"all like it's voices coming over while you twiddle a dial on a radio," says one friend. His English is more British than American. David Greenbaum, a cellist in the Chicago Symphony who was born and reared in Scotland and was an impersonator of any conductor's moods, gestures, and language, remembered that some members of the orchestra were mystified by some of Solti's "English-isms" when he first came to Chicago. "He was calling quarter notes 'crochets,' eighth notes 'quavers,' and half notes 'minims.' People used to come up to me after rehearsal and ask, 'What does he mean, this crochet is too long? What is it, a crochet?' "

The English of Solti is memorable for its accent, tone, and pace. And for its quaintness. He often uses the wrong word for something which is close to what he means: "too good" in correcting the orchestra may mean "too much." But his enthusiasm and his guilelessness conquer all. "This is as we would never did it," he once said of something that was done well. Or "Here we have some swimming," to indicate that the sound of the orchestra is getting a bit muddy. To one utterly baffled group, he kept saying, "Here we have mad cows! Mad cows!" He meant 'mad chaos." On another occasion, he rushed up to a singer who'd substituted at a performance in a quite difficult role: "Congratulations," he said. "I thought it would be twice as bad!"

In no sense is Solti static or dull in rehearsal. He makes the rehearsal tense and exciting so that the performance that follows may be less tense and more exciting. "Tense at the rehearsals so we concentrate," Aitay has said. "Relaxed during the performance so we relax." His body motion ranges from deep knee bends, as if he is trying to dig the sound out of the violins, to still serenity when he barely beats with the baton while he stands in deep concentration—in meditation—to listen to the orchestra. At one point in rehearsal, he stopped the orchestra and discussed with the woodwinds and strings their pace, relative and absolute. Then he prepared to start the orchestra in a very small motion; he was bent in a very precious stance, almost as if he was intent on hearing a confession. He paused: "I am not praying, I assure you." The change of pace was nerve-releasing. There was a small ripple of laughter as he prepared to start the orchestra again. And when he did, he talked and cajoled all the way through. To the violins: "Excellent. Excellent. Would you play that a little softer in concert please? A little softer?" He did not stop the orchestra but instead kept the beat and the music going and turned to the cellos: "More espressivo in that crescendo, please. Would you be so kind as to give me more espressivo?"

"With other conductors, we are used to playing softer," explains Frank Miller, the principal player among the cellos. The cellos and the bass carry the smooth surging rhythms of the first movement of *Eroica*, and in a sense it was symbolic of this season's start of the Chicago Symphony: no section was led more ably or by a more distinguished player than the cellos were led by Frank Miller.

In this season, the cello was distinguished by the tragedies of its leadership. Pablo Casals died. Jacqueline du Pré, it was revealed, suffered from multiple sclerosis. They were soloists, of course; Frank Miller has been, perhaps, the leading orchestral cellist in the world for many years. Partly it is because, even within the orchestra, he recognizes the individuality of the instrument. Its full name is violoncello, which means "little bass viol." (In the contraction to "cello," only the "little" was preserved.) Its demand was based in the classical orchestral repertory of the seventeenth and eighteenth centuries on the need for an instrument to play the bass notes along with the double bass. For a long while, it served to underpin and strengthen the bass section of church choirs and, from the early days of the string quartet, it served *as* the bass, rarely in the early days being given a melody to play. Yet it has many characteristics of the violin. It is tuned in fifths, as is the violin (whereas the double bass is tuned in fourths), and it can play almost everything that the violin can play—chords, harmonics, arpeggios, etc. Even the eye of the most casual concertgoer can see the double relationship of the cello. It is played while the instrument is set on a tailpin on the floor, as is the bass (and not the violin); yet it can be played while the player is sitting in a normal-sized chair, as the violin (but not the bass).

Frank Miller's individuality goes deep into the playing of the instrument. Historically, the cello is described in terms of the art of the fingering. The strings of the cello are thicker and heavier than those of the violin—indeed, some of them are often made of metal—and thus demand stronger pressure by the fingers. But since the distances that the player must span are greater on a cello than on the violin, the fingers must be not thick and prodding—as one would imagine in dealing with heavy, stiff strings—but quite nimble and stretching. Of course, there is an ideal combination: very strong, even thick fingers, but long ones set in a hand with a small palm.

However, Miller puts the emphasis on the other hand. "The great art is in the right hand, in the bowing," he says. "You can teach a bricklayer how to work with his left hand and make the fingering. But the greatest artists are those who bow most wonderfully."

Miller's bowing is wonderful and distinctive. One reason is that he has a "heavy" right arm. But he is a heavy man. Not many years ago, he weighed well over 300 pounds; he'd gone on a diet and lost 145 pounds, though he still weighed somewhat more than 200 pounds. "I manage to lean into the strings very heavily," he says.

That, he suspects, is the reason he breaks the A- and D-strings so often. "Every fourth day—every *fourth* day—I have to replace them," he says. "Whereas many colleagues of mine can keep a string on for six months or so." He's had the instrument checked, the bridges inspected, and still is unable to find a reason —other than his heavy right arm—that the strings should break. "So I don't take a chance anymore. I just change them every fourth day."

He knows what it is to be caught making the change too late. Some years ago, he played in the NBC Symphony under Toscanini and, in those days, the strings broke every five days. ("I don't know why it is shorter now, but I suppose it is because I got older and heavier and had a heavier right arm.") One day the orchestra was playing a broadcast concert in which the cello had a solo near the beginning of the second number—"absolutely nothing else playing; just the one cello," says Miller. Toward the end of the first number, the A-string on Miller's cello broke.

He sat there stunned for a moment. Then he got up and rumbled furiously offstage—he is a big man but an athletic one, and he could move swiftly for his size. Toscanini watched him in absolute astonishment. He had no idea what had gone wrong, other than the possibility that his solo cellist had gone berserk. But he could not stop the orchestra to inquire. Nor could he, when the first number had ended, make any sharp, scorching inquiries; the radio microphones were still "live."

Offstage, Miller changed the A-string with great speed. He turned and rushed back to the stage—where Toscanini was waiting, bound to silence by the sensitivity of the microphone. "Fortunately there was a long commentary between numbers and I was able to get back in my chair for the downbeat," says Miller. But all through the solo by Miller, the puzzled Toscanini kept giving him dark, suspicious glances, as if he was not quite sure what would set off his cellist next. "But he never really said a word to me"—which was unlike Toscanini—"except to inquire later if I was all right."

Miller, now in his sixties, has been a principal player under some of the greatest conductors: Toscanini in New York, Solti and Reiner in Chicago, Leopold Stokowski at the Philadelphia Orchestra, Dimitri Mitropoulos and Eugene Ormandy with the Minneapolis Symphony. His memories of them are touching, spirited, musical, and human.

Mitropoulos, he remembers, was a very jerky and calisthenic conductor—"One might think that Solti has angular movements, but Mitropoulos didn't use a baton and his jerky movements were sometimes very difficult to interpret. He would just conduct with a fist or an elbow, not a baton—and it makes a difference." But that is not all that Miller remembers about his calisthenics. The carpeting where the Minneapolis Symphony played in the 1930s was not often cleaned. "When I first started playing under him, sitting up close as a first cello, he used to stamp his feet a lot as he conducted. And the thing I remember is the dust—it used to come billowing up out of the carpet and fly like mad around all of us that were up close."

Frank Miller played an important part in the touching events of Toscanini's last performance. The two men were relatively close in Miller's years with the NBC Symphony, as close as a player could get to Toscanini and his "old school" style of relationships. Indeed, Miller had occasionally been given certain responsibilities within the orchestra for leadership.

Toscanini's last concert took place on April 4, 1954. About a week earlier, on his eighty-seventh birthday, he'd submitted his resignation as conductor of the NBC Symphony. "He did not actually want to do that last concert, or even the one before it," says Miller. "All that season, he'd had memory lapses and we could see that he was coming to the end." Miller remembers Toscanini's own admission:

"He said, 'I am an old man and I am finished and I do not want to conduct.' " But the executives of the National Broadcasting Company, knowing that they had contracts for commercial sponsorship of the orchestra, put great pressure on him to conduct this one last time. He finally agreed.

"We were doing Wagner"—*Tannhäuser*—"as the next to the last number," recalls Miller, "when suddenly the maestro simply stopped conducting. We had half the piece to go and he stopped conducting—his arms just dangled." The orchestra was able to keep going, though the members were soon thrown into confusion over the lack of a beat and into apprehension over the maestro's failing. Never had he so clearly demonstrated that his memory was going—that he couldn't remember the score. "There was quite a bit of faltering," says Miller. They were in the Bacchanale when it happened, so Miller turned and—still sitting down—started giving cues and trying to maintain the beat. The orchestra kept going under his direction, but up in the radio control booth the engineers, executives, and sponsors were in panic. Somebody there gave an order to make a switch and so Toscanini and the orchestra were cut off the air and a record of Brahms's *First Symphony* —by Toscanini and the NBC Symphony—went on the air. In any case, Miller managed to keep the orchestra together and coherent, and after thirty seconds or so, Toscanini seemed to recover. He raised his baton and resumed conducting. The control booth cut off Brahms's First Symphony and put Toscanini back on live with Wagner's *Tannhäuser*. "Very few of the listening audience really knew the difference," says Miller. "Only musicians and connoisseurs."

But that was not the end of the drama. Or of Miller's part in it. For when *Tannhäuser* came to an end, Toscanini started to walk off the stage. He'd forgotten that there was more on the program. "I stopped him and said, 'Maestro, the *Meistersinger* Overture. You must conduct the *Meistersinger* Overture.' He looked at me, nodded, and went back and conducted the *Meistersinger* Overture."

But he didn't finish it. "We came down to the last three bars and he threw his baton down on the floor and walked off, while we were playing those last three bars."

The broadcast executives got the message: Toscanini had resigned.

And his memory was gone with him.

"It was like a funeral afterward," says Miller. "Everybody in the orchestra was crying."

But Toscanini remembered Miller and what he'd done for him. He gave Miller eight of his batons, finely wrought, marvelously colored instruments that, says Miller, "were made for him by his neurosurgeon " He also gave Miller one of the rarest possessions within his vast treasury of gifts: a recommendation to conduct a symphony orchestra.

This is the irony of Frank Miller's illustrious career: he's always had other ambitions—two of them, to be precise.

The first was to be a baseball player. "When I was younger, I played all kinds of sports," he says. He still loves sports, though the musical disciplines tend to interfere with them. He's left-handed in everything, including sports, and it is the left hand that must do the fingering on his cello. "I stopped playing tennis quite a few years ago because I held the racket in my left hand, and my left hand would become cramped after three sets of tennis." Similarly he had to be wary of bowling: "After lugging that sixteen-pound ball for a while, my left fingers get very stiff." He still plays golf, however: "it's a game in which both hands hold a small shaft"—so there is no tension on them. But baseball was the game that he loved: "first base"—naturally, as a left-hander with power—"and the outfield." He had, as a youth, plans all made out that fit the young people of his time. "I always wanted to go to Yale, the reason being there was a great baseball coach at Yale: T. A. D. Jones. My great love was to go to Yale and study baseball under Tad Jones."

But Miller ran afoul of his musical talent. At the age of fifteen, he won a scholarship to the Curtis Institute of Music in Philadelphia and he faced a crisis in his life. "I only wanted to play baseball for a living," he says quietly. If he accepted the scholarship to Curtis, he'd never finish normal high school and then go to Yale; he'd be locked into a career in music. His older half brother, who also played the cello, helped him make up his mind. "He 'talked' me out of baseball." On the face of it, the decision was a sound one: at the age of seventeen, Miller signed a contract to play in the Philadelphia Orchestra, a feat considerably more singular than starring for a major-league baseball team in his teens. But he's never quite forgotten those years of hope and nascent glory—that might have been devoted to baseball.

His other great ambition is to be a conductor. A full-time conductor. For he does it on the side now and he's always had a firm, strong hand—the right one—in conducting. He was conductor of the Florida Symphony Orchestra for five years in the late 1950s; that's the orchestra for which Toscanini gave him a written recommendation when the NBC Symphony was broken up in the wake of Toscanini's retirement. Later, he was associate conductor of the Minneapolis Symphony and conductor of its summer series of pop concerts. ("Between 1955 and 1960," he says, "I conducted four hundred concerts.") He's conducted the Chicago Symphony on several occasions and he's the resident conductor of the Evanston Symphony in that suburb just north of Chicago. The latter plays six concerts a year, has eighty-five members, and is entirely amateur. "I don't engage outside symphony men, as in other community orchestras; they don't want me to," he says. He had eight rehearsals for a concert compared to the four-rehearsal schedule of the Chicago Symphony Orchestra. But the Chicago schedules those four rehearsals into one week and the Evanston spreads them over eight weeks. "Still, I don't feel too bad—that the Evanston Symphony needs eight rehearsals while the Chicago Symphony needs four," says Miller.

It's been forty years since he first started playing in a symphony orchestra and he still has his old high resolve: that one day he will return to full-time conducting. He's spent these years conscientiously studying conductors as well as superbly playing symphonies.

He remembers, for example, what Toscanini told him about the pace of the orchestra. "Toscanini often would go right ahead with the violins when they are rushing. I would ask him, when we were visiting in private, 'Maestro, what can

you do with the violin section when they are running? How can you hold them back?' He would say, 'Don't hold them back. Go along with them. Because it would make chaos if you tried to pull the reins and they would fall apart. So sometimes you have to go along with them, even if they are running.' "

On the other hand, he is more inclined to adopt Solti's attitude of conducting from a score instead of conducting from memory, as do so many young conductors in aping Toscanini. He says: "Toscanini was almost blind, and to see the music without glasses he would put that music right against his eye, smack against his eyes—he was that nearsighted. That was the only way he could conduct—he had to memorize because he could not conduct from music." It is, Miller thinks, not necessary for other conductors to follow Toscanini's habits if they don't have Toscanini's limitations. "Many of our conductors today do the same thing, but I think it is only for show. . . . It does not make one bit of difference in the performance. . . . And the performance is the thing, whether the conductor is doing it from memory or not."

And he is not likely to adopt Mitropoulos's technique of conducting without a baton, even though he recognizes the limitations of the stick. "The baton does not do anything at all—it's just an extension of your arm to show the men in front of you where the beat is. But still, I don't like batonless conducting. I don't object to it strenuously but I prefer that a conductor use a baton"—even if the conductor is named Miller.

His conducting experience has been extensive but not all-absorbing. One reason is that he's been so eminent an instrumentalist. "I would love to have a conducting job, if it were possible," he says. "But nowadays, the only ones who get the jobs are young men." Despite his ambition, he does not think less of the responsibility that he has. "I don't like the system"—of picking young, virtually unshaven men to conduct and ignoring the superbly experienced men of the orchestra. "But I don't put down my cello in disgust and say that I won't play because I can't have a conducting job. Instead I·play the cello harder for it."

Indeed, he is dedicated to his work. He teaches six or eight students. He takes his cello home after many a performance so that he can practice the next day—which means that he totes twenty-two pounds of "big fiddle" onto subways and buses to his suburban home. He plays thirty or forty or fifty chamber music concerts every year with the Chicago Symphony String Quartet.

Moreover, he is, like any virtuoso, terribly sensitive to the conditions of the hall that he's playing in. The shape of the stage of Orchestra Hall, for example—which was designed more like the organ loft of a church than the proscenium arch of a concert hall—does not project the sound of the strings beyond the stage. ("I wish we had a shell in this hall," he says.) The center doors of Orchestra Hall open into a foyer which opens into the box-office lobby, which opens into the street. ("Why don't they close those center doors and make people come in through the sides? Have you ever been able to come into a theater and go right through the center door into the theater? No? You have to go into the auditorium from off to the side. . . . There is not one other theater or concert hall in the United States whose

James Palecek (left), stage manager, and Lional Sayers, librarian.

Frank Miller (right), principal cellist, and Leonard Chausow, associate principal cellist.

center doors open at the center so you can see from the stage right out into the street or from the street right into the stage.") The air changes in the hall are direct and swift. ("It changes the pitch of our instruments. The woodwinds find it difficult because their instruments change pitch immediately and they have to adjust terribly. I am constantly tuning my own instrument because of that.")

Solti himself has trouble with some of the sounds in the hall. "Dry. Very dry. Too much dry," he said early in the first rehearsal. He means there is little reverberation; the sound goes up to the very high ceiling of Orchestra Hall and then disappears through openings instead of being reflected downward so that there would be a rising crescendo of sound within the hall. The "highs" off the high tones are lost altogether and there is no gathering of the low tones, like rollers on a seacoast, to help in the rich sense of growing power.

But that is not anything that Solti can change. And so he does not agonize much about it.

Instead, he played the Beethoven for just over an hour, then at 3:25 called for an intermission.

Backstage, one of the crew resisted the temptation to light up a cigar. "The maestro hates cigar smoke," says Jim Palecek, the stage manager. "That's the one order he gave for backstage—no cigar smoking."

"Look, you're just going to have to get somebody who can play," said one musician to another as they clattered down the stairs to the players' locker room and lounge during intermission. "I just don't think he can do it," continued the musician, somewhat vehemently. "Why, he hasn't had a racket in his hands for years."

"He got terribly sick one night and before we knew it, he was having a heart attack," said another player during an intermission conversation. "So we rushed him over to the vet's and the vet gave us the diagnosis—'He hasn't got a dog's chance.'"

Valerie Solti approached Jim Palecek with a request-that-was-a-suggestion-that-was-an-order: had he noticed that one corner of the podium had been rounded off, like a cardboard box dropped on a corner? Did he suppose it could be fixed before the performance?

"He could fall off it," explained Lady Valerie. Because he is so gymnastic a conductor, Solti moves around on the podium a great deal. He has a metal U-shaped stand, with a horizontal bar set at a height just above the small of the back, locked upside down into the floor of the podium so that he can't back accidentally off the podium.

"But he learns the podium, every square inch of it, with his feet," says Lady Valerie. He has it memorized and reacts to it as reflexively as blinking: he knows every uneven meeting of the boards, where every squeak might develop, just what the signals are to his feet if he's getting too close to the edge.

"If there's a spot that's changed it may surprise him and"—referring to the crushed corner—"since that's so close to the edge, he might even fall down," explains Lady Valerie.

How does a podium suddenly turn up with a crushed corner?

It just sits there in the dark of the hall while the orchestra is away. Nobody attacks it or sets termites upon it.

Not quite. "The podium goes on tour with the orchestra," says Lady Valerie. "It goes where the orchestra goes—to the recording studio, to New York, to Hanover, everywhere."

But why? Wouldn't it be just as easy to use the podium that's already in Carnegie Hall or in the recording studio or anywhere else?

Not really. For one podium may be different from another. "It may be higher or lower—maybe he doesn't get the same perspective of the orchestra," says Lady Valerie. "Or it may squeal or squeak—he couldn't tolerate that during a recording session. Or it may be of a different size. Or maybe it doesn't have the bar at the back."

It is part of Solti's attention to detail: he learns this podium and for him it is "perfect"; he does not want to "learn" a new podium in critical concerts, such as those in Carnegie Hall, or at a recording session.

"So," explains Lady Valerie, "this is a 'touring' podium."

Undoubtedly it got the crushed corner while being trucked and flown around on the orchestra's last tour. It had been a long one, to the East—Philadelphia and New York—and then on a number of college stops in the Southwest and on the Pacific Coast. Normally the orchestra's own stagehands fly with the orchestra and then meet equipment being trucked from stop to stop—clothing, the trunks, the big instruments, the podium. That way, they can make sure that everything is handled carefully. In fact, the same truck crew is usually maintained all through a tour, so that it can fit smoothly into the continuing plans—and learn how to protect the cargo—instead of having the management break in a new crew at every stop. But this tour was so long and fast-paced that planes, not trucks, had to be used for shipping. And the podium had been dropped or severely bumped so that one corner was rounded off.

It had been used after the tour, but not by Solti. He'd gone back to Europe immediately.

There'd been a few weeks of guest conductors. And then the long hot months of summer in which the podium sat unattended.

So it was not until Solti got back that anybody noticed that the podium had a defect.

And then it had been noticed in moments: Solti's perfectionism.

"Don't worry, Mrs. Solti," said Palecek. "We'll take care of it." He is as fiercely protective of Solti's good health as Solti's wife is.

The podium was not only fixed but repainted white—in time for the first concert.

The buzzer sounded in the office of Radivoj Lah, the personnel manager and string-bass player. He waited for one minute. Already some of the brass players were onstage and working on their parts in the next rehearsal number: *Men and Mountains* by Charles Ruggles. Then he took two steps across the hall and opened the door to Solti's dressing room. "Ready," he said.

A minute later, onstage, Solti turned the pages of the score. Ruggles was a most curious composer. A "wiry, salty, disrespectful, and splendidly profane man," he lived until he was ninety-five years old—he died in 1971—and yet produced only eight works preserved in the musical literature. (One reason may be that he was also very deep into painting. His works are included in several major American collections.) Despite this spare output, Ruggles has had a deep influence on American concert music; his concepts were always of great forces meeting, and his musical painting of these confrontations had a touch of the apocalypse. Indeed, *Men and Mountains* was taken from a line by poet William Blake: "Great things are done when men and mountains meet."

Now Solti indicated the first movement. "Let us just play it. Up to the very end," he said. "Except for the beginning." As the orchestra swung into the deep sonorities and pounding rhythms that were to interpret the wild, gigantic, tortured symbols of Blake's imagination, Solti conducted with his head down. He was watching the score carefully. He'd studied it, of course, but he'd never heard the music. And his first movement was a curious one. It was actually the last movement of an earlier Ruggles work, *Men and Angels*. That work had not won much renown, except for a central movement called "Angels." Indeed, part of it had never been published or performed. So Ruggles took the last movement of that symphony and made it—through rewriting and reorchestration—the first movement of *Men and Mountains*.

Though the work demanded concentration on everybody's part, there was a variety of emotions and experiences running through the orchestra. The string bass, or double bass, section was characteristic. It had the player oldest in continuous service with the orchestra, Alfred Kovar. He was in his fiftieth year with the Chicago Symphony and, as the momentum of the rehearsal gathered torrential force, he could think of the long weeks in which the orchestra had not played together—eight weeks, almost, since their last performance at Ravinia. "Now it was like we'd never been apart," he says. The section also included the newest man in the orchestra, Roger Cline. He is in his late twenties, a strong-looking, large, somewhat rounded youth with a mustache and easy good humor. He had the "bass player's walk," a careful spraddle-footed pace with the feet set wide apart, as if he were pushing a six-foot-tall string bass in front of him. (One day one of his colleagues in the orchestra described the walk with earthy eloquence —and high accuracy—as "the walk of a man who's got a load in his pants.") Roger is not the youngest member of the orchestra; there are several people younger than he. But he is the newest one: he'd gotten out of the army just under four months earlier—he'd played in the Special Forces band at West Point—and he'd flown out to Chicago for an audition. ("They paid half fare for my bass," he said. The bass occupied the seat beside him.)

"Auditioning is a kind of horror," he says. "It takes a lot of concentration." He'd grown up in Tacoma, Washington, and started playing the violin when he was in fifth grade. But then when he got to the ninth grade, the junior high school got a new string bass and he was nominated to become its master. "I was the largest violin player, so they figured I could handle the bass." The key to the bass, in his view, is not the physical size of the body, but of the hands. His hands are large and meaty, not lean, long, and aesthetic. "It helps to have hands that don't have too long fingers so that you don't have a problem of being too far away from the focal point of the muscle," he says. The part of the bass string that actually sounds—the part above the bridge—is unusually long: three and one-half feet. Since the bass is tuned in fourths, not fifths (as are the other stringed instruments), the left hand need cover only a quarter of that distance, ten and one-half inches, to span a fourth before moving over to the next string. (If it were tuned in fifths, the fingers would have to stretch fourteen inches—and probably couldn't make it.) But Roger Cline is not worried personally about the stretch of the hand so much as the muscular power it develops to bring the proper pressure on the proper string—which is, of course, heavier and stronger than the strings on the other instruments. In his view—which is not necessarily the universal view of bass players—it is better to have a large palm with strong, even if medium-sized, fingers. "If your fingers are too long, you get much farther away from where the muscles are pushing down, so it takes a little bit more effort to bring the pressures that you want on the string," he says.

He didn't spend his entire youth playing the bass. He was more interested in astronomy, and he went to the University of Michigan to major in it ("I was always interested in science"). It was not until he was a sophomore that he switched over to majoring in music. He got his master's degree in music before going into the army. He was at West Point, in the last year of his enlistment, when he began studying trade papers for auditions. He was ready to try out anywhere, but when he spotted a notice about auditions for bass for the Chicago Symphony Orchestra, he decided to start at the top. He wrote to the Chicago Symphony's personnel manager, Radivoj Lah, who now plays beside him in the bass section, and got the proper papers. He filled them out, sent them back, and got, in return, a letter telling him when and where the first auditions would begin.

The first auditions were in November of the season before. They were held in Orchestra Hall and forty-three candidates showed up to seek this job. That is not terribly unusual: for one job in another section more recently, 126 candidates applied for auditions. The stage of Orchestra Hall is specially fitted out for the auditions. A screen is mounted so that every player will be hidden from the view of the audition committee—made up of members of the orchestra—and eventually of the conductor. The Chicago Symphony was, for a long while, the only symphony orchestra in America which held "blind" auditions. "So that if there are any women among the candidates, or any ethnic groups, they won't be discriminated against," says Roger Cline. The candidates are identified only by number so that the name can't tip off any of the listeners.

"The preliminaries lasted all day," says Roger Cline. It was evening before the forty-three had been narrowed to five and then to three. Solti was supposed to hear them that night, but a conflict came up in his schedule and the final session was

Roger Cline, *bass player.*

Radivoj Lah, *bass player and personnel manager.*

postponed. "They called us all back late in December—the five of us, not just the three," says Cline. He played a bass part out of Beethoven's Fifth Symphony and part of the Paganini *Variations*—just standard literature; nothing tricky at all."

He got the word that he was the choice before Christmas. And then by summer—now out of the army—he was heading for Chicago. He played briefly during the Ravinia season but this was his first glimpse of Solti in action. "He's like I expected. He's very musical and he seems to be very easygoing. That's one thing I noticed about him—a lot of other conductors put themselves on the podium, so to speak, and he doesn't do that. He seems to be a little more outgoing." The small talk, of course, had been a help. "But he's very quick and professional in his work."

The work was going very well, at the moment. Solti appeared satisfied with the first run-through of *Men and Mountains*. He had only a few comments before his mind went on to the next problem. ("The whole orchestra gives my wholly notes," he told the violins at one point. "You alone have the eighths." Then when the violins went at it with zest: "Don't rush me. Don't rush me. Oh lee . . . oh la . . . take your time, now. Ah—with confidentiality . . .") The next problem was the Bach Suite no. 3 in D Major. He would not need the full orchestra for this, but he did not know how much of the orchestra he'd need.

He wanted to make a decision early because the players that weren't needed would be free to go home. That's why the Bach suite was last to be rehearsed, though it would be first to be played on opening night. (If it had been kept in the number-one slot in rehearsal, as well as performance, all the players would have had to stay through the two and one-half hours of rehearsal. This way, roughly three-quarters of them would get a half-hour or forty-five minutes off.)

That's one of the union agreements that works a certain tension on the professionalism of Solti. Under the contract, the rehearsal schedule must be posted in the players' quarters on the Friday before the Tuesday-Wednesday-Thursday rehearsals begin. That tends to limit the conductor while freeing the player. Solti is not opposed to a schedule which will give players free time on numbers on which he doesn't need them. One trouble is that he doesn't know ahead of time how much work—and thus how much time—will be needed for each number. Yet he is committed to each number in a certain order in the two-and-one-half-hour limit. "So we must be better organized than ever," he says. The biggest trouble is on numbers with vocalists or soloists. They often do not arrive in the city until Sunday, Monday, or even Tuesday morning. So they have no voice in the rehearsal schedule; it's been posted for two or three or four days before they show up. "What it means," says Solti, "is that if you have a singer coming, you cannot ask him whether he wants to rehearse in the afternoon or the morning." To be sure, Solti knows the preferences of some singers, but he does not always know the state of their mental or physical fatigue when they arrive in Chicago. He would prefer to schedule their work to fit their own needs, but under the union restrictions, he cannot do that.

On this day, he experimented with orchestras of different sizes. But he narrowed the number of bass players he'd need to two; the other seven were free to go. Only six of them left. The seventh was the man who had been in touch with Roger Cline, and forty-two other bass players, for the audition; he was the man who was responsible for posting the orchestra's rehearsal schedule so all the players could see it; he was responsible for everything from getting rare instruments to putting weekly paychecks into the players' hands.

His name is Radivoj Lah. He is the personnel manager. And now, as the other members drifted off—or stayed onstage to work on the Bach suite—he plunged into his basement office to solve a problem.

Could he—or should he—get a heckelphone?

This is a rare instrument. Sometimes years go by without the orchestra's needing one. The heckelphone is a baritone member of the oboe family. It appears—when it appears at all—mainly in the music of Delius and Strauss. Nine days from the first rehearsal, the orchestra would be playing two pieces by Strauss—the tone poem *Macbeth* and the Dance of the Seven Veils from *Salome*—and the question was whether the orchestra should go to the trouble and expense of getting the instrument.

Lah had examined the scores. He'd considered whether another instrument might play the notes of the heckelphone. That might be a likely alternative: the orchestra does not have a heckelphone in its inventory of instruments. "They cost about a thousand dollars," says Lah, "and you use it once, maybe twice a year. Usually not that often. So it's just sitting around and they get out of repair just sitting around." What he'd been doing is using the friend-of-a-friend approach. Grover Schiltz, the oboe and English horn player, had a friend at the University of Illinois in Urbana who has a heckelphone. "So what we'd been doing is borrowing his. We'd send somebody down there—or he'd send somebody up here—and we'd repair it and have it put into good condition for him, and use it whenever we needed it badly enough," says Lah. And, of course, the orchestra pays for the privilege of using the instrument.

But it is a lot of trouble—involving the 275-mile round trip to Urbana—when the notes might be played by another instrument. Not quite the same, of course, in tone and coloring, but close to it. But Lah thought he should ask Solti whether to get the instrument or make the substitution. "We try to accommodate the conductor whenever we can," says Lah.

So he'd taken a moment of Solti's time during this first rehearsal day to ask: "Do you really want to get that heckelphone? It's a lot of trouble and . . ."

Solti interrupted him. He did want the exact tone and coloring and so he wanted the exact instrument. But he was looking also to the future.

"My dear Mr. Lah, look, we do not talk about programs a year away. But I will tell you something," he said expansively. "We play *Salome* full next year. So we need a heckelphone then. We need a heckelphone now. Let us get the heckelphone." There was one thing which he did not tell him about the still-secret program of the future: that Birgit Nilsson would appear in it.

So Lah got the heckelphone. Not only for this one week but for a year. "The man who owned it just said to go ahead and keep it to use again next year. We'd need it more than he would."

This is just part of the everyday tasks of Radi (pronounced Rahdi) Lah: he may be asked to come up with anything from a musical saw—"Frank's Drum Shop has one that we use"—to a thunder sheet which was used in *Men and Mountains* to express the clash of the elements. ("We have," he said of the upcoming Henze piece, "all the cowbells in inventory.") He may have to come up with a quick replacement for a player who's suffered a nosebleed onstage—as one did not long ago—or one who's suffered an attack of bleeding ulcers (Lah himself has ulcers—"had 'em since I was sixteen"). He may have to recruit new members for auditions or pass on to other players some information on outside job opportunities. ("The other orchestra phones here, not upstairs"—to the management or staff—"to get leads on positions they have to fill.") He has to make sure players know the bus-departure times when on tour—and that if they miss the bus, they meant to miss the bus. His toughest task so far: asking the wives who'd joined the players on the European tour of 1971 to get off the bus and make room for the players when going to and from the concert hall. He is a very equable man and he does not like to hurt people, but "the bus *was* for the players and some of them complained that the buses were getting filled and they couldn't get on them because some players' wives were getting on them first and filling them up. So . . ." the attitude of the nonaccompanied players was that it was up to the husbands to get their wives to the concert on time, not up to the orchestra's bus.

In short, the personnel manager handles everything that concerns the player in his day-to-day dealing with management—when to get paid, when to work, where and when to get on buses, what the player must know simply to function. The personnel manager works on the player's level, not on the management floor, but he is considered part of management by the players—which is to say, he is considered suspect by many players. This is hard on Radi Lah, partially because he does not like corrosive confrontations, partially because he was union steward and head of the players' committee before he became personnel manager. But in the past, the feeling was thoroughly justified.

John Weicher was Lah's immediate predecessor and was, as we've seen, an iron-fisted type who tended to intimidate the players: he represented management to them more than he represented them to management. Lah thinks that Weicher was highly motivated. "He was a little more fierce, I think, because he had this high esteem for the orchestra so that he used to do things that were not even—that did not ever seem to me like they were fair." He cannot be specific. He gropes for an expression of Weicher's attitude in phrases such as: "He had these kinds of feelings: 'You're in a great orchestra, behave yourself, don't get out of line, and don't ask any stupid questions.' " As the union representative, Lah was intimidated and frustrated by him. "He used to brush me off and I didn't know what to do because I wasn't used to this kind of treatment. The people I associated with were nice and polite and he'd brush me off, you know?" Even today Lah is aggravated by the memory. "I'd go in to see him and he'd be playing cribbage and he wouldn't pay attention to me. I didn't know how to handle this. I'm not a guy who comes on strong. I do not like that kind of an attitude and I do not do it myself to the other players." But Lah was persistent and insistent. His stewardship with the union was in the tense times of the late 1960s and "I decided he had to have some kind of respect for that relationship." So one day, when he went to Weicher with a problem and got the usual brush-off, "I said to him, 'Look, John, this is something serious and if you don't want to talk to me right now, something is going to happen that won't be good for the whole orchestra.' He finally said, 'Okay, if it's a serious problem.' " Thereafter, Lah knew that he could always get Weicher's ear, if not always his cooperation.

He was so successful that John S. Edwards picked him to succeed Weicher. Edwards discerned, not long after he came in, that the "Weicher problem" would have to be solved. John was getting up in years; he'd already given up his post as conductor of the Chicago Civic Orchestra and he'd moved from concertmaster —that is, leader of all the violins—to the first chair in the second violin section. He was, in fact, soon to die of cancer. So Edwards persuaded Weicher that a change would be beneficial, and an announcement was made that Weicher had elected to give up his post as personnel manager. Then Edwards asked Lah to take Weicher's place.

"I was taken by surprise. I didn't know what to say," says Lah. "This position was seemingly on the other side of the fence for me. It was in opposition to all I was and all I felt at the time, and I did not know if I could make an adjustment." Before he took the job, he talked candidly with Edwards. He told him that if the squabbles between management and the players became worse, "I will go with the guys in the orchestra. He said, 'Okay, that is what we want in the job. We want somebody who has an interest in what's happening downstairs.' " So Lah agreed to try it out for a year. At the end of the first year, he decided he wanted to stay on as personnel manager, and he has. "It was amazing. All of a sudden I became a father confessor—the guys came in with all their personal problems and it began to shake me up a little bit. They wanted advice and all of a sudden I was a man of great enough knowledge to tell them what to do about their personal problems." That isn't still always the case, but yet Lah feels that he's "in a position to do things for people."

The position of player doubling as personnel manager is so little known, yet so important, that it is useful to examine just how a Radivoj Lah rises to the post. This is not to suggest that there are a simple formula and constant temperament for the job. Radi Lah's temperament, for example, is not so pungent or pugnacious as that possessed by John Weicher. Indeed, he tends to force himself to the "public" manifestations of his life. He gets up at six o'clock in the morning, for example, to go jogging, because it's dark at that time and he doesn't want to be seen. "I'm a little self-conscious about it—I think that all my neighbors are watching from their windows—which is ridiculous; they're all sleeping still. But it bothers me, anyway."

Nor does he have the pugnacious man's looks. In fact, he doesn't even look like a man named Radivoj Lah: he's light-skinned with bright blue eyes and blond hair turning to white. The look of anger or irritation is quick to pass over his face but not the rigid self-satisfied look of the boss. He is not Indian, as some might think from his name. He is Slovene—"the northern provinces of Yugoslavia," he says. Many of his people are blond and blue-eyed, but not all: "I have several cousins who look very Italian, because they are very dark and swarthy, and yet there is no Italian in my family anywhere." His name, like that of many old European families, stems from the work that the family did in the Middle Ages. "*Lah* is actually derived from the word *vlah*. A *vlah* was a person who worked in the vineyards, who picked grapes and squeezed grapes." Over the centuries, the V was dropped from the word, and the name, and all that remained was *lah*.

Lah wasn't born in Yugoslavia; he was born in Waukegan, Illinois. His family had a sense of inner liberation and a tradition of hard work. The former can be seen from his name of Radivoj. It wasn't his father's name. It was the name of one of his mother's before-marriage boyfriends. "I was the last of five kids," says Lah, "and so she thought, 'By, golly, I'm going to name this one 'Radivoj'—she liked the name and she thought this might be the last chance. So here I am." What did his father think of having a son named for an old flame? "He thought it was okay. He didn't mind."

His father wasn't working in the vineyard, of course, in Waukegan, Illinois. Nor was he working in music. He operated a crane at a tanning company in Waukegan. "My mother did a little work in the factory when they needed a hand. I have a picture of her in her factory uniform—black blouse and long bloomers all the way down to her ankles." His mother thought it was proper attire for young Radivoj. He used to go swimming on the lakefront off Waukegan with all his clothes on: "My mother insisted that I wear all my clothes because"—with his fair skin—"I burned too badly."

He got into music because of a brother, not because of his parents. "He played the fiddle. Jazz. He wasn't really interested in the classics," says Lah. "He just said one day, 'You take up the bass and I'll get a dance band and you can play in the band!' " So Lah took up the bass. But not in a seriously musical way.

He did not drift into becoming a musician of a symphony-orchestra quality. He willed it for himself. The turning point came when he was at the University of Missouri at Columbia, not long before the start of World War II. "A friend of mine, another bass player, wanted to go bicycling through Europe. You know, take a freighter over and then go bicycling all through Europe? We had it all planned—and then up popped the old practical side of me.

"I thought, 'What am I going to do? Just be a bum? Kind of enjoy life doing things like this? Or am I going to get practical and settle down and decide what I'm going to do?' " This was, as we've noted, before World War II, when the answers were different from those a later generation of college students might offer. "I thought, 'I'm going either to be a good bass player or a bum,' " he goes on. "So I pulled out of the project. My friend eventually got somebody else to go with him. What I did was stay down there in Columbia one summer and I practiced eight hours a day—the whole summer. I figured that if I were working in a factory, I would have to work eight hours a day. Why don't I practice eight hours a day? So I did." That gave him a strong base of rising skill. "And from there the momentum just kept going."

He didn't stop at that point and cruise. He took on a harder discipline. He decided to study under a superb bass player named Warren Benfield, just a few years older than Lah and then living in St. Louis. He'd hitchhike to St. Louis—it was a two-and-one-half-hour drive each way in preexpressway days. "I'd start early in the morning and get there about nine or ten o'clock," he remembers. "I'd have a lesson usually whenever I got in. If I had to wait, it was because Benfield was down at a rehearsal with the St. Louis Symphony and I'd usually end up downtown. Then he'd drive me to his home, and I'd take a lesson, and he'd drive me over to the highway and I'd start to hitchhike back home again." He did that twice a week for a couple of years. "I traveled forty thousand miles hitchhiking back and forth between St. Louis and college," he says.

It turned out to be a valuable investment. For Radi Lah not only learned to play the bass but acquired a deep friend and longtime admirer in Warren Benfield. For Benfield himself was to carve a singular career, playing bass in the Philadelphia Orchestra and then moving to the Chicago Symphony. When the Chicago needed another bass player, Benfield nominated Lah. By that time, the latter had gone into the army and been discharged because of his ulcer; he spent the next six years with the Minneapolis Symphony before being summoned to Chicago. That was in 1949. He's celebrating his twenty-fifth anniversary with the orchestra in this season.

He maintains, of course, the same practice schedule that every other player keeps. He's never gone in much for a heavy teaching schedule outside the concert hall. At one time, he played a lot of jazz in his other hours: he was in a combo at the famed Preview Lounge in the Loop for several years (some of them before he joined the Chicago Symphony). The bass player he idolized then—and whose records he still collects—was Slam Stewart. His skill as a jazzman was such that Stan Kenton once phoned him and asked Lah to join his outfit. Lah had just signed to play at Ravinia with the Chicago Symphony and he was playing several nights a week at a nightclub called Mangam's Chateau in Chicago's western suburbs. So he had job security and income available without leaving home to go on the road. And yet he was ready to say "yes—I'll take it" when Kenton asked him to think it over. "I pulled all my Kenton albums out and I was figuring out all the things I would have to do to get ready to join Kenton," says Lah. The next day Kenton called back and said he might have to withdraw the offer. He thought he should give his current bass player—who'd been drinking a little too much —another chance. And he doubted the wisdom of tempting a player like Lah to leave the Chicago Symphony. Lah wasn't convinced. He knew that Kenton was going to be playing at Chanute Field, near Champaign, Illinois, a few nights later and so he drove down there to see Stan Kenton in the flesh. And let the situation help him make up his mind . . . to join the jazzmen.

"All these people are crowded around the stage door, getting Stan Kenton's autograph—he really is a marvelous guy, just a beautiful fellow. And I'm standing there and my hair is long—I always wore it kind of long—and he looks at me and smiles and says, 'You must be a musician.' So I said, 'I'm Radi Lah.' And he pulled me into his dressing room."

To talk. And talk. And talk.

They went outside—"it was a very hot night"—and they talked some more.

And the burden of Stan Kenton's conversation was, "Why do you want to do something like this? You're a symphony man."

"You have to be kidding! Man, I've been dreaming about this! to play with a band like yours!"

Well, Kenton was very pleased. And very savvy. He could judge the balance of the quality of life for a sideman in a jazz combo and a string bass in the Chicago Symphony. And so he urged Radi to go home and stay with the symphony.

"I didn't have the courage to tell him I had my bass in the car"—just in case he asked Radi to join the outfit that night.

"That was my total experiece with Stan Kenton."

Today Radi Lah spends his nonplaying time in the administrative work of personnel manager. He'll soon have to make a choice of how much he loves it. For the union contract this time specifies that he'll have to choose between being a bass player and a personnel manager; the union no longer wants a player doubling in the role. He appreciates the reason. "They don't want anyone in management taking part in the players' pension plan," he says—as he might. "I'm torn between the two because I'm in a position to do things for people," he says. "I get a kick out of doing the good things. I do not like to do the bad things—that upsets me. It's going to be a rough decision to make."

In the meantime, as personnel manager, he goes about duties that are sometimes very simple and often very complex. Simple: he signals the players when to be onstage to tune to the A. Under Reiner, everybody had to be onstage and tuned five minutes before the conductor arrived onstage. "Five minutes—that seemed sort of a waste," says Lah. So he cut it down to three minutes, then two minutes, and now one minute. By the time the orchestra gets settled and is tuned to the A, Solti will be precisely forty seconds late in getting onstage.

He keeps track of who is working extra hours in the orchestra and whether they've played the extra services. "An extra rehearsal"—a full rehearsal—pays around $40 per man," he says. "An extra concert pays $60 per man. The base pay is $350 per week. So if a guy has one extra concert, he's going to get $410 a week."

Just as important, he finds out what—and who—will be needed to play a certain piece or perhaps an entire concert. "Take a look at this week," he said, picking up a score for the concert of an upcoming week. He'd studied the score and quickly found that the full orchestra wasn't required. Sometimes it's the composer's idea. Sometimes it's the conductor's idea. He may have sent along a marked copy of the score indicating what he'll need for the various parts. "Twenty-four violins —twelve and twelve," says Lah of this score, instead of the customary thirty-two, sixteen first and sixteen second violins. "Ten cellos"—instead of eleven or twelve—and "ten violas and eight basses"—instead of the full complement of twelve violas and nine basses.

If he finds that fewer players are needed in any section, he'll check a scrupulously kept rotation schedule to find out who is eligible for the time off. In this case, for example, he could free twelve strings. Just who they'll be is posted on the bulletin board so the players themselves—and everybody in the orchestra—will know who is free in that piece. The idea is to make sure that everybody is equally

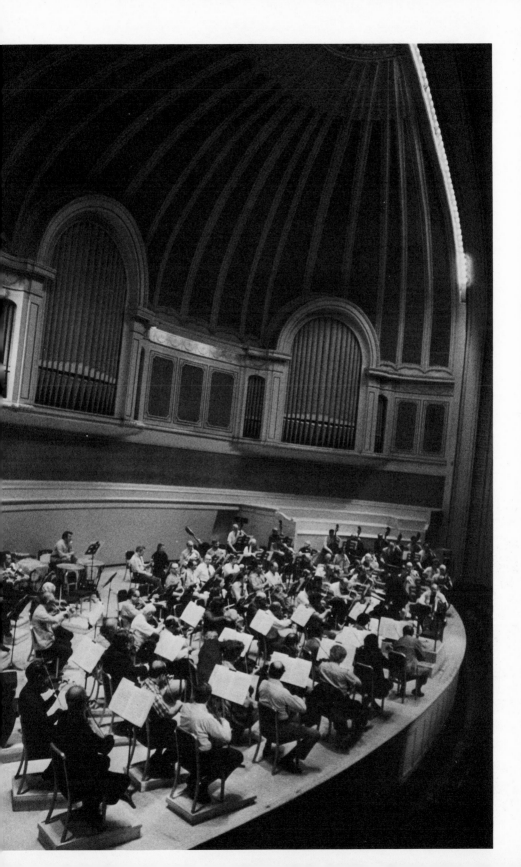

utilized and everybody is given an equal shot at time off. In addition, the section leader may want to play a solo in one number but not another: "Clevenger will take the solo in this piece," says Lah of the French horn section, "but he'll let his associate, Tom Howell, have the solo in the other." Again, he takes a look at the score and finds out the number of woodwinds that will be needed. There's a passage calling for four saxophones. Though the orchestra has some spectacularly skillful saxophone players—most conspicuously Burl Lane, the bassoon player —the saxophone is not normally a symphony instrument. "So it looks like I'm going to have to hire four saxophone players," he says. He's got plenty of sources for them: his own lists, accumulated through the last five years or so, and the recommendations of the men and women in the orchestra.

But there are always situations such as the current one with the Bach suite, when Lah doesn't know how many men will be needed to play the piece. In fact, Solti himself didn't know. Onstage, he was working through passages of the Bach with different numbers of strings. At full strength there were sixty-four strings in the orchestra as the season opened: sixteen first violins, sixteen second violins, twelve violas, eleven cellos, and nine basses. Solti wanted to make something of a chamber music ensemble of this aggregation, so he knew he would cut those numbers in half, and then cut them in half again. But he did not know quite the balance among the strings he'd have left. He tried different numbers—at one point he had more than thirty players onstage—and then dismissed them one by one, occasionally adding a player here while dropping one in another section. Until finally he had it: "Would you play six, please," he said to the first violins. He meant "Would six of the first violins remain?" Similarly with the second violins—"four, please." He went through the string section until he had every-thing balanced as he desired. There was no time wasted on his part in choosing which men in each section would stay; it is the conviction of the players in the Chicago Symphony that any six of the first violins can—if they can play in the Chicago Symphony in the first place—meet the needs and demands of any conductor; he does not have to choose the *first* six among the first violins. Nor does he have to know who will stay and who will go. Thanks to the rotation system of the players, and the schedule-keeping of Radi Lah, that has all been decided and the men themselves know which of their number will leave and who will remain onstage for the Bach. And when the conductor chooses a number, the rest simply leave. Quietly.

"Quietly," says Solti. "Ah! Now: 6-4-4-2-1." It sounded as though he were calling out signals for the defense in football. But it was merely his code for remembering the balance for the Bach suite: six first and four second violins, four violas, two cellos, and a bass. To these he added a harpsichord, three trumpets, two oboes, and a contrabassoon. Twenty-four players in all, out of the 105 in the orchestra. When Bach did it, he had at his disposal—thanks to his royal patron —an ensemble of eighteen men.

Though the tiny, gracious, precise sound is not what the Chicago Symphony—or Solti—is noted for, there was great satisfaction among some of the men in playing this Bach suite. On the one hand, the air which follows the overture is one of the most beautiful and loved movements in the classical repertory. On the other hand, it demonstrated the variety of skills of the Chicago Symphony, that it is not, in truth, a "single-sound" orchestra—that it can produce the vast variety of sounds, with equal skills, that are demanded by a cultivated audience.

Solti himself reacted to the dimensions of the music with a much smaller, more secluded style on the podium. At many of the points during rehearsal he did not indulge in the broad, angular sweeps of his Teutonic response. Instead he kept his arms close, often barely beating with the stick, indicating the tempo by bouncing up and down on his toes, then moving to a simple, intimate, clean, firm beat with the baton. ("Stay piano . . . stay piano," he whispered to the harpsichord.) Then at 4:26 P.M., four minutes before the deadline, he gave the final cutoff. "Okay," he said. "I thank you very much."

But it was not really the end of the preparation or his participation in it. A few of the players remained onstage to practice their parts for a few minutes longer. Ray Still was among them. The oboes had a significant role not only in the Bach suite but in the Beethoven Third. In the first movement of the Beethoven, the oboe introduces a new theme—following a climax—in the somewhat remote key of E minor. In the second movement, the oboe takes up the melody between the principal themes—a sad, lonely, and lovely melody, a resigned answer to the funereal mutterings of the bass. In the fourth movement, the oboe takes up one of the variations—a melody or tune—that Beethoven intended to be played against the theme that is played against the bass. These parts, as well as the Bach suite, are so important that Solti continually turned and looked out into the darkness of Orchestra Hall and asked, "Can you hear the oboe? Can you hear the oboe?"

From the darkness, Henry Mazer, the associate conductor who was sitting in the hall, following the score, would answer. Not only in the affirmative but in terms of the quality of sound. For the oboe is the soprano of the double-reed family of the woodwinds. (The bassoon, naturally, is the bass of the family.) The danger is that those high tones of the oboe—the total quality of the instrument's music—will be lost in the peculiar acoustics of Orchestra Hall. Solti, of course, can hear the oboe. His podium is only a few feet away from the instrument. But he is never quite sure that the audience can hear it. Or can hear the total quality of Still's sound. At one moment in the rehearsals, he climbed down off the stage and went back into the darkness to talk with Mazer. He simply signaled the orchestra to start and gave it a downbeat while he could still be seen in the halo of light on the main floor just off the stage. Then he moved back into the darkness and, while the orchestra played in perfect unity without a conductor, moved about to determine how well the oboe could be heard in different sections of the main floor. "That is one of his chief concerns," says his wife, Valerie. "He is not just playing the music for himself or for the orchestra. He is playing it for the audience and he wants the audience to listen and to hear."

After the rehearsal, as Still—among others—engaged in a little personal practice, Solti was engaged in conversation at the podium. In the wake of his first rehearsals, there are always a few players who approach him to chat for a few moments, perhaps about the music, perhaps about his availability for a game of bridge. Solti is an enthusiastic, even passionate bridge player, and one of the inner contacts he has with the Chicago Symphony is playing bridge. One of his constant partners is co-concertmaster Victor Aitay, like Solti a Hungarian, and one of the few players who is likely to show up—invited, of course—at a social gathering put on for, or by, Solti. And so Aitay was one of those who fell into postrehearsal conversation with the maestro on this day.

As the conservation wore on, Solti was caught—momentarily at first—by the sound of the oboe. He glanced once or twice at Still, then returned to the conversation. Again the delicate beauty of Still's playing caught his attention. "No—a B-natural," he said at one point. Then again, on the playing of a grace note, "No—not in the second measure." Still played the second measure again, with the grace notes. He was not improvising it; the grace notes were written on his score. Solti broke off the conversation with Aitay and went to Still's stand. There, marked in black pencil, were the grace notes—marked in by an earlier player under another conductor. "Not on my score," says Solti. He went back to the podium to compare his score with Still's. They were different—and he could not tolerate the difference. All the players should have the same score, marked in the same way, as his own. This is not, in fact, always the case: some of the scores have been used for decades under the Chicago Symphony, and the players who mark in notes and notations remember their markings in the concert of the moment, but they don't remember them the next time they play the music under a different conductor. Or it may happen that a different instrumentalist is given the score.

The first time the Bach suite had been played by the Chicago Symphony, for example, was on October 24, 1891, only a few weeks after the orchestra had been organized by Theodore Thomas. The last time it had been played was under Jean Martinon on April 2, 1965, some eight and one-half years before this rehearsal. Either way, it's a long time for a player to remember accurately the meaning of the markings on the score—a Martinon, for example, is more likely to seek a grace note than is a Solti, if only because of the French lilt compared with the Teutonic sonority.

"Somebody get me Mr. Sayers," says Solti. Lionel Sayers is the head librarian for the Chicago Symphony. He has the responsibility for some six thousand compositions in the custody of the Chicago Symphony and for delivering any or all of them in good condition to the players. "Many of these pieces are too messy," muttered Solti of the score being used by Ray Still. That is inevitable; they've been used over the years by many players and some of them are so old that they must be patched together with translucent tape by the library staff before being put on the music stands. But his staff does not remove the markings from previous performances or rehearsals because many of the players consider them valuable; the markings tell them what the previous conductor—or perhaps the same conductor, after a number of years have passed—preferred in the way of a particular performance: v's and some inverted v's to indicate up-bowing or down-bowing for the violins, scribblings on tone or loudness (mf., p., sf.), or simply notes that the conductor of the moment wants emphasized or accented. In some cases, scores that are black with the markings of previous users have been delivered to the musicians.

In this case, the three men—Solti, Still, and Sayers—huddled over the scores for a short while. There was no doubt that Solti would get what he wanted—that all the scores would be brought into complete harmony with his own. But it was symbolic, and characteristic, of the contribution of Ray Still: it is in his nature to work to the perfection of these moments, to bring out the utmost in the beauty and capability of the orchestra. And of the oboe.

"That's what I work for," says Still. "What I'm working for constantly is to make the oboe—to be able to play the oboe—so that it doesn't have to have any excuses made for it as a unique instrument of any kind. So many times the oboe is—excuses are made for the oboe because of the so-called extreme difficulty of it." He wants to banish the image of difficulty while expanding the appreciation of the instrument. "In other words, when I play with a fiddle player—the Bach *Double* Concerto, for instance—I don't want the oboe to have any special concession made to it because of its reed and its difficulty. I feel that it should express the same kind of musical ideas that the fiddle player has."

The oboe has had a long tradition of difficulty. The players who worked at the Greek oboe, called the aulos, had to gulp huge quantities of air and exert great—if gradual—pressure on the reed because the instrument took so much strength to play. The legend is that the players' cheeks were strapped in a leather belt so that they would not burst. Even so, it is said, "they blew until they suffered abdominal hemorrhages."

The modern oboe is hardly as taxing. But great legends have built up around it also. One is that the oboe player goes slowly insane from years of playing the instrument. A few of the more droll oboe players disagree. They claim that insanity is the cause, not the effect—that you have to be crazy to take up the instrument in the first place. In general, the idea is that the vibrations of the instrument come slowly to affect the brain. Nobody knows precisely where and how the rumor was born, but Still has a notion about it. "I think the myth got started years ago when there was a New York oboe player who had a monopoly on oboe jobs. There weren't very many oboe players around at the time"—and he didn't want any more. "He was extremely eccentric and I believe he cultivated this business of pretending that the oboe caused you to become insane. There *are* people who try to discourage competition."

He considers the rumor itself preposterous. He ran down a list of oboe players in their seventies and eighties, great figures in the modern history of the oboe—"sharp as a tack . . . steady as a rock and a highly intelligent gentleman. . . . I don't think there's any higher percentage of eccentricity, or insanity, among oboe players than among any other instrument."

Still does not even consider the oboe to be the most difficult of the woodwind instruments. "The clarinet seems to be, even though it's the most common of the woodwind instruments." Yet there are a lot of clarinet players on the high school level and post-high school. "At the professional level, there are just as many oboe players around as there are clarinet players; in fact, there seem to be more good

Ray Still, principal oboist.

oboe players than clarinet players at the highest artistic levels."

This is not to say that he considers the oboe an easy instrument to master. "Probably the most difficult thing about the oboe is that the instrument itself is very delicately adjusted. The mechanism is very hard to keep exactly in adjustment." That is a reason that the oboe is used to give the A to the orchestra in the tuning-up period just before the concert starts—because the oboe's basic pitch cannot be changed, subject almost to carpentry. The oboe, like the clarinet, has a series of holes that are closed or opened to provide the different notes. "In the clarinet, your fingers constitute the pads for closing the holes, for the most part," says Still. "But on the oboe, your finger never touches the actual hole. Your finger touches the silver key, which in turn activates the pad that closes the hole. So consequently, all those pads have to be finely adjusted and when any tiny bit of adjustment goes out, the instrument doesn't play right. So you have to be—or have—a marvelous repairman, and you have to know a lot about the instrument itself."

Still also concedes that the oboe inspires an acute physical reaction in some people, but not because of the vibrations or because of the sound. It's because of the air control vital to playing the instrument. "I mean, students will many times get dizzy when they're playing," he says. "I used to do that when I was a kid. I used to get dizzy and kind of keel over, almost." The reason is the conflict between the need of the players for air—and oxygen—and the need of the instrument for almost no air, for a very slow input of air with no gulping by the player. "I had one student who actually vomited all over and fainted dead away on the rug," says Still. "I had him go see a doctor." Still knows that many young people, without matured lung capacity, "get a little dizzy, light-headed, hyperventilated, and so forth." But the reaction of this one, he says, "scared the hell out of me." The youth had a complete checkup and came back to Still with all the proper medical credentials. "The doctor said he was all right—nothing wrong with him. So I took him back again and first thing you know he fainted and vomited all over the rug—the same thing again. So I got rid of him. I said, 'You shouldn't play the oboe if you've got something wrong with you that way.' "

The problem suffered by young people is not from having to blow so hard. Quite the contrary. "It's difficult because it takes so little air. You get bottled up with air. You *look* like you're blowing your brains out because it *doesn't* take much air at all." The look of exertion is caused directly by keeping the air in the body and controlling the muscles of the face, throat, and chest to let the breath out very, very slowly. A player doesn't blow into an oboe as he does, say, into the clarinet or flute. Instead he lets air escape—seep—into the instrument at a very slow and carefully controlled rate. The idea is that the player has enough air to play the most complex of phrases without opening his mouth for a new gulp of air—for that gulp will destroy the tone and the phrasing.

"I can hold a note for eighty seconds," says Still. "I haven't tried it lately 'cause it's a kind of silly thing to try." But for exercises, or as a demonstration, he'll take a taxing oboe solo from the repertory and reel it off breathlessly—literally. "The Tchaikovsky Fourth Symphony, you know, where the oboe starts the second movement"—in a very slow, sweet lament—"I'll play it all in one breath." Clark

Brody, the principal clarinet of the symphony, timed him the other day and said he "couldn't believe it." The reason? "You played that whole thing on one breath and it takes at least forty-five seconds to play." Says Ray Still: "Well, forty-five seconds seems like an awful lot. But you can hold your breath I'm sure, for forty-five seconds if you practice just a little bit. Especially if you practice letting it out very slowly"—like a swimmer under water. "But it would seem interminable if you didn't practice it, work up to it bit by bit, if you didn't keep your cool.

"So with oboe playing, you have to kind of keep your head. Even though you don't seem to be getting rid of any air, you just have to hold your breath.

"The difficult thing is that even though it doesn't take much air, you're required to have an extremely steady flow rate of air. And to use the muscles of the body in such a way that it feels that you're getting—you have to pretend to yourself that you're getting rid of huge quantities of air so that the muscles stay in a nonisometric state. You almost have to psych yourself into believing that you're getting rid of much more air than you are."

As it happens, Still knows exactly how much air has to bleed into the oboe as compared with, say, the clarinet. The oboe, he says, uses only 3 liters of air per minute. "It's a very artificial instrument in that sense. It's ridiculous." The clarinet, he says, uses "at least three times as much. I would say it would be more like 10 to 15 liters per minute, normal sound. Maybe more in the low register and less in the high." The tuba, of course, might demand a flow rate forty times that of the oboe—120 or more liters per minute. (The tuba player in the Chicago Symphony, Arnold Jacobs, has made a decades-long, highly scientific study of the flow rate of various instruments—which is why Still knows his flow rate so precisely.) "When you get up to a tiny, high baroque trumpet, why it almost approaches the oboe in the high register," says Still. "Of course, it takes a lot more pressure within the mouth but it has a very low flow rate."

Out of all this emerges a feeling that Ray Still believes that the greatest difficulty in playing the oboe involves the psyche—what you know versus what you believe. "I realize that the hazards of oboe playing involve getting this bottled-up feeling all the time," he says, "So I'm constantly psyching myself into believing I'm *not* getting bottled up. I psych myself into believing that I'm inhaling instead of blowing, sometimes. I use any psychology I can to reverse the process." He tries to insinuate to his mind that he's inhaling when he's really exhaling at an excruciatingly slow pace. It is considerably more convoluted and sophisticated than all this, but the fact is, as Still says, "It's simply a lie. You're actually getting rid of air, no matter what you tell yourself." But the telling prevents the muscles that are involved in breath control from getting locked into a static state instead of being flexible and bellows-like. "See, if you hold yourself down here," says Still, indicating the diaphragm, "without doing it from your chest—just sit tall—and you'll see these muscles come in like crazy. You learn to blow that way so that they don't tighten up. It's a very difficult thing to do."

Still is in his early fifties now, a tall, slender, dark-featured man who wears dark clothes that give him a vaguely clerical look. (He lost twenty-five pounds before this season began. He was keeping in muscular shape by going up every stairway he encountered two steps at a time—four stories of two-stepping to his fourth-floor office and studio at Northwestern University.) He grew up in Los Angeles and got into playing the oboe through the normal route: by playing the clarinet. "I had a clarinet teacher who played second clarinet in the Los Angeles Philharmonic," says Still. "He was fairly pessimistic and very short. I'd say he came up, oh, maybe just above my belt." Still was sixteen at the time. "But I was six-feet-two even at that time and he was about four-feet-eight and he was, oh, he was very pessimistic—with all his students, I'd say. One time I was having some squeaks and he said—in his Italian accent—'Maybe the clarinet is not for you. Maybe you take some instrument like an oboe, a trumpet, a saxophone. You could make some money with those instruments.' He was always disappointed about his ability to make money, you know"—as were most symphony musicians of forty years ago. "He saw the guys in the studios and the recording industry out in LA and Hollywood making lots of money and he was stuck as second clarinet in the symphony. . . . Now things have changed and the recording and the movie industry out there is very, very hard hit because they're doing everything in Europe these days. It's switched around: the symphonies are making the money."

His teacher's advice, and his own inclinations, tempted him toward the oboe. "I used to usher at the Philharmonic Auditorium out in Los Angeles and I'd been watching the oboe player, who was a much greater artist than the clarinet player was," says Still. He also noticed that "clarinet players are a dime a dozen in high school and there aren't many oboe players"—at least not at that time. He has that peculiar strength of character—that determined will—to master the instrument and to give it a range of thought, tone, and expression that is endemic to the superlative artist. It took him to the Kansas City Philharmonic, the Buffalo Philharmonic (under William Steinberg), and the Baltimore Symphony before he came to the Chicago Symphony in Reiner's first year, 1953. The exceptional sound that he brings to the oboe section of the Chicago Symphony begins but does not end with him. For the other members of the section—Richard Kanter, Grover Schiltz, and Michael Henoch—all studied under Still, if not exclusively (as did Henoch), then for a significant time. (Kanter had also studied at the Curtis Institute of Music in Philadelphia.) "So one of the reasons we have a very well integrated oboe section," says Still, "is because we do play the same style and we blend very well."

For his part, the studies have never ceased. "I stress a little different approach than most of the oboe players in the major orchestras of the country in that I've gone much into singing—a lot more deeply than most instrumentalists do." He was absorbed in the sound, particularly as it might apply to he oboe. For he is endlessly seeking a more thoroughly rounded sound, a deeper-dimensioned sound than the wheezy, thin, nasal sound that is so often associated with the oboe, particularly in Europe. He also thought the insights of a singer's breath control would be profoundly useful to playing the oboe. It turned out that the very experience of singing had its own rapture.

"I studied as an amateur for about eight years," he says, "and during that time I would vocalize as much as four or five hours a day. Way too much. I mean, I got obsessed with it. And I—in this period I practiced the singing much more than I practiced the oboe." He was never thinking of taking up singing as a career—of becoming an operatic performer. "But I was just fascinated by singing. To see if I *could* sing. To see if I could apply the same technique used in singing—which must necessarily be very efficient—to the playing of the oboe, which tends to be very artificial. The oboe player always wants to sound like a singer. But what they do physically with a breath—because of the extremely low flow rate the oboe takes—makes them end up grunting and straining and doing all kinds of things that a singer could never do and get away with it. So this is one of the reasons that I studied singing so long." He tended to ease off the obsessive aspects of singing in the late 1960s, though "I still vocalize a little now." He also still uses what he learns. "I teach all my students these techniques—techniques that are basically used to counteract the evil tendencies of the oboe. That is, the tendency that the oboe has to make you play in a tight, constricted way."

And yet all these efforts are only the visible parts of mastering the oboe; the invisible work involves a technical skill which few people—other than woodwind players—ever consider: making the reeds for the instrument. "I'd say it takes four or five years before you really can begin to make reeds," says Still, "but the thing is that your reed-making ability goes hand in hand with your ability as an oboe player. So that as you progress as an oboe player, you also progress as a reed-maker, and vice versa." How long does that take? "I'd say reed-making takes twenty to thirty years to learn." Why is it so vital? "You can't really become a fine oboe player, with great control, unless you can make reeds. Now it's true that in Europe they don't have quite the tradition of spending so much time on reeds. Many times they tend to, well, minimize, the art of reed-making. Consequently they accept a more nasal sound—I would say that's why our critics many times call, when they hear Europeans, they call them the 'bagpipe' and 'duck-hunting' school of oboe playing. I mean it sounds like duck calls to them." The traditions of the oboe in the American orchestra were—until Still—strongly influenced by the sound of the oboe that emanated from Europe. The reason: the top players in the Boston Symphony, the New York Philharmonic, and the Philadelphia Orchestra in the past—of the days when these, and not the Chicago Symphony, were the preeminent orchestras in America—came out of or followed the European school. But Still did not study under them. In general, he feels that the European school of the oboe is a little more "devil may care" than the new American school. He feels the latter is more cautious—and that caution may have something to do with all the time invested in making reeds. "Our players become obsessed with reed-making a lot of the time," he says. "And by being obsessed with reed-making, they don't practice as much as they should; they spend all of their time on the reeds."

He feels that this discipline affects the personality of the oboe player. "There are some oboe players who are very neurotic about reeds. Maybe they all tend to be a little that way." Still describes with third-person objectivity—almost as if he weren't involved—the kind of person who has his role and the impact that constant reed-making has on such a player. "The first oboe player in the orchestra many times is a kind of prima donna type and, in a sense, temperamental. He tends to be a little neurotic because of this reed situation, and always feeling at the mercy of his reeds."

Well, how long does it take him to make a reed?

"You can make one in ten minutes. But sometimes you'll spend two hours babying it and touching it up and testing it." Moreover, not all reeds will work, and the player doesn't know it until after he's invested all the time and skill in making the reed. The estimates of throwaways among reeds runs as high as eight failures in nine tries. "If you have a really good reed, it'll work for everything," says Still. "But since you don't have really good reeds all the time, you tend to accept fairly mediocre reeds." Of course, he adds, "What is a mediocre reed to me might be, to a student, a marvelous reed. But what you have to do is learn to play on fairly mediocre reeds because you're not going to get the great ones all the time. If you have a great one, it'll play Debussy, it'll play Bach, it'll play anything.

"But there are certain reeds that simply have greater requirements. You might have a piece, like a concerto, that calls for very high notes and very low notes, played at all dynamic levels. If you're playing the *Unfinished* Symphony of Schubert or *Le Tombeau de Couperin* of Ravel or the Brahms violin concerto, you'll have greater requirements in a reed. For the Brahms violin concerto, you want a reed that is easy to play very long phrases on without getting exhausted. If you're playing the Tchaikovsky Fourth Symphony, you want a special—you simply want a finer reed. Well, maybe not just finer, just one that is easier to control." The demands on the conscientious player to produce the right reed are all the greater because composers write scores for the oboe that demand everything from an earthy blatancy to a dreamy, melancholy, detached, tender quality. "It brings a ray of hope," said Berlioz of the oboe, "in the midst of torment."

The material for the reed is a cane that comes from special fields in southern France. "It's cured and dried a certain amount and then they send it to us, for about $20 a pound," says Still. The cane is really a stalk of bamboo that is cut to a

certain length, and then split by the player in three parts. The segment is then put into a planing device—"it costs about $300"—which gouges out the interior of the segment, "with a curved blade, not a straight one. It scoops out the cane from the inside."

The tip of the reed then must be cut and shaved so that it has an almost imperceptible thickness. "You get it down to a couple thousandths of an inch tolerance," says Ray Still. He estimates it as .0023 inches. One reason is that the reed of the oboe is actually a double reed—two reeds bound together through which the air is allowed to seep at an eloquent rate and produced a controlled vibration. The clarinet, by way of contrast, has a single wide reed which vibrates against the mouthpiece of the instrument. And its reeds can be bought ready-made and then shaved to perfect quality.

The reeds that Ray Still makes last for "about twenty hours of blowing. Five or six rehearsals and three or four concerts—that's a good long life to get out of an oboe reed." He usually has twelve reeds with him at any one time, and he carries them all onstage. ("We're the only ones who are permitted to take satchels like this onstage. Because we have all our tools and reeds in there," he says, indicating his bag.) Usually, Still has three reeds that are ready for activity. All three have been tested and kept "wet" in case they're needed during the performance. The failure factor he listens for in good reeds is fatigue. "This is living material," he says of the reeds, "or at least ex-living material. The high frequeny of the oboe vibration tends to fatigue the materials quicker, for instance, than an English horn reed." The English horn is the alto cousin of the oboe; it is five tones lower than the oboe and "it is slower-vibrating, even much more than a bassoon reed."

Not only do fatigue and the demands of the music affect his choice of reeds, so also do the temperature and humidity. "We like about 30 to 40 percent humidity to make the reeds act normally," says Still. "So in the wintertime, when the heat is on—a low humidity—we have to make quite different reeds than in the summer time at Ravinia, with the high humidity." As it happens, Orchestra Hall is a very low-humidity auditorium. "Willard Elliot, our first bassoon, goes crazy with it," says Still. "He says that it's so dry that it collapses his reeds. You see, the minute you take the reed out of your mouth, it gets dry in the atmosphere. So we have to keep sucking the reed to make sure that it doesn't dry out."

This is why he has three reeds ready for use. And why two of them are always in a state of "wet ready." "I've got the current reed that I've decided to go with on that day. But I've also got the standby reed, and I have to know whether the standby will play if I pick it up after it's been sitting there for quite a while. It has to be the kind of standby reed that'll play when you need it in a hurry." It is not unusual for Still to change reeds during a concert. Or even, for that matter, during a particular number or during a solo. "I've changed reeds between the second and third movements of the Mozart oboe concerto—I was standing up in front of the orchestra and found that the reed I was playing on was giving out. And I had to switch and play the last movement on a different reed."

The professional imperatives for shaping reeds and the personal imperatives for improving the sound of his instrument tend to bring a great deal of pressure on the conscientious oboe player. For extraneous reasons, Ray Still came, in the 1960s, under a greater pressure; he became renowned more for his embattled stand in the orchestra than his exalted skill on the oboe. In a sense, he thinks it followed from his early days—even in Baltimore—in favor of a players' committee and a unified voice in talks with management. "I'm an old union agitator," he says simply. He feels privileged to have been in the very crucible which brought about the changes in the Chicago Symphony Orchestra. "They've been through terrific turmoil," he says of his fellow players. "Much more so than other orchestras." He feels that his position was endangered once and is honored today because he was one of the few first-chair players who threw their fortunes in with the *tutti*—the back-stand players who felt, through the years, that they were ignored or abused by management. "They would split the orchestra purposefully," says Still of the management of the past, "by keeping the *tutti* down in their salaries and by paying very high salaries to some of the first-chair men." He fought the system, though he had the benefits of being a first-chair man. "The men know what I've been through—even though I was a first-chair player, I stood up for them. I was active when it was dangerous, you know, and that's what the guys appreciate." He's been elected to various posts within the players' committee many times over, but now he's not quite so active in that area. The orchestra is unified now and does not need the kind of determination that Still is likely to bring to it.

Nor is he a congenital complainer about conductors. To the contrary. He feels—with the sole exception of his abrasive relations with Jean Martinon—that he gets along with conductors quite well. "My relationship with Reiner was marvelous," he says. "I felt almost like a son to him. Because he brought me here, and I was the first change he made—in the sense of firing someone and replacing him with a first-chair man. . . . I've gotten along with every conductor well, except this Martinon character. I mean, I get along marvelously with Giulini and with Solti. I've never had any trouble with conductors."

Solti realized the tension that the "Still situation" created in the orchestra and, because of the man he is, decided to try to resolve it. That players do not speak to each other is not unusual in the symphony orchestra: the Philadelphia Orchestra had a situation in which the first oboe and the first flute—as in the Chicago Symphony—didn't speak to each other. The Chicago Symphony itself has two trombone players and two viola players who are not on speaking terms. It is, perhaps, more acute in terms of the first oboe and first flute, if only because they are part of the "woodwind quadrangle" set up just in front of the conductor. "You want the first flute, the first oboe, the first bassoon, and the first clarinet to be close together right where they can hear each other," says Still. But the distances are so great, personally, that they can't reach each other with words.

Solti undertook an effort which involved him in something he, and most conductors, carefully avoid: the private lives—and enmities—of the players.

He called Still aside one day and said, by way of preamble, "Mr. Still, I am very, very happy, delighted that you are playing with us. I consider you a great artist." And then, as Still remembers it, he got around to the point of the conversation:

"There's only one thing. Everything is so marvelous about this orchestra, we're

getting along so well and everything, but I have understood that—you don't *speak*
to certain members of the orchestra." Only to three other principal players; he got
along fine with the rest. "Now I'm not criticizing you for this," said Solti. "I don't
really know what took place but I understand there's some bitterness there . . ."
There was the classic awkward pause. "I understand certain people were involved.
But if I can be of any help in smoothing things over, I would love to do this, because
I hate to see any unhappy situations existing here." It was, all things considered, a
remarkable effort on the part of Solti. As an archetype, he shares—with all
conductors—a preference for distance from the players and their problems. But
here he was taking the risk of his persona and his professional credentials. And all
to heal a rupture in the symphony.

It didn't work.

Still has his standards, just as Solti has his.

He turned down the offer of Solti's intercession. He explained that he was not
that eager to talk with those who, he felt, had not done right by him. "I just said, 'I
play better with Peck now than when I used to speak to him.' "

And that is where the matter ended. In simmering antagonism.

There were four rehearsals for the opening concert. One on Tuesday, two on
Wednesday, the dress rehearsal on Thursday morning.

After the last rehearsal, the patterns of the players were fixed. Some—like Victor
Aitay and Frank Miller and Milton Preves, all principals—lingered to practice with
the Chicago Symphony String Quartet. . . . Some, like Arnold Jacobs, the tuba
player, went to their university classrooms and workshops to spend the afternoon.
. . . Some, like Don Koss, went home for the interim period. . . . A few, like
Donald Evans, a violist, Joe Golan, Jim Hansen, and Frank Fiatarone, all violinists, stopped in the lounge for another game of bridge.

Georg Solti left quickly after the last rehearsal. He'd promised to take his
daughter Gabrielle for a walk. "We walked for a block along the lakefront," he
says. The waves were gathering into breakers and crashing onto the Oak Street
beach that fronts the hotel. He was very grave and Gabrielle was very lively. She'd
recovered from jet-lag faster than her father. Shortly after two o'clock in the
afternoon, he was back in the hotel. He had to sleep, or at least to rest. "I could not
sleep," he said later. He suspected the antibiotics for his cold were bothering him.
He suspects pills. Even when he cannot fall into a deep sleep before or after a
performance—because he gets so worked up over the events—he will refuse to take
tranquilizers. ("But sometimes," says one friend, "his wife will prevail on him.")
On this afternoon, he tossed and turned without a deep sleep. He would not take
anything to deepen sleep.

Just before six o'clock, he got up. To dress. To have tea and a snack. He felt very
tired. But the season was just an hour or so away.

The Performances

"**F**inally."

That was the one-word lead of one critique of opening night.

Finally. After years of planning, of months consumed in correspondence, of weeks of angry labor negotiations, and days of preparation, it all came down to this:

—An opening night in which the programs ran out early, leaving hundreds of upset customers, while nobody noticed or remembered the thousands of programs stacked neatly on a dolly in the building's basement.

—An opening night in which the usual elegances—notably a festive black-tie dinner—were canceled, as being too wry or too belated a commentary on the season.

—An opening night in which there was a stir of apprehension after the first number. It was the national anthem and once the closing strains were done, the members of the orchestra got up and marched offstage. Some viewers stirred uneasily; they thought perhaps it was a sudden and unannounced walkout by the players over some new union issue. ("I'll bet a lot of them thought they'd come all this way, dressed in their finest, to hear the Chicago Symphony play *The Star-Spangled Banner*," said one man.) Actually, the players were leaving to allow the twenty-four players for the Bach suite to take their appropriate places onstage—the chairs and music stands had to be moved to place them close to Solti instead of spread out across the width and depth of the stage.

Then after it was over—after the bows and applause, and more bows, and yet more—the corridors downstairs were abuzz with excitement and satisfaction. Louis Sudler waited, with all the others, outside the maestro's dressing room, to exchange a word of congratulations. "I feared this night would never come," he said, his eyes suddenly tearing over with emotion. For it was he who'd broken the deadlock—even by remote control—by somehow negotiating for the extra money to pay the players what they wanted.

A few feet away, in business clothes, stood Stuart S. Ball, president of the

Orchestral Association (since Sudler had been elected chairman). He is a huge, bulky man who looks more like a retired stevedore than the president of a symphony society. Actually he is, by vocation, a corporation lawyer whose clients have been among the most conservative in the land. Yet his brother, George Ball, long an adviser to Adlai E. Stevenson, and to Presidents Kennedy and Johnson, was the sole State Department figure of the 1960s with the prescience and insistence—but without the success—to urge that the United States get out of the Vietnam war, at a time when this view was not widely held, or even parochially acknowledged. And his son, Stuart Ball, Jr., was one of the brighter young men on the defense staff of the Chicago 7—at a time when the embattled judge in the trial, Julius Hoffman, was, as a member of the Establishment, a very close friend of fellow Establishment-man Stuart Ball, Sr. Word got back to the father that a lot of people, in the court and out of it, were outraged that he'd let his son take part in such "disreputable" activity. The implication was that "treason" was transferable, presumably through contact with the Chicago 7 to young lawyer Ball to his father. The elder Ball was unperturbed. He defended his son on the basis of love, of intelligence, and of basic rights: he suggested that a lawyer can and must decide whom he is going to defend without the pressure of society, and family, deflecting him. Furthermore, it was his son's duty and privilege to respond to that notion, and to his own set of internal urgencies, and what's more, Stuart Ball, Sr., was proud of him. Whatever decision he might reach, he'd make, suggested his father, a better lawyer than most.

Now Ball stood near Solti's door, happy at the result of the opening night, just as unperturbed that—in the nearby players' quarters—many musicians regarded *him*, not Louis Sudler, as "the enemy." He saw Victor Aitay emerge from his dressing room—the concertmasters and a few principals have their own rooms, separate from the orchestra's quarters—and walk down the corridor.

"I had my first coronary forty years ago," says Ball, to no one in particular but toward the now-recovered Aitay in general, "and I've managed to survive every one since."

Aitay stopped, realized the president of the Orchestral Association was speaking to him and for him. He was deeply affected, and for a moment he didn't seem to know what to do. He is a thin, slight, disciplined man, not given to public spontaneities. Yet now he came up and laid his head on Ball's chest and the two men embraced, like a bear clasping a cub.

The critics were, as usual, baffling, elevating, eloquent, and contradictory. Karen Monson in the *Chicago Daily News* commented about the Bach suite that "No attempt was made to flavor the Overture with French double-dottings"—a device in which the second dot adds half the value of the first dot, thus lengthening the note by three-quarters of its original value. But Roger Dettmer in *Chicago Today* commented that the Bach was "beautifully turned with double-dotted rhythms."

All of them loved the air within the Bach suite. ("How good it was, for example, to hear the orchestra playing the Air properly," wrote Robert C. Marsh in the *Chicago Sun-Times*, "with continuo, after all the times it has been played without this essential element of the texture.") All responded amply to Ruggles's *Men and Mountains*. ("Comprehensive, taut, and massively sonorous, though imprecise at moments," wrote Dettmer.) But it was the Beethoven Third Symphony, the *Eroica*, which captured their attention and their prime critical stance. "Since March, 1969, when he last conducted *Eroica* here, Solti has both deepened and broadened his conception," wrote Thomas Willis in the *Chicago Tribune*. "The strong off-beat accents which do so much to propel the music onward have sharpened. The transitions dance now, and there are touches in introspection in the pianissimo sections of the outer movements. . . ." And Robert Marsh echoed in the *Sun-Times*: "Certainly not the least of the achievement of Solti and his musicians is that the stature of the work was made fully apparent in a performance filled with inspired insight into the score."

From the windows of his suite in a hotel overlooking Lake Michigan, Georg Solti can see the sun come up as he bends over his scores. He is so intense in his studies that he does not always notice it. Nor does he notice it edging away in the autumn—moving to his right, until finally it is out of sight—and returning again in the spring. He has many other things to worry about, not the least of which is the state of his health.

"I arrived in Chicago with a very bad throat, which just went on and on and on," he says. "The first week I am conducting, I am having that cough. I have a doctor friend who says, 'I hear you coughing all the time and I don't like it. I ask you, please check with somebody.' "

Solti had gone to a doctor in London and gotten X rays. Out of it came the assurance that it was nothing worse than a cold—no long-term lung condition. Next he went to a doctor in Chicago who told him, "You have an infection in your throat. And you won't get rid of it unless you do something about it."

"I said, 'I have to work. I can't quit.'

"And he said, 'You can practice but you must take these antibiotics.' " Solti does not like taking pills of any kind for any reason. He suspects them. "I took these antibiotics for four days but they added to my problems in Chicago because, of course, they make you very weak. I lost the cough. But I lost a great deal of energy also."

The disciplines that go into all this—indeed the disciplines of living a season in Chicago—are not Solti's own. They are imposed on him, in a style that has a good deal of charm, guile, even bewitchery, by the women he has around him. For Solti, though very much the *macho* in his professional attitudes, would have difficulty surviving in a world with so many plaguey devices—pills, phones, cars, planes, lost socks—if it were not for the diverting style and sagacious management of the women around him.

There are six of them altogether. Three are family: his wife, Valerie, and his two daughters, Gabrielle and Claudia. Three are staff: his secretary, Enid Blech; his housekeeper, Patricia Hughes; and the nanny for the children, Jill Ferguson. He has been known to travel without them, but only reluctantly. Because he prefers to "keep household" around him, even when on the road, rather than leave the family at home. "I just could not do it any other way," he says. "So either I earn as much money as I can to keep them with me, or I am in trouble. That is all. I simply won't live my life without my family. It just does not make the slightest bit of sense. If I can't afford it, I stay home. I am not coming to America."

Each of the women in his life has not only a place but a function. The children, of course, have transformed not only his life but also his personality. "He goes absolutely ga-ga over them," says one close friend. "He'll be going along very tense, very brusque and brisk when one of the girls will toddle into the room and suddenly he'll be on the floor, on his hands and knees, making faces and ga-ga sounds with them," says one longtime friend. Solti, of course, is aware of this. And is delighted by it. But he tries, rather dutifully, to disguise his delight behind a sense of mock gruffness. "My life will be lived," he said to Enid Blech one day, "with Elgar's *Enigma Variations* in one hand and a Babar the Elephant book in the other."

Each of the staff keeps watch, in effect, on the members of the family. Jill Ferguson, who comes from a nanny school and from Dorset, looks after the children. Mrs. Blech, of course, looks after Sir Georg. "And Miss Hughes is my right-hand lady," says Valerie Solti. "Pat is really my alter ego. She organizes everything—she cooks the meals, she makes sure the laundry gets out and gets back, she makes sure the suite is booked for the next time, she makes sure his tails are cleaned, she packs the trunks. And she calls the housekeeper in the hotel so that she'll know exactly what we are leaving—pots, high chairs, clothes, and so forth."

The key to it all is, of course, Valerie Solti. She is a woman of superbly easy and open temperament whose particular grace is that she prevents Sir Georg from meditating at length—or even at all—upon the complicated and acrid flavor of his existence. For his is not an easy life. He is one of the uprooted. He has not lived in his homeland for thirty-five years. He has a home in London but he is there only a few weeks of the year. Otherwise he is a transient, traveling to Paris, to Chicago, to Italy, on tour to Germany, Switzerland, New York. He spends forty to fifty days a year in airplanes—and they torment him. ("He is absolutely miserable at flying," says Mrs. Blech. "He's nervous. It upsets his tummy, upsets his head, and he just hates it. But he has to do it.") The gift of Valerie Solti is that she creates the illusion of a home in whatever place they settle, for however long they settle there. "I think as a family we are aware of the disadvantages but we don't complain about them. We try to be quite happy with the arrangement."

The advantage is living in luxury surroundings most of the time. Actually, Solti tends to avoid the more ostentatious hotels in favor of smaller, more comfortable quarters. He stays at the San Regis in Paris, at the Stanhope in New York, for example. "But when you are living in such circumstances, it is not for the luxury of it but because it is a necessity," she says. "We endeavor to make it as comfortable as possible to conserve our energy. You need to be comfortable—if you are giving a performance, you must be technically comfortable to be physically strong in order to do your best."

The disadvantages are singularly human—"you never have any continuity"—and peculiarly feminine. "You never seem to achieve—to get what you want done. My photograph album is never quite finished. And I would like to do some writing. But when I am going to do it—well, I just don't know.

"On the other hand, all this is compensated by his marvelous enthusiasm for life. He is an intensely happy man—a very inspiring person to live with." And: "He is completely immersed in the things that fascinate him."

These things are music. He is a compulsive worker who has little time and virtually no inclination for play. "We don't need to go to parties to be happy," says Valerie Solti. "We are perfectly happy being at home." It is part of the privileges of their lives to be free from the nine-to-five syndrome, even if Solti has replaced it with a seven-to-eleven syndrome—7 A.M. to 11 P.M. "Other people are going out to cocktails, out to dinner, out to the theater"—they are living a life to get away from their work. "Our work is all-consuming and our leisure is essentially just leisure." Sir Georg throws very few parties while in Chicago, usually one a year for the members of the orchestra, sometimes another for the members of the chorus. "But our real retreat is the beauty of our place in Italy," says Lady Valerie. "We don't have to dress up and we really don't have to *do* anything. We live simply, wander around in simple clothing and devote ourselves to our family and our friends."

In his nonconducting moments, Solti is very selective, very disciplined, in both his professional and personal pursuits. It does not bother him at all that he does not match the image-making pacesetters in either field.

Professionally, for example, he is indifferent to the examples of Leonard Bernstein and Pierre Boulez, among others, to be composer-conductors. He has no interest in composing or in the opportunity, exploited by some conductors, to sell compositions from the podium.

"I stopped composing at an early age, twenty-one or twenty-two," he says. "For the simple reason that I am not good enough. A good composer will be an eclectic conductor and vice versa. I can put my mind and soul into other people's minds, but my mind and soul are not good for creating original pieces, really good ones." When he was very young, when he was still working at the Budapest Opera, he tried composing. "But I am not proud of the work. And I don't think I will start going back to it at the end of my life and start composing again. I don't think so."

Personally, Solti is not—among the many and furious other divertissements attributed to great artists—a great gourmet. In fact, he is not a gourmet at all. "He'd be perfectly happy, perfectly happy, living on cottage cheese and salad," says Mrs. Blech (counters Lady Valerie: "He wouldn't be!").

Partly this is because he wants to avoid fat. "He can't bear the idea of getting fat," says Mrs. Blech. "He likes good food but he won't eat it because he thinks he's going to get fat."

Part of it is because he likes food only if it meets certain internal specifications. "He's impossible to design a dinner for," says John Scott Trotter, a longtime friend who was music director on the Bing Crosby radio and TV shows for years. One reason is that he won't eat any fowl—"he will not eat anything that flies," says Trotter. Solti attributes his aversion to fowl to a childhood experience "when I was

Lady Valerie and Sir Georg Solti.

taken by my mother to a very small town and I entered a kitchen and saw a row of these poor little animals there, all plucked and hung up by the neck." One of his close friends and associates once designed a dinner that included capon, then had to change all the plans at the last minute on learning that Solti would not eat it. "And there is no use trying to disguise the menu with an exotic name," says one friend, "because he speaks so many languages that he can decipher virtually any name you lay on it." There is some perception, even concern, among his party-giving friends that he is beginning to avoid the meat of recognizable animals—lamb, beef, etc. ("I don't like to see a corpse when I am eating.") This is not to say that he's becoming a vegetarian. He loves sausage and other meat cuts. It's just that his aversions are more pronounced than his affections. "Wait," says Lady Valerie with only a small distant sense of desperation, "until he finds out what a sausage is made of."

Otherwise, Sir Georg has very few, but very compulsive leisure-time activities. One is bridge. Another is reading the newspapers. "Summertime is my book-reading time," he says. "In the wintertime I am avid newspaper reader. Have always been since a young boy. It was a pattern of life with Middle Europeans that they would read newspapers in the morning." He often has *The Times* of London flown to him wherever he is performing, and he deplores the advent of television in news presentation. "Television has done great harm to newspapers," he says. "Its news is prefabricated. To read, you have to think, to make up your own mind. With television, you get the prefabricated news and have it with your breakfast."

Solti is an intensely competitive man and—in contrast to the popular image of the aesthete—an intense sports fan. He does not take part in many sports himself, but he follows spectator sports religiously and makes the customary transference.

In Chicago, he took a liking to ice hockey and soon was following it in the paper and on TV. For Christmas one year he was given the Bobby Hull tabletop hockey game and, after a brief practice period of twiddling the knobs that activate the various "players," imperiously challenged all comers. "He's incredibly competitive," says one man who was there. "He played that game with utter concentration, just like he does everything else."

In England, he follows soccer religiously and has been known to change rehearsal times so that he can get to a game or get home in time to watch it on the telly. The tactic did not arouse much antagonism in his co-workers at Covent Garden. "There were always a couple of basses—David Ward was one—and an Australian tenor who'd come and say, 'Make sure he doesn't put in a rehearsal on Saturday afternoon,' " says Mrs. Blech. She'd ask why. "Because it would conflict with the big game—the Wolves are playing the Eagles or something, you know." Mrs. Blech does not rank sports and team names among her enthusiasms. "And I'd say, 'Oh, my God, no! We must try and avoid that, mustn't we?' " And very quietly, she would make a note to keep that afternoon open—for soccer for Sir Georg and friends.

The role of Lady Valerie in all this inspires memories of *Moses und Aron.* Instead of going to Sir Georg for the resolution of many day-to-day problems, people come to her—"instead of going to Moses, they come to Aaron." For Aaron was the detail man with the gift of tongues. That is exactly Lady Valerie's role. "I coordinate everything," she says, and she does it with an easy cheer that makes those she's dealing with—including Sir Georg—gratified at her skills. "The wife of an artist or musician has a very important job. She has to become part of him and part of his work," she says. "The wife of a business executive, the president of a corporation, for example, is always involved in a separation of life—he has his work at the office and she makes his home away from the office. But the wife of an artist is an integral part of his working system."

She answers the phone for him, for example; he doesn't like to do it. She goes to certain other people's performances when he's working elsewhere and gives him her impression of the performers. She once worked in the theater and in TV and she studied drama at the Royal Academy, and she knows show business if not all the inner details of music. "He won't take my word alone," she says. "But my going is a place to start." She catalogues the scores for him and she knows what kind of batons he uses and where and when to get them. ("He uses a light baton, with cork on the handle end." It's made of plywood, she says, and the tip of it is no longer pointed as it was in the past; ever since he stabbed himself in the hand with a baton while conducting a recording session in Veinna, he's turned to using a stick with a blunt end.) She knows what cities have the rehearsal clothes that he prefers—or she looks up new sources when old sources die out. For instance, he must have suede-soled shoes, so that he maintains good contact with the podium in rehearsal. He insists on wearing, at rehearsal, a loose pullover made of wool that has a collar and three buttons at the neck that he can undo as he gets worked up. ("I can't get them anymore; they've discontinued the line—I bought up the last thirty or so that I could find.") He wears a rehearsal jacket that she gets in London to help absorb the sweat of his work ("he loses about two pounds in every performance") and helps keep him warm. He wears baggy trousers that she gets in Chicago and she makes sure they have very wide cuffs: he's a fiend for efficiency and, like many men, he hates to take off his shoes when he changes his pants—"so with these cuffs he can change these trousers without taking off his shoes."

Most of all, she keeps track of where all these things are. "We arrived in Chicago," she says—without desperation—"with twelve suitcases and a pram." The pram was for six-month-old Claudia, of course. They would leave Chicago with an extra suitcase or so, just from the accumulation of living in one place for five weeks. One friend brought in two Hubert the Lion stuffed toys, each large enough to fill a trunk. Another friend, John Scott Trotter, stopped by with a book that Solti wanted not only to read but to take home. Then there were the rehearsal clothes that Valerie bought in Chicago and the problems of the extra schedule: he'd need an extra bag—smaller than the ones he goes intercontinental with—to take care of the tails and shoes that he'd need to carry on the eastern tour that would conclude this visit to the United States.

Valerie must look to the tiniest of details—soap, for example. "The hotel soap, generally speaking, is rather dry," she says, "and so you need a fatty soap when you're away from home so much." She or Pat Hughes simply goes out to a supermarket and buys soap—"we just use regular soap"—but they hate to leave the soap behind in one hotel when they're going on tour and may need the soap in the next hotel before they have a chance to go shopping. "So if you find a soap you like, you end up taking along six tablets"—or bars—"with you when you go on tour," says Valerie. All this tends to more than fill the capacity of the luggage they bring to town. "It always seems as if you start out with an extra pair of socks and you have to buy a trunk to take it all home," she says.

The luggage is as well planned as everything else. "We have a certain range of suitcases we buy in Switzerland or Germany and we have another range which we buy here in Chicago. We always buy the same ones in either place. The ones here are black, the ones in Europe are gray. We have X's written on them so that when the plane comes in and the baggage is unloaded, we can find them without much trouble."

The last thing she does is make a careful list of everything that's going to be left in each city. The Soltis do not carry all their clothes with them from place to place. Lady Valerie leaves a complete wardrobe in Chicago, for example, so that he doesn't have to carry the clothes back and forth with her between Europe and the United States. Similarly with Sir Georg: he leaves certain relaxing clothes and some formal wear in Chicago, as in Paris and, of course, in London. Even Mrs. Blech leaves clothes in storage in Chicago—"the shoes, the things that tend to be heavy," she says. But very detailed lists of what goes into hotel storage must be kept, and kept available, so that when the Soltis—one man and six women—return, they won't be bringing things that are already awaiting them in the hotel—the things they've stored there before.

The response of Solti to all this activity ranges from blasé innocence—he does not understand it all in the first place—to euphoric delight. In between is a sort of little-boy humility, a guileless appreciation that all *this* could be done in a world which astounds, baffles, and confounds him. There is an enormous appeal in this, and no amount of contradiction—he *is*, after all, a sixty-two-year-old man—can quite quell the attractiveness of his personality.

His personality is rather potent under any circumstances. For many women, he seems to possess—even on the podium—a powerful sexual attraction. ("I first saw him conducting Wagner in Europe when I was nineteen," says the wife of one of the richest men in Chicago, "and the first thing I can remember thinking was that he's a very sexual man." The reason she remembers it, she says, "was that I wasn't even sexually aware at the time.") In the years before he married Valerie—so goes the gossip—Solti put the theory to more intimate tests and did not find it wanting. The talk was that any number of women were passionately interested in him and he rewarded their interest and their passion by giving each a white fur coat. Nobody today dares venture whether this is true, but there was a time in London when the feeling was that a woman who wore a white coat on certain social occasions not only compromised herself but identified her lover.

In any case, the fact is that two women have left their husbands to be with Georg Solti and eventually to marry him. He met his first wife, Hedi, in Switzerland during the war. She was married to a professor of history who was also a member of the Swiss parliament and had two children when she decided to leave the family, divorce, and marry Solti. At the time Solti was unknown and, until he won the assignment at the Munich State Opera, unemployed. Hedi was a remarkable woman—mondaine, ambitious, intelligent, and very deeply in love. She cut the rough edges off Solti, polished and honed his personality and his manners, and gave him the style if not the substance of the great conductor. Beyond that, she mothered him and supported his ego and offered a sympathetic ear for his tensions and complaints. But success and the passing years loosened their ties. In 1964, Solti met Valerie Pitts, then a BBC announcer who was married to a lawyer. They fell in love while maintaining their individual personalities ("It was a violent affair," Solti was quoted by *Time*). In 1966, both Solti and Valerie were divorced—the grounds were adultery—and a year later they were married. Whatever Hedi felt at the time, she also soon remarried and now she sees the Soltis frequently.

Valerie is seen by mutual friends as being more spontaneous and effervescent than Hedi. She was not as intent upon his success but more intent upon him as a human being. "I think," one friend has said, "that Valerie understands him now as Hedi understood him in Munich and Frankfurt."

She also gave him children. That was something missing in his life with Hedi. Solti was fifty-seven years old when, on April 26, 1970, Gabrielle was born. Solti was on tour in Germany and he was so excited that, as the time of birth approached, he gave orders, "There will be no concert, no concert!" if the baby came before the concert did. For he intended to be there when the baby was born. Valerie phoned Solti in Germany at 3 A.M.—long after the concert had ended—to say that the baby was on its way. Solti spent the rest of the night at the airport, trying to get a flight from Berlin to London. Around five o'clock in the morning, he

Orchestra Hall in Chicago: players' locker room (top) and fans outside.

finally got a cargo flight to London, and he arrived at the hospital just as the baby was being born.

"This is my mother," he said the moment he saw Gabrielle. And so she was given the second name, Theresa, after his mother, Theres.

Solti took no chances with the birth of the second baby. He canceled the first of the Beethoven recording sessions with the Chicago Symphony so that he could go back to London and be with Valerie in the final weeks of her pregnancy.

Today the children fill his life as music does. He schedules his free time so that he can be with them around two o'clock in the afternoon—for a little play, a short walk, before he goes to the bedroom to toss and turn through the preconcert hours. ("But I will *not* take tranquilizers"—unless Valerie can persuade him to.) It is a discipline for him to take this time out of his day. But it is another discipline that the children—and all the women around him—have helped him to learn to love.

Even as Georg Solti tries to nap, or study, or simply take respite with his children from the intensity of his labors, the work at Orchestra Hall goes on in methodical and even anticipatory ways.

In no endeavor is the phrase "what is past is prologue" more accurate than in music. For on Friday, with opening night barely gone and with the rest of the week's performances not yet played, work is well under way on the next week's performance. The conductor has, of course, made out the schedule of rehearsal for the next week; Radi Lah has posted it and with it posted the personnel requirements, by name, for the next week's work. But unseen behind all this is the work on the scores of the next week by the concertmaster. To most concertgoers, the concertmaster is the violinist who sits in the first chiar—under the conductor's left—and who plays whatever violin solos turn up in the score. Actually, this is only a part of his duties. "The concertmaster is responsible first of all to prepare the music—the bowing, the phrasing, try to match it up with the other string sections," says Victor Aitay, in his slight Hungarian accent. "You get from the library the parts and you mark one part, the bowing and the phrasing into the other parts, so that a great deal of work is done before the first rehearsal." Solti relies on the concertmaster to do the marking of the parts; Giulini is much more likely to do the marking himself for the concertmaster to read. "Then, naturally, you have a rehearsal to correct certain things according to the conductor's wishes," Aitay goes on. "Sometimes the conductor wants something more powerful; then you have to change the bowing and the phrasing, and that is done in consultation between the conductor and the concertmaster on the stage. And according to that, the rest of the section is marking it."

He cited, as an example, the case of Strauss's Dance of the Seven Veils, from *Salome*, which would be played in the second week of Solti's season. "In the *Salome* just at the rehearsals we used to take certain liberties. Some conductors are doing it slowly at the end which needed different bowing than Mr. Solti, who plays it exactly in tempo. So we have to change the bowing accordingly. Now if another conductor will conduct that with different things in mind, with different interpretations in mind, we might have to change it again. Or three times, four times —there are many, many different ways to interpret the same piece."

Thus the concertmaster is one of the conduits through which the conductor seeks to get his particular sound out of the orchestra. "It is really up to the conductor who balances the woodwind, brass, to the percussion and strings," says Aitay, "and with this balance you get a certain kind of sound." The balance involves not only the loudness of the various sections but their method of attack, their tone—blaring, mellow, lyric—and their style in various parts of the music, perhaps staccato, perhaps vibrato, perhaps muted. It is the combination of all this and countless other small, subtle elements that makes the sound under one conductor so different from that of another—it is an intellectual process and not simply an inspired leading. Says Aitay: "Now that sound is created by the conductor because he has that kind of a conception of the orchestra's sound"—the conception that is in his mind and is played through the inner ear of his imagination. "Every conductor has a different perception—I am talking now of outstanding conductors. Obviously some conductors have no conception at all," says Aitay. "Then you just play the ordinary way. But the major conductors do have conceptions and the same pieces sound different under different conductors."

It is not enough to have a singular conception of a piece of music, suggests Aitay. It must be a convincing conception. "If it is convincing, the piece is good several ways," he says. "If it is not convincing, then it is no good *any* way. So the conductor has to be powerful and very convincing. A conductor who, when he conducts a particular piece, gives the impression that it cannot be performed any other way except that way—if the conductor doesn't get that, then the audience just can't react. So he can't be vague in his conductor interpretation. If you do, then there is something that is already wrong. You have to give the impression, 'This is it and nothing else is good.' And the other one can do the same thing in a different way but that is why, to be a conductor, you have to have powerful personalities, besides being an excellent musician. The personality has to put the stamp on the performance. If you do not have that, you just have a wishy-washy."

The personalities of the men who've led the Chicago Symphony over the last twenty years are much in tune with Aitay's understanding. For he attended the same school that Solti did—the Franz Liszt Royal Academy. "I did not know him. He was in a generation which finished earlier than I did at the Academy." But they know each other well now; Aitay is one of the few members of the orchestra Solti prefers to relax with, playing bridge and talking Hungarian. He was also close to the "earlier Hungarian," Fritz Reiner. It was Reiner who persuaded him to join the Pittsburgh Symphony in 1946. Aitay left to become concertmaster at the Metropolitan Opera from 1948 to 1954, then left the Met to rejoin Reiner at the Chicago Symphony in 1954.

But he is not the only man on the job as concertmaster. The Chicago Symphony has a co-concertmaster, Samuel Magad, and two assistant concertmasters, Jacques Israelievitch and Francis Akos. The reason is the work load. The Chicago Symphony Orchestra might play a maximum of 146 concerts a year, excluding the summer schedule. This includes not just the subscription concerts but the youth concerts and the Saturday Night Specials—Arthur Fiedler led the orchestra in one during the first week of work—and the concerts in Milwaukee and at the various colleges. Then the Ravinia summer schedule is added to that. "We play three, maybe four different programs a week out there," says Sam Magad. "Downtown we play one program a week"—one program for the subscription audiences (but perhaps two others for the Specials and the Youth Concerts). This is far too heavy a work load for one concertmaster. Samuel Magad and Victor Aitay share the duties and functions of the concertmaster. They are precisely the same in power, tone, and influence. They "cooperate by alternate"—they simply alternate on the top duties week by week. "Instead of choosing by saying, 'Well, I would like to play this piece' and he says, 'I would like to play that one'—that would be impossible; we would never decide. And so we say, 'Fine, you start or I will start, and then week one is yours, two is mine, three is yours, four is mine,' and it goes all the way. No matter who the conductor is, no matter what the piece is." In this season, Victor Aitay had the first week, the actual opening week. Magad would have the second week—two Strauss, a Berlioz, and also the responsibility for a key role in difficult moments with Josef Suk, who flew in to play the Martinů violin concerto. Then

Victor Aitay, co-concertmaster.

Samuel Magad, co-concertmaster.

Aitay would take over again for *Missa Solemnis*, while Magad carried on in the last pretour week on Mahler's Sixth Symphony.

They are, quite naturally, equal but not identical. Whereas Aitay is thin and angular, Magad is round and leans to weight. Aitay is pointed in demeanor whereas Magad appears somewhat diffident. Actually, Magad is quite articulate.

In talking about the labor of the concertmaster, for example, he cites the many factors that go into it other than the conductor's preferences. "If my week just happens to include Beethoven's Fourth Symphony and Tchaikovsky's Fifth Symphony—well, this is usually our own music." That means the scores are in the library; they aren't being shipped in from elsewhere. Also the music has been played by the Chicago Symphony so often that the scores are pretty well marked—"they're prepared the way that I, as the concertmaster, would probably play them." There are, of course, conductor's changes but many such scores are so familiar to the orchestra that even these can be made easily. "We've played the piece last year or the year before; we made preparation then and nobody's changed it." On the other hand, he may encounter scores that have not been played or have not been marked. "So you have to take care of that. I've run into a week where there's a great deal of modern music. That means more preparation for the concertmaster. You may run into music where there's a tremendous amount of solo playing. Now that's your own professional preparation—you take care of that yourself. You have to come prepared to play it at the rehearsals. And well. But sometimes you get a week that doesn't have one note of solo. So from that point of view you have less to do."

In one sense, perhaps, Magad and Aitay symbolize what has happened to the symphony orchestra in the last decade or so. Aitay came to the Chicago Symphony after being concertmaster of the Metropolitan Opera. Magad came to the Chicago Symphony after being in the U.S. Army Band; his concertmaster experience was with the summertime Grant Park symphony in Chicago. ("You treat them a little differently. There are certain things—although it's a good orchestra, it's a pickup orchestra. It's nowhere near the class of the Chicago Symphony. I think you would treat the sections of the strings a little differently. You have to explain a little more to them, things that we assume in the Chicago Symphony. You have to give details in an orchestra like Grant Park. If you give an indication of what you want at a rehearsal in the Chicago Symphony, the section will pick it up immediately.") In the Chicago Symphony, Magad had to fight his way up from the back stand —where he spent six years—to win an audition for concertmaster. Aitay, on the other hand, came to prominence in the American symphony orchestra at the behest of a countryman; he was named concertmaster by a countryman, and he prospers today under a countryman. This is not to say that one plays better than the other, but only that their skills became apparent in different ways. The route of Sam Magad is likely to be more characteristic of the way of success in our time and the future.

Sam Magad's name comes from the storyteller of ancient Hebrew—"The *Magad* went from village to village to tell stories of the Bible," he says. His father loved music and played the violin part-time. "But he couldn't do that for a living," says Sam. So he had a mattress-manufacturing firm. "It was a small, small operation where you produced everything yourself. I think the time eventually put him out of business, because he couldn't compete with the big firms, mass-producing mattresses, box springs. And there was very little market for the handmade personalized bedding items." So when the market died out, he retired. "He plays violin out in the Los Angeles area in all the amateur orchestras. He loves it. He's wild for it. At the age of seventy-five!"

Young Sam began studying the violin at the age of five. He had turned thirteen when his father took him to a teacher who so enchanted him that he followed him all through high school and even through De Paul University. Then Sam was drafted and, having heard of the U.S. Army Band at Fort Myer, Virginia, near Washington, wrote for an audition and was transferred there. He was assigned there for three years, 1955 to 1958, and his duties included playing background in a string ensemble—"about five to eight people, with a piano"—at receptions and cocktail parties and embassy gatherings throughout Washington. When his time was up, he auditioned for the Chicago Symphony and in 1958 won a position there.

"I sat in the back of the orchestra for six, maybe six and a half years. On the last stand in the days when we didn't have rotation. You just continued to sit there unless perhaps somebody died. There wasn't any democracy like we have today in our orchestra. It was an autocratic-government type. You know, Reiner rules, he plays like a king, and if he smiled at you, your life was made. If he frowned, you never knew what the consequence might be." He remembers it now as a most frustrating time. "Like there was no tomorrow. It was foreverness."

When Reiner died, Martinon ran auditions for a number of posts and Magad tried out for, and won, assignment as an assistant concertmaster. He'd also been working at Grant Park, but he gave that up to play with the Chicago Symphony at Ravinia in the summer. Now he was about to spend another six-year term sitting in the same chair of the Chicago Symphony, but this chair was considerably closer to Ultimate Success. There were times in all these years when he got discouraged and wondered about following another course: he might become concertmaster in another, if lesser, orchestra, for example. But all through his career, he's been able to find outlets and satisfactions outside the symphony: he plays in the Chicago Symphony Strings, he teaches at Northwestern (chamber music classes as well as the violin), he plays in a string quartet. So when Sidney Weiss, one of the co-concertmasters of the early 1970s, resigned in order to go on a recital tour with his wife, who plays piano, Sam Magad was one of those who auditioned for the privilege of joining Victor Aitay as co-concertmaster. The finalists included applicants from orchestras all over the country—"Pittsburgh, Cleveland, other places," says Magad. Sam was the man Solti chose and in March 1972 he moved up to the first stand as co-concertmaster.

There is a personal cachet as well as a public one that goes with being co-concertmaster: both Aitay and Magad play instruments made in 1715 by Stradivarius, owned by the orchestra, and given to the concertmasters to play. "You know there *are* other violins," says Magad. "I own a brand-new modern-made instrument—just finished a month ago—and it has a big volume, a big sound. But it doesn't have the quality and richness of tone, and beauty, that suave sound the Strad has." He does not think, however, that antiquity is the total secret of the sound of the Strad. As a musician of high skills, he thinks there's another element. "Of course I'm an egotist—I think it's what I put into it. A lot of people—very often you play a concert, a chamber music concert—they say 'It's such a lovely sound. What kind of an instrument do you play?' And I say, 'Well, it's a Strad.' And they say, 'Oh, yes, I thought so. I could have guessed that.' Well, I hate to start a discussion with them, but there's something else that goes into the best of Strads. I've never seen one play by itself."

As co-concertmasters, Aitay and Magad work together with easy grace. "We are two completely different individuals," says Magad, and we get along very well, I must say. We have different lives, we have different life-styles, and we may have different musical ideas—everybody does. Naturally. But when he is concertmaster, I go along with him, and when I am concertmaster, he goes along with me. Which is really the only way we can do it. I don't think we try to impose each other's way on the week we are not the leader."

He has, of course, slightly more detailed views of what the concertmaster does and how he does it. "What I do is, before the week comes up, I take the music home. You have to prepare ahead of time—you study and decide according to what you think or according to the dynamics or according to the music, the interest, whatever it is—you decide what bowings might be used."

The bowings mean not only whether the bow is going up or down. "Each bowing has its own inherent qualities that one may play louder than the other. A short bow. A long bow. A bounced bow. A legato type bow. One drawn nicely, one hit hard. This is what brings variation and interest to the music, as we are trying to bring out the composer's wishes."

On occasion, the decision is made for them. "Very often it happens that the conductor will send his personal scores ahead of time, completely marked —maybe played with a different orchestra some time before, but completely marked. Now in this case we are certainly not going to change it, because this is what the particular conductor wishes—he is on his way here and the music has arrived and that is what we play. But what so often happens at a rehearsal is that if I don't like it or it does not seem right, comfortable, or whatever, with the conductor's agreement we change it right there, even though it is his part. I mean, he decided last week it sounded good; maybe this week it will sound better some other way. . . . Change is going on all the time, because sometimes what you figure at home by yourself sounds good and should work out, but when you get there in the whole section, maybe the brass section is drowning you out completely and you didn't expect that much sound from them. So you want to make more volume. You want to make more bows. You change it right on the job; right then." What about the conductor's view? "You have a conductor who will see that you want to do something, you want to make a change, and he will stop. Or if it is time for a break, or there's a minute when he stops to say something, you turn around and pass what you want. You mark it in your part so that they can see what you want. Then you turn around and let them know there is a change, and usually it is picked up by the second stand and third stand and they pass it back. It is rather quick; they do it fast."

The conductors deal with the problem in many different ways.

"Solti," says Sam Magad, "is a little less concerned with the bowings per se than some other conductors. Some other conductors are very interested in what goes on—you know, bowing-wise, they think it will make a great deal of difference in the music. Sometimes it does and sometimes it doesn't."

Giulini has a different approach than does Solti. "He has a different style completely. He prefers to send his own scores ahead of time—he thinks it saves time and to an extent it does. It saves rehearsal time. I mean it is all in what he wants. If he decides at the last minute for one or two changes, that is easier than thirty-five changes—it takes less time. But Solti doesn't bother too much unless it offends him, unless it is not what he wanted out of the music."

The concertmaster must also consider the problem of the other strings. "You are always involved with the rest of the strings, as concertmaster," says Magad. "I may have marked something for myself but maybe the second violins or the violas are doing some thing else. Should they do similar, or the same type bowings, or what?" The way he resolves the problem is by getting together with the principal players for the other string sections—Frank Miller for the cellos, Joseph Guastafeste for the string bass, Joseph Golan for the second violins, Milton Preves for the violas. "What I usually do is go through my own part first, and then I will have the second violin principal and the viola principal look at my music and coordinate where they can. So that by the time the rehearsal comes, everything is assembled and everything is ready to go."

The result is that some of the scores are pretty heavily marked. "Ninety-five percent of the parts we play are marked from before." He often recognizes the markings—"I see my handwriting constantly," says Magad. "I see my own handwriting on everything I wrote from previous years, even when I sat in the second stand." Those parts that are not heavily marked can cause problems. The score for the Martinů violin concerto was one example. It came out of the archives of the Moldenhauer collection at Northwestern. It had never been played in public before. The original score had been copied by some unknown person—"and it was a terrible manuscript." The copy was made in such a tiny, sloppy hand that it was all but indecipherable; the notes were too small, and frequently they weren't placed with precision in or around the musical staff, or even linked to each other in a credible way. The score was enlarged photographically and copied, but even Solti had trouble reading the score. It did not even seem to be complete; there were no tempo markings on the score. Solti simply decided himself to play it allegro moderato in the first movement, then andante in the second movement, and finally, allegro—moderately lively at the outset, then more slowly if flowingly, and finally, merrily. But the decisions of the conductor could not relieve all the problems of the score. "The men had a terrible time playing it and, of course, I had to bow from scratch."

The rest of the players felt the same thing. "The lines are so blurred and sloppy

that they extend over three notes so that you really have to analyze the chord structure," said one player, sitting in the lounge one day.

"How do you know what to do then?"

"I don't . . . none of us do."

"He [Solti] told us to try not to worry about that. Not right now. Not in the first rehearsal. It was more important to grasp the overall style and flow of the piece than to worry about one bad note here or there."

But it was a difficult concept to communicate. With many orchestras, there is a great tolerance—even a fondness—for an occasional bad note. Not in the Chicago Symphony, even under the most trying of circumstances. "We'd like to play the right notes," said this player—if they could discern what they were.

Solti was very much aware of the players' problem. He'd been trying to decipher the Martinů manuscript since Roccamare. "It was very difficult, the Martinů," he says. "We had a very bad manuscript—a score which was unreadable. So it was partly guessing. Even the parts for the players were partly guessing. I don't know how many wrong notes we left in. I have no idea because I cannot ask anybody"—the composer was dead and those close to him not even aware of the concert. "It sounds very strange, but I did not want to change [any notes to make them clearer to the players]. Because I did not know what was right. The score is a manuscript which a copier writes very quickly; you just cannot make every note out. Deciding on tone, it could be that one, it could be this one, it falls between the lines. So you really don't know which one—some of them are logical, some of them you can guess, but some of them is a wrong guess. So it is a great deal of problem."

In fact, the players' committee weighed a resolution to make a statement to management about the condition of the score—though it was not the fault of management. The only score that existed was this one, so the choice seemed to be between a bad score and no score.

This was to be a world premiere of the work, and it was to be involved in a number of other problems.

For example, a good many of the players thought soloist Josef Suk, the fine Czechoslovakian violinist who flew to Chicago to take part in the premiere, was admirably well prepared—but on the wrong Martinů violin concerto. The reasoning was that, when Suk had been engaged to play a Martinů violin concerto, he thought, naturally, of *the* Martinů violin concerto—there was only one that had ever been performed. When he got to Chicago, he found that the Chicago Symphony was ready to rehearse another Martinů concerto, one that had been unknown for years. "He is a very excellent musician," says one player. "He sat down and learned the new concerto by the time we were ready to go with it."

The players might, of course, be wrong. "This is typical musician talk," says John Edwards. The players do have an affection for legend, and there is some reason to believe that Suk was aware of the two violin concertos before coming to Chicago. Edwards insists that the violin part of the "unknown" concerto was Xeroxed and sent to Suk before the performance. Suk has not confirmed it, one way or the other, but whatever happened, the episode remains a scholar's—if not a musician's—delight. For one thing, Martinů was born in eastern Moravia but was, at an early time in his life, attracted by French music and art and, indeed, felt somewhat stifled by the German-Romantic atmosphere of the Prague Conservatory where he studied. Thus the preferences of Martinů do not seem to match the preferences of Solti and the Chicago Symphony. For another thing, Martinů was a twentieth-century composer who defined the sources of his works as—among other things—the Elizabethan madrigal; his compositions generally reflect a taste for the style of the baroque, using very simply thematic "cells" which, carried along on a rhythmic current, tend to develop into full-blown melodies. Again, nothing in this taste or example fits in with the predispositions of Solti and the Chicago Symphony. Finally, Martinů wrote more than four hundred works before dying in 1959; they included fifteen operas and twelve ballets. But this particular work, to be premiered by the Chicago Symphony, had been lost, or hidden, for many decades.

It was known that Martinů had written a violin concerto. It was composed in or before 1943 for violinist Mischa Elman. In fact, it was performed by Elman with the Chicago Symphony in 1944. (Altogether, the Chicago Symphony had, by late 1973, performed nine works by Martinů.) But the existence of a second violin concerto was not known. It began surfacing in 1961 when Boaz Piller, once contrabassoonist in the Boston Symphony Orchestra, sought a place to preserve his collection of musical autographs and manuscripts. He chose the Hans Moldenhauer Archive, a portion of which is preserved at the Northwestern University Library. The Piller papers included original manuscripts by Martinů, and in going through them, Dr. Moldenhauer discovered the second violin concerto. "Strangely enough, not even Martinů's closest associates ever knew of the work's existence," writes Dr. Moldenhauer. He traced the supposed origin of the work to a decision by Martinů to compose a concerto for Samuel Dushkin, the Russian-born American violinist, in the early 1930s in Paris. But when Dr. Moldenhauer asked Dushkin about it, he expressed only a faint recollection of having seen the draft of one movement. He was surprised to find that the work had been carried to completion.

Nevertheless, Dr. Moldenhauer had a complete copy of the violin concerto and he set about setting a world premiere of it. In 1970, he heard Josef Suk play a Mozart violin concerto with the Chicago Symphony, and he developed a method of exposing the work through Suk's skills. Suk is, after all, Czechoslovakian, as was Martinů. He is the great-grandson of Antonín Dvořák, who composed, among other things, the *New World* Symphony. He is the grandson of Josef Suk, a violinist and composer who studied under Dvořák (and eventually married Dvořák's daughter). So the instrument and the nationality fitted. Dr. Moldenhauer had in mind a world premiere in Chicago and also in Prague, and he says that Suk agreed to this. Thus the suggestion is that Suk was aware that he was tackling a new work.

In any case, he carried it off beautifully. A tall, square-faced, powerfully built man in spectacles, he seemed not in the least intimidated by the difficulties of the score. "Suk, when he could be heard, played with tenacity and gusto," wrote

Karen Monson in the *Chicago Daily News*. ". . . A thoroughly sympathetic account of the material," wrote Robert C. Marsh in the *Chicago Sun-Times*.

In fact, he carried it off one night under circumstances more difficult than the critics knew. For on Saturday night, when the critics were absent, one of the strings of his Stradivarius broke while he was playing his solo. Solti stopped the orchestra while Suk went offstage and mounted a new string on the instrument. Then Suk came back and began playing—and another string broke. This time not only Suk but Solti was surprised. "The first time, no. But the second time, that never happened to me before." Solti went on: "I have broken strings. I have broken strings, one here, one there, in months. But two broken strings in one night, that has never happened to me before."

Suk had a right to be shattered by the experience. Here he'd come so far to play a world premiere with the finest orchestra in the world, and all he'd encountered was a difficult score and two broken strings in one night. But he remained quite poised. He examined the second broken string onstage, then turned and handed his Stradivarius to the concertmaster, Samuel Magad. Magad, in turn, gave his Strad to Suk so that the soloist could resume his performance. "Usually, when I break a string," says Magad, "I would pass the violin to whoever is assisting at the moment. He gives me his violin and I continue to play on his violin, so the the play of the concertmaster can go on." What happens to the assistant? "He can either change the string or pass it on to somebody else to change the string"—so that the assistant concertmaster can continue to play his score.

In this case, Magad did not pass the Suk instrument back. "It was towards the end of the concerto so I tried to play on his instrument without the string," says Magad. "I just improvised a little bit." And considering the shape of the score, the improvisations would hardly be noticed by anybody—if only because so many players were improvising.

Solti was not discouraged either at the difficulties or at the results. "It was difficult but the concerto was interesting. Very interesting. It was the first performance of that piece at all and I thought it was very good."

All but lost on the drama and difficulty of the Martinů premier were the other efforts of the second week of Solti's season. In that week, Pablo Casals, the great cellist, had died at the age of ninety-six, and Solti opened the Thursday night performance with a memorial to him—the Adagietto from Mahler's Symphony no. 5. ("The performance may have been technically flawed, but it was emotionally rich and beautifully shaded. And it was an apt tribute from the Chicago Symphony to a great musician and humanitarian," wrote Karen Monson in the *Chicago Daily News.*)

For the rest of the program, Solti returned to the sound and the composers of the sound that he likes best. He chose the overture to Berlioz's opera *Les Francs-juges*, one of the composer's more youthful works which had never been quite finished. In fact, the score was cannibalized by Berlioz—much in the way old autos or warplanes are cannibalized by mechanics—and the music used in other works, including the *Symphonie Fantastique* and the *Symphonie Funèbre et Triomphale*. The work had been performed only once in history by the Chicago

The Soltis receive admirers after a performance.

Symphony, exactly seventy-nine years to the day of Solti's Saturday night performance. The critics did not particularly care for the choice (". . . makes up in amusing brassy bombast what it lacks in subtlety," said Monson). Nor did they care much for the choice of two Strauss works: *Macbeth*, a tone poem, and the Dance of the Seven Veils. (". . . two examples of juvenalia kept alive by greater things from the same men," wrote Robert C. Marsh of *Macbeth* and *Les Francs-juges*.) But the criticism seemed aimed at the choice of music, rather than the playing of it. The audiences gave their own views, with demands for repeated bows—more than on opening night, in fact—and by staying in their seats to the end, instead of trying to beat the traffic jam out of the hall.

The Time of Testing

$\mathbf{A}$s the autumn deepened, Georg Solti did not progress through the season. He fought his way through it.

The next two weeks would make the difficulties with the Martinů work seem like recreation. "This was one of the hardest two-week periods I have ever had," he says.

Essentially, it would involve three weeks of work in two weeks of time. Onstage at Orchestra Hall, he would perform two of the mightiest works of the season: the *Missa Solemnis* of Beethoven and Mahler's Symphony no. 6. He would also spend, in that time, the equivalent of a week's work in recording Beethoven's Symphony no. 3, his Symphony no. 5, and his Symphony no. 8. Beyond all this, he was running rehearsals for the eastern tour that would follow these two weeks. "All that, in a fortnight, was a mammoth, a mammoth task," he says. "I was overtired by that time. I would not like to repeat those weeks again very quickly."

In one sense, Solti was vaguely bothered, distracted, by what was happening elsewhere. In moments of professional tension, he's always been able to rely on a particular kind of professional woman—self-sufficient, self-confident, able to anticipate his needs and wishes without stepping on his prerogatives. Margaret Hillis, director of the Chicago Symphony Chorus, is such a woman: she would play an enormously important part in resolving the tensions of the upcoming weeks. Another such woman is Enid Blech, his secretary. She hadn't made this trip to Chicago and, though she was replaced by a thoroughly competent young woman, Elizabeth Allen, there was the worry of Solti over what was happening to Mrs. Blech.

"You know, of course, that I had cancer of the esophagus?" she said when we first met.

"Yes. I was quite lucky, you know. I've had it about five months only. That's the tragedy about cancer, so many people have it and they don't know that they've got it."

She is a bright, matter-of-fact woman in her fifties, the sensible-shoe type. There is a classic British-older-woman's beauty about her and a sense of the unconventional within her: she flies her own plane and, until now, had casually smoked very discreet cigars. "He hated it, of course," she says about Solti's reaction. "He's violently antismoking. But that was the one thing I never gave in about. Until now. The irony is that since I've had this operation for cancer, I feel exactly the way he feels about smoking. So he's had his victory after all, hasn't he?"

She's been with Sir Georg for twelve of the last thirteen years. She was married to a musician, Harry Blech, who was a violinist in the BBC Symphony Orchestra and later conductor of the London Mozart Players. Her husband's manager, Joan Ingpen, was also a co-worker on different projects with Sir Georg. She was controller of opera planning at Covent Garden while Solti was music director there and more recently has worked with the Paris Opéra. "She knew I was looking for a job—this was long after I got divorced—and she rang me up one day and said, 'Look, there's a new music director coming to Covent Garden. Georg Solti. I know he's looking for a secretary and I somehow think you two would click.' I was madly interested. I started life as a singer and I wanted to get back to opera, so I went along and saw him." But then there was a mix-up and delay; the opera front office wanted his secretary to know a good deal about radio. So it was all put off for a while and after six months or so, Mrs. Blech concluded it was all off. "What a pity," she thought. And she put it out of her mind.

These were difficult months for Solti. He was learning a new language: his English then had not achieved the high polish and "distinction" that it has today. He was learning a new culture: the English way of doing things is considerably different, of course, from the German, the Swiss, and the Hungarian ways. And he was even learning to respond to the combination of culture and language in its simplest form: people kept calling him "George" and he was baffled by it. "Maestro" was the least he expected—and "George" was not the right name at all. Not then. For his name has been a reflection of the various incarnations that he's gone through. When he was a boy and a young man in Hungary, his first name was György. The affectionate adaptation was "Gyuri." Even today, his wife and a very few intimates call him that: it comes out now as "Yuri." In any case, when he moved to Switzerland and later to Germany, he changed the spelling and pronunciation. It became "Georg" or "Gae-org"—pronounced quite swiftly so that the two syllables become almost one. In England, people noticed the missing e on "George" but they didn't let it bother them: they called him after their kings, anyway. In time, Solti came very much to like it. He would have liked to have formally added the e to "Georg," and thus have become thoroughly Anglicized, when he was knighted. But there seems to have been a mix-up in the passport documents and his name was printed out once again as "Georg." So Georg he's remained in print—though he's George in conversation.

The acclimatization of Georg Solti was very much in progress when Joan Ingpen phoned Mrs. Blech again, just as the latter was about to go on a summer holiday. "Are you still interested in that job with Solti?" Yes, very much. "Good. He wants you immediately. He needs you at once. You must cancel all your plans and go to him now."

"This was the sort of thing—well, I should have known right there what my future was going to be," says Mrs. Blech.

The future as present is always "quick-quick-quick hurry-hurry." Mrs. Blech does not find this disagreeable. "I like doing things quickly. And besides, he's very, very tidy-minded. He's very, very clear. Never wastes time and can't bear anybody else who wastes time either. Very decisive; makes decisions quickly. Inclines to make decisions too fast but you're never left in any doubt about what he wants: he's very clear, for an artist. I mean, most of the artists I know are inclined to—you use that expression in America?—to sort of *waffle*. 'I'm not sure—maybe we do this, maybe we do that, or on the other hand we might do something else.' " This is not to say that every decision that Solti makes is a final one. "With traveling—I mean I never get the tickets until, if possible, the midnight before, you know, because everything gets changed twenty times over. But then I'm used to that." When he makes a decision that turns out to be a mistake, he takes the blame himself. "Believe me, there are a lot of men who do not do that. If they make a mistake, they try to palm it off on the secretary or anybody else who happens to be around. But Sir Georg is not like that a bit. He always admits his own mistakes."

His flaw is trying to cram so much into a day—his musical studies, his rehearsals and concerts, his administrative work, his planning. At one point in 1974, he scheduled a concert for Sunday afternoon and a flight to New York Sunday night so he could be in a dentist's office in Manhattan at seven-thirty in the morning so he could catch a ten o'clock plane to London. "He has the most unbelievable energies," she says. But what about his state of fatigue? One of the newspapers in Chicago would comment soon on his "continued pallor." That is real, of course, when he has a cold or is suffering from jet-lag. "But the day he doesn't say, 'I am dead,' I shall know he's really ill." But the variety of his day gives him a sense of renewal, she says. "He relaxes from conducting by having a business meeting, sitting down and planning like mad. And then he relaxes from administrative work by going down to the orchestra and conducting."

She has many functions—some of them spontaneous—other than helping Sir Georg in his business approach. He hates inattention when his orchestra is playing. At a performance of Wagner one night, Mrs. Blech hit a bothersome and inattentive operagoer with her handbag, just by way of focusing his attention on the music. "It is only right," said Sir Georg probatively, "that Wagner should provoke a passionate response."

His own passionate response during one Wagnerian episode was handled, as always, by Mrs. Blech. He was conducting *Götterdämmerung* at Covent Garden when a man in the front row, close left on Solti in the pit, began coughing and barking like a seal. Solti can't stand noise under any circumstance—"he absolutely hates it," sayd Mrs. Blech. In particular, he can't stand noise during a perform-ance. The trouble with this man is that he just didn't cough; he coughed long and hard, with the reflexiveness and persistence of a consumptive. The experience was all but shattering to Solti. "He was really quite upset," says Mrs. Blech. At intermission, she came up with a solution: she put a couple of cough drops in the tails of his formal wear so he could take medicine to the man. Just before starting the next act, Solti turned to the cougher and said, "Here, take these." And he handed the cough drops to him. It did no good; the cougher dropped them and, in the dark, couldn't find them on the floor. So he continued coughing. At the next intermission, Solti was even more distraught. "I mean, he was practically in tears, he was in such a state," says Mrs. Blech. "He said he could not go on with the performance unless this man was gotten rid of." She came up with another solution: she'd swap seats with the cougher, giving him her seat in the grand tier for his in the front row. Because of the view of the stage, hers was considered a better seat and he'd likely accept the swap. "All right," said Solti. "But I am not starting the next act until I am seeing you sitting in that seat." She negotiated the swap and—when she took the seat in the front row—got almost as much applause as Solti did on mounting the podium.

She sometimes has to play Solti's fears and phobias off against his drive for efficiency. When the Chicago Symphony was on the West Coast in the spring of 1973 on a nationwide tour, Mrs. Blech scheduled him to take a chartered light plane from San Francisco to Fresno. She'd love it; she simply loves flying her own plane. But he didn't. "He started getting in a panic about this," she says. Sir Georg has only barely reconciled himself to big-plane jet travel, and he was not about to go up in a tiny plane that can practically fly around the interior of a 747. "Weeks and weeks before we ever came to America, he was saying, 'I don't go. I don't go.' " He was told that he'd be wasting a frightful amount of time if he didn't make this trip by light plane. "So by the time we got to America, he was saying, 'I don't go—if there is no airline flight, I don't go. We check the airline schedules.' " Each time, he was faced with the inefficient alternatives and each time he backed off to different excuses: "I don't go. If the weather is bad, I don't go." Mrs. Blech calmed and cajoled him. "Of course we won't go if the weather is bad. We'll take the car. Of course, it *will* take a great deal more time . . ."

By such hints, by such reassurances, by sweet words and suggested conflicts, she got him to agree to go to the airport. Then to get on the plane. He sat deep and suspicious in the seat as the plane took off and headed for Fresno. Then he began getting interested in what was going on around him, and finally in the fact that he could see the ground. Soon he was peeking over the pilot's shoulder, and by the time the plane landed, he was bounding off to greet those who'd met him at the Fresno airport with assurances that it was "Splendid. Just splendid. You really must try it. It is a splendid way to travel."

Every time Mrs. Blech introduces him to some of the amenities of modern life, there is resistance, then doubt, and finally resolution. The same thing happened when he first got on the subway. "He'd never been on the underground and I told him it was disgraceful, that he couldn't possibly live in London without having been on the underground." But she waited for a moment when he had to get from his home to a recording studio very quickly—"it would take hours to get through the traffic by car and get back in time for a concert." She traced the subway route for him and said: "It will be three times as quick as going by car."

"You really think so?"

"I don't think so. I know so."

"All right. We do it." But then he had second thoughts as the time for departure neared. "I think it's better if the chauffeur, Franko, comes with me."

"Oh, no," said Mrs. Blech. "You're not getting out of it now."

He went with her to the station, exhibited a great deal of astonishment—and no little wonder—at how people got tickets through a little hole in a window, and proceeded to deep doubt when she chose the eastbound platform to wait for the train.

"He said, 'How do you know we go eastbound?' "

"Because we are in West London and we are going into the city, which is east."

"You are sure?"

"I am quite sure."

But *he* was not sure, particularly when a train came and went on the other platform.

"I don't think you are right. I think you are wrong. I think we should be on the other platform."

Finally, the train came, pulled to a stop, and Solti stood with his toes and nose against the doors. "Why doesn't it open? What happened? It is not opening. Where is the man to open it?"

Mrs. Blech explained that there's a few seconds' lapse between the time the motorman brings the train to a stop and the doors open automatically. When it opened, he rushed in (" 'Tis empty. 'Tis empty."—"Yes, it usually is in the middle of the day") and then began worrying. "It won't start—why won't it start?" The train started and, says Mrs. Blech, "He was like a little boy. His eyes were popping out when we went into the tube. 'We are under the ground? You are *sure* we are under the ground?' Then he kept looking at his watch. 'How do you know when we have to get off?' "

It went on and on like that, as Mrs. Blech got him to the studios and then back to the opera. "When we got to Covent Garden, I just felt, you know, completely exhausted."

Not Solti. He felt renewed. He went bounding up to a friend and co-worker, saying "I must tell you something—I have just discovered a splendid way . . ."

In those days, Solti spent a good portion of the year in London. Since his main assignment was as music director of Covent Garden, he did his planning and administrative work there and left only on guest-conducting expeditions. It was easier for him to acquire a sense of "belonging," to begin to learn the everyday aspect of living. He has yet to do it in Chicago, and one of the reasons is the staccato nature of his Chicago ventures.

In 1973–74, Solti would make three trips to Chicago rather than schedule the two six- and seven-week stretches of the past. He would play four programs in this stretch in Chicago, then two programs in January, followed by five weeks in the spring. The two weeks of tour in the east—one in the autumn, one in the spring—would then fill out the thirteen weeks he devotes to the Chicago Symphony.

"He finds it terribly exhausting, having those long stretches," says Mrs. Blech. "Because the pressure here is enormous. I mean, one is going full tilt all day, every day, and he found that doing it for six or seven weeks at a stretch a killing pace." On the other hand, the extra travel—one more round trip between London and Chicago a season—and the extra drain of jet-lag reduce his personal sense of efficiency enormously. He would go through the three-trips-a-year schedule one more time, and then he would return to the two-trip basis. "What he's going to do is stay a longer period, but have one week free from conducting, a little break where he can get his breath, don't you see," says Mrs. Blech.

This is something akin to his pace in Paris. "When he conducts the Paris orchestra, they have concerts only every other week, so he has two weeks for one program. Mind you, he needs far more rehearsal with that orchestra than with Chicago, because in Chicago the players are so quick that you can prepare a very complicated program in just three days' rehearsing, which you probably couldn't do with another orchestra."

But even the singular skills of the Chicago Symphony do not take all the problems off his shoulders. For there are always complications and, in the week of *Missa Solemnis*, they reached a climax with a series of cancellations by the soloists he'd labored so hard to book three years earlier. In fact, the most unpleasant experience of the season, he would say later, "was the *Missa Solemnis* cancellations. I had eight soloists instead of four. And for only three performances. Four of them never had any rehearsal. I know I come from an opera house, so I am not easily disturbed by singers, but that was rather a bit hard, a bit hard. And you must make these changes when you are tired and you don't really want to go to rehearsals."

There is always a scramble when singers cancel. The stability in such situations is offered by Margaret Hillis and the Chicago Symphony Chorus. For she always has reserves for the most hectic of situations—and this was the most hectic situation. For every focal work with the orchestra, for example, she doesn't just have stand-ins. She has *two sets* of stand-ins, in case there has to be a substitute for a substitute. This is not, of course, done just to provide for emergencies. The stand-ins sing the solo parts in the rehearsals of the chorus, long before the big-name soloists ever appear. "They use those stand-ins to cover the first time the conductor meets with the chorus," says John Edwards. "This is usually two weeks before the first performance." So the center of stability, in these frantic days of the preparation and performance of *Missa Solemnis*, was the Chicago Symphony Chorus and its director, Margaret Hillis. Both this character and this characteristics have made Margaret Hillis the most successful woman conductor in the world.

Now fifty-two, Margaret Hillis is a strong-featured, well-tailored woman who lives in a rambling yellow-brick, green-roofed, gabled home on Chicago's North Shore, with a cat named Menelaus. She has been conducting, or trying to conduct, in a man's world for forty years. It has taken persistence, direction, design, and delicacy. For there is never any assurance about how the Chicago Symphony and its chorus might attract attention.

Maloney was ready to go out for breakfast. He walked by Coatsworth who was sitting in a chair with a forlorn look. There was a handcuff on his right wrist.

It was from a story by Tom Fitzpatrick, Pulitzer Prizewinning columnist for the *Chicago Sun-Times*. Maloney, Bill, was a sergeant in the Chicago Police Department. Coatsworth, James, was a thick-haired man of twenty-five with serious deep-set eyes and a worried look. He'd been a music major at Roosevelt University but now he had a job outside music, assistant manager of a Sheraton hotel in Chicago. He also had a sideline: acquiring keys and slipping into hotel rooms to steal what he could. At least that's what he was charged with. Now Maloney was trying to get him to open up about his activities—to open the first crack on which personal admission might be built.

"You studied music, he?" Maloney asked. "Tell me about it."

"I'm a bass-baritone," Coatsworth said. "I also play the piano. A couple of times I sang in the chorus with the Chicago Symphony."

"What did you sing?" Maloney asked.

"Well," Coatsworth said, "Carlo Maria Giulini was the conductor. We sang *Stabat Mater*; one time it was the *Gloria* by Vivaldi."

"How far did you get in school?" Maloney asked.

Coatsworth shook his head. His face was drawn.

"Well, I went two years but I guess you could say I only got as far as Burglary 101."

And so the singing started. About burglary. It was the most singular, but not the most memorable, performance by a member of the Chicago Symphony Orchestra Chorus that season. ("The strange thing is that I don't remember him," says Margaret Hillis. "He must have been in for only one or two performances and then drifted away. Because people who've been with us for a year, I remember. Even though there are two hundred of them.")

The memorable performances were to be *Missa Solemnis* in the upcoming week and the *St. Matthew Passion* in the Easter week. There was only one demand: they had to be better than the tradition established by the chorus in the last few years. Though the chorus trains separately from the orchestra—until the rehearsals just before and in the week of performance—there is a perfectly fused relationship between orchestra and chorus that exudes a kind of magic, a music which hits like a tidal wave, engulfing one in energy and drive, yet with the tones sharp and focused, the phrases clear and strong. The result can be illustrated by the reaction when the orchestra and some of the members of the chorus performed act 3 of Wagner's *Die Götterdämmerung* in a concert version in New York in the spring of 1973. Harold C. Schonberg of *The New York Times* summed it up in this way:

"Sir Georg slowly brought his arms down in the great Redemption scene that ends the opera. The audience could not wait to start cheering. There was a rising ovation; nobody made a move towards the exit; it was as though all present wanted to let the tonal images remain in their minds and ears, meanwhile paying homage to a great conductor and orchestra, and a brilliant group of singers."

In one sense, the singers make it all possible. The orchestra obviously flourishes on its own sounds, but it reaches beyond greatness when Solti brings the chorus and orchestra together. For there *is* the dimension of the sound of the human voice. There *is* the dimension of drama that is inherent in the great choral numbers. Most of all, there *is* the dual skill of Solti, as a conductor of opera—thus knowing the quality that singers must achieve—and a conductor of the symphony orchestra.

He uses those skills on singers in the same remorseless way that he uses them on the orchestra. In the autumn of 1971, he was in Vienna, preparing for the recording of Mahler's Eighth Symphony. The Chicago Symphony Orchestra would stop in Vienna during its European tour that year—its first European tour—to provide the music. But the Chicago Symphony Chorus, which works almost reflexively with the orchestra, would not be there to provide the song. ("It just was financially completely impossible—$150,000 just to take them over for that recording session," says Miss Hillis.) And so Solti and London/Decca, the recording company, turned to the Vienna Singverein, the Vienna State Opera Chorus, and the Vienna Boys' Choir to accompany the Chicago Symphony.

The quality was not what Solti was used to hearing from Hillis's chorus in Chicago. "They were singing sloppy, like an opera chorus," he said. "I told them, 'I am bringing you an orchestra that can play Mahler for twenty minutes and never make the smallest mistake. Will we have to sop the recording session because the *chorus* makes mistakes?' " In Chicago, this was unthinkable; the chorus there does not make mistakes—it knows the quality of the orchestra. But in Vienna? "They didn't believe me. But then they heard, and they believed."

In Chicago, Solti is just as demanding. He does not let Chicago know what Vienna is hearing. He expects and gets more out of the chorus, just as he expects and gets more out of the orchestra. But he sometimes appears more demanding of the chorus and its members. For one thing, there are so many more of them—170 in the stripped-down version, 201 (or almost twice the number of players in the orchestra) when all are onstage at the same time. Thus he must seek ways of getting all their attention constantly. And he does: "When Solti's around, everybody sits up and pays attention," says Dick Carter, manager of the Chicago Symphony Chorus. But he also believes that the chorus, like the orchestra, must constantly surpass itself.

"We are trained only to go within 10 percent of our maximum vocal fortissimo," says Carter, who also sings in the chorus. But when the orchestra and chorus were performing Beethoven's Symphony no. 9 (the *Choral*) several seasons ago, Solti asked—on one memorable phrase—just a little bit more than 100 percent. The phrase was that which ends the section in which the chorus and the quartet of soloists—tenor, bass, soprano, and mezzo-soprano—close on a climactic *"Und der Cherub steht vor Gott!"* (". . . And the cherub stands before God!") It is a place of rising emotion and, as Carter has described it, "everybody was wide open at the invocation of '*Gott!*' "

Solti wanted something more.

In particular, he wanted it out of the sopranos, who already were singing at a pitch and an intensity that were causing them some discomfort. The tone almost inevitably deteriorated under the length of the stress and Solti became impatient. He did not ask them to hold the note steady. Instead he said, "I think I would like a *crescendo* here." The sopranos were appalled. They did not think it could be done. But when the moment came in the performance, Solti—who is, as we've seen,

somewhat vocal—cued the sopranos and screamed: "*Vor Gott*, for God's sake!"
The shocked sopranos went blue in the face. But they managed their crescendo.
And they stayed on pitch.

"Some day, I am sure," says Dick Carter, "we will be known as the 'chorus of
bleeding throats.' "

That the chorus can respond with blood—and guts—is because of the skills and
drives of Margaret Hillis. She is the prime example of how a man with the *macho*
of Solti finds his substance, and some of his success, in the work of a woman. A
woman in his profession—for she has every bit as much authority on the podium
as does Solti, if a slightly easier temperament and a readier run of humor. And she
is just as well organized in her rehearsals as is Solti.

"I went through many years of disciplining myself to a smooth working rehearsal
technique so that I knew exactly what had to be done next," she says. "For many
years I would plan out every rehearsal, minute by minute. If you asked me what I
was going to be rehearsing at seven minutes after ten, I could tell you what note was
going to be sounding.

"Then I would go home from the rehearsal and look carefully over what worked
and what didn't work. For what didn't work, I'd try to figure out 'Why not? What
was it that I did that kept that from working?' Then I would try something else the
next week to see if it worked."

She got many of her basic principles in choral work when she studied under
Robert Shaw at the Juilliard School in New York. "But I had to refine them
myself, and there was a good ten years when I planned and replanned every
rehearsal, I don't know how many times. Hundreds of times. Just to get that
technique developed to the point where rehearsals would run smoothly, where the
discipline of the chorus came out of the music making and not out of a whip being
cracked over their head. Which I can't do. I'm not temperamentally suited to that,
any more than Mr. Solti is."

The full-chorus rehearsal is held once a week—from seven o'clock to ten o'clock
on Monday evening. Then there are separate workouts with the different sections
of the chorus. "I work on Saturday afternoon from two to five with the altos, and
four to seven with the sopranos. Then on Sunday afternoon two to five with the
basses, four to seven with the tenors." There's an overlap in times that allows her to
work the two sections together for a while. "But there are certain numbers that
require a change. The Mahler Eighth Symphony"—which the orchestra and
chorus would do the following summer at Ravinia—has a double chorus. So Miss
Hillis splits the full chorus into two and rehearses them as two choruses instead of
as sections. "It will be chorus one on Saturday and chorus two on Sunday, and
then on Monday night we put them back together again."

The times for the rehearsals must be chosen carefully to allow the members of
the chorus to carry on their activities. Those members of the chorus who are
professional musicians usually have Monday night off and usually can make room
on a weekend afternoon for a rehearsal. "There are 93 professionals we carry on the
rolls this season," says Miss Hillis. "That means that 108 don't get paid, just more
than half." They get paid by the concert ($35 for one, $48 for two, $60 for three),

and they get paid for rehearsing ($3.15 an hour for some, $4.15 for others), and they get paid for the warm-up period before a concert ($3.15 for the first hour, $3.50 for the second). So the top professionals earn about $203 for the typical performance—thirty hours of rehearsal, three performances, and warm-up periods. The amateur members of the choruses are students, lawyers, anything. "We have lots of nurses and doctors. One part-time archaeologist—her husband is a professor, specializing in the Hittites, at the University of Chicago. Accountants and housewives. We had a garage mechanic several years ago. We have lots and lots of public school music teachers; many of those came in to smile on me, as they say, for a year and suddenly they find they've been here for ten or twelve years. They were just going to learn for a year and somehow they ended up seduced and stuck with it."

So the motives and drives of the members of the chorus are as different from each other's as those that animate the players of the Chicago Symphony Orchestra. For most it is a hobby, an unpaid outside activity peripheral to their main lives; even for the professionals, it is not a way to make a living, though students who hold a union card can expect to be paid for their labors. But such paid students are not in abundance. "I would say that the average age of the chorus is between thirty and forty, where people are still in a very mobile state of life," says Margaret Hillis. They are mobile for all kinds of reasons. The lawyers get a better job with another firm in another city: "we just had one lawyer, Fred Houghtelling, who was with the chorus for five years and suddenly got a marvelous job with the State Department in Washington." Others simply go on to more exalted singing careers. "Sherrill Milnes"—a leading baritone at the Metropolitan Opera—"was with us two years as an amateur and three years as a professional. It must have been close to fifteen years ago." She'd been conducting the Chicago Symphony Chorus for only two years at the time he appeared for an audition. "When he came in and sang for me, he was not vocally ready at all," she says. "But there was a very special quality—now and then you meet somebody who has that star on his head. And he was very bright, very intense, and zeroed in on what he was doing. Very careful about what he was doing, and very musical. He had that sort of extrasensory perception that many great artists do. I've conducted when he's been a soloist and we never knew when he was following me or I was following him—we just went, we know, each of us knew exactly what was going to happen."

The chorus has turned out many another promising operatic talent. Richard Best, who's already gone on to the Metropolitan, is an example. "We have another tenor, a marvelous young artist, Bill Wahman, who's now with the Western Opera company. And another, Barbara Pearson, who went to Europe and started out as an apprentice a year or two years ago in the Cologne Opera House and then she was signed on as a leading lyric soprano." Many of the more ambitious young singers go to Europe to seek jobs in opera. "We don't have many opera houses in this country," points out Margaret Hillis. "The Met is the only one that has a year-round season. But Germany has sixty opera houses and many of them are light opera"—which opens an opportunity to more voices than does grand opera. "That's why Germany has more American opera singers than America has. They have to go there to get their experience."

But all this is up to the individual. The Chicago Symphony Chorus is not a school and not a placement organization. It has a primary function: to perform with the Chicago Symphony Orchestra with the same skills, or higher ones, that the orchestra itself possesses. The remarkable thing is that so many people respond to the discipline of the chorus with no greater reward than an abstract one of excellence achieved. There are very few people who take spontaneous leaves from the orchestra, for example. "We have a few people who earn their way entirely by music, and they occasionally have to take a leave of absence because they have a big job someplace," says Margaret Hillis. But the regularity and punctuality are, on the whole, astonishing. "We have a remarkable rehearsal attendance record," says Miss Hillis. "I think the average for the whole season may be sixty calls"—to appear perhaps three to six times. "That includes rehearsals and performance. And the average number of absences at each rehearsal may be around three and one-fourth." That means that, on the average, 98 percent of all the people in the chorus show up when they have to. "The morale is exceptionally high," she reports. "There are many factors that enter into that, but I think that probably Mr. Solti is the strongest factor that enters into it. Simply because of the excitement of his performances. Plus the fact that we are now casting small roles for the *Salome* that he will be doing next year and the *St. Matthew* that we're doing in the spring. So that our singers can see that some of them will have a chance to appear as a soloist with a major orchestra."

The chorus is also aware that more and more voices are coming along—more voices and better ones. "I reaudition the chorus every year," says Miss Hillis. "It's the only way you can keep the standards up." Prospects, and present chorus members, begin applying for the auditions as early as April or May for auditions that will take place in the last week of August and the first week in September. In this season, Miss Hillis would be preparing to take on thirty new members. Not so much to replace people who are fired—"that doesn't often happen in this chorus"—but to replace those who've gotten married, or taken new and more demanding jobs, or simply moved away. Those who do win a place in the chorus get a learning experience as well as a singing experience. "I attempt in the rehearsals to give them principles by which they can work," says Margaret Hillis. "To get them related to the score, to the insight that the sound they make is expressive of the inner quality of the music and not just a bunch of notes that sit up there." Beyond this, there are formal classes for the singers who want to take them. "I'm under obligation to turn in a first-class performance whenever we go onstage," says Miss Hillis. "But my feeling is that if we don't educate them—well, I think the worst thing I can do is send the professionals away with nothing but money."

So free classes for those interested are held in Orchestra Hall on Monday nights, an hour before rehearsal time. These are very practical courses, useful now and in the future, rather than being devoted to theory. "We have classes in punctual harmony, so that they know how to tune, how intonation works when it comes to harmonic motion. We have classes in German diction, in French diction, Italian diction. This gives them—particularly those who are potential soloists—an insight into their own work on lieder, the French repertoire, any opera roles they may encounter. And when we're working on an Italian piece, we have Italian coaching. So their morale is very high simply because they feel they're learning something of value. And I think they are."

There is a large talent pool for prospects for the Chicago Symphony. Not only among the musically inclined and talented but among children being formally trained in voice in Chicago. The Chicago Symphony Chorus recruits from a children's chorus that often supplements the chorus. It is called the Glen Ellyn Children's Chorus (because it is headquartered in Glen Ellyn, a suburb of Chicago). "I think their age limits are seven to twelve—on your thirteenth birthday you're out," says Miss Hillis. "They audition any kid who wants to apply—I think they choose about 150 kids out of 400 auditions." The best of these then get a chance to sing with the Chicago Symphony Chorus in those numbers in which younger voices are needed. "There will be seventy of them involved in the *St. Matthew Passion*," she explains. "There will be one hundred of them in the Mahler Eighth this summer at Ravinia."

There is another children's chorus in Chicago that provides voices on occasion for both the Chicago Symphony performances and the Lyric Opera. It is called the Chicago Children's Choir and it is headquartered in the First Unitarian Church in Hyde Park, in the shadow of the University of Chicago. There are 550 youngsters in the chorus, ranging in age from eight to eighteen, and they sing a regular schedule of summertime performances—in the summer of 1973 the best of them took part in a production of *I Pagliacci* in Grant Park. The director and founder, the Reverend Christopher Moore, studied at Harvard University and with the Vienna Boys' Choir. The repertory of his choir ranges from sixteenth-century motets to gospel-shouting. It is open to youngsters of any race or religion. Because it is in the inner city, in an integrated neighborhood, it is a little more accessible to black children than is the Glen Ellyn Children's Chorus. (There are no black members of the Chicago Symphony Orchestra. There are about a dozen black performers in the Chicago Symphony Chorus. Classical music is not exactly the "thing" in the black community; the traditions and historic instruments of the black culture are not the European tradition which is the foundation of symphonic music. For that reason, the orchestra instruments have not usually been the route of the blacks to symphonic performance. But the great voices, which are common to any culture, give blacks an opening into the classical repertory on the highest possible levels—in grand opera and with major symphony orchestras.) In the case of the Chicago Children's Choir, an effort is made to keep the unit open to every youngster from any neighborhood who has the voice to gain entrance to the choir: it maintains a busing operation to bring children from distant neighborhoods three times a week to the church for rehearsals. They do not charge for this. The choir exists only on fees from its performances, support from a sponsor, Urban Gateway, and on contributions through the church. ("People are just reluctant to give to any organization," says Mrs. Jane Mather, administrative assistant for the choir. "The handwriting is on the wall—people just aren't giving.") To make sure that the opportunity is there, the admission standards are eloquently simple. "We will take anybody who walks through the door, can sing 'My Country, 'tis of Thee,' and has a voice that can be trained," says Mrs. Mather.

Putting all of these skills together is, for Margaret Hillis, an enormous problem and remorseless stimulus, particularly with Solti raising his standards. At the first rehearsal of Berlioz's *La Damnation de Faust* a year or so earlier, Solti was concerned that, in Orchestra Hall, he could not get quite the projection of sound he wanted in certain parts of the score. He couldn't add people to the chorus: it already fills the rear shell of the state on a number of tiers, making the musicians appear a little crowded.

"Do you suppose it would look phony if we used megaphones?" he asked Miss Hillis.

Well, it would make the chorus look like something out of Rudy Vallee. But Margaret Hillis and Dick Carter were willing to experiment with the idea.

The only trouble is that it wasn't easy to come up with two hundred megaphones, simple in color and discreet in size. There were problems beyond projection: where could the members of the chorus put the megaphones when they weren't being used? They have no storage facilities onstage; they couldn't even put them on the floor—no space because of the crowd—so they'd probably have to hold them in their hands throughout the performance, which caused problems with holding of the music folders. And how could they bring them to their mouths without causing a snicker, or outright laughter in the audience —since there might be a Rudy Vallee image in it all? Thus using the megaphones for projection might defeat the whole purpose of the performance, by focusing the audience's attention on the megaphones instead of on the music. Nevertheless, Solti's order is Hillis's command and she assigned several of her aides to check out the megaphone inventory in Chicago. "They called stores and couldn't come up with anything." But Dick Carter had a workable idea. He went out and got two hundred small Dixie Cups—"with the bottoms knocked out of them." The chorus tried the cups at rehearsal the next day and found that "they really projected the sound out. Terrific!"

They solved the other problems, too. "We could flatten them and put them in the folders or the men could put them in their pockets," says Miss Hillis. "We felt the singers could sort of sneak them out and get them rounded so that there'd be no motion out in front of the bodies—so the audience couldn't notice the motion." From that point, the Dixie Cups had to be brought to the mouth with precise uniformity—so that there was no ragged movement of arms all across the stage —and with great subtlety. "We practiced movement the way we practice song—"one, two, three, four—one, two *Sing!*" It took work and it took persuasion. "Solti was afraid it would look phony. 'Does it look phony?' he kept asking me," says Miss Hillis. The concern was understandable: Solti didn't want people laughing at the Chicago Symphony for singing through Dixie Cups. The chorus got the discipline down perfectly—"and I told him 'No, it didn't look phony.' " Solti accepted her view: the Dixie Cups did give him the sound that he wanted and the movement was not enough to distract the audience from that sound.

"So we went ahead and used them," says Hillis.

"And not a critic made a comment on it."

In her own work on the podium, Margaret Hillis has the skill to put all of the needs of the chorus in perspective. "Here you must be Presbyterians and have a strong sense of predestination," she tells the chorus at one point during a rehearsal. Or: "Think a forte here, don't sing it," she says, understanding that many members of the chorus are—like chorale singers everywhere—inclined to sing a little piano so that they can hear each other. Or: "It's just like a Frenchman chopping a salad—chip, chip, chip—the eighth notes must be *even*."

"She really penetrates each work—she really studies the music," says one of the members of her chorus. "She has a most kind personality. I've never heard her utter a harsh word that reflects on a personality of a singer. All of her comments are directed towards the development of the music." To be sure, she is not—in the view of this singer—perfect. "She has almost no left hand. There is no indication, in her conducting, that it is different from her right." But: "She has unending patience. She is really like the phoenix. She was born and, to reach her peak, she has to die—she must come back to work within the personality of another conducter." Such as Georg Solti.

The evidence is not common. For the common evidence is that Margaret Hillis works on her own at a variety of labors. She is chairman of the Department of Choral Activities at Northwestern University. She's music director of the Elgin Symphony Orchestra, in the suburb of that name about forty miles west of Chicago. She shares conducting responsibility for the Chicago Civic Orchestra with Gordon Peters. And once a year or so she conducts the Chicago Symphony Orchestra.

"When I rehearse the Chicago Symphony, I still have a little fear on the podium," she says. "They're such a extraordinary orchestra that any mistake I make, I hear immediately. Of course, when I make one, I look at them and they look at me and they know that I know." So there's a lot of rapport—"but there's still a little fear."

Conducting on the major scale—of a major symphony orchestra and chorus —has been her major ambition. But there is no chance that a woman will be given such a major post. It is more likely that a woman will become president—or perhaps pope—than conductor of a major symphony orchestra. She concedes that there's no breakthrough visible—"not for me." Not at the age of fifty-two. "There might be a chance for a younger woman coming along." But it's not terribly likely. "It takes an enormous combination of luck for a man to make it," she says —without having any extra burdens. Such as womanhood.

It hasn't gotten to her yet. "I'm too busy doing what it's all about, and where I've come to now," she says. "I don't feel a sense of frustration. I did for a long time but I don't now. I feel I've had a very rewarding musical life. People ask if I'm a member of women's lib and the only answer I can give is that I'm too busy."

A man might admit that temperament has barred Miss Hillis from a top conducting job—the male temperament of orchestras—but Margaret Hillis is not likely to use that cop-out. She has a very acute, a very objective mind. A *male* mind, in the view of some male chauvinist pigs. And so she is quite able to analyze the situation in very dispassionate terms. They are both general and personal.

Among the general problems is acquiring the experience with a classical repertory. "You can't get the experience, the repertoire, because you're a woman," she says. "Between the age, say, of twenty-five and fifty, you can't get the experience because you are a woman and then you can't get the job because you don't have the experience." She has been unusually experienced and enterprising and she's conducted a good many works in the choral field that many men never encounter. But not in the orchestral field. "I do orchestral works but I don't have the standard repertoire in my hand. The Brahms symphonies—I've conducted only one. The Beethoven symphonies—I've conducted only five. The Schumann symphonies—only one. That's a great repertoire for a twenty-five-year-old. But I'm fifty-two years old. It isn't that kind of background that the sort of commercial run of the major orchestras need." She would not need as many orchestral works in her repertory as she has choral works. Of the latter, she estimates that there are 600 in her own repertoire. That comes from focusing on the choral effort for so many years. "A major conducting post? I would say no simply because I haven't done 100 performances of Beethoven's Ninth Symphony. I've never conducted the work"—in orchestra and chorus—"and in that sense I'm not qualified even to be an associate conductor with the Chicago Symphony. Because I don't have the repertoire in my hand. "How large an orchestral repertory would she need? "Now if I were to be the conductor of a major symphony, I would have had to have, I would say, a minimum of 150 orchestral works," she says. "At least that much experience with the orchestra repertoire before I ever step on that podium. Choral works, yes, I have—maybe six, seven hundred of them. But not 150 orchestral works."

She admits to career idiosyncrasies. "My rehearsal technique with an orchestra is not of the same order as it is with a chorus. If I had a rehearsal technique and the repertoire with an orchestra that I have with a chorus, I would be qualified for a major conducting position. But I don't have that because I didn't have the opportunity to develop it. That takes time—going away from a rehearsal and thinking it over and 'Aha! That's where I went wrong.' And 'Aha! That worked very well. Now I know something.' "

And finally she concedes some personal idiosyncrasies. She responds beautifully, for example, when she's asked to do a work or assigned to do one. "When it's my assignment to conduct, I prefer to conduct. But the preparation doesn't go as far as when I'm preparing for somebody else," she says. "It goes as far when it comes to the studying of the score, the knowing of it, knowing exactly what's going on. But I don't sit down and mark the parts, and I don't go through the individual instrumental parts, and make sure 'Ah, this man, he's got to know that and so-and-so over here is doing that.' "

She does take this kind of care in choral work, perhaps because it is at the center of her life. Indeed, it was her skill in such assigned work that first brought her—however vicariously—to the attention of Solti. For she was asked to do something for him—really for the Northwestern University Chorus: she didn't know him—and the assignment was classically successful.

She was living in New York at the time—she'd lived there for fifteen years before moving to Chicago. "One summer I came out to do a three-day teaching stint at Northwestern—as a guest lecturer—and I had things all planned out for a certain literature, things that we were going to go through, things that I thought a chorus should know." She was barely settled in when the assistant to the head of the department—the boss was away at the time—came to her with a problem. The Northwestern University Chorus had its major performance every year, and this summer it was going to be at Ravinia singing Haydn's oratorio *The Seasons* with the Chicago Symphony Orchestra under a guest conductor named Georg Solti. "He said, 'They've got a performance next week and they haven't even seen the last five choruses, and the rest of them they don't know very well.' " The implication was that it was up to Margaret Hillis to whip them into shape during her visit to Northwestern. She didn't know *The Seasons*. But he was helpful: he got her a score of it and brought it to her hotel. "This was seven o'clock in the morning. I took it upstairs and I sat down and I studied it until midnight," she says. "I learned the work. Then I went to the singers and I started with the final chorus, which they had not even looked at yet, and I went backwards, chorus by chorus." She managed to do a thorough rehearsing job on the last five choruses before her time was up and she had to leave.

She didn't hear anything about what happened at Ravinia until several years later when she ran into the young assistant who was, by that time, teaching at the University of Wisconsin. "I said, 'Hey, how did that performance ever come out?'

"He said, 'It was the funniest thing. Solti started out at the beginning of the piece and things really didn't work—they weren't rhythmically clean, they weren't in tune. He kept going. He kept going. And getting more and more discouraged. And suddenly he gets five pieces from the end and they're brilliant. The character is there and they know what the piece is about—they know what kind of characterization they're supposed to do. And he couldn't understand what happened.' "

Some years later, when Solti had taken over as music director of the Chicago Symphony, Hillis asked him if he remembered *The Seasons* at Ravinia. He said yes: he couldn't understand what had happened but he was told that somebody else had prepared the Northwestern Chorus in the last five segments.

Margaret Hillis nodded.

"And Solti knew then that I'd done it."

There is no certain route for a woman seeking to become a conductor. There may be, in fact, no route at all. But the struggle of Margaret Hillis is illuminating, if only for the decision which she faced and the decisions which she made.

She was born and grew up in Kokomo, Indiana, in the 1920s before the Depression—the classic small American town ("then about 38,000") in the warming summer of easy prosperity. Her own family knew prosperity: her grandfather Elwood Haynes had been one of the early inventors and producers of the automobile. "The reason he invented the automobile was that the first job he got, the reason he moved to Kokomo, was that they needed somebody with a chemistry background to be an inspector for the natural gas wells around Kokomo. He got sick of riding around behind a horse so he decided that there must be a way to make a horseless carriage. He made it in 1900 and he and my mother drove to New York City in that car—you can imagine what it was like on the roads." He was also, she says, "the first man ever arrested in Chicago in an automobile." She thinks the charge was disturbing the peace—akin today to refusing to bribe an alderman. The idea that he could make a success of all this was, to the rest of the family, incredible. "He was the dreamer in the family. He was the one the rest of his brothers thought they would have to support. But he could put it all down on paper and he could build it to see if it worked," she says. It worked: his original car sits in the Smithsonian Institution, she says. It is a monument to his innovation and his individuality. For when Henry Ford came on with mass-produced cars, Elwood Haynes refused to go along. The result: he went out of business—about 1924, she says. That did not exactly leave the family destitute. For, as a dreamer, he'd developed a number of other devices and thoughts. "I think seven or eight of the things flying around now in space were originally his patents," says Margaret Hillis. Among them: a method for making stainless steel—"he was primarily a metallurgist and stainless steel was his," she explains.

So there was always money for the family as she was growing up in a small midwestern town. And there was also a cultural drive built on antecedents. "The people that settled the town came mainly from Massachusetts and they carried with them a great deal of their cultural heritage. There were literary clubs, where people reviewed books. There were concerts and recitals—when I was a kid I heard Paderewski, for example." Both the money and incentive were there to travel afield for a musical experience. Since young Margaret loved to sing and was fascinated by the radio broadcasts of the Metropolitan Opera on Saturday afternoon—"I wouldn't miss one, or of the New York Philharmonic on Sunday afternoons"—her parents were willing to give her more exposure to music. "My mother brought me to Chicago just to hear the opera," she remembers. "On one Christmas vacation, my mother and I went to New York—I was about fourteen, then—and I remember that in ten days we went to eight concerts, four recitals, and six plays."

On one such venture, she heard Kirsten Flagstad in *Tristan und Isolde*. Given a miniature of the score, Margaret tried to follow the performance right to the point where she heard a microtone shift in the midst of a long-spun note: the orchestra changed chords and, accordingly, Kirsten Flagstad had changed from a D-flat to C-sharp. *That*, to Margaret Hillis, was great musicianship, an attention to detail as well as to volume. It established Flagstad forever in her private Valhalla. "I just adored her," she says today. "She's still my heroine."

Today she can even remember her first introduction not only to singing but to sound, or at least the concepts relayed to her that seem to stimulate memory. Her grandmother was a church organist and, since the family could afford it, she had an organ in her home—a pipe organ of massive expense, not the electric organs that are common today. The pipes were in the basement, under the floor, "and the sound came right up through the floor when she would play it. And I'd crawl out there in the middle and demand that she would play more," says Miss Hillis. "That was really my first introduction to sound."

She experimented with all musical sounds when she was a youngster. Her mother got her started on the piano when she was five and later she played in the grade school and high school orchestras, everything from the trumpet and the saxophone and the French horn to the baritone horn and the tuba and the string bass. "I taught myself to play the string bass, and when I went to Indiana University, I became the principal string bass in the orchestra." Though she loved singing, she didn't get much into choral work. "I just loved sound, never dreaming that I'd get into choral work. I hated choruses." She had not yet, she says, conceived of the chorus as a "valid musical instrument."

Like Solti, she can remember when she first became fascinated by conducting. "I was about nine and I was taken to a band concert, the old Sousa band," she says. John Philip Sousa was seventy-eight years old then and he'd die within a year. "But it was a great band. Then I heard my first symphony orchestra when I was thirteen and that was it. There was no doubt. It just took hold of me and from there on, everything was in that direction. I'd already learned several instruments but I learned more. I managed to talk the high school director into letting me become his assistant conductor both of the band and the orchestra. Which was just as well because the poor man was so overloaded and harried that it was a relief to him that somebody would do some of his work."

In college there was no opportunity in conducting on the undergraduate level—particularly for girls. So she started at Indiana University by majoring in the piano before interrupting her college career to do some flying for the U.S. Navy during World War II. "My brother taught me to fly," she says. He's now a U.S. congressman, Elwood Haynes Hillis, and he represents the Fifth District of Indiana. "He owns his own plane and commutes between Kokomo and Washington," she says. After entering the navy, and then completing her tour of duty, Miss Hillis returned to Indiana University to find that she couldn't get—in the rush of students back to campus under the GI Bill after World War II—certain courses in her piano major. "Such as counterpoint." So she switched to musical composition and got her degree in that.

She'd had experience in conducting as a high school student. "I was a sophomore in high school" and it involved a piece with the school orchestra that she didn't know "as well as I thought I knew it. But I rehearsed it and we got through it and we didn't break down. I don't think it was well in tune but it sure has a lot of enthusiasm." Now at Indiana University, she was to be given another and much delayed chance—one that was ten years in coming. "There was a concert being given on which a chorus was to appear and a piece by Randall Thompson was being done," she recalls. It involved an honorary sorority "and somebody who had a semester of conducting was asked if she would conduct it. Well, she just had a terrible time with the rehearsal. So she was flustered. She didn't want to do it. And she asked if somebody else would take over.

"So I went up to her and I said, 'Look, I don't know anything about choruses.

But I think this man is a solid composer in the sense that he knows voice and wouldn't ask anything that was unreasonable. If we follow his directions, it should come out all right.' " Obviously the next question was whether Hillis would take over the conducting of the chorus. "I said, 'I haven't conducted a chorus in my life. I've never liked choruses. But I do know a little about conducting. So I'll try.' Well, we started in and I got them to the point where they could count, where they could phrase, where they could 'color' sounds. And that was the first time that I realized that a chorus was a decent human being—I started to say, 'a decent musical instrument.' "

That proved to be a turning point in her life. For she'd been studying composition at Indiana University under Bernhard Heiden, a distinguished composer. He wanted her to continue her studies in composing at Yale under Paul Hindemith. But she kept insisting that she'd rather be a conductor.

"He said, 'You have a great compositional talent.'

"I said, 'I don't think it's a great talent. I think it's a pretty good talent, as a composer, but I want to conduct.'

"He said, 'Oh, you're a composer, don't go into that conducting stuff.' "

But he went to the choral concert, with Hillis conducting.

"When it was over, he came backstage and he said, 'You're right. You *are* a conductor.'

"But he said, 'Don't go into the orchestral conducting. Though I know that's where your heart lies . . .'

"He said, 'Start your career in the choral field and do the choral and orchestral works that are not commonly done. There are plenty of great works that you can do to fill in the gap in performance and, thus, through the back door, you can get into orchestral work.'

"He said, 'It's hard enough for the men but for a woman—you're not going to have a chance. And you're too good a talent to lose.' "

He changed his mind about Yale as well as about composing. He urged her instead to go to Juilliard to study choral work under Robert Shaw.

She accepted his advice this time and at Juilliard she began to understand what she didn't know. "I had the whole repertoire to learn—I didn't even know Bach's B-minor Mass, for God's sake. And I had to learn rehearsal technique. And I must say that Bob Shaw"—now conductor of the Atlanta Symphony—"is the greatest teacher in the world. He's just incredible."

Eventually, she became assistant conductor of Shaw's Collegiate Chorale. She became an instructor at Juilliard. She became choral conductor for the American Opera Society. And she established the American Concert Choir and Orchestra; in that way she was able to get an orchestra to conduct. But she still felt inhibited about it. "I did a few orchestral works, not very many because I was in the limelight as a choral conductor," she says. "I could hold my own but I felt that doing major concerts in New York City, with no more orchestral experience and background—well, I simply should not get up and perform and try to get the backlog of experience there." She did organize a small chamber orchestra at the Union Theological Seminary. "There was a certain repertoire that I got there, but not the big Beethoven symphonies and things of that kind," she says. So the big problem remained: how to get the experience conducting the big orchestral works so that she could qualify for conducting an orchestra.

If there were frustrations in these years, there were also a number of successes. Her choral group was the only one invited to represent the United States at the Brussels World's Fair. She became choral director of the New York City Opera and the NBC-TV opera. She became conductor and choral director of the Santa Fe Opera. And she attracted the attention of Fritz Reiner, then conductor of the Chicago Symphony.

It was one Christmas season in the middle 1950s and Reiner was in New York with the Chicago Symphony. At the time the Chicago Symphony had no chorus or children's choir. So Reiner scheduled a rehearsal with a local school choir, to work with the symphony on a Christmas program. There was one problem: nobody remembered that the schools would be closed, and the kids away on vacation, at the time of the rehearsal and performance. "They wired the kids, they called them by telephone, they tried to get as many of them back as possible," says Miss Hillis. When Reiner showed up for a rehearsal, he had only one-third of the chorus, says Hillis. He canceled the chorus and changed the program rather than go onstage with this group. And of course he went home in a simmering rage.

In February the next year, recalls Hillis, he was back "looking for a professional chorus." He heard of Margaret Hillis's work and he auditioned her American Concert Chorus, then consisting of sixty singers. Reiner subsequently invited Hillis and her choir to Chicago to accompany the orchestra in a perform- ance of Verdi's *Requiem*. "I said, 'I won't do Verdi with sixty singers. Mo- zart, fine. Other pieces, fine. But not Verdi with sixty singers.' " She felt that the *Requiem* demanded 100 to 120 voices onstage to mesh gracefully with a properly symphonic sound. She also pointed out that the expenses of moving a huge chorus from New York to Chicago were outrageous, and maybe the Chicago Symphony Orchestra could find better ways to spend its money than on airline fares. At Reiner's suggestion, the general manager of the Chicago Symphony—it was then George Kuyper—phoned her and asked her for an estimate of what it would cost to bring her choir from New York to Chicago for one program. "I said, 'Look, just basic expenses—even without a fee for me—it's $8,000.' He gasped, as I knew he would. And he said, 'Well, we were thinking around maybe $14,000 or $15,000.' So I said, 'Look, if you're thinking about $14,000 or $15,000, why don't you keep the money in Chicago. Establish your own chorus and use the money for the development of musicians in Chicago instead of for just one program.' "

There was no conclusive response. So the matter ended there—briefly.

"The next morning, the phone rang at nine o'clock. 'Margaret?' I said yes.

" 'Reiner.' As if I didn't know.

"And he said, 'Where do ve get the singers?' "

It just so happens she had the answer to that. For she was so sure that Reiner would call that she'd gone—on the previous night—to a large New York hotel, one that had out-of-town phone books. And she'd gotten the yellow pages for Chicago to look up under "Music" the names and sources of schools and singers in the

Chicago area. So when Reiner asked the question, she had the answers ready for him. She also had a plan of action to accompany it.

"I had it all outlined on a little pad of paper," she says. "I just read it off to him—how you have to plan back from the performance as to when the rehearsals begin, and you have to plan back from that to when your auditions begin, and you have to plan back from that to when your publicity to get singers for those auditions begins.

"He said, 'Fine. Ve get the singers. Who conducts?' "

Hillis volunteered, as humbly as she could, to come out and help them set up the chorus and find a conductor in the Chicago area.

But Reiner didn't go for that. "No, ve don't do it unless you conduct."

She didn't expect it to come, at least not so readily. So she had to do what everybody does in music: look at her futures book.

"I found that I had almost every Monday night free. I could get on a plane on Sunday afternoon, fly to Chicago and get a good rest on Sunday night, go to the office on Monday and do what work needed to be done there, go to the rehearsal that night, take a midnight flight back to New York, and be ready to teach on Tuesday morning."

Reiner agreed to the schedule. "I made that trip for five years," she says.

In those years she kept her choirs and orchestras and jobs in New York, and she kept her apartment on West 79th Street in Manhattan—until finally she was offered the post of music director of the Kenosha Symphony Orchestra. She promptly moved to Chicago to be near the Chicago Symphony and to be near Kenosha (some sixty miles north of the city). "I never really had a full-size symphony orchestra before," she says simply.

It was in these years also that she found a tutor for her orchestra conducting. "It wasn't until I was forty-five," she says, "that I really thought I found somebody who knew how to teach orchestra conducting. A man by the name of Otto Werner Mueller. He was at that time at the University of Wisconsin, and he is now teaching at Yale." He'd been born in Germany, survived World War II—as a precocious musical teen-ager—with help, and under the sponsorship of Richard Strauss, according to Hillis. He immigrated to Canada where he found work copying music and making arrangements for jazz musicians in Montreal. He eventually got work in opera, in ballet, in conducting symphony works on television. "So every week," says Hillis of the last-named job, "he could sit down and watch the kinescope, watch his mistakes, and find out what worked and what didn't work. And he evolved a theory of conducting that works."

She remembers the first time she ever encountered his insights. It was at the summer session of the University of Wisconsin when she was in charge of the choral institute. She invited him to lecture to the institute—"he got up and started discussing Bach's orchestra and I thought, 'O boy! here's somebody I can learn from.' " She stayed at Wisconsin for three summers to study under Mueller. "Of course, we were all students of each other on the faculty. That was the philosophy of the program—we sat in on each other's classes." The things that she learned did not prevent her from leaving Kenosha—"I didn't feel I was getting the support of the board there"—and taking an identical post in Elgin. But what she learned did develop her total being on the podium.

"For the first time, I really felt stable on my feet, as it were, in front of an orchestra," she says. "I felt that I knew how to conduct and I knew the principles behind what I was doing. So when I made a mistake, I could anaylze it and I could correct it. It wasn't a matter of imitating. It was a matter of knowing the principles."

She also spent these years working delicately with the men who were already conductors. Reiner was an education in himself. "With some musicians, he was a terror," she says. "He was a terror with anybody who didn't do their job. For me, he was always deeply appreciative. Often after a performance I would be called backstage and the only thing he wanted to say was, 'Thank you.' "

She does remember times when he could be touchy. One of those times was in 1959. "Right after the cancellation of the tour. He was sure the whole world was against him. He was sure the chorus was going to be against him, too. So he started to accuse the chorus of things there were not doing." It was a most delicate moment for her and for the chorus. "It was almost as if he was deliberately trying to get the chorus to turn against him." So at one point she just asked him if he'd stop on a particular note. He did, and the chorus held the note. It turned out that the chorus was singing precisely what was written; the basses were not singing the bottom end of a particular chord—as he'd been accusing them of doing. They were singing the note exactly as written. "I sort of looked at him, and we locked eyes for a moment, and then his eyes began to twinkle," she says. "He knew then that I was loyal to him because I'd made the point in such a way that I did not shame him. I was able to prove to him that I knew he was upset and I wasn't about to take his tactics, but I wasn't about to shame him either. He was terrified of somebody calling him down or shaming him about something."

She found in Solti a bearable skeptic when he first became music director in Chicago. "He had been told what a beautiful chorus it was but he had no idea how true it was," she says. For, though he'd often conducted the Chicago Symphony Orchestra as guest conductor, he'd never conducted when the chorus was performing with it. "Of course, I've been told many times that a particular chorus is beautiful and I get there to conduct and it's lousy," she says. "I'm sure he's had that happen to him many times. So he wouldn't believe what anybody told him, and I don't blame him."

The first time he conducted the chorus, with orchestra, was in Haydn's *The Creation*. "He was floored by it," says Miss Hillis. The second time was for Mahler's Second, the next effort was Beethoven's Ninth Symphony. "I think that's when he decided to record the Ninth."

His attitude toward her changed dramatically in that period. At first he questioned her quite closely and checked her markings on the scores she used. Now he simply assumes that everything will work quite well without his excessive intercession: Miss Hillis is a superb conductor who responds—as he does—to the responsibility of perfection.

So also does the chorus: to perfection and to responsibility. Solti gave it plenty of the latter and the chorus gave him the former in return. In 1970, he used the chorus in *Fidelio*. In 1971, he used it in *Moses und Aron*. In the fall of 1972 he used it in *La Damnation de Faust*. In the fall of 1973 he used it in *Missa Solemnis*, and in the spring of 1974 he followed it with Bach's *St. Matthew Passion*.

His attitude toward the chorus is suggested by the labor involved in the Chicago concert-hall performance of *Moses und Aron*. The singers were sent the basic scores, with analyses of variations, months in advance of the performance. Then they jammed fifty-one rehearsal hours into six weeks of preparation, while carrying on with their other work. ("I think," says Margaret Hillis, "that it was only because it was impossible that they did it.") When Solti arrived for the final rehearsals, he was gratified. In London, when he'd staged the opera at Covent Garden, he'd accepted that the singers could only approximate the score of Schoenberg. In Chicago, he found that the chorus had only the problem of extreme precision ("Even *I* don't know every note!"), which tended to squeeze out passion: "You must scream! You must scream!" The chorus gave him his screams.

All this turned out to be what Solti and the symphony needed in the week of this season that embraced *Missa Solemnis*. It was indisputably one of the "big" pieces that Solti designed for this year. He would have nothing else on the program on the night of the *Missa*. But what he did not know—could not know—is that, despite the best planning, it would also be a race against disaster. For one soloist after another had to drop out and be replaced: the only soloist in the original booking who actually appeared in all three performances was the mezzo-soprano, Julia Hamari.

In this situation, the annealing agents were the chorus, its talents, and the wit of Hillis, Edwards, and Solti in coming up with replacements.

As is the custom, the chorus had been working out for several weeks on *Missa Solemnis* under the direction of Miss Hillis. The soloists weren't in Chicago at that time and so she simply had people from the chorus stand in for them during these rehearsals, so the solo parts could be sung in rehearsal.

All this went smoothly enough until six days before the first performance. The only difficulty was a request from tenor Peter Schreier to skip the first rehearsal so that he could fill another engagement. But Solti was adamant; he wanted all the soloists on hand for all the rehearsals.

"A piano rehearsal was scheduled for Sunday," says John Edwards. On Saturday night, with a performance scheduled for the hall, Edwards walked into his seventh-floor office to clear up some work. The next day he would enter St. Joseph's hospital to have an infection in his foot treated. Edwards has diabetes, and any kind of cut, sore, or infection in the foot might lead, if unattended, to gangrene.

As he was working, he heard the office teletype chattering away. He went and took a look at it and found a message from Peter Schreier. He was canceling the Chicago date. "Laryngitis, something like that," says Edwards. He was more than a trifle agitated. "But Schreier sent along a doctor's certificate later—all the bona fides—that he was genuinely ill," says Edwards. "And there's no record of him singing anywhere else that week."

Solti couldn't go to work on the problem. He was conducting a concert. So Edwards had to do—in a matter of hours—something that had taken months in the planning three years earlier: find a tenor.

His first response was typical: he made a list.

He looked up immediately the two tenors who'd sung *Missa Solemnis* with the Chicago Symphony in the previous five years or so. They were Richard Lewis and Robert Tear. He looked up in a catalogue—"the Schwann catalogue"—who'd recorded *Missa Solemnis* and found the names of Nicolai Gedda and George Shirley ("who I might not have thought of, just offhand"). He jotted down the names of other tenors who'd worked with Solti in the recent past—Stuart Burrows, for example, was the tenor on the recording of Beethoven's Ninth Symphony made by Solti and the Chicago Symphony.

Then he made a few phone calls to get more ideas, to see who was available. One tenor was in England. Another could make the rehearsals but not the performances. Another was not considered up to singing the work because of the strain it might work on his throat. It wasn't easy. "It was Saturday night, of course, and their managers weren't in the office," he says. He did find some at home. But he knew that many of them would be at the various musical performances that are so abundant in New York City on a Saturday night in the autumn.

He had one colleague he was sure he could talk to. The Metropolitan Opera was playing that night in Manhattan—"*Salome*, I think it was"—and he phoned there and got Paul Jaretzki, assistant artistic administrator, on the phone. "Two of the names on the list were operatic," says Edwards. They were those of Nicolai Gedda and George Shirley. "It turns out that neither was singing at the Met that year," says Edwards. Jaretzki didn't have any idea where Gedda was. But he did know about George Shirley. "It so happened that Shirley had been in to visit him just a few days earlier, and he'd mentioned that he had the next two weeks free," says Edwards. Shirley's home was in New Jersey, just outside New York—an easy plane commute to Chicago. So a flurry of phone calls went off to George Shirley. He couldn't get to Chicago for the rehearsal on Sunday but he could make it Monday. Edwards checked with Solti. He agreed to postpone the piano rehearsal for a day. And Shirley agreed to play the date.

On Sunday afternoon, Edwards entered the hospital for six days, thinking that he'd covered that crisis rather effectively.

Little did he know . . .

Under normal circumstances it was going to be a strenuous time for Solti. He had a concert—the Martinů performance—on Saturday night. He had the piano rehearsals with the chorus on Sunday afternoon, now put off until Monday. But he also had a concert in Milwaukee with the orchestra on Monday night. Then he had to open rehearsals for *Missa Solemnis* with the orchestra on Tuesday, have a double rehearsal on Wednesday, and a rehearsal and performance on Thursday. The fierce schedule seemed almost a visceral response, an effort to make obsolete a comment about *Missa Solemnis* by a pianist Artur Schnabel—that this is music "that is better than it can ever be played."

All this time, he was fighting a cold, of course. And he was worrying about the vocalists and what was happening to their throats. They'd all rehearsed through Wednesday. "But I felt very uneasy on that Wednesday evening," says Solti. He thought he could hear trouble in the voices of soprano Wendy Fine and bass Karl Ridderbusch. "I knew, I thought I knew, that the soloists would get so tired that it would just ruin the performance if I asked them to come one more time to rehearsal," he says. "I did not want to play along with it any further and so I said, 'All right, we will have to risk it without the final rehearsal.' " He ordered the Thursday morning dress rehearsal canceled. He did not think the soloists' voices could last through both rehearsal and performance in one day. "Better to have a performance and no rehearsal than to have the rehearsal and no performance," he says.

It helped—but not much. For on Wednesday night, Ridderbusch came down with "Chicago throat." He phoned Solti to say that his doctor prohibited him from singing *Missa*. Solti was distressed but understanding. "With singers, you have always the problems of colds," he says. "Coming from Europe quickly and flying over and arriving on Sunday on short notice, and singing Tuesday, the climate change is just too big. This is what happened to Ridderbusch. The poor fellow arrived, made all the rehearsals, and then could not make any of the concerts."

To replace him took some very quick diplomacy. To get a bass, Solti turned first to Carol Fox, manager of the Lyric Opera. He'd worked with her and for her in the 1950s in Chicago and they were still friends. Lyric had performed Wagner's *Siegfried* at the Opera House on Wednesday night. Solti wondered if the bass in *Siegfried*, Theo Adam, would be free on Thursday night. A few phone calls confirmed his hopes. And Carol Fox had no objection to the arrangement.

Though Theo Adam had sung a taxing role as the wandering Wotan in *Siegfried* on Wednesday night, he was willing to step in and sing the bass in *Missa Solemnis* on Thursday night.

The patchwork—and the chorus and orchestra—worked beautifully.

"Singers Scale the Missa Summit to Score Another Solti Success," read a headline in the *Chicago Tribune*.

"One heard more of the music Beethoven created than at any performance I can remember," wrote the *Tribune's* critic, Thomas Willis.

"Solti Rises to Missa Impossible," read the headline in the *Chicago Sun-Times*.

"Solti is a conductor of enormous range," wrote *Sun-Times* critic Robert C. Marsh, "but the essential Solti, I believe, is a man of the theatre, a dramatist and one especially gifted at joining words and music, of combining the strong and weak accents of a phrase with the patterns of tension and repose in an unfolding melody. Thus in a score such as this, his prime emphasis is on the words. Getting the words across, enforcing their meaning with the full resources Beethoven has provided, becomes the primary goal. That, surely, was the overwhelming quality of this performance."

But it was no time to relax and enjoy success. For the problems with *Missa Solemnis* were still alive and becoming more acute. For one thing, Theo Adam was free only to play the Thursday night and Friday afternoon performances; there was no conflict with the Lyric Opera's schedule. But on Saturday night, the Lyric would be presenting *Siegfried* again and Adam would have to honor his commitment there. That meant that Edwards and Solti had to come up with another bass—their third of the week.

They turned to Thomas Paul. He'd sung the role under Martinů with the Chicago Symphony and he'd worked with Solti on Beethoven's *Fidelio* in 1970 and again in Wagner's *Das Rheingold*. Most of all, Edwards knew where to look for him: Paul is a full professor of music at the Eastman School of Music in Rochester, New York, one of the most distinguished such schools in the United States. Edwards, now working from his hospital bed, phoned him there, "and he was able to get away for Saturday night."

It wasn't over yet. For on Thursday night, there was just a hint of yet another disaster. It could be heard onstage, in the problems encountered by Wendy Fine, the soprano. It could be seen in the reviews. Said Roger Dettmer in *Chicago Today*: Miss Fine, however, lacked power and consistent intonation in music for a Birgit Nilsson voice. . . . In the *Chicago Daily News*, Karen Monson wrote: "The weak link in the quartet was debutante Wendy Fine. She had trouble making herself heard, and either her intonation was way off or she was singing wrong notes."

Solti knew—though the critics did not—that Miss Fine was also succumbing to throat problems and perhaps a cold. He was just hoping she'd make it through the week. She didn't. "On Friday at eleven-thirty in the morning she told us she could not sing," says Edwards. Now all he had to do was find and prepare another soprano in two and one-half hours.

That's where Margaret Hillis and the Chicago Symphony Chorus stepped in. For she'd been preparing the understudies—really stand-ins for rehearsals when the guest vocalists weren't in Chicago—for weeks. "Sometimes we don't have a voice that can really do the concert, but most of the time we do," she says. "In this case we did have four who really could have stepped in." There were, perhaps, reservations about the stand-in bass: "He was really a bass-baritone and the bottom notes were not quite bitey enough to cut through the orchestra yet. In another couple of years, he'd be able to sing it with anybody. He's just not quite ready." She felt the soprano, Sarah Beatty, was ready—though she was all but brand-new to the discipline of the soloist.

"I first knew her when she was a graduate student at Northwestern," says Margaret Hillis. "She hadn't really blossomed forth yet as a voice, but there was a certain sort of seriousness about how she thought about things and I thought, 'Well, we'll just see what happens.'

"But she disappeared from view after that. It turned out that she was working as a waitress in order to help her husband finish law school. She'd given up the voice, whatever hopes and expectations she had, to help her husband in his career —working as a waitress.

"Then when he finished law school, he turned to Sarah and said, 'Honey, you can do anything you want to do.' So she went seriously back to the study of the voice."

She was twenty-seven now and this was her second season in the Chicago

Symphony Chorus. "So I gave her some understudy stuff," says Miss Hillis. "Usually the first year a person is in the chorus, I want to wait, to find out whether they've got it all together—whether they're reliable—and gradually move them up. Sarah was so reliable and she worked like a Trojan." Normally Miss Hillis builds two sets of understudies in case something happens to them. She began working Sarah Beatty into the second group of understudies. "When she was assigned an understudy role to do, she would come for her coaching session and she knew the score, and there were no notes missed, no mistakes made, complete assurance. So that being the case, I could move her into the first group of understudies." In that role, she'd sung for Solti at his *Missa Solemnis* piano rehearsal. "She'd sung, but not the whole work." Yet she emerged from the experience excited at having sung for Solti, renewed in confidence at having performed ably for him, even in this private manner.

"So when I got the call at noon and was told that Wendy Fine had no voice, nothing, I was sure that Sarah could do it," says Margaret Hillis. She couldn't ask Sarah; the chorus call for the two o'clock performance was twelve-thirty and Sarah hadn't arrived yet at Orchestra Hall. "Then Solti called me and asked, 'What do you think? Should I come down to the hall ahead of time or just meet her backstage before the concert starts? Which would make her feel more secure?' " Solti, of course, prefers to come in at the last moment; he doesn't like to arrive at the hall early and then hang around fretting for the starting moment of the concert. This time, Miss Hillis suggested he come down early. She pointed out that Sarah Beatty had sung the part in rehearsals for him but hadn't gone through the entire score with him. "She probably would feel a little better about it if she saw you for twenty minutes beforehand. Maybe you could go over a few things on the piano with her," Hillis told Solti. "He said, 'Fine, I will be there.' "

Now all Miss Hillis had to do was break the news to Sarah Beatty.

"She came in about twenty minutes after twelve and I said, 'Sarah, how are you feeling? How's your throat after that strenuous performance last night? She said, 'Fine. Just fine.' I said, 'Well, Wendy Fine is ill and Mr. Solti wants you to sing today.' She said, 'You're kidding!' And I said, 'No, I'm not kidding at all. He's going to be here early to go over some of the points with you.' "

Her reaction was calm.

"Well," she said, "I've got to go warm up."

Dick Boldrey, the assistant director of the chorus, was standing by, ready to go to a studio on the sixth floor of Orchestra Hall where he could work with her in the warm-up period.

As she was about to get on the elevator, Sarah Beatty turned to Miss Hillis and expressed her most immediate concern—something that, in the excitement of the moment, she had neglected. She turned and said, "Oh, Miss Hillis, would you please check in my attendance at the concert?"

Her performance was a deeply satisfying one. It satisfied every high demand, every subtle dimension of the work. "She was spectacular," says Edwards. Solti was so gratified that he immediately scheduled her for a small role in the *St. Matthew Passion* in the spring and in *Salome* the following season. The major roles, of course, had been booked for years, but in this way he could not only give her more experience, and presence, as a soloist but make sure—through *Salome*—that she got exposure in New York. It isn't easy for her to consider what a solo career might do to her life. "She knows she has to go ahead on a solo career," says Margaret Hillis. "She knows definitely where her life will lead. The only really sad thing is that she'll have to leave the chorus to do it."

The impact of the chorus could be seen in the person as well as the professionalism of Sarah Beatty. On Saturday night, when she might have chosen any glamorous gown for her second solo performance—she obviously had no time for a choice on Friday afternoon—she chose instead to appear in the black, austere "chorus" gown she'd been wearing all week. As a signal of what she was as well as what she might be.

The impact could be seen also in the overall judgments made on the *Missa Solemnis* by the critics. "As for the chorus," wrote Robert C. Marsh in the *Chicago Sun-Times*, "can there be a finer, more sensitive vocal group of this type to be heard today? I rather doubt it. Thank Margaret Hillis for that."

Within the orchestra itself, there are only six women. It is not by present desire: "I think many of us would like to see more accomplished women come into the orchestra," says Sam Magad. Nor is it by present design: the "screened auditions" are an effort to pick symphony players on the basis of their skill, without prejudice of sex or color. But this has not always been the practice; the result is that the only women in the orchestra include two in the cellos (Margaret Evans and Leonore Glazer), one in the violins (Betty Lambert), one in the flutes (Louise Dixon), the pianist (Mary Sauer), and the second harp (Lynne Turner).

This is not to say that women are not important to the orchestra, both as players and as the wives of players. The latter, like the former, have their tests, their hopes, their high reach, their black despair. In this week, Vicki Graef would undergo an operation to remove what—she now feels—the doctor believed to be a malignant tumor. The operation would take place two days before *Missa Solemnis* opened. This time of testing is an opportunity to suggest the style, tone, and amplitude of a young family caught up in the glories of music and the problems of life. And the conflicts that come up when a man must balance his personal needs against his professional imperatives.

In this season, Dick Graef was thirty-one years old. He is an alert, intelligent man, square of face with dark hair and dark mustache. He had been playing the flute in the Chicago Symphony Orchestra for five years. In this season he'd been on the negotiating team for the members' committee during the contract discussions and as the talks and the work stoppage went on, he—perhaps more than anybody else in the orchestra—faced, as we shall see, a critical conflict between the players' interest and his family interest. For if management decided to bring counterpressure by canceling premiums on insurance benefits, he'd be paying for the operation himself. There was no sign of it in his position: he stood unwaveringly by the players' need all through these tense weeks, at a time when, in fact, he had reason to believe that his wife would die without an operation. "He figured there was a sort of duty in working on the committee," says Vicki. "He felt that every few years, you have to take your turn at something like this. I think he was very good at what he did. He is very diplomatic—he knows how to handle difficult situations. He tends to smooth people's tempers out and keep things at a low boiling point most times. Stu Bernstein"—one of the lawyers involved in the negotiations—"said he should have been a lawyer. He just has a good mind for that sort of thing."

It is an objective mind, curious and candid. It does not run swiftly with the crowd. He does not, for example, accept the easy ritual of ranking orchestras by "the greatest" or "the best" but rather identifies them by their characteristics. "We are the only brass-oriented orchestra in the country," he says. "I think of the New York Philharmonic or the Cleveland Orchestra as being woodwind-oriented. I think of the Philadelphia Orchestra as being string-oriented. It's reflected first in what we all play. We do a tremendous amount of Wagner and Mahler and Bruckner. This is what we are famous for. The Cleveland Orchestra, in its heyday under Szell, was most famous for its interpretation of Mozart, Beethoven, the pieces which so often feature woodwinds and which feature a smaller sound—a very controlled sound. The Philadelphia Orchestra, of course, has always been famous for that lush, beautiful string sound; also the hall, the Academy of Music, is extremely flattering to the strings." The predominant sound of the orchestra tends to enforce a discipline on the various players, he feels. "We play in such a way that the brass predominates. This means that the other sections might have to compromise. It seems that the woodwinds are more concerned here than any- where else with projection," he says. "How do you keep up with this big, glorious enormous brass sound that is so famous with Chicago?"

He's given a lot of thought to this, and to the sound of the flute, in general. "I think it's hard to talk about it," he says. "There are all sorts of terms which people use—light and dark sounds, bright and dull, focused and unfocused. I find that even when you talk to people in your own section, what I would call a bright sound they would call a dark sound. It is unfortunate that the description of sound is not all as specific as sight, where we have color to deal with.

"I think generally what flute players look for now is the sound—well, first of all we're concerned with projection, the flute being one of the softer instruments in the orchestra. I think most of the other wind instruments were designed originally for outdoor use and the flute was always an indoor chamber music instrument. Now we are faced with—how do we keep up in strength with the Chicago brass? And at the same time come out with a sound that is still beautiful and still sounds like a flute. Every flute player wrestles with this problem and everybody has a slightly different solution. We've experimented with different metals, with differ- ent weights, with the density of silver alloy, with gold—years ago flute players gave up the wooden flutes, even though they had a beautiful sound.

"So what I heard and learned was a certain basic concept of sound which I think maintains the original wooden flute sounds, but at the same time can be opened up and pushed to the extreme in much the same way the oboe achieves projection. This was basically what I heard in the sound—very big and full, yet very rich in quality." There are, he feels, decent limitations of the search for projection. "A lot of flute players go to the extreme of putting in certain buzzes, certain other noises, which give the sound great projection. The only comment that I like about that is that it projects—but a truck horn also projects. You want to have some refinement and not sound like that."

That this would ever be a concern of Dick Graef is, perhaps, one of those improbable happenings that give depth to life, and a sense of the unexpected. He grew up in Fort Wayne, Indiana. His father was a factory worker—"for International Harvester. He was in the service parts department as a stock manager—he had the same job all his life," says Dick. As a child, Dick had a disputatious beginning with the piano and a dubious beginning with the flute. He preferred, as we've seen, to play the trumpet. "You know why I wanted the trumpet? They gave a little demonstration—the high school kids came to the grade school and they showed all the different instruments. I looked at the clarinet and the flute and I saw all those keys and gadgets. And I thought 'Oh, brother!' Then the kid came with the trumpet and I saw just three things, and I thought, 'What a snap!' "

He didn't get his wish. His mother talked with the piano teacher who, as we've seen, urged that Dickie take up something easy, like the flute. ("Believe me," says Graef, "it is not easy.")

His first flute teacher was a clarinet player. "He really didn't know the flute that well and he taught me all sorts of wrong fingerings. He taught me the wrong fingerings for the whole upper register." Later Dick went to an authentic flute player, "but even then some of the basic approaches were taught completely wrong. I practically had to relearn the instrument when I went to college, my freshman year."

His father's ideal was not that he would send his son to college to learn to play the flute.

"My father's idea of sending his kids to college was so they could make more money," says Dick. He was no different from the rest—"a lot of parents thought that." In fact, the college itself leaned toward aggrandizing that theory—"you read reports where college grads make 'so much money' in their lifetime." All this was escalated, in the Graef family, by the background and ambitions of the times: "My father went through, I think, fourth grade, and always felt like he missed out on something." He wasn't going to let his kids miss out on that same thing. "His feeling with both my sister and me was that we would go to college and we would make so much more money than he'd ever had a chance to to."

His sister introduced his father to the New Thinking. "When she announced that she wanted to be a philosophy major, my dad hit the ceiling. He said, 'What are you going to do? Hand out a sign that says *PHILOSOPHER?* Do something practical!' " But his sister won.

Dick went to Oberlin and, by way of doing something practical, started to major in music education. "I was going to be a high school or grade school band director." But it took him only his freshman year to discern that this was not the route for him. "So I came home and said, 'Look, I'm going to be a flute major.' "

"A flute major!"

"So there was a big argument," says Dick. "And I said 'Look, this is what I'm going to do. Either I spread the degree over a period of six or seven years and get a job to pay for it, or I'll be out of school. Because this is what I am going to do.' And he—like a loving parent—he finally gave in."

The irony is that the first job Dick Graef ever got, after he finished college, was as a flute player in a symphony orchestra at $200 a week—ten times what his father earned in some of the hard days of the Depression. And Dick now earns well over $20,000 a year, a figure which doubled and tripled some of the best years his father had ever known in his younger days.

Today? "Today, he's very proud. Overwhelmed. I'd say both my mother and father are a bit overwhelmed. Sometimes I have the feeling that my dad would have been a little happier if I had ended up like—well, like Lawrence Welk. Maybe not so much that, or like driving a truck. Something a little more manly. For a guy who worked with his hands in a factory all his life, he can't hardly envision his only son as a flute player."

Two years younger than Dick, Vicki had grown up in Hillsboro, just outside Portland, Oregon, and she'd gone the same route that Dick had—into the piano and later into the flute. But her impetus and her direction were somewhat more amenable. "My mother was a piano teacher and a classical pianist," she says. "She had like twenty students who came to the house weekly, and I was hearing some little songs over and over again. And I was going to the piano and picking them out with one finger. So in order to curb bad habits, which I was learning, my mother got me started on piano lessons at the age of three. I was playing pretty well in a short time but I was hampered because my hands were very small and when it came to playing certain pieces, I just didn't have the hands for it.

"So when the band program came around, when I was in grade school, I started on the flute. I really did not have anything to say about it. It was the flute because my mother knew classical literature and had fallen in love with Brahms's First and she wanted someone who could play that. A little later on, I guess when I was about in seventh grade, I started playing the organ at our little church." It didn't hamper her to have small hands in playing the organ. "You can always pick up a note with your foot which you could not normally reach with your hand—it's easier to play the organ if you're affected by the problem of small hands." In any case, she played both flute and organ, won a spot in the Portland Junior Symphony, and through it eventually won a scholarship to the summer institute at Aspen, Colorado.

That's where she met Dick. It "kinda was" like love at first sight. When the summer ended, he went back to Oberlin and she went back to Portland State University, where she was a freshman. But she didn't wait much beyond that. In her sophomore year, she transferred to Oberlin and in the summer following that she and Dick got married. "Then we both finished up at Indiana"—Dick getting his master's degree, Vicki getting her baccalaureate. By the time they were finished, Dick was well on his way to fathering a family. And to needing a job.

But he couldn't get one. "All through my college training, I never really intended to play in a symphony orchestra," says Dick. "I was thinking of preparing for college teaching work—that sort of thing. That's why I went on to get my master's, because I thought it was essential." He wrote to a number of colleges seeking jobs. No offers came. "Of course, they get all the applicants they can find. They look them over and then decide who is the best qualified, and interview him, and offer him a job. And of course he sits on it for a while to see if a better offer comes along. If you're the sixth or seventh man on the list, you might not hear from them for months."

There was always the alternative of seeking orchestral work. Moreover, there was, in Vicki's view, no trouble about his playing the flute in an orchestra. "I think his greatest problem, for a long time, was self-confidence," she says. "When we came out of college, he really did not believe that he could play in a major orchestra. He did not feel that he was that good. I kept saying, 'Yes, you are. You're going to do it.' But he really didn't believe me. I don't think it was false modesty or anything. I really think he did not feel that he had it. And I don't think it's been until the last year or two that he realizes how good he is."

In any case, Dick began applying to various symphony orchestras and was invited to an audition at the St. Louis Symphony. "I really prepared for that audition," he says. "I had learned the orchestral repertoire. I had memorized the big solos. I thought I was all set. But the baby was coming, and the pressure was on because I had to find some work because the bills were piling up and we were in debt like crazy. I went there and by the time I went out on the stage to play, I was so scared and nervous that I blew the whole thing.

"This was a terrible experience because jobs for flute open up so seldom. Maybe one or two a year . . ."

"Across the country?"

"All over the world."

Next he heard about an opening in the New Zealand Broadcasting orchestra. He and Vicki were enchanted by the notion—the cost of living was low and "it's really supposed to be a beautiful place to live in. "We wrote and sent tapes and after a lot of correspondence, we were offered first and second flute—both of us, in the same orchestra." Now it was their turn to pause. Dick heard about an opening in the Minneapolis Symphony and he applied for an audition, all the while putting off the New Zealand venture. He got a letter back from Minneapolis that said, in effect, "Thank you for your interest but we're looking for someone with much more experience than you have." What they were trying to say, according to Dick, was "Don't bother to come. It will be a waste of your time and money." He was put off by this and he mentioned it to a friend on the faculty at Indiana University who'd been concertmaster in the Cleveland Orchestra. "He said, 'That is not right. They should at least hear you. In Cleveland, Szell used to hear everybody. Maybe only for a few minutes but he heard everybody.' " He urged Dick to write back to the personnel manager in Minneapolis and to use his name. "I can't believe I had the nerve to do this, but I wrote back and said, 'You should hear me because Mr. Z. told me that an orchestra like yours should do so.' " So he got the audition—he didn't know that old friendships endure in orchestral politics and the use of this man's name was like a key in the door. "So I went up there to play and

Betty Lambert, violinist.

Below: Leonore Glazer (top), cellist;
(clockwise) Robert Swan, violist; Phillip
Kauffman, violist; Ted Ratzer, cellist (not
a regular member of the orchestra).

Margaret Evans, cellist.

*Bottom left: Richard Graef, associate
principal flutist.
Bottom right: Michael Henoch, oboist,
and Louise Dixon, flutist.*

my feeling was that, 'No way I'm going to get the job.' I was very relaxed about playing because I figured I did not have a ghost of a chance of getting the job." It was not magic: there is no formula for a sublime indifference that wins jobs. But he did not get a complete turndown. "They said they'd let me know."

By now, things were piling up, what with Vicki's time of delivery coming closer and the bills gathering ominously. His next shot was at the New Orleans symphony. "I was thinking very seriously that I would take that job," he says. He went down for the final audition, played for the conductor, and sat in the orchestra for a rehearsal. He got the word. "We want you for the job, but we can't give you a contract because we've promised to hear some people in New York." In effect, they were working the old "pressure" game: they wanted a firm commitment from him—that he'd take no other job—while refusing to give him a firm commitment in return. "They really know you're at a disadvantage, when there are so few jobs; they know you're pleading for work," says Graef. But he insisted on his rights as an individual. "I said, 'Look, I can't do that. Either give me a contract or I'm a free agent.' He kinda looked at me and said '*Sure*, kid.' " So Dick walked out and went back to his hotel, plagued with a feeling of desperation and of opportunity lost.

"There was a message waiting for me to call the personnel manager in Minneapolis—they wanted me to come back for the final audition."

Because he refused to play the management game in New Orleans, he had a chance at a much better job in Minneapolis.

He won it.

"I was so amazed. I can remember the personnel manager said, 'We'd like you to come in the office and talk about pay.' Suddenly I realized I was going to get *paid* for this!"

His opening salary in Minneapolis was $200 a week. It was $20 over the base scale. "They could have given me $180 and I would have been delighted," says Graef.

He had no money. He had no insurance. Just to get started, he had to pay the hospital when his son, Ricky, was born by borrowing money from the bank in Fort Wayne, where he'd grown up. "His father had to cosign the note to get me and Ricky out of the hospital," says Vicki. The family moved to Minneapolis where "we furnished our first apartment on $30."

He considers himself lucky. "The usual course is you leave school and if you decide you want to play, you end up in your first job in Birmingham, Alabama, or some other southern orchestra and you try to make ends meet on four or five thousand dollars a year—for twenty to twenty-five weeks"—precisely what the Chicago Symphony players were earning only a few years earlier—"and you try to work your way up or you go to New York and you become a tour rat." The latter is a New York musician who is waiting for a permanent orchestral job to open and who goes out on tours with the various shows or performers until a spot opens. "And they wind up spending their whole life on the road," says Vicki.

In his route, he spent two years in Minneapolis and then learned of an opening in Chicago and went down for an audition. "It was a lousy audition. I was very confused. I had never been in Orchestra Hall before that, let alone play there. And the preliminary auditions were behind a screen. I had no conception of what the hall was like. Sometimes you can walk out and get a look at the hall and get some idea of what it's like, what it will sound like. I walked out and here's a screen." He couldn't see anything. He had no idea of the need for projection. "The first couple of notes I played, I was shocked. It was a funny kind of sound. It took me at least half of the audition to get used to the sound in the hall." He felt he played so poorly that "I think they asked me back for the finals simply because I was from a major orchestra and they felt they had to hear me again."

They heard him again and they picked him. Dick and Vicki moved to Chicago and bought a home in Glencoe, far up on the North Shore—only ten minutes or so from Ravinia, the summer place. They had another baby and they took in students—Dick had eight a week at $20 an hour in this season—and they made music together.

For Vicki was also an accomplished flutist. She'd hoped to get jobs in and around Chicago—ideally even in the symphony—to be with Dick. But for some reason, the jobs just weren't there. "In Minneapolis, there was a lot of work," she says. "I played in the opera there, did a lot of jobbing. It was the kind of thing I could do at night, when Ricky was in bed and a baby-sitter could take of him." She played for a couple of summers at Grant Park in Chicago but gave that up, as Ricky got older, to spend her sumner evenings at home with her son and—when he was free of Ravinia—with her husband. Still, she hungered after some assignments to play the flute. But the jobs didn't seem to be there. Not in the abundance of Minneapolis—which, she notes, is a smaller and less active city, musically, than Chicago. She can't put her finger on the reason, but Mary Koss, the wife of Don Koss, feels much the same as Vicki Graef did. Mary also is a fine musician and she won appointment to the Grant Park Symphony one summer under her maiden name. But when, she feels, it became known that she was married to Don Koss of the Chicago Symphony, she didn't get the job at Grant Park anymore. Or any other jobs. Nothing wrong with Don Koss; it's just that he *has* a job. And the feeling among the women is that the jobs are being parceled out, not according to skills—which some of the wives possess in abundance—or according to sex, but according to economic units; that is, one job in music to a family. This is difficult for them to prove. In fact, it is easier to disprove. Willard Elliot's wife, Gladys, plays in the Lyric Opera Orchestra. And two of the six women in the Chicago Symphony are married to men in the symphony. Margaret Evans, the cellist, is married to Donald Evans of the violas. Louise Dixon of the flutes had just married Michael Henoch of the oboes. In the end, the explanation may be the resigned expression of Vicki Graef: "There are a lot of good flutists in Chicago and not enough jobs to go around."

In any case, Vicki Graef did not wait to be consumed by frustration. She decided to begin studying the organ seriously again, in the belief there was no opportunity for her—locally—in the flute. Then she decided to go back to Northwestern where she's now getting her master's degree in church music. "I went back not really for the degree but for a course that I wanted to take that I felt I needed to make myself a better church organist," she says. And she found a job playing the organ at St.

Philip Episcopal Church in Palatine. "It's a half-hour trip by car," she admits. But it's the kind of work that beckons for an organist. "And we are Episcopalians."

It was, in fact, her dedication to church music that brought Vicki to the personal crisis of this week. For she'd gone to Colorado to work in a church workshop for two weeks during the summer. When she came back, she noticed the growth on the left side of her face. She had it examined and diagnosed as a possible parotid tumor. And all the while it grew quite sharply. And she got the urgent suggestion that surgery take place immediately.

She wanted to put it off, as we've seen, because of the press of her church work. On the other hand, she was plagued by a small nagging doubt about the wisdom of waiting. For there was the problem of medical insurance. Many of the expenses of the operation would be covered by group insurance if the orchestra had a contract. In New York, the striking members of the New York Philharmonic were stripped of their medical benefits just before some ninety-three or so of them undertook a strike-time tour of Spain. The same thing, she feared, might happen in Chicago. And nobody could know it more than her husband: he was on the negotiating team for the players' committee.

So Dick Graef was faced with the classic conflict. His wife needed surgery. He stood, like the rest of the players, in danger of losing medical benefits. By fighting for his colleagues, he might be hurt seriously in the pocketbook. By rushing his wife into surgery, he could, perhaps, meet both the doctors' imperatives and his own financial needs. But not the internal aspirations of his wife—to carry out her obligations to the church on All Saints' Day.

In the end, the doctors won—and the crisis disappeared. Dick Graef stood firmly by his colleagues in the contract negotiations; not many of them even knew the conflict he faced. But the contract was signed and the medical benefits of the players were never endangered.

"Thank God," says Vicki.

At nine-thirty in the morning on October 30, Vicki underwent surgery at Presbyterian–St. Luke's Hospital in Chicago. She was returned to her room at one o'clock in the afternoon. Dick stayed with her until six o'clock that night, telling her not to worry.

His was the right prescription, for tests showed that the growth was not malignant. "It wasn't until later that I found out that all the doctors I saw really thought it was cancerous," says Vicki. They determined what it was not, but not what it was. "They seem to be calling it a granular nodule which, as I understand it, is a sloughing off of dead cells which form a very, very hard surface. They know it was caused by some kind of infectious disease, and until they get me on some kind of antibiotics, it could crop up again."

Just what disease, and where she got it, were still under exploration. There was some conjecture that it might be histoplasmosis, a disease caused by the inhalation of dust carrying the dung of certain kinds of life, including bats. And Vicki remembers that there were bats in the ancient organ that she played during the church workshop in the summer, "that dust came out when I tried to play it."

Now there were changes necessary in her life, as a result of the illness.

There was a change in her looks. She redid her hair so that it effectively disguised the scar of surgery that trailed down from her left ear into her neck. She gave up wearing contact lenses and returned to wearing spectacles. The reason was that the surgery had impaired certain muscles on the left side of her face. One effect was that she could no longer close or blink her left eye. It just remained open and staring. "At night I have to tape it shut," she says. During the daytime, she has to blink it manually. She just puts a finger on it and closes it. The blinking is important to keep the surface of the eyeball covered with liquid—which is why she turned to specs and away from contacts: it is hard to keep the eyeball "lubricated," so to speak, with a contact lens if the eyelid does not move reflexively. "I have eye drops to keep it moist," she says. "But it gets to be a problem when you're outside, and the wind blows . . ." The changes dampened her spirit a bit. For she is a happy and guileless woman who can speak of herself and her looks without an arch self-consciousness. "I guess I'm getting over it but I have always—I always thought I was an attractive person. And it's kind of difficult not to feel very attractive now."

There were changes in her musical skills—"I kind of think," she added, "that it's more of a problem not being able to play the flute." For the muscle problem that inhibits her blinking also affected the whole left side of her face, including her mouth and lips. "I can't play the flute because these muscles are not working properly." That means she could not continue teaching individual students, because she could not play along with them. "I've given some of my advanced students to other teachers temporarily, because I can't help them."

There were fun and oneness, as well as income, in her teaching. For both she and Dick would be available for the problems of their various students. "If there was something that I thought he could explain or illustrate better than I could, I'd always ask him to join us for a few minutes," says Vicki. Similarly, Dick might call on her to get her ideas on a particular problem. Thus their mutual absorption in the flute, and in the students of the flute, pulled them more closely together.

One day her playing and her teaching would resume. "The muscles are much better than they were right after surgery," she says. In the meantime, she's playing the organ, going to Northwestern, and working at the church in Palatine. And she's counting the riches of the threat of cancer and the surgery:

"We learned then how much we'd had together in the past."

The week or ten days after Vicki Graef's operation were not easy ones. Not for Dick Graef. Not for Georg Solti. Not for any members of the Chicago Symphony Orchestra. For it was the recording week.

It began at an unlikely time—long before dawn on a Monday morning.

It began at an unlikely place—the alley behind Orchestra Hall.

It began in an unlikely way—with the evacuation of Orchestra Hall.

The weather was bitter cold. It was the night of the first "hard freeze" of the season. Shortly before six o'clock in the morning, a truck pulled up behind Orchestra Hall. The orchestra's stagehands, already on duty, began carrying out trunks filled with instruments, with music stands, with musical scores. They also began carrying out all the chairs on the stage of Orchestra Hall. The reason: the

chairs go where the players go, whenever there's a recording session. "Our chairs don't squeak," says stage manager Jim Palecek. "Single-frame aluminum. There's no chance for a squeak when a player shifts around on them."

The stage was left bare. So was the basement. Everything was moved a mile north to the stage and backstage of the Medinah Temple. It would all be brought back to Orchestra Hall in midweek for a rehearsal, then moved out again for another recording session later in the week. And brought back once again for the final rehearsals and performances of the week.

For the week of recording sessions was being enclosed within a normal week of rehearsals and performances—Mahler's Symphony no. 6 was on the program this week. Indeed, an extra rehearsal or two was expected to get the orchestra in shape for the eastern tour that would follow.

Why go to all this trouble? Why bother to leave the natural home of the orchestra to seek the local headquarters of a men's lodge?

For two reasons.

One is that the Chicago Symphony Orchestra has a long and revered history in recording. It was the first American orchestra to record commercially under its regular conductor. Its first records were made in 1916 under Frederick Stock for the old Columbia Gramophone records. The orchestra has recorded nearly three hundred different works or excerpts since then, many of them more than once. The success of its most recent efforts was both professional and commercial. In 1973, the recordings of the orchestra, under Solti, won four Grammy awards as the best of their kind in the field. Its recording of Mahler's Symphony no. 8 (The Symphony of a Thousand) was named Album of the Year. It was also acclaimed as having the best choral performance and for being the best-engineered classical recording. Its record of Mahler's Symphony no. 7 was acclaimed simply as "the best classical performance by an orchestra." In 1974, Solti and the Chicago Symphony won another Grammy for London/Decca's four-record set of Beethoven's five concertos for piano and orchestra, with Vladimir Ashkenazy as soloist.

The other reason is that its home hall is considered acoustically deficient. Even for live performances it falls short of the high quality of Carnegie Hall in New York, of Symphony Hall in Boston, and of the Academy of Music in Philadelphia.

This was not always the case. Orchestra Hall was once considered the jewel of U.S. recording sites, a little brilliant in the early years of recording but virtually perfect when stereo recording first came into existence.

Time and man changed all that. But then time and man brought the hall, with all its original beauty, into existence in the first place.

The hall was the conception of Theodore Thomas. Through the first thirteen years of his direction of the Chicago Symphony, he had to play his concerts in the Auditorium. This is a magnificent architectural specimen, located on Michigan Avenue, and designed by Sullivan and Adler, the incomparable architectural team of and before the turn of the century. It is still one of the great large theaters of the world (after having been recovered from a wartime incarnation as a bowling alley for servicemen). But it was designed at a time when opera was the prime musical form; you will recall that concert-hall music, by symphony orchestras, trailed opera in prestige and chronology through much of the nineteenth century. The Auditorium was really too large to provide an ideal acoustical home for a symphony orchestra—even one that is "the loudest in the world."

Thomas was dissatisfied with it on a number of counts. He kept shifting players around on the stage in an effort to bring the sound up to an ideal level—and felt he was failing. He had to compete with other attractions for time in the hall; frequently rehearsals of the Chicago Symphony could not be held in the hall where the concerts were to be played. Finally, he told the trustees that it had too many seats—some 3,500 of them. Thus it was seldom sold out for a symphony concert. Moreover, that meant that people who followed the symphony did not feel compelled to buy season subscription tickets because they knew they could always go up to the box office at the last minute and get a ticket.

Conductor Thomas had very firm ideas on what the ideal concert hall should be. He did not favor the proscenium arch stage, for example. He though the entire orchestral chamber should be a single space, not unlike the interior of an eggshell, enclosing both audience and orchestra. The orchestra should merely be set on a platform within that single physical entity. Its music then would not be developed within the proscenium arch, and projected outward from it; rather it would rise upward and outward from the orchestra and enclose the audience in what has come to be known—in the days of quadraphonic speakers—as "surround sound." Accordingly, he favored the construction of a very high, deep gallery, but he specified that it should not overlap the main floor of the concert hall. And, to further resonance and clarity, he felt that the walls should be finished in wood and, to the extent possible, that its seats should also be wooden.

Ultimately he got his concert hall: the trustees raised some $750,000 from more than 8,000 contributors in every walk of life, and Orchestra Hall—just up Michigan Avenue from the Auditorium—was designed by Daniel Burnham, the planner and developer who set up a long-range plan—executed a generation or more later—for Chicago's lakefront park system.

But he did not get quite the hall that he envisioned. For one thing, the Iroquois Theater fire took place on December 30, 1903, long before Orchestra Hall was finished. Some 602 persons lost their lives in that blaze. It was the most calamitous "city" fire in U.S. history—only the Peshtigo forest fire in Wisconsin took more lives—and it led to a spurt of reforms and regulations in the building code of Chicago. Thus the wood-finish concept of Theodore Thomas was greatly restricted and the traffic flow within the hall—aisles, exits, and so forth—was somewhat altered. (One can see in the design that arouses Frank Miller's ire—the ability of people to look from the street directly onto the stage—something of the wake-of-the-fire concept. For the front of the hall is broad and lined with many doors—many more than one encounters, for example, in Carnegie Hall or in the usual Broadway theater. Perhaps the theory was that where there was visual access there might also be physical egress. That has not worked out in fact, as the crowds patiently attest as they shuffle out of a hall after every concert. But then there were many things in Orchestra Hall that did not quite work out.) Thomas got his high

galleries and deep ones, but they do overlap the main floor. He got the smaller seating capacity he wanted; there were 2,581 seats in the hall. But the shape of the hall was not the perfection that he dreamed. The lot on which Orchestra Hall is built is too shallow, from street to alley. Today, the rear-row musicians have their backs against the wall which abuts the alley. (Trumpeter Adolph Herseth says that on cold and wintry nights he can feel a chill wind cascading down the wall onto his shoulders.) Thus the stage, though an oval without a curtain or a proscenium arch, is somewhat too shallow. And finally, an organ was built into the hall for religious services and the pipes were built—in stunning array—into the wall behind and above the orchestra. The result is that there is no solid wall, or shell, behind the orchestra, to reflect the sound out over the audience; the organ pipes, with their openings, capture a good deal of the sound rising from the stage.

Despite all this, Thomas himself was not displeased with the hall. His comment after his first rehearsal in the hall was, "Gentlemen, your hall is a success, a great success." But he caught cold in the drafty, unheated building and, after conducting two or three programs, he fell ill with pneumonia. He died within a month after that first rehearsal.

On the whole, the hall came to high esteem in the years that followed. There were, to be sure, dead spots; some patrons under the balconies could not hear precisely what was played in all its depth and glory. There were other problems onstage. Precise attack tended to be visual and psychological rather than aural: the violinists at the rear stands on the left could tell that the string basses were playing on the far right of the stage, but they couldn't hear the bass. The sound reached the

audience all right, but it did not often reach the conductor. Edward Druzinsky, the principal harpist, who's played in the Chicago Symphony since 1957, once detailed for me the difficulties he encountered. "You always try to play so that the music sounds right to you," he said of those days—before renovation. "But in Orchestra Hall the music sounded all right to the audience but not to the musicians." The sound of the harp, coming from the extreme left of the conductor on the very wide, shallow stage, was muffled by the time it got to the podium. "If the conductor stood out among the seats in the audience, the sound of the harp came through clearly," said Druzinsky. "But when he returns to the podium, he immediately begins signaling for the harps and the basses"—on the far right extreme—"to begin coming up. My friends in the audience always wondered why I played so loud, particularly with guest conductors." The reason is that the guest conductors were not aware of the sound peculiarities of the hall, whereas the regular conductors became adjusted to the fact that—though they could not hear the harp with great clarity—Druzinsky was playing exactly as the music and the conductor demanded.

The interior of the hall offered other problems for Druzinsky. "If the concert is at 8:15, I'll get there at 7 o'clock because I like to feel comfortable and relaxed during a performance," he says. "I'm at my best a half-hour to an hour after I'm completely warmed up." The trouble is that the temperature and the humidity of the hall were so variable that—even during the concert—he always had to keep tuning the harp. "The tuning changes when the doors are opened and the winter air rushes in," he said of those prerenovation days. "Then it changes again when the doors are closed and the hall heats up. "The strings are very much affected by temperature," said Druzinsky. "You can never stop tuning."

He rubbed his fingers thoughtfully. They are large and strong and many of them were long framed with calluses. In years past, he had to keep filing down the calluses. He even carried a black emory file—"Dr. Scholl's callus remover"—onstage with him. "Sometimes I'd forget to file down the calluses until the tone of the harp got really bad." It was not always easy to do, particularly in the very dry air inside Orchestra Hall in the wintertime. "When the humidity is low," he said, "the skin on my fingers will harden and start to crack." As the cracks deepen, there's a rise of blood to the surface. He tried putting hand cream on his fingers at night and also covering them with Band-Aids. But none of this helped during the concerts themselves. He simply had to learn—at certain times during the winter—to play the harp with his hands turned so that unaffected portions of his fingers could pluck at the strings. Otherwise, he says, the harp might begin sounding "like a banjo."

Despite all these facts and feelings, Orchestra Hall came to be highly regarded in its first three decades or so of use. For the human ear, it seemed to have the ideal balance of highs and lows, the desirable mixture of reverberation and clarity. To be sure, some of the record companies were wary of it back in the days of monaural sound and 78-rpm records. For it was a very "live" chamber. "Too much resonance," says Milton Preves, the first violist. He's been playing in the orchestra since 1934—under Frederick Stock—and he's been the principal in the viola section since 1939; not only has he occupied a first chair longer than any other principal in the symphony, but he's done it almost ten years longer than anybody else. "I remember in my first days with Stock—the first recordings I sat in with the symphony—they used to run heavy draperies from the gallery all the way down to the main floor. In those days, the records just couldn't take it."

Then recording technology improved. High fidelity and stereo systems appeared and with them many advanced techniques for making the most of the resonance of Orchestra Hall. It became, in those days, virtually an unparalleled chamber for reproducing on records the sound of a symphony orchestra. "It became ideal," says Milton Preves, "because they had an echo effect, a twelve-second echo effect in the hall."

As Preves and many other players remember it, some of the finest records ever made by the Chicago Symphony Orchestra, notably those during the Reiner regime, were made in Orchestra Hall. For stunning effects of reproduction could be achieved in Orchestra Hall with relative simplicity. Burl Lane, the contrabassoonist, says that "some of the Reiner recordings were made in Orchestra Hall with the use of one microphone suspended in the center of the hall. These days, no matter where we record, they use fifteen or twenty microphones scattered throughout the orchestra"—some companies use double that number or more—"and still they are merely hopeful that they can catch the quality of the recording made in the old days with just one microphone in Orchestra Hall."

Then, in 1966, Orchestra Hall was renovated. It was made a much more comfortable hall, particularly for the players. They now have a large, carpeted

Milton Preves, principal violist.

James Palecek, stage manager, offers Solti his choice of batons.

locker room in which each member of the orchestra has a full-length locker and a half-length locker. There are a lounge, toilet facilities for the men and the women, warm-up rooms, and private dressing rooms for the soloists and some of the principals. It was made more comfortable for the audience. High-speed elevators were built to take concertgoers to the galleries, the wood-based seats ware covered with cushions of plush and velour. A more efficient temperature-humidity system was installed. It was made more attractive to the eye. Walls of off-white—called Orchestra 66—were muted into a golden sheen by new lighting that set off carpets and seats of a deep, profoundly elegant shade of red. Altogether, more than $2 million was spent on the renovation.

There was only one trouble: it became an acoustical calamity.

"I'll never forget the first day we came back and played *The Consecration of the House Overture*," says Milton Preves. The number had symbolic significance: it was composed by Beethoven for the opening of the Josephstadt Theatre in Vienna in 1822. "We hit that big C-major chord that would usually raise the roof," said Milton Preves. "We just hit it and it just went completely dead—the sound. The hall had no reverberation at all"—the twelve-second echo had almost completely disappeared.

Thus the sound that was left was—in the musician's language—much "drier" than in the past. The orchestra no longer sounded balanced; some instruments could be heard more clearly but others sounded muddy. From a few dead spots, there now seemed to have grown many dead spots; people in certain spots in the galleries could hear a much better sound than those on the main floor.

The players don't identify any one cause for these problems. They tend to identify a score or more of them. Perhaps the most common was the removal of a thick layer of plaster in the ceiling and walls and its replacement by perforated aluminum screens. It was believed by the renovators that this would increase the available volume of air in the hall and make reverberation time longer. Then invisible panels above the stage, designed to be acoustically reflective, were to help improve hearing onstage and in the auditorium dead spots. There is no doubt that the latter was a success; the players themselves can hear the sound of the orchestra better than in the past. It's just that they don't like what they hear. Says Edward Druzinsky: "The curious thing is that I don't have any problem, as I did in the past, in getting the conductor to hear the sound of the harp." He paused. "But now the audience can't hear it so well."

There have been efforts to undo the damage. Burl Lane cites cause and effect in this way: "The ceiling and the walls behind the orchestra were solid plaster, several feet thick. A hard reflective surface. And the balcony and gallery seats were sort of antique wooden seats. Again a hard reflective surface. In the renovation, the hall was completely gutted and a false interior ceiling and back wall were installed in the form of a wire-mesh screenlike material and the hard gallery and balcony seats were replaced with plush seats, velvet in some places, leather in most. This effectively did away with all reverberation in the hall. There have been attempts, many different kinds of attempts, to restore the hall and restore the sound. These attempts have not succeeded at this time."

"The sound goes through. What used to be a reflective surface is now an absorbent surface," says Gordon Peters, the principal percussionist, of the many planes of Orchestra Hall. "Perhaps the most important thing is that there's nothing above us"—the orchestra—"there's no shell, nothing to throw the sound back at us. Hence we have to play with our eyes rather than with our ears. And that's very unnatural because you've been trained all your life to play with your ears."

Burl Lane points out that several recording companies tried heroically to salvage the hall for recording purposes. "They've tried covering the upper seating area of the hall with plywood sheets to increase the reverberation. They've tried piping the sound into the foyer upstairs"—for recording purposes—"and rerecording it with another set of microphones to recapture some reverberation. All of this has failed."

To a large extent, it's been up to the players to compensate for all this. They've all reacted, in different ways of course, but few have reacted more than Donald Peck, the principal flutist. He is a student of sound as well as of the flute and he speaks of the impact of the renovation in this way.

"Before they remodeled it, the hall was very bright. I don't like to sound flute-y or bird-y, so I tried for a full sound that was dark. It was marvelous in this hall at that time.

"After the hall was remodeled, they destroyed completely any quality of sound that they might have had. The hall now has a gray, dull sound. It has the pitch of the note but it does not have any of the glamour of the note. Like when the orchestra plays in New York, or in the other better halls. In almost any other hall the orchestra has a glamour or sheen, which can never be achieved in this hall because the acoustics are so 'dry.' It is not dead so much; it is just lacking in quality. Like someone took a knife and cut all the high overtones off everybody's sound.

"So I could not play my original flute in this hall anymore. I've been searching for four years for a flute that will have more glamour on the sound—not be quite as dark.

"Let's face it, I even went to different metals. And I just recently found the best thing that I can find for this hall."

What is the combination of metals?

"Well, I have been playing a platinum flute for over ten years. But most of the flute sound is in the head joint"—where the mouthpiece is—"and I got one made out of palladium, which is a platinum by-product metal—this is a substitute for platinum in certain dental plates and radio frequency material. It was very good. But it lacked something—it had something which I was not quite pleased with."

So he went to a flute made of different metals in different parts. (The flute, being a tube, comes apart at its seams, for easier carrying and packaging.)

"So what I am using now is a flute—the main body is platinum. The head joint is also platinum. But the chimney"—the hole into which the flutist stabs air—"the wall of the chimney is gold. This smooths out and gives a certain mellowness to platinum, which has tendency to get hard. Just a tiny bit of gold and it smooths out the sound and makes it brighter and adds more glamour.

"The foot joint, the small third section of the flute, is silver. This opens up the sound a bit for this hall, and I find this very good."

Donald Peck, principal flutist.

How did he ever assemble a flute of such majestic mixture?

"Well, the head joint had originally come with my platinum flute. I merely had them"—the flute makers—"strip off the mouthpiece and remake it. The mouthpiece was made of platinum but, as I say, the wall (we call it the chimney) is made of gold and that was completely redone.

"The foot joint I got from another flute and had it fitted onto this one."

How and why did he begin thinking of this combination?

It started with his platinum flute. He identifies it with a proud pedigree. "It was made by Verne Powell; he was a famous flute maker in Boston." It was made for a flutist in the New York Philharmonic. "He did not like it," says Peck. "He did not sound good on it. He played a bit hard anyway and platinum was just what he did not need. He got a gold flute which mellowed out his sound. He sounded marvelous on the gold flute"—though, says Peck, "silver is the more usual metal." He listened closely to the sound of his teacher on the flute, William Kincaid, who played for years with the Philadelphia Orchestra. "William Kincaid had played a platinum flute." So he started with platinum and built gold on one end and silver on the other to develop the sound he wanted—in the hall that had been "renovated."

All this effort by Donald Peck is directed at live performances. The record companies have another way of solving the problem of Orchestra Hall: they no longer record there. "We examined seventy-six halls in and around Chicago to find a suitable place to record," says Ray Minshull, producer of Solti's Beethoven series and manager of the classical artists department of the Decca Record Co., Ltd. (In England it is Decca; in the United States, its label is London Records.) The best place in the Chicago area is, in the view of most experts, the Krannert

Center on the Urbana campus of the University of Illinois. It is where London/ Decca recorded the Solti version of the Beethoven Ninth Symphony, and it is where Deutsche Grammophon planned to do the Barenboim recordings before they were put off by the work stoppage.

Just why did London/Decca choose to go to the garish old Medinah Temple?

There were many stories put out, and one of them might even have been true.

One was that Solti found the acoustics at Krannert Center suitable for something heavy in the way of musical sounds, such as the Beethoven Ninth or much of the Mahler series, but thought that the texture of the other Beethoven symphonies required a different kind of acoustical frame.

Another was that the players didn't want to be away from home for three days; they'd have to go to Urbana, about 135 miles from Chicago, to record in Krannert Center. But since they'd already done this in the past, this didn't seem altogether likely.

Another was yet a different dimension of the same problem of travel: London/Decca didn't want to pay the per diem ($30 per day per player) and travel expenses for the trip to Urbana.

Still another was that time did not allow for much in the way of travel between Chicago and Urbana, considering that rehearsals and performances were scheduled as usual during the recording week. And that extra rehearsals were scheduled for the tour. Even if the recording sessions were scheduled so that only one round trip was needed, it would make the recording sessions more than merely demanding; it might have made them beyond the players' ability to endure—and still play effectively.

The truth probably lies in the overlapping facts that the orchestra didn't have the time and the record company didn't have the money to go to Krannert Center. So they settled on Medinah Temple on the near North Side of Chicago (for RCA Victor had previously made some of its Chicago Symphony records).

That they had the money to come to America at all is the notable fact. For classical recording in the United States has all but disappeared. Only a few record companies maintain contracts with U.S. symphony orchestras (though some set up deals for individual discs). One reason is the way the classical market has plunged over the years. In 1910, classical recording accounted for 85 percent of all record sales. It was not likely that classical works could ever retain that dominant a portion of the market, once pop recording came along. Ten years ago, the figure had slipped to somewhere between 10 and 20 percent. The dire fact is that things have gotten dramatically worse since then: *The New York Times* estimates that in the early 1970s, the classical cut was figured to be around 3 to 5 percent of the total market.

Whereas a pop record often makes a million sales routinely, a sale of 15,000 copies of one record is considered a satisfactory result in classical music. "Forty thousand and up is a hit," says Terry McEwen, head of London/Decca's U.S. classical operations. That doesn't mean that a 40,000 sale is what's needed to make money. "A piano solo record that sells 40,000 really makes a lot of money," says McEwen, "because that doesn't cost you anything to make." But an opera is very costly to record, because what is required is not just one man but two hundred or three hundred musicians, soloists, and singers. A version of *Lohengrin*, made with the Boston Symphony Orchestra in 1964, cost RCA some $170,000 and very nearly convinced the board of directors to take the company out of classical recording altogether. (RCA did not drop out; it subsequently negotiated a quite costly recording package with the Philadelphia Orchestra.) And the recording of *Carmen* that won a Grammy for Deutsche Grammophon in 1974 reportedly cost that company $250,000.

Of course, the decline in the classical recording market in the United States is not the only consideration of the recording companies. For they still have a healthy market in Europe, where classical recordings are said to represent 30 percent of all sales, and in Japan, where classical music records represent 40 percent of all record sales.

But the economics of classical music recording is still very demanding.

Figure that $1 to $1.25 of the $6 list price of the typical stereo recording goes to the cost of the artists and the basic engineering costs of the recording session. (The figure varies from company to company, depending upon their bookkeeping, their overhead, and the sophistication of their recording equipment and production-and-engineering personnel. In the case of the recording of the Chicago Symphony at the Medinah Temple, London/Decca has to bear the cost of renting the hall and shipping all the instruments and chairs back and forth between the two sites —Medinah and Orchestra Hall—twice. In the past, the Orchestral Association helped subsidize certain recordings made with the Chicago Symphony but that is said not to be the case today.)

Then balance that figure—say $1.25—against a sale of 15,000 records. It's $18,750.

Or balance it against a "hit" sale of 40,000 records. It's $50,000.

That theoretically is what can be budgeted for artists, musicians, and other recording cosss for making a classical record—from $18,750 for a "good" selling record to $50,000 for one that's expected to be a hit.

Now compare that with the cost of hiring the Chicago Symphony Orchestra for one four-hour recording session late in 1973. It would be $14,140.35. This includes only the basic payment to each player—$134.67 for a four-hour session. It does not include the fee for Solti, the extra payments—if any—made to certain principal players, or the costs of moving the recording equipment and the engineers and producers from London to Chicago. It is simply the very basic cost of paying the 105 players of the orchestra.

(It should be noted that this cost was not set by the Chicago Symphony or its parent Orchestral Association. It was set by negotiation between the various recording companies and the American Federation of Musicians. In late 1974, the new four-hour recording rate for a major U.S. symphony orchestra would rise to $14,839.65—minimum.)

So the edge on a four-hour session, producing one excellent disc, is thin, even if one considers only the recording costs alone and not the promotion, advertising, and distribution costs.

To be sure, a three-hour recording session is more customary in the United States. In 1973–74, it would cost London/Decca $10,605 to hire the Chicago Symphony Orchestra—or any major U.S. symphony—for a three-hour session.

Compare that with the cost of using English players and recording in London: $1,575 minimum for the London Symphony Orchestra, a first-class symphony. The reason: in England, the players get about $15 for a three-hour session while in the United States they got $101 in 1973 (and they would get $106 a man starting in late 1974).

Thus it is easy to see why recording companies prefer to use English musicians rather than the top American symphony orchestras. And, indeed, why they turn even farther east: some of the Eastern European orchestras—which were making tours of the United States in 1973–74—undercut even the English orchestras on their prices.

It is also easy to see why the record companies want to have the numbers to be recorded by U.S. orchestras thoroughly rehearsed (for concert-hall performances) before the orchestra comes to the recording studio—if only because rehearsal time would cost the record companies something on the order of $3,000 an hour.

Given all this, it seemed a bravura defiance of destiny for London/Decca to come to Chicago to record the Beethoven symphonies with the Chicago Symphony Orchestra. For fourteen hours of recording, spread over three days in one week, would cost the company a minimum of $49,490.70 in basic payments to the musicians. In those fourteen hours, the company expected to record three Beethoven symphonies, plus fragments for the "Showcase" albums, Berlioz's *Les Francs-juges*, and the overture for Weber's *Oberon*. If it took three such sessions to get all the Beethoven symphonies recorded, the basic cost would be $148,472.10. (Actually, the Beethoven Ninth was already recorded, so that was not a problem in this series. And London/Decca expected to record a few other numbers to release under a Chicago Symphony "Showcase" series.) Of course, London/Decca did not go into this venture expecting to lose money. It figured to sell the Beethoven-under-Solti as a single-package album and, when the market was pretty much exhausted, to sell the symphonies as individual discs. Between the two, it was likely to sell far more than the 40,000 copies—in albums and as individuals—to make a "hit." Certainly there was no danger of their losing money. "I'm very happy to say that nobody has lost any money with the Chicago Symphony recordings with Solti—that's for sure," says McEwen.

Indeed, these records seem to do exceptionally well. In 1973, the Chicago Symphony under Solti had five records in *Billboard*'s charts of classical best-sellers—five of the top forty. They were the Mahler Eighth, the Beethoven Ninth, the Mahler Fifth, the first "Showcase" album, and the five Beethoven Piano concertos with Vladimir Ashkenazy on the piano. Only three other American orchestras were represented in the *Billboard* Top 40 list. They had one record each on the list. "I don't know if it's ever been true that one orchestra and one conductor have had five hits on the [Top 40] chart," says McEwen. "It certainly has probably never been true of an American orchestra."

There are, of course, other benefits of making the records, more for Solti and

the symphony, perhaps, than for the record company. It spread the renown, and
presumably the appreciation, of the symphony well beyond the borders of
Chicago. "Do you know that we sell more records by the Chicago Symphony in
San Francisco than we do in Chicago?" asks McEwen. "I would imagine that we
probably sell more in Hamburg than we do in Chicago. It's absolutely extraordinary."

This esteem can be converted into dollars when the Chicago Symphony makes
its tours. By the time it reaches San Francisco—or Hamburg—it's got enough of a
built-in following that it can charge top prices for tickets to its concerts. And expect
to sell them to the Chicago Symphony enthusiasts in town.

Similarly with Solti: his records helped him achieve a wide renown at a time
when he was not widely known in America, or in Europe for that matter. He has
never regarded records as a decorative frieze on his career or an extra source of
income (though by now, that income from record royalties is very formidable).
Rather, he's regarded it as part of the foundation of his career. ("Yes, yes. I think
so. I think so. Really more than a half, probably.") Indeed, it can be said that some
of his recording efforts border on the historic. It can be said that thousands upon
thousands of music lovers bought their first stereo sets because Solti's stereo
recording of *Rheingold* came into existence. That was in 1958. After that, he
undertook, with London/Decca, the Herculean task of recording the entire *Ring*
cycle of Wagner. The record-making was spread over seven years; he did not
complete *Die Walküre* until 1965. It was the first time that so vast an enterprise,
and so meaningful a one, was put on stereo, and even the years of being sated by
sonic marvels has not reduced the significance of those works: "The Solti
Rheingold," said *High Fidelity* magazine of the first album in the *Ring* cycle,
"seems undiminished in its musical and technical excellence."

Since then, Solti has gone back to Wagner. He recorded *Tannhäuser* in 1970
and *Parsifal* in 1972. He's now done seven of the ten works of Wagner that remain
in the repertory. (He has not recorded, as of this writing, *Die Meistersinger*, or
Lohengrin, or *Der Fliegende Holländer*.) He had also done Mahler's symphonies
nos. 5, 6, 7, and 8 as well as Mahler's *Das Lied von der Erde*, all with the Chicago
Symphony. And now he was doing the Beethoven symphonies; he'd already done
the five Beethoven piano concertos (with Ashkenazy) and he'd planned to record
Missa Solemnis—though the idea of doing it at the same time as the Beethoven
symphonies finally died.

So that is how Solti has begun to spread-eagle the field. He's captured the
musical zealots who follow orchestras by using the Chicago Symphony on so
many of his records. He's also captured many of those who follow composers by
doing virtually all of the Wagner, the Mahler, and the Beethoven. Whatever or
however fervid the discipline of the classical music follower, he is likely to find
Solti standing athwart the path of his own interest.

For Solti, all this provides not only an immediate income but a longtime
annuity. Many of these records will be producing royalties twenty and thirty years
from now and will be producing income for Solti when he is no longer recording or
will be producing income for his children. It also produces a living record of his

own work. Live performances die forever, but the records are a permanent testimonial to the man and his music.

They are also a permanent opportunity for his critics. Peter G. Davis found, for example, the record of Beethoven's Ninth Symphony by Solti and the Chicago Symphony Orchestra to offer a "surprisingly bland and even at times slack reading." He conceded that his was a minority view—almost spectacularly so —but, in a critique in *The New York Times*, he said, "it does raise some questions in my mind about Solti. In the earlier recordings, after one has digested the jabbing enthusiasm and the trim athletic drive, is there really a potent interpretive mind at work here or will history judge him a homely if occasionally excitable second-generation Toscanini disciple? Does the famous first-ever *Ring* cycle, after the initial thrill of hearing this mighty epic in its entirety so beautifully engineered, now sound a trifle prosaic when placed beside Furtwängler's less perfectly recorded version or even Karajan's interesting if problematical statement?"

Davis did not venture the answer. What he did was raise the question—and thus suggest the dangers and drawbacks of recording one's works.

There are other, more subtle risks. One is in the nature of the record-buying public. The classical music fan will, of course, buy the first of everything but not always the best of everything. Solti's records of the *Ring* cycle were the first and—Peter G. Davis to the contrary—the best of their kind. Thus they sold extraordinarily well: there are reports that some of the albums in the series have sold more than 100,000 copies. But it was being first that was important—not being best. Take *Carmen:* when Fritz Reiner and Risë Stevens made a recording of it some years ago, almost everybody with a record player and an interest in *Carmen*—or in opera in general—represented the potential market for the record. Today, everybody in that market—everybody with a record player and an interest in opera—is likely to have a copy of *Carmen*. No matter how well a subsequent *Carmen* is made—let us say a new one *is* the best—the vast market that existed for the first record is no longer in existence; many people have their record and are likely to be satisfied with it. Thus Deutsche Grammophon had a severe merchandising problem on its hands when it invested so much money in producing a new *Carmen*. It was not plunging into an unfulfilled market.

Similarly with Beethoven: since the celebration of Beethoven's two hundredth birthday in 1970, some fifteen package albums of all nine of the Beethoven symphonies have been released. Not to mention the continued existence of prebicentennial albums and of a sizable number of single-disc releases that included one or more Beethoven symphonies—Fritz Reiner and Seiji Ozawa made excellent ones with the Chicago Symphony Orchestra and Solti himself made not only the Ninth with the Chicago Symphony but the Third, Fifth, and Seventh with the Vienna Philharmonic. Does the world really need another album of all the Beethoven symphonies?

Of course there's a cynical answer to that. It isn't what the world needs, it's what can be sold that counts.

There's a practical answer to that. There were ten complete stereo sets of Beethoven's five piano concertos before Solti and Ashkenazy recorded them with the Chicago Symphony and yet the Solti-Ashkenazy version climbed onto *Billboard*'s chart of the Top 40. (That seems to endorse the conviction that record buyers buy performers—that is, Solti, Ashkenazy, and/or the Chicago Symphony —as well as buying composers or their works.)

There is also an answer to it involving aesthetic expectations: ". . . only reason any record company should record a Beethoven cycle," says Terry McEwen, "is because they have a conductor who's reached such eminence that not only he but the world expects him to do a Beethoven cycle. I mean, it is the crown of a conductor's achievements." And besides, London/Decca's existing album is by a respected conductor, Hans Schmidt-Isserstedt, who has an ample parochial reputation—chiefly in Germany—but not a worldwide renown; he is, McEwen concedes, "not a household word in the United States." The Beethoven cycle, he says, "was made primarily for the European market. Solti's new Beethoven cycle is for the world market . . . everyone in every country who buys a lot of records expects a Beethoven cycle from Solti now." And it is up to London/Decca to convert these expectations into hard sales.

In any case, Solti was scheduled—in the autumn of 1973—to record Beethoven's Third, Fifth, and Eighth symphonies in Medinah Temple. In the second session at Medinah in May 1974, he was to record Beethoven's First, Second, and Fourth symphonies. And then when the Chicago Symphony made its European tour in the following September, the orchestra would pause at the Sofiensaal in Vienna to make Beethoven's Sixth and Seventh symphonies.

The whole project had begun eighteen months earlier. "When he did the Beethoven Ninth, we thought then that if it came out well, we'd do the whole Beethoven cycle," says Ray Minshull. The Beethoven Ninth came out spectacularly well and planning went ahead for the start of the cycle. The first plans were to start in May 1973, but they were wiped out by the imminent arrival of Claudia, Solti's second daughter. That was coveted time lost, not only because the musicians got a raise for making records in the interim but because that first week would have been devoted exclusively to making records. Now it was split up among record-making, rehearsals, and performances.

The site of the record-making was both a problem and a blessing. It had a dazzling background. On the one hand, it is a Shrine temple, the third largest among the 174 owned in North America by the Ancient Arabic Order of Nobles of the Mystic Shrine. On the other hand, it's the scene of one of the circuses that hit Chicago semiannually, and the players and record staff joke about following the circus in the temple—there is, they claim, a rather perceptible odor on first entering the hall and a problem of cleaning the peanut shells from the galleries.

One reason the circus goes into Medinah Temple is that it has a large stage—the largest of its kind in the Midwest. It is a "thrust" stage—a proscenium arch with a platform extending far out in front of the curtain line. Overall, the stage measures 68 feet by 68 feet. Some 48 of those feet extend out from the proscenium arch; that means the platform—on which the musicians are placed—is 48 feet deep by 68 feet wide, or a total of 3,264 square feet. That allowed for roominess and a certain flexibility in placing both the members of the orchestra and the microphones.

Minshull and his crew would try to get by with ten microphones. When one company did the Mahler Eighth Symphony with another orchestra, they'd used forty-two microphones.

But there were difficulties with a stage of this size. For back of the platform —which is actually the stage under the proscenium arch—is an area some 20 feet deep and 68 feet wide. That is fine for storage during recording sessions; the stagehands can simply haul in the trunks and set them up to the rear of the players, giving them easy access to their equipment. But that rear area is very high, and the danger, acoustically speaking, is that some of the sound will escape into the vast area behind the proscenium arch, and thus be lost to the record-makers, when it might be used as part of the resonance in the recording chamber.

There is a metal fire curtain that can be lowered to any distance between the platform and the rear-stage area. It could be used to add to the resonance, if it could be set at the ideal height. When London/Decca had recorded here on one occasion in the past, the first curtain was kept raised to its full height; the word is that the English staff—not under Minshull at that time—had disagreements with the Americans maintaining Medinah Temple, and the Americans would not move the curtain to accommodate the record-makers. Thus the record engineering staff had a great deal of difficulty with the sound.

Now Minshull and his staff had come early to tackle the acoustical problems. His chief engineer, Kenneth Wilkinson—a small, quiet, almost cozy man who'd worked on many, many Solti recordings through the years—and a technician named Peter Van Biene had arrived four or five days early to set up some $50,000 worth of equipment in a control room off the recording chamber. Minshull, quick, intense, so fast in his speech that it sounds almost like another language, arrived on the weekend to look over the hall.

He found a dirty brown-brick building, some sixty-two years old at this time, a cross between an Arabian mosque and a Chicago warehouse. The entrance through the recorder's office is walled in bright, gleaming varnished plywood. The auditorium itself is large, a main floor with two balconies containing a total of 4,500 seats. The dome, centered with stained glass, is seventy-five feet above the floor; some of the cables and equipment for the trapeze and high-wire acts of the circus are fastened into girders around the dome. There are eight banks of spotlights on the front of the second balcony. They would help in the lighting for the musicians, but they would provide only a portion of the light needed for the closed-circuit television system that Minshull and his engineer would set up: they'd mount a small TV in a corner of the balcony to the right of the podium and connect it to a monitor in the control room. Thus Minshull and his colleagues in the control room would be able to see Solti as well as to hear the orchestra all during the recording sessions.

The fire curtain was thick—perhaps a foot thick with metal panels on each side. It was decorated with scimitars and half-moons, the symbols of the Shrine. On the morning that the first recording session was to start, it was down all the way—right to the stage floor.

The time was 10 A.M. on a cold Monday in November. Nobody was late; the orchestra was tuned and ready to go when Solti gave the downbeat. When there's so much money involved in payment of musicians, not a moment can be lost. The first thing they played was a segment of Beethoven's Fifth Symphony. It was not for recording. It was to test the equipment and the balance of the room.

At 10:12, Solti halted the orchestra. Dale Clevenger, the first horn player, spoke up for Solti's information.

"They have one microphone back here and it's turned the other way," he said. It was out of the ordinary, compared to the bristling forest of microphones that had been used in past recording sessions. But there was a danger that the brass—always powerful in the Chicago Symphony—would come up too strong on the recording. Nevertheless, Solti picked up a beige telephone from a table behind the podium.

"Mr. Clevenger says there's only one microphone in his section and it seems to be turned away." He listened for a moment and hung up. "They say, 'Don't worry. They don't want it too much. Too much.' "

The music resumed, again with Beethoven's Fifth as a test.

Peter Van Biene, in a black turtleneck and black pants, emerged from the control room from time to time to turn a mike here, to lower one there, to move one a few inches in other places. In the control room, Minshull and Wilkinson listened carefully, studied their batteries of instruments, moved a red-knobbed lever here or a black-knobbed switch there. "The first half hour was the key to the whole thing," said Minshull. If he couldn't get the perfect balance and the desired resonance—if he couldn't get that fire curtain raised or lowered to the proper height—he'd be faced with the decision of whether to scrub the whole project or to go ahead with a high chance of failure.

The music stopped again.

"Hey, this curtain is up behind me," called out one player on the rear stands. The players knew the trouble the raising of the fire curtain caused in an earlier session. Solti nodded. He'd seen it raised. The temple's staff was working with the record company's staff and that was a good sign. It meant that the problem would not be whether the curtain might be raised or lowered but at what height it should be held.

Solti himself went to the control room to listen to the tapes of the opening minutes of the record session. "Solti has developed an incredible ear for studio dynamics," David Harvey has said. He was producer for London/Decca on the recording of the Beethoven Ninth Symphony and later he was an assistant general manager, under John Edwards, for the Chicago Symphony Orchestra. "On a playback, he not only spots wrong sounds, but also knows precisely how to correct them."

In this case, he did not need to correct the sound. He had only to work with the engineers in determining how to get the best sound. Their conclusion was to lower the fire curtain not to the floor but to a height about equal to the shoulders of an average man—say five feet above the floor. That would give the entire chamber exactly the resonance that Minshull and Solti wanted out of it.

There would still be details; Van Biene would still be turning microphones and adjusting their height and Wilkinson would be laboring over his dials and levers all

Willard Elliot (left), principal bassoonist, discusses fine point with Georg Solti.

through the session. But the main problem had been solved: at 10:30—just a half hour after the first downbeat—Solti was ready to record.

"We suggested doing the *Eroica* first," says Minshull. It was the "biggest" piece of the first week's work—"and the biggest piece tends always to be first in our recording sessions. It's a matter of getting something accomplished"—of the feeling of having accomplished something. The orchestra is at its high; later on in the week it would be very fatigued and thus likely to be less alert on the "biggest" piece. Neither Solti nor Minshull wanted the orchestra to be worn out—or get worn out—on the "big" pieces of Beethoven. There would be other works— smaller in scope and in recording time—to occupy and preoccupy the orchestra later in the week: the Overture to *Oberon* by Weber and Berlioz's *Francs-juges* that would be made for another "Showcase" album. "Somehow," says Minshull, "the small thing always takes more time."

In the hall, the playing of Beethoven's Symphony no. 3 started with the two staccato E-flat major chords and then swept deliberately, confidently into the first movement (allegro con brio), with the theme expressed by the cellos, then with the violin statement of the first theme, and into a transitional idea followed by the statement of a new theme that starts with the woodwinds and comes to involve the strings. Solti has, within his mind, the precise notion of how far he wants to proceed with each theme or each movement. But his notions are allayed by the union regulations: twenty minutes of every hour must be devoted to a break for the orchestra. He would time those intermissions to coincide with his own plan for the proper break in the music. (He could store up the intermission until the last hour; thus he could hoard sixty minutes of intermission and use them after the orchestra had played without a break for two hours. But that would not satisfy his need for hearing the tapes immediately and then making notes on how they might be improved.)

In this case, he took an intermission just before the clock passed into the second hour of recording. He did not have to make all the intermissions twenty minutes long; some might last only ten or fifteen minutes but they had to total twenty minutes an hour. At the outset of the recording session, Solti was inclined to take the intermissions early, so he could monitor the progress of the tapes quite closely. Now he had some first-hour time left.

"Quiet, please," he said. There was hubbub in the yellow-walled control room when he entered and sat down to listen to the first takes. He had the score and a half dozen or so marking pencils in front of him along with a stopwatch to check the time of the take. It was a broad table with nothing in front of it but a set of stereo speakers and the TV monitor showing the podium. On the walls around the room were hung pictures of potentates of the Shrine—in their exotic, jewel-daubed robes—looking like newly crowned queens or newly consecrated popes. Some were covered by quilts hung from pipe frames—"sound-dampening mats"—rugs hung on the wall to reduce the reverberation within the room.

In this session, to Solti's left sits the concertmaster—Victor Aitay for Beethoven's Symphony no. 3. To his right sits Ray Minshull. The one will relay Solti's notes and instructions to the string section. The other will relay them to the engineers, usually through his own orchestrating of the engineer's labors.

Though he's listening to the tape, Solti is reacting emotionally, viscerally to what he's hearing. His head bounces—up and down, jerking spasmodically from side to side—to the beat, his shoulders shift, his torso twitches. It is all he can do to keep from raising his arms and "conducting" the music—and sometimes he doesn't altogether succeed in that restraint.

"The timpani is too loud," he says, almost to himself—though his companions can hear him and make their own notes. "Should be a bit softer, a bit lower. The horns are always generally too loud." He will repeat these thoughts to the orchestra when he resumes recording. Now he half turns to Ray Minshull about the cello part on the next take: "If you don't get that *espressivo*, stop me." He knew now he was going to tape it over. To Aitay, he said, "The strings, we can do better." Back to Minshull: "Too much shock at the beginning?"—meaning the two chords that open the work. Says Minshull: "Yes, it was rather a bright shock."

At eleven o'clock, he is back on the podium. "Curtain down, please," he says. The fire curtain had been raised at intermission to give the players a little more roaming room. "Now we have just a few points," continues Solti. "The horns, too loud—Mr. Koss, please, too loud. . . . The woodwinds and brass, please, my dears, every first note shorter. You are trying with the strings but you are hanging over. . . . Strings, wasn't spectacular. We could do better, my dears." Then in general: "It wasn't so good as we did in concert. . . . Too loud the second horn. A little bit less, please. . . . First violins, I didn't hear the last tone."

He throws his towel over the rail of the podium and raises his arms. "Take three," says Minshull in the control room. The tapes are rolling before the first two chords are sounded—the brightness reduced a little by engineer Wilkinson—and the orchestra moves once again in the first movement of *Eroica*.

"The cellos," says Minshull very softly. He is reading the score as the music proceeds and he cues in engineer Wilkinson so he can move his hands and be ready to make the electronic most of the playing of one instrument or another. "The violins," says Minshull in his clipped, soft tones. He hates noise; he darts quick angry glances at anybody who comes into the makeshift control room and lets the door thump or scrapes a chair ever so softly on the floor. "Bring the bass down a bit," he says. "The oboes, *now*"—as a climax subsides to a new theme. Then a little later, "The violins . . ."

Kenneth Wilkinson is hunched like a gnome over his battery of dials and levers and switches. He is as concentrated as Minshull but not as tense. His lower lip is thrust out as he weighs and considers the sound that he hears and the sound that he must record. In response to Minshull's cues—and to his own inner drives—he touches a lever here, a dial there, with all the delicacy of a surgeon on his first incision. He is, in a sense, as important to it all as is Solti. For Solti manipulates the orchestra while Wilkinson manipulates the instruments that record the orchestra. Minshull is an interpreter, a liaison man, an executive. Wilkinson is the man who can make or ruin this recording—by a touch that is a fraction of an inch one way or another.

Now Solti stops the orchestra. "Very good," he says. "Could we take twenty minutes, please?"

He returns to the control room to hear the takes. The players drift—or bolt—off to their own pursuits. Some go to the phones or hear how the stock market is doing. Some resume their nonstop card games, either on the tops of trunks backstage or on two vast plywood sheets thrown over the first two rows of seats on the main floor. A few follow Solti into the control room. They are concerned with the sound that they or their sections are making.

"The drums still sound 'tubby,' " said Don Koss to Ray Minshull at the end of one intermission.

"Still?" asked Minshull. He had talked out the problem with Koss very briefly before and thought the problem was resolved. "You and the basses are still having problems," Minshull went on. "Where were you standing?" he asked.

Koss indicated a spot in the makeshift control room where the sound from the two stereo speakers might intersect—the ideal spot for hearing the sound.

"It must be the room," said Minshull. He is an old hand at dealing with musicians. He must have an explanation for them all and he must not admit the truism that exists between them: that he is aiming for the sound that the record company wants, not the sound that the musicians are accustomed to hearing and think best.

He marches to one wall, sweeps back a dampening rug, and pounds on the wall. Thus he sows the reverberation within the control room that he and his engineers were hoping to control by the dampeners.

"It *is* this room," he says. "It'll be all right when we get out of this room"—that is, when the record is heard in a normal setting.

Koss nodded and went back to work. But there was still a look of skepticism on his face. The players in an orchestra hear the sound of the orchestra in a way different from the way an audience does; it is necessarily so, since they are immersed in the sound, not standing outside it. The records and tapes invariably sound different to them; some of them worry about the sound on the tapes when the session is in progress, others merely hate it. They suspect that the record company is striving for a different sound than they have historically produced. And, of course, with all that great gadgetry, they suspect—darkly—that the record company can take any sound and redevelop it in the way they want. So there is an underlying uneasiness among some players that the engineers are doing more to produce the sound of the record than they are. And that the engineers are not on the same wavelength—literally—as the musicians are.

"I concede," says Ray Still, "that tapes, many times, will sound lousy to the performer because he idealizes what he was playing. And he thinks he got a certain sound. That can throw you into a turmoil and give you an insecure feeling."

He was the target of a Solti inquiry during one intermission. "Mr. Still," he said, turning from his table and looking through the array of musicians crowded ten feet or so behind him. "Mr. Still, could we have more oboe on that?"

Still shook his head in a very small motion. "We're fortissimo now." His implication was clear: the engineers would have to adjust since the musicians could not adjust.

Solti nodded and turned back to his score. He would have a way to solve the problem later.

Dale Clevenger of the French horns felt his section had a problem in being heard. "That third horn solo," he said during one intermission, "he's playing as hard as he can and he can't be heard." The suggestion was that the microphone wasn't picking up the sound of the horn, since Clevenger felt it was still turned away from his man in the section. "He's blowing his head off. There's just no microphone near him. He's playing right out to the audience"—and there was no audience.

Solti dismissed the thought. "We don't want a horn concerto at this point," he said. He was quite satisfied with the sound that he'd heard from the podium and on the tape. Clevenger nodded. He knows he is held in high respect by Solti and his own respect for Solti is just as high. But he would agitate just a little with the English crew to get that microphone turned.

It is this devotion to detail that, Clevenger thinks, makes the Chicago Symphony unique and makes the horn section within the symphony so singular. "There's nothing abut blowing it that's different," he says of the French horn in the orchestra. "It's the attention to detail that the general level of player in our orchestra has— the attention to fine detail and the fact that it's on a little higher musical level than most other orchestras. There are horn players in other orchestras who have just as much technique. But the combination of sound that we get in the orchestra—well, it's because we work together at the kind of sound that we have in the horn section and in the brass in general. Stylistically, the way we play, the kind of rhythms we play, a feeling of what we have—we sort of think individually but we immediately apply it to what we hear around us and try to make it all blend. There is apparently more of that thought process in our orchestra than there is in most others. Because we get better results. It's been said—and I think it's a very good way of putting it—there is a standard below which we rarely ever fall. And that standard is already higher than in most other orchestras in the world. We rarely fall below it and most often we are way above it."

Clevenger is one of those aging prodigies—he's thirty-three and has been in the orchestra since 1966—whose gray-flecked beard and gray-flecked temples give him the look of a bright, engaging, and self-confident Mephistopheles. Candid, secure, and restlessly ambitious, Dale Clevenger has a musical skill that creates a highly idealistic, moralistic, and intelligent principal who seems to grace every prideful remark with the turn of truth and the highly polished veneer of collective achievement. "Our brass section, everybody tells us—I'm not always in a position to compare—but everybody tells us that it's unparalleled by any other orchestra in the world. But, frankly, we work at it. We work real hard at it. We don't have sectionals together, practicing as a brass section, but we talk to each other and we think alike. We try to sound as best we can.

"We have a lot of stars in the orchestra. By stars, I mean really virtuoso players, soloists in their own right who play extremely well but who are adaptable at orchestra playing, too. Who can blend in very beautifully with the orchestra. I learn an awful lot by sitting and listening to these men play their solos—what they do is just marvelous.

He is himself one of the great virtuoso players of the orchestra. He has mastered

the sound of the horn—perhaps the most beautiful, the deepest, and the mellowest of any brass instrument—by sharpening the focus of the instrument. He's not trying for noteworthiness by following the general pattern of horn players. "It's not too dark or too bright," he says of his own style. "The general concept of American horn players—the sound is often tubby and woofy and unfocused. I don't think I indulge in any of those things. In fact, I know I don't. We have been compared as a section, and I as a horn player, to Viennese sound with American flexibility." He can and does demonstrate the sound of the horns in other orchestras and in other nations—in Germany, in Prague, in Vienna. "What I try to do is put the best of all of them into a style of playing." That style is subject to change—or to growth. "I didn't come in here as a finished, polished solo horn player. I've been learning and I'm still learning and I don't expect to stop learning."

He talks with a southern drawl and he has many of the southern imperatives. "My daddy," he says, "is president of a manufacturing company." It was his daddy who got him started in music when Dale was only seven and began playing the piano. At the time, his daddy was president of the Chattanooga Opera Association. "He presented three or four operas a year down there." His daddy began taking Dale to the opera and sometimes to rehearsal and the fact that it *was* opera created a situation that stimulated Dale's interest in music. "In the opera, with the orchestra sitting in the pit, I could see the musicians and I got more interested in what was going on in the pit than on the stage. I used to ask daddy if I could go down and sit beside them and—this was in the high school auditorium—I would go down and sit in the front row next to the horns. So I got to know the horn players."

That did not lead to automatic success. It did not even lead to immediate horn playing. When he was eleven—a fifth-grader—he had a chance to get into the school band. "My father would not buy me a horn because it cost too much at that time," he says. "A second choice was the trumpet. So I played the trumpet for two years"—all the while looking for the opportunity for the horn. When he was in seventh grade, and thirteen years old, the school bought a French horn and he clamored to switch to it. "I put the trumpet aside and I began playing the horn. . . . I knew then that this is what I would like to do. It was probably more a fantasy, a dream rather than really knowing. But I had a good idea that's what I wanted to do." His father was a trifle skeptical. "I didn't know anything about professional music and neither did my father. He assumed that professional musicians were all like Chattanooga Symphony musicians, all of whom had secondary jobs." His father was right: this was in the early and mid-1950s and symphony musicians *had* to have other jobs. Dale was still going down to sit in the front row during rehearsals and performances. "I remember promising one of the horn players in the orchestra that I would be sitting with them one day, because I was going to work hard to get there."

It took him very few years. At the age of sixteen he auditioned, somewhat audaciously, for a place in the Chattanooga Symphony—and was hired. "So I spent my last two years in high school playing in the Chattanooga Symphony." He was the fourth horn player. Beside him sat Imogene Sloan, the third horn player who'd befriended him in the days when Dale was hanging over the front rail—"she was sort of my mentor; it's her horn that I play on today in the Chicago Symphony Orchestra." One day Miss Sloan asked him if he'd like to study under her teacher. Dale would and his father agreed and so Clevenger spent a summer stydying the horn in Chautauqua, New York, under Forrest Standley. He, in turn, asked Dale if he'd like to continue studying under him at Carnegie Tech. Dale would and his father agreed. "As I tell my students, it's not where you go to college or what music department you're in or what subjects you take per se. In music, it's who your teacher is. That is the important factor."

At Carnegie Tech, the emphasis was on music education rather than on playing in symphony orchestras—or playing professionally at all. But Clevenger plunged into a dizzying round of horn playing. He played summers in one symphony, winters in two symphonies—as an extra in the Pittsburgh Symphony and as a regular first horn in the Wheeling Symphony, some sixty miles away. (One of his conductors was Henry Mazer, now associate conductor of the Chicago Symphony.) "I played in all kinds of ensembles, orchestras, bands, brass ensembles, woodwind quintets." He played duets with his roommate and solos whenever and wherever he could. "There were four or five of us at school who were determined to play professional. And all of us did." In the summer after his junior and senior years, he went to New York to study under Joseph Singer, principal horn in the New York Philharmonic. "With Singer I added touches with a different point of view. But with the same basic style of playing," he says. He also got the "feel" of New York. He was a southern boy but he was not exactly intimidated or backward, in "the big city." After graduating from Carnegie Tech, he moved to New York and—after another summer with Singer—played three auditions. "And got all three jobs."

One was playing the second horn in the New York City Opera Orchestra.

Another was playing in the pit orchestra for the Broadway musical *Stop the World—I Want to Get Off*.

The third was playing first horn in the Radio City Music Hall orchestra.

He chose the Radio City Music Hall job.

"Being young and not knowing really which is best, I would probably do it again. But from what I know now, I would have taken one of the other two."

The job had no glamour. "It's a factory. It's a very hard job. The orchestra does four shows a day. You have only two hours free in between each show—for the movie—and then you have to be back. You can't do much in those two hours. The orchestra—the players—for their own survival kibitz, kid around, and joke, have fun backstage, and so forth." The *older* members of the orchestra do that. "The new players just can't do that." Clevenger made a deep impression—"they were always complimenting me on my playing"—but not on his surging self-confidence. For he began acting like some of the older members: joking and kidding around backstage—just as if, at the age of twenty, he was one of *them*. "The conductor at that time apparently was offended by the fact that I was so carefree." Clevenger lasted a month there, one month of his six months' probation. Then he was fired.

"It hurt me. It hurt my feelings deeply. As a matter of fact, I cried. I didn't know what to do," he says. "I thought the bottom had fallen out. Here I'd turned down two other jobs. And the Broadway show was with a New York contractor"—a musician who lines up other musicians for specific jobs—"who was, notoriously, very hard on players. If you turned him down, people thought you might never work for him again."

He had a chance at other income. For at the very moment he was fired at Radio City, he was playing as an extra horn at the New York Philharmonic. "That week we did Tchaikovsky's Seventh Symphony; we recorded it." So he had both money and friends. So he soon began playing in other orchestras as a free-lancer, and a couple of months later he went back to the same Broadway contractor and won a job in the pit orchestra of another musical, *Oliver!* "It ran a long, long time but I played only nine months of it." For now he was growing increasingly busy, not only playing in orchestras but doing jingles and commercials for TV and making records for the pop music industry.

"My first commercial recording session was April 1, 1963—I'll never forget that date. We had a sixty-piece orchestra—we did Marty Gold's *Sounds Unlimited* on RCA Victor—and I was just flabbergasted at the quality of the musicianship. I still am when I hear the record played." That got Clevenger started heavily in the pop and commercial music industry of New York. He had the skills but he also got—through commercial recording—exposure to the various contractors and to the New York system. "Contractors like to help other contractors out and—since they're all musicians and like to appear on records—there would be a lot of contractors at the recording sessions," he says. "They would hear you—they'd see a new face and ask, 'Who is that playing so-and-so?' So you'd get a call to play another thing and the whole thing began to snowball."

One call was to do ten minutes of overtime for a jingle for a Kellogg's cereal. "That introduced me to the jingle world and it was a fascinating world," he says. "It's done very quickly and with very high quality musicians who can adapt to different styles and idioms extremely quickly."

All this time, Clevenger's heart was still in classical music. So while he was making records and doing jingles for TV commercials, he was also playing extra with the New York Philharmonic, playing with the Bach Aria Group, playing with various ballets, working in pickup orchestras for concerts around town—"four or five different orchestras," he says. "They don't function anymore because they just can't pay for them. There are so many outside orchestras that come to New York now"—including the Chicago Symphony—"that they can't fill a house with a local pickup orchestra."

So deep was his feeling about classical music that he left New York one time to make a European tour with the Pittsburgh Symphony, left it again to play for six months with the Kansas City Philharmonic. But he had his eyes fixed on an improbable, almost impossible goal: to play first horn—and only first horn—with one of the top symphony orchestras in the country. He tried time after time—and he failed time after time after time. "It may be of encouragement to those younger players who have taken auditions and haven't made them," he says, cataloguing his failures.

Clevenger auditioned for assistant first horn in the New York Philharmonic and was turned down (though he played as an extra with the Philharmonic). He auditioned for first horn in the New Orleans Philharmonic and didn't make it. He sought an audition for first horn in the Boston Symphony and couldn't even get heard—"they already had thirty players for the audition and they said, 'That's enough.' " He auditioned at least three times for first horn in the Pittsburgh Symphony and was turned down every time. ("Even though I played with them on the European tour and they knew my playing—I could be in that orchestra right now without ever having auditioned, but it wouldn't be as first horn.") He auditioned for first horn with the Metropolitan Opera and won plaudits—"one of the first horn players who heard me said it was the best audition he ever heard played"—but the job went instead to a first horn player from the Chicago Symphony. So Clevenger promptly sought an audition for the first horn opening with the Chicago Symphony and came in as one of the two finalists. "But they didn't take anybody at that time."

One day in December 1965, he got a phone call from conductor Alfred Wallenstein, under whom he'd played from time to time. "He said, 'I've spoken to the conductor in Chicago about you. You should go out and audition for them.' I said, 'I just did audition for them, back in April, and I didn't make it.' He said, 'You go out again. You play for them again. They want a first horn player.' "

So one Sunday night, after playing a concert with Leopold Stokowski in Manhattan, he flew to Chicago and at nine-thirty the next morning he ran an audition. Chicago didn't hesitate: this time he got the job. In fact, he was named the principal horn player. "There is no way to describe what it's like to finally land a job as No. 1 in an orchestra like this. But for it to be principal chair in one of the great orchestras of the world—something which you've been looking forward to all your life—there is no way to describe it. You laugh, you cry, you holler, you shout. I was alone when it happened"—when he got the word from Chicago—"and I just couldn't believe it."

In Chicago Clevenger not only solidified but expanded his reputation in the symphony. But he is a restless and an ambitious man: the horns are much sought after for commercials and jingles even in Chicago and, when he had time free from the symphony, he'd work that side. He did the signature music for the "Wild Kingdom" show on TV. "We did it back in 1967; they're using the same music ever since then—I've been paid for that since 1967." He did the commercials for United Air Lines, the Mazda car, Schlitz Beer, Sears tires, Sears paint, American Petroleum, Toyota. "Many, many more. I can't remember them all."

At the same time, he worked hard and long hours on other pursuits and other hopes. He's a devout and dedicated member of the Church of Christ and he's developed a philosophy of personal philanthropy: he helped organize a people-to-people giving campaign for the poor in the Christmas of this season—in which gift-givers searched out and offered what was needed by a particular family, instead of indulging the impersonal charity of massive campaigns. In addition, he conducts his church choir, which has led him to another ambition: he candidly would like to become a conductor.

"I wouldn't want to do it unless I could be—I don't mean to sound egotistical

—but I wouldn't want to do it unless I could do it on the same level that I'm playing here. I wouldn't want to be a third-rate conductor. It wouldn't be enjoyable to me. And, frankly, I don't think I would be." He studied conductors and conducting for years. "I went to a conductor's workshop for seven summers," he says. "I watched many young students—saw the mistakes that they made. I've watched the great conductors and tried to put together the best attributes of all of them. You must have great inner rhythm. You must have a reasonably clear beat. But you've got to have a heart; you've got to have a feeling for music. And you've got to know the music."

Clevenger identifies, for example, the musical style of conductors such as Leonard Bernstein, Solti, and Giulini.

"Bernstein is a rhapsodic type conductor," says Clevenger. "He's very romantic in nearly everything that he does. Very rarely does he describe a very precise baton technique—it's always a flowing sort of thing. . . . He did things like the *Rite of Spring* extremely well because he can build mood through style. He knew some of these pieces well enough do them from memory. But that doesn't matter in and of itself. That could get in your way if you had a memory lapse.

"Giulini's music always comes across as very, very linear—the long, long phrase. It's smooth and sometimes overly romantic.

"Solti's music is usually a little more straightforward, sort of angular, quite rhythmical. Solti's inner rhythm—although he might not always show it in the stick—his inner rhythm is always there and it's always evident."

In terms of personality: "Here again their depth of music, their understanding, comes out in what they're able to tell the orchestra. Primarily, we hope, with their hands, with their stick technique. Sometimes with their mouths. We don't like it when they have to do it with their mouth."

The danger of using the mouth is that it erects some barriers and breaks down others—it creates a crisis of respect. Bernstein, for example, was on a first-name basis with many of his players whereas Solti maintains a "maestro" and "Mr. Clevenger" relationship, Bernstein might build a "Lenny" and "Dale" kind of relationship. The difference, of course, is that Solti comes from an old European tradition whereas Bernstein "grew up with a lot of these people. They knew him from the time he was virtually a kid and he was just 'Lenny.' " The relationship didn't damage the music he made: "Because he's such a fine musician, he did raise the standards of the New York Philharmonic, both monetarily and playing-wise. He was good for them and he was a genius for the public because he was an attraction. And whether an orchestra likes a conductor or not, if he brings the people in, that's what it's all about. If you happen to do good music on top of that, great." But sometimes the verbal give-and-take was accepted under Bernstein in the wrong way. "Sometimes Bernstein would be a little undiplomatic in the way he calls somebody on, say, an intonation problem," says Clevenger. "I remember one time a first oboe player played a note and it was obviously out of tune. Bernstein said, 'Harold, that note was out of tune.' Harold looked at him, stared at him for a moment, and said. 'I heard it too, Lenny.' Which he did."

"Solti and Giulini never insult the orchestra. They never come close to it.

Dale Clevenger, principal horn player.

They never—well, they rarely ever flinch if something goes wrong. Solti may look back and smile or something if there's a little careless error that maybe only the conductor hears. But other conductors will look back and frown or stare you down. At this level of playing that's not necessary. Because if a mistake has been made, the guy who made it is the first to know who did it. The first to recognize it. And the last to want it to happen. So you don't have to tell us that we did it."

Clevenger's experience at conducting is limited and he's astounded at some of the experiences of working the other side of the street, such as when he conducted select members of the Chicago Symphony in the sound track for a Sea World film.

"I must say, it was quite an exhilarating experience to conduct the orchestra in that recording session," he says. "It's amazing how quick they are, what they do with your tempo, with the little inflections of your hands."

These hopes and this ambition haven't prevented him from undertaking the singular task of the principal horn player. It involves more than playing solo. It involves, as far as Clevenger is concerned, building the horn section within the symphony. That is why he was fighting so persistently to have his third horn player heard in the recordings of the Beethoven symphony; he felt that the work that the player put into it would be perfect but that the sound would not. And he wants the sound of the section to be heard and to be perfect.

"In America, it's hard to make a section," he says. "In a place like Prague, where every first horn is a professor, he teaches and his students hopefully come along in the orchestra. Here it's not possible because you can't get that kind of student." One exception, he concedes, is the Philadelphia Orchestra. "Philadelphia is a place where the first horn player had literally all his own students playing for him—Mason Jones. That's one of the last places where that's taking place."

In the Chicago Symphony it has not been possible to develop a professor-and-pupil relationship. One reason is that Clevenger came in as the principal player, at the age of twenty-five, to an orchestra which had veteran horn players such as Frank Brouk and Joseph Mourek, who'd won their own renown many years earlier and who'd been in symphony orchestras since the 1920s and 1930s. "So I sort of adapt a little bit to what I do. Then when you audition, and somebody comes in from the outside"—since he had no pupils to funnel into the section—"you try to get somebody who plays basically like you. And you hope that once you get it together, it sort of meshes and becomes a unified sound."

Under Clevenger, the horn section has the burnished confidence of the veterans and the surging confidence of youth. There has been a constant inclination to youth ever since Clevenger proved himself. The auditions are strict and screened, of course, but it's been young men—rather than older men from other orchestras—who've moved into the horn section of the Chicago Symphony. There was a time around 1970 or 1971 when three of the six members of the horn section were thirty or under, including the principal player. And the fourth was just over thirty.

One of them, for example, was Richard Oldberg, who joined the orchestra in 1963 at the age of twenty-five.

Another was Norman Schweikert, who was making $110 a week playing, at eighteen, in the Rochester Philharmonic Orchestra (it was costing him $8 a week to rent a room in a boardinghouse—which is not the usual style of the symphony player). Like Clevenger, he didn't take up the horn until he was thirteen years old—a trifle late for a symphony-scale musician. He started on the piano, later played the piano ("in some training orchestras in Hollywood"), and later switched to the French horn. "It was, I guess, the sound of the instrument. The moods it could evoke. The masculine kind of feeling as opposed to . . . in a sort of way—you know how kids are—the sissy look of a violin. At least this was a more masculine, a more manly instrument. I felt I wanted to be part of that." He's thirty-six years old now and he started playing in symphony orchestras half his lifetime ago.

Perhaps the most spectacular example of the youth who came into the horn section is Tom Howell. He was twenty-one when he won his audition for the symphony, he was twenty-three when he became associate first horn. And yet he wasn't picked just because he was young: he had to beat out seventy-eight other candidates to get the job.

If there is anything singular in Tom Howell's rise, it is in both his natural and instinctive gifts.

The natural gift was having perfect pitch and good rhythm—and having it discovered at an early age. He was in grade school in Midland, Michigan, when he was given—along with all the other children in his class—a test of pitch and of rhythm. "I scored perfect on all the pitch problems and I did very well on the rest of it," he says. So the school suggested to him and to his parents that he take up the French horn. ("It takes a good ear to play the French horn," he says.) That was okay with nine-year-old Tom: he'd seen the French horn, among all the other instruments, demonstrated at a school assembly put on by the high school orchestra and he'd fallen in love with it.

The instinctive gift is his embouchure—the way in which the lips and the mouthpiece meet when playing the brass or flute. "When I picked up the French horn and started playing it, I put it on my lips right," he says. This was not a learned process. "They didn't have that many great horn teachers around Midland, Michigan." It was instinctive and he would not know how right it was until many years later. "I just put it on the center with about the right amount of the upper lip and lower lip, and at a good angle coming out. In other words, with the French horn you don't want to be playing it straight out. It comes down a little bit to match with the overbite. It just sits right on there and I never had to change it—it's the same now as when I started. And that was an awful big break."

He was barely in his teens when a nationally renowned French horn player named Joseph Eger came to Midland to conduct the local symphony orchestra. Tommy played an audition with him and Eger agreed to accept him as a student. "I believe it was my third lesson with him, when I was in ninth grade, that I decided that this is what I want to do for the rest of my life. I was fifteen and I started working hard at it." He played in the local high school band and the orchestra; that amounted to two hours of work a day there. He played in the Midland Symphony—"I was first horn in that orchestra when I was in tenth grade." At the same time, he was third horn player in the Saginaw Symphony—"by the time I was in eleventh grade, I was first horn there, too." Plus the Germania Club in Bay City: he played first horn there. So three or four nights a week he played in various symphony orchestras and ensembles and every day of the week he played for two hours in the school groups, and on weekends—if he didn't have anything else to do—he'd practice a minimum of three hours a day.

He didn't play in the usual dance bands around school. "I like rock music. I love jazz," he says, "but all I ever wanted to do, as a horn player, was play in the symphony orchestra."

Howell was just about as compulsive when he went to the Juilliard School of Music in New York. His father, who is a doctor in Midland, could pay his way, but Tom won a scholarship in his junior year and decided to make it on his own. "I still remember the day that I called home and told them not to put any more money in the bank," he says. "It was the greatest day of my life." But he had plenty of opportunity to earn money as a musician in New York. He played in the American Symphony Orchestra under Stokowski. He played extra in the Musica Aeterna Orchestra. He played in a woodwind quintet from Juilliard School, he was playing in a series of operas in New Jersey and a series of symphonies in Connecticut, and he was playing extras in orchestras around New York whenever he could.

And, like all students of his generation, he didn't let classwork interfere with his

Thomas Howell, principal horn player.

interests. "I remember especially a class in music history," he says. It's astonishing that he remembers it because he hardly ever got to it. "It met for four hours on Wednesday with another class on Friday afternoon to clarify whatever the lecture had been. And in the whole semester I believe I went to two of the lectures and slept through one of the two that I went to." At least he wasn't dogmatic about it: he missed the tests as well as the lectures. "I had a dress rehearsal during midterm, so I didn't make that."

All this caused a little consternation when, in his senior year, Howell competed with seventy-eight other players for a first horn job—"assistant or associate, they didn't say which"—in the Chicago Symphony and got the job. He was twenty-one when he auditioned and he was just two weeks past his twenty-second birthday when his appointment was announced. But he'd not quite finished half his senior year at Juilliard. He didn't want to delay another six months before reporting to Chicago, so he prepared to drop out of Juilliard. But the school's administration approached him: if he'd make up his work and take appropriate courses in Chicago, they'd give him the degree. He made the deal: he went to Roosevelt University in Chicago, took some private tutoring, and went back to Juilliard during his summer vacation for makeup and final work, and he got his degree.

In Chicago, he fit neatly into playing first horn. "I think that one of the reasons that I ended up playing first horn as a professional is that I had so much practice at it when I was young. Horn playing, like a lot of things, is quite a psychological thing. The pressure is there of playing solo, and unless you have a lot of experience, you might get psyched out. In other words, I grew up playing first horn. That was what horn playing was." In symphony orchestras in general, the first and third horn players take the high passages and the second and fourth horns take the low. Just like belonging to the Episcopal clergy: one is either "high" or "low" and, once so, usually stays that way for life. "I could have played anything else," says Howell, "and when I was in New York, I did play other parts. But somehow I had a lot of experience playing first horn"—and a first horn player he remains.

Howell started as assistant first horn and after a few months became associate first horn. Both terms and customs are locked in the increasing work load of the horn player.

"Many times Dale will play a major work—say a Mahler symphony—which is a very difficult part. There's a lot of tension involved. If he had to play every single thing on the program, with all the tension, week after week after week—well, the track record for first horn players who have tried to do that is not good. They fall apart. They can't take the pressure after a while.

"With the schedules what they are today—fifty-two-week seasons with heavy repertoire every week—for somebody to play first horn every week, well nobody can do it."

And so the Chicago Symphony has an "associate first horn" who takes the pressure off Clevenger by playing certain of the first horn parts in his stead. In the first week of this season, for example, Clevenger played the *Eroica*, Beethoven's Symphony no. 3; but Howell played Ruggles's *Men and Mountains*. When the orchestra reached Carnegie Hall, Clevenger would play Mahler's Symphony no. 6 and Howell would play the first horn parts on Henze's *Heliogabalus Imperator*. ("I like to play contemporary pieces," says Howell, who was already working on the tour solos. "I don't happen to feel that the Henze was a very good piece at all. In fact, I thought it was a rotten piece, but I played it.")

The assistant first horn player, Norman Schweikert, has a slightly different function. He doesn't usually take over complete solos unless the principal or his associate is ill. The assistant's function is to keep the continuity of the solo going when the soloist runs into problems. The assistant, says Howell, "will sit beside either Dale or myself while we play first horn and help us out. In other words, if we need a spot to take a breath in a solo, he'll sustain a note for us. Or if there's a loud, long, heavy passage—something where we'd become very tired and not be able to play a subsequent solo very well—then we have the assistant play it."

The relationships of age and sophistication in the horn section are baffling. Dale Clevenger is only eight years older than Tom Howell, yet he seems, in poise and manner, to be old enough to be his father. Indeed, he is two or three years younger than Norm Schweikert, yet seems to be somewhat older than Schweikert. It is the particular asset of Tom Howell, in this circumstance, to look like the youth-in-residence while possessing a very mature sophistication as an artist.

In this season, Tom Howell, the "youth," wears shoulder-length hair, stays up all night ("I was up until four o'clock this morning"), loves backpacking with his girl friend ("she's a candidate for a Ph.D. in human development at the University of Chicago"), cultivates many and furious hobbies from playing chess to raising parrots. He also accepts the common dogma of his generation. ("I don't have in mind to get married. Maybe five or ten years from now. I like being single . . . and I wouldn't have time to have children right away so I can't see any reason to get married.")

As a musical sophisticate, he can articulate in detail everything from the sound of the symphony—its horns—to the reason he won the audition for a role in the Chicago Symphony. "In Chicago we have a certain style and because I play quite a bit like they do in Chicago is probably one of the big reasons that I was asked to join the orchestra."

How would he describe that sound? That style?

"First, we play on brass horns whereas orchestras such as Cleveland, New York, and Philadelphia play on German silver horns. In other words, they're white metal"—whereas the Chicago Symphony horns are yellow metal. "This is 'pure' brass and the tone of the section—because of the horns—is a little bit different. In playing style? We don't play quite as covered—you might say quite as 'woofy'—as some horn players in the New York Philharmonic and other orchestras do. We have, I'd say, a more clear, open style of playing and we also have a little bit more brass in our tone when we play loud. Whereas the orchestras in Philadelphia and Cleveland and New York don't like to get that brass in the sound. They try to play very loud but with no brassy sound. So the tone is essentially the same when they play loud as when they play soft. It's the same type of sound, loud or soft, whereas our sound would tend to get brassy and nice and projected when it's loud. I like the way it sounds here to me. To me, it's nice and woodsy-like—hunting horns and things like that."

The power of the horns and their magnetism are such that they can unhinge the careful balance of sound that Solti is seeking. That is why he was restrained in changing the microphone attitude during the recording of the *Eroica*. For he was playing the most difficult of roles: as a conductor during the moments of recording, and as his own best critic during the intermission playback.

On the podium, he was—as seen through the monitor—a soft, gray, shadowed figure, almost wraithlike in the underlight of the hall.

In the control room, he was the taut, purposeful, all-is-business figure. ". . . string too soft and bass is too loud. So we change that," he said during one intermission on *Eroica*. Then at a crescendo: "That's hot! That's too hot!" At one point: "The G minor, after that the color is not very beautiful yet." And at another point when the bass came in heavy: "Ah-h, that's a good sound"—and everyone in the control room beams.

Toward the end of the first day's session, Solti decided to plunge ahead with a retake on one section. There was very little time left and if the session runs even a fraction overtime, the record company has to start paying higher rates to the musicians. "We just have time," said Solti confidently. "1–2–3–4–5—last five bars please." ("Take seven," said Roy Minshull.) Solti started the orchestra, played for a few bars, and stopped everything. "Sorry," said Solti, "the last *six* bars." There was some uneasy glancing at clocks; Minshull has several of them mounted on his control console. ("Anybody got the correct time?" he asked nervously. Like the English, he had the feeling that time was running out on him.) Solti took the orchestra through the phrase that he wanted to correct, finished it, and ended the session with a crisp "Thank you."

There were twenty-one seconds left in the session. David Harvey, sitting in the control room, smiled slightly. "Wasting money," he said dryly.

Not everything ran smoothly all the time—not on the technological side. At one point, a microphone broke down. "You never can tell when they're going to fail," says Peter Van Biene, "because it happens so seldom."

On another occasion, a photographer prowled the vast recording chamber, snapping pictures of Solti at work. When there was a brief break in the flow of the music, one musician—as irritably as a professional golfer—called out to Solti, "There's somebody clicking a camera around here."

Solti turned and made a general announcement into the darkness where the cameraman lurked.

"My dear, I will *kill* you," he said. It was done without rancor—though Solti was aware that the microphones were sensitive enough to pick up even the click of a camera shutter. "Now, nicely, sit down, please. See the beautiful chair . . . ?"

At another point—during a scherzo of Beethoven's Symphony no. 5—there was a growing grotesquerie of sound in the control room. A clank. Then another. Then a rattling series of cranks. Van Biene stood by the front wall to see if it was coming from the next room. It wasn't. The music was continuing and he stood by the left speaker. It was coming from the recording chamber!

Ray Minshull immediately flicked on a microphone connecting to Solti—an alternate to the telephone system. His first words brought the flow of music to a stop.

". . . Yes," said Solti. "I was wondering if you noticed it." While Van Biene rushed off to check the huge auditorium, speculation broke out in both the control room and the orchestra about what, or who, was causing the noise.

"I know who was sending us that hideous noise," said Solti lightly to the orchestra. "It was the New York Philharmonic."

Actually, it was the radiators.

The building had steam heat. When there was a change in temperature, the radiators began clanking. Van Biene was trying to find the building staff to get them to change the rate of heat into the pipes. Even the shortest delay in ending the clanking would be costly: if it took but six minutes, London/Decca would lose about $300 worth of recording time.

It took just about that much time. The clanking was smothered now but it would arise again later on. In each case, the staff of the building worked quickly and smoothly with the Britishers—instead of letting them suffer for a few hundred dollars.

The interruptions annoyed Producer Minshull. He became exceptionally sensitive to sound: "Watch the truck," he told Wilkinson as a vehicle ground into gear in the street outside the Temple. At another point, he grimaced as the technicians stripped a tape to mount it on the machine. Three tapes were running incessantly: Minshull was recording in two-track stereo and in eight-track quadraphonic, and he had a "safety-first" tape accompany the other two. Before the session was over, he expected to run some twenty-four miles' worth of tape through the recording machines.

As time went on, there were conscious efforts to break the tension. On a trunk in the rear of the control room was a Dorothy Sayers book—a Lord Peter Wimsey mystery called *Whose Body?* In the room next to the control room was a cloakroom with hangers and coat frame—and a posture chair where Solti would lie down, on rare occasions, to let the tensions flow from his body. In the hall, Frank Miller plunged into an impromptu rendition, on his cello, of "The Swan" from Saint-Saëns's *Carnival of the Animals.*

But for the most part, the players—the first-chair men and the principals—drifted in and out of the control room to listen, during intermission, to the particular sounds that they'd created. They were aware of, even sensitive to, the special demands of record-making.

"When you do a recording—it's funny, so many conductors will hear all of a sudden something on the playback that's different than what they imagine," says Joseph Guastafeste, the principal bass player in the orchestra. "This could be for many reasons. It could be just the way the engineers are picking up on the mikes—they'll make changes right then and there, differently from the way we performed it completely. The opposite in fact. We'll be playing much more aggressively, or much less, more volume or less."

His bass section has important parts in all of the Beethoven symphonies being

Joseph Guastafeste, principal bass player.

Below: Horn players (from left): Norman Schweikert, Rudy Macciocchi (not a regular member of the orchestra), Thomas Howell.

recorded in this week. But Beethoven's Fifth Symphony was historic for the bass section in a particular way. For in it, Beethoven brought the double bass into orchestra prominence by having it pair with the cellos in a highly rhythmical melody in the third movement. It is said that, from that time, players of the string, or double, bass, considered themselves responsible for the loudness or softness, the blandness or aggressiveness, the length or shortness of the overall tone of the orchestra.

Guastafeste, then, was aware how changes in the recording sessions were different—for him as for the orchestra—from the concert-hall performances. "At least once or twice in the bass section we had to give a heck of a lot more than we were ordinarily giving," he says. "Lighter sections as we play them in the hall, but in order to come through the way he wanted to hear it on the tapes, we had to play much more articulately than we ordinarily had been performing." All this, plus the way that Solti handled the requests of the horns for a different microphone placement, suggests that he wanted to hear the strings much more prominently on the tapes, whatever the reputation of the Chicago Symphony for being a "loud brass" orchestra—or perhaps because of it.

Guastafeste has always been involved in the strings, but they did not always thrill him. "I started out on the mandolin, of all things," he says. "It sort of fit in with the Italian scene and I think the neighborhood teacher—that was the only instrument she was strong in." He was born in Brooklyn and his father had a barber shop there and later in the General Electric Building in Manhattan. The family is Italian; Guastafeste interprets his name as translating into "spoil the feast." ("I must have had," he says with a dark, small, Italianate smile, "a great-great-great-grandfather in Roman times who was taking part in these bacchanals and he just got sick and tired of it all—the whole scene, the whole mess. So he said, '*Basta!* I've had it! I'm leaving!' And as he walked out, the host naturally said, '*Guasta feste.*' ") The trouble with the mandolin was that it didn't excite him. "I fell asleep when I was studying the mandolin," he admits. When he was in junior high school, he switched to the violin. "I started getting serious about music when I did that," he says.

His older brother, Eddie, couldn't believe it. "My older brother was the neighborhood swinger," says Guastafeste. "He had a jazz band going and he played at the local church; he was doing the dances and all those things." Eddie listened to Joe and "decided I wasn't going to be a Jascha Heifetz." Besides, he wanted a bass player in his orchestra and he wanted it to be Joe. "He said, 'Why don't you lose the violin and study the bass and I'll have you working with me.' " He went a step further; he got Joe a teacher. He also got him a teacher of unquestioned excellence, though his methods of discovery were very basic. "He looked in the union book and he came across Fred Zimmermann, who was at Juilliard. He also played in the New York Philharmonic. So he said, 'This guy must be good. Let's go see him.' " And with nothing more formal than that, Joe Guastafeste went to see Zimmermann, bowed the bass for him—"since I had some training in the violin, I could hold a French bow, so he was interested. He said he saw something he could work with and so I started with him. I was fifteen."

The thing that the teacher saw was "talent." For Joseph Guastafeste went to Juilliard when he finished high school, but only for two years. Then he won a job as a bass player in the New Orleans Philharmonic Symphony orchestra when he was eighteen or nineteen years old and a year or so later became principal bass player for the Dallas Symphony. He was there for ten years; he met his wife—a cellist—there; they both played not only in the symphony orchestra but worked regularly making jingles. ("At that time, Dallas was a center for commercial recording; I was recording for four commercial recording companies down in Dallas.") Then the Chicago Symphony called and he came to play for Fritz Reiner in Reiner's hotel room. ("At that time, the auditions were set up that way. It's no longer that way now.") So, barely into his thirties, a veteran of ten years as a principal bass, he became the principal in the Chicago Symphony.

In many ways, he does not fit a traditional concept of a bass player. His fingers are long, for example, and he is not deeply concerned about the shape of the hand. "Every hand is different," he says, "so you have to adapt to your own equipment." He does agree with Roger Cline, however, on the importance of the strength of the fingers and the way they touch the strings. "If you have long, skinny fingers," he says, "they'd better hit down harder. They'd better strike with force so that you keep the string really depressed. Yet the finger is relaxed. Everything has to be done with strength but relaxed—that's in anything you do. On the bass, it has to have that combination, otherwise it shows up on the sound." But he thinks it's all bound up less in the shape of the hand than in the sound in the ear. "If you have a sound in your ear, that's the sound you're going to reproduce. And whatever you have to do to reproduce it, you're going to do—somehow work it out so that the muscles coordinate and react the right way to get the sound that you're listening for. But you have to have that concept in your head. It's got to be there before you can produce it."

Neither is Guastafeste the bulky kind of bass player with the "bass player's walk." He is slim, wiry, as noiseless as a ghost in his movement, sharp, dark, Italianate in his being. But he is not athletic or sports-minded. But he is very practical and so now, in his forties, he's taken up karate. Not for self-defense but to keep in shape—mental and physical—to play the bass better.

"It's a strenuous thing, actually, to play the instrument," he says. "You put an awful lot of energy into it and you have to learn to utilize that energy in the best way. You have to be able to relax at the right times and give out with tremendous intensity at other times. I think karate teaches you that. Like yoga—I fooled around with that for a while. Still do. It teaches you when you should be tensing and when you should be relaxing. Part of our business—when you're on the spot and you're performing, you'd better know how, even though you're under tension, how to control that tension. How to lower your speed, relax, and still get the job done in the right way." Moreover, the changes come fast and hard during a concert, if only because the tensions—for a principal—of playing superbly within the orchestra are changed to the tensions of playing magnificently in a solo. "You think, 'My gosh, this is a big, big thing.' Even if it's eight bars, it's a big thing. The bass is playing a solo and you've got to have a pretty cool head. When you're playing with eight other guys in a section—all playing at once—you're hearing yourself as a part of the eight. You don't hear your instrument as a solo instrument. Then all of a sudden the eight others drop out, and you're standing there as a solo instrumentalist.

"It's different than the first oboe playing his own part all the time—just him alone. He's always playing a solo part. First trumpet, first horn—all the others, aside from the strings. They're always playing their part and it's always one part—one person. But this is a different scene in the bass. It takes a different kind of reflexes, a different kind of thinking and conditioning. So I try and keep my head and physique in shape from karate.

"Some guys look at me and say, 'You're out of your mind. What about your hands?' That was the first thing I mentioned to my instructor. 'Look, I'm a musician. I make my living with my hands. I can't hurt my hands.' So he guided me with that in mind." The guidance was into that form of karate called Tae Kwon Do. "The Tae Kwon Do school teaches more of how to use your legs than your hands. You use your hands in defense." Eventually, he did learn to break a board—"a good inch thick"—but he learned to do it with his feet. "I didn't even try to break it with my hands." The whole idea was to meet Guastafeste's need, just as karate might meet the needs of any student. Nobody, and particularly Guastafeste, wants to engage so strenuously in a pastime that he is laid up and knocked out of work because of the enthusiasms of the moment. It happens that the school has an instructor who "enforces the no-contact rule very strictly. He gets very angry when a student goofs and happens to hit somebody, no matter how slightly. He insists that we follow the no-contact rule because otherwise guys can get hurt pretty badly. So it ends up more as an exercise than as a ritualistic kind of thing in hitting."

That was tough enough on Guastafeste. "It's quite complicated trying to do these forms in a correct way. You have to move your body—I'm not one who was always interested in body movement; I never studied the dance." He thinks it helps him—as a man in his early forties—keep his body limber. "There are a lot of guys shriveled up before that, mentally as well as physically." He also thinks it helps him keep a clear head and an alert one for the changes in tempo and tone that are so much a part of his orchestral life. "When you engage in free-sparring, you have to have your head very much in place, just to watch what the other guy is doing, in order to engage in it at all. Otherwise, you stand there like a goof—you could really get laid out if they were hitting you instead of just getting points checked against you. You have to be able to move and judge those movements by what is happening with the partner. You have to have a clear head to do that."

He's only been at the karate for a year and a half or so. "It takes a good three and a half years for a pretty steady, solid student to become a black belt," he says. He can't be steady: he often goes on a different day each week because the rehearsal schedule is changed or other orchestral obligations intrude. Beyond that, he is aware of the need to keep at his physical and mental peaks during the concerts. This is difficult because he's a morning person and a light sleeper: if he hears his kids get up at night, "if anything's wrong," he'll wake up and stay awake.

Particularly if it's four o'clock in the morning or afterward: he tends to come fully awake very early and very easily. "One of these days I'm going to work out a system where I'll just stay up for those hours, get whatever work I want done, and then if I can get back to bed and zonk out again, I'll probably do it." But the morning rehearsals interfere with that plan now. And he knows that he's going to be worn out at night; his whole creative and mental energies—high in the early morning—are going to be a low ebb. So he makes strenuous efforts to harbor his energies: he goes home after the morning rehearsals so he'll be fresh for the Thursday evening performance. That's why he bought a home that is—though it's in the suburb of Wilmette—only two blocks away from the end of the "El" subway line going into Chicago. "So that I can get home at every opportunity—I'd rather have my meals and rest at home. If I don't get that nap in the afternoon, I don't feel too great for the performance. I don't like that at all." If he feels a little foggy or logy after the nap, he does some stretching and shoulder-standing, as in yoga. "The blood goes right to your head." So he takes a nap, does yoga, and "goes downtown with high energy that night."

In essence, this is what Solti tries to do—without the yoga. He naps in the afternoon and preserves his energies. The players know this and note it, not always cheerfully. They feel the awkward hours of the recording sessions were designed by Solti to give him the maximum opportunity to rest. The first record session ran from 10 A.M. to 1 P.M. Monday, for example. Then there was a four-hour break until the next record session—5 P.M. to 8 P.M.—got started. That was plenty of time for Solti to get to his hotel suite for a good rest but it pinched the time of the players, who have to travel an hour to two hours or more to get to and from their suburban homes. It also wrecks the schedule of those players who have students on Monday (which is usually free of orchestral duties). One bass player made it up—and adjusted for his expected absence during the upcoming tour—by taking eleven students, each for a one-hour session, on the following Monday. In any case, there is grumbling over the split shifts but there is no action: it is part of the function—and the burden—of playing in an orchestra that is in demand.

By week's end, there was a numbing sameness about the sessions:

Minshull signaling to Wilkinson, almost "conducting" the record with quick, imperative movements of his fingers: "Here come the cellos. . . . Now a burst —now! . . . After the oboes, now. . . . Keep the strings as high as possible." Wilkinson responds with his small intimate movements of dials and levers. He is the hunched, intense listener; he is listening to Minshull, he is listening to the sound, and he is listening to the music of his inner ear: he has been the engineer on at least eight different recordings of Beethoven's Fifth Symphony.

Solti working in the control room between takes, making notes on what he's heard and what he must change on the next take, and talking with the orchestra about the changes. "The second movement here, we must do to relax. . . . The horn solo, it sounds a bit muddy on the tapes. . . . When we come to the piano, the piano must be less than the piano before. . . . The pizzicato quality is very good. But we don't need quite so much pizzicato."

Sometimes Solti talks directly to Minshull through the microphone hung on a

T-bar directly over the podium. "Ray, would you do me a favor?" he said before one take. "If you can feel that the horns are not clear, please stop me."

Minshull can talk back directly to Solti either on the audio system or through a telephone. The latter involves talks of a candor which he might not want to share with an overburdened orchestra: "On these long notes, if they can be even a bit louder . . . when the first movement is done, I should like to hear the second movement again. It is not easier on you but it is easier on me."

When finally the three Beethoven symphonies were done, the orchestra could not relax. Solti and Minshull planned to go on and record the Berlioz *Les Francs-juges* and the overture to Weber's opera *Oberon*. Even then, no matter what the burden, the humor between conductor and orchestra remained high. At one point, Solti made a few corrections after intermission without saying exactly why he was seeking them.

"May I ask what the problem was?" called out a voice from somewhere in the orchestra.

Solti grunted, "I won't tell you," he said. "I'm too much of a diplomat."

And through the orchestra there echoed a wave of appreciative—or cynical —laughter.

But there comes a time when it must end. A few minutes before the scheduled end of the last four-hour session, Ray Minshull talked via microphone to Solti on the podium. "Can we," he asked, chipper, bright, "run through that just one more time?"

Solti's shoulders sagged. He was already reaching for the towel to wipe off the sweat of this last effort.

"I'm sorry," he said. "I just can't do it."

He stepped from the podium. The lights were dimmed.

Solti went to his makeshift dressing room to relax on the posture couch for a while. The orchestra broke up and began rushing through the autumn night to get home. In the control room, Peter Van Biene began dismantling the recording equipment.

The London/Decca group had run three reels of tape all week for fourteen hours of tapes—twenty-four miles of magnetic tape consumed. In four days, Minshull would be listening to the tapes once again in London. Then would come the cutting of the disc records. He had two more record sessions to go, just to close the cycle of the Beethoven symphonies. He thought it would be thirteen months after the first session before the album would be on the market.

In the deepening chill of an approaching winter, it is difficult to remember the warmth of spring. In the ardor and demands of this week, it is difficult to remember how the week came to be:

Work on every day for seven consecutive days. Double sessions on Monday, Tuesday, Wednesday, Thursday, Saturday. Ten services in that time—concerts, rehearsals, recording sessions. Some thirty-two and one-half hours of playing. And all that was to follow was tour week, with three concerts and two out-of-town air junkets in three days. It was tougher on the orchestra than on Solti, for in the

Recording session playback at Chicago's Medinah Temple: *(from left)*

span—ten days of work out of eleven—the orchestra not only played under him but, in addition, had both rehearsals and Youth Concerts under Henry Mazer.

It was in this week that Solti chose to play his "Mahler of the Year." In a sense it was fitting, for Mahler was known, within musical circles, as a noted interpreter of Beethoven, though not so faithful a one as Solti. "Of course, the works of Beethoven need some editing," Mahler once said. He never hesitated to retouch Beethoven's works. He doubled the oboes for the little cadenza in the first movement of Beethoven's Fifth. He doubled the use of the woodwinds in Beethoven's Sixth. He apparently felt that Beethoven, who was deaf by the time he composed his Ninth Symphony, needed a little help on the instrumentation; thus he added a trombone, a piccolo, and an E-flat clarinet in various places, and he inserted a new horn part in the D-major passage of the scherzo. Mahler was, as a conductor, full of these tricks, which would shock the musical world today. At the time, Bruno Walter, who idolized Mahler, explained away these curious invasions of the composer's prerogatives as being directed "against the letter and towards the spirit" of the composer.

Thus, even as a conductor, Mahler seemed to be acting out the role of composer. He is renowned today as a composer but in his own lifetime he was just

Ray Minshull, London/Decca producer; Sir Georg Solti; Samuel Magad, co-concertmaster.

as renowned as a conductor. He conducted the Vienna Opera for ten years, until 1907, and these years are commonly described as the golden years of the Vienna Opera. He later conducted both the Metropolitan Opera and the New York Philharmonic. In fact, he once described the Philharmonic as "the true American orchestra—without talent and phlegmatic."

As a conductor, Gustav Mahler had a temperament familiar to many musicians, even of a more modern era in Chicago. "He was demonic, neurotic, demanding, selfish, noble, emotionally undisciplined, sarcastic, unpleasant, and a genius," wrote Harold C. Schonberg in *The Great Conductors*. "His actions throughout his life strongly suggest those of a manic-depressive"—he would plunge into periods of deep depression and alternate them with periods of great vehemence, energy, even violence. Today people remember his genius; not in those days. Mrs. Charles Dana Gibson once asked Mahler's wife—after observing his complaining, constantly arguing, and making life difficult—"How can a beautiful woman like you marry an old, ugly, impossible man like Mahler?"

He gave his musicians the full force of his charm. Like some latter-day conductors, he would pick on weak players and do everything he could to embarrass and humiliate them before their peers. One of his tactics was to ask rear-stand men to play a solo, and then to flay them verbally for what he felt was their lack of skills.

Schonberg tells the story of the double bass player in the New York Philharmonic who was asked to rise and thus perform—to submit himself to the sacrificial rites staged by Mahler. The double bass man finally rebelled and asked why he picked only on the rear-stand men.

"Why don't you ask the first flute or the first oboe to get up and play alone like this?"

Mahler stared at him bleakly.

"I'm afraid," he said, "to take a chance on what I might hear."

Perhaps some of the public torment of Mahler was a reflection of his private torment, for he felt that his mission in life was to compose. But his celebrity in life was conducting. His chores on the podium, and the administrative duties they imposed, stripped away much of the time he would have liked to devote to composing and seem to have left him deeply frustrated. Yet he composed ten symphonies before dying in 1911, at the age of fifty, and these symphonies have become a prominent part of concert hall programming in the last few years. Indeed, they've become the "signature" of the sound of the Chicago Symphony —the works of Mahler and the works of Anton Bruckner. Says Robert C. Marsh in the *Chicago Sun-Times*: "The Chicago Symphony is now, very probably, the greatest Mahler-Bruckner orchestra in the world. . . ."

For this week, Solti chose Mahler's Sixth Symphony. Mahler called it his "Tragic" symphony. The external evidence is that he experienced nothing tragic when he composed it in the summers of 1903 and 1904. "The summer was beautiful, serene and happy," wrote his wife of the 1904 period, adding that she and her husband walked arm and arm through the woods to the hut where he composed, so that he could play the work for her. The usual interpretation is that

Mahler was mordantly anticipating the tragedies that might yet befall him. In two or three years his older daughter would die, he was stricken with a devastating heart condition, and he had to give up his cherished position as director of the Vienna Opera. In any case, the Mahler Sixth is edged with a portentous, tragic coloring and moves through to a last movement that echoes with a sense of final resignation.

In a sense, the Sixth is the most classical of Mahler's works, viewed from a structural point of view. It is also classic Mahler in that it relies so heavily on the sound of the brass of the orchestra. The sound of the brass is a sound that Solti not only elicits but exports—to France, of all places. He had Jay Friedman, the first trombone player, go to Paris after Solti took over the Orchestre de Paris, and tutor some of the brass players there in the way he achieves his sound for the Chicago Symphony.

Friedman did not sense that sound as being uniquely German. He feels it has some qualities of the French as well as the German school. It fits Mahler because "it started with the German style of brass playing, which was a very big sound, as opposed to the French style, which was a small, sort of piercing kind of sound. But very clear. We try to take that very big rich sound and give it the advantages that the French style has—make it very clear, very precise." Combined with all this, he feels, the Chicago brass has a facile sense. "Flexible. Being able to change styles. Like if you play a French piece, you try to play like a Frenchman," he says. "When you play different kinds of music, you adjust your style to suit the music. There are orchestras that play all one style and it sounds all right. They play the notes and it's there, it's one style. But I feel that it's much better to be able to be flexible and to change your style to the mood of the music."

But he didn't know if the French would know this. So he was a little apprehensive when he was asked to go to Paris to work with the brass in Solti's orchestra there. "When I got there, I thought I wouldn't be surprised if these guys say, 'Get lost. Nobody is going to come and tell me how to play.' Because if somebody did that to me, I might be bugged. So I was a little bit nervous." His Parisian hosts were far from bugged. "They were just fantastic. They said, 'We're glad you're here. We can exchange ideas. We'll learn from each other.' So for the rest of the time, things were just fantastic." In fact, they became very close friends—Friedman from Chicago and Marcel Lagorce, the first trumpet, and Marcel Galigue, the first trombone, of the Orchestre de Paris. "Those were two of the greatest people I ever heard in my life. . . . I didn't want to leave those guys, they were so nice."

There was no "teaching" to change their style or their sound. The three men just sat down and played in their own ensembles, talking over the sound they were getting and its quality and uses. Friedman also brought records of the Chicago Symphony to reflect the sound of the trombone in concert. "They were much closer to the way we played than I would have thought," says Friedman. "But they were the exceptions. Those two guys, they like the American way of playing, the style of playing, and so they were going in this direction. The rest of the musicians over there thought they were crazy, because that wasn't the French style." He was interested to find that they were playing American instruments—"everybody seemed to be using American instruments." But the bore size of the horn was smaller than that used by Friedman and most other brass players in Chicago. "That was typically French. The smaller the bore, the brighter and harder the sound. And that's what Solti doesn't like. He likes a very broad, sort of Vienna-concept style—I mean the Germanic concept, which is a broad sound. When you play instruments with a large bore, then the sound tends to spread more. But it's a warmer kind of sound. It blends better. So they changed to those instruments because they liked the way we sounded." To get the bigger, mellower, somewhat Teutonic sound, and yet get the clarity of the French sound, was not easy. "You have to work harder," says Friedman. "It takes more physical energy to play something larger than it does small."

The irony is that Jay Friedman is not sure whether the brass in the Orchestre de Paris *should* sound like the brass in the Chicago Symphony. He admits this is the trend—for orchestras in different nations to sound more and more alike. "You can go out and get a record of the Timbuktu Philharmonic and you say, 'Well, that sounds good. Maybe I should do that.' So the thing is getting in sort of a melting pot, which is too bad. The standard of playing is going up, but it's no fun to go to Vienna, or some other big city, and go and hear their orchestra—the Vienna Philharmonic—and see that they're all using American instruments, American style. The fun," he says, "was in listening to all these really different styles. You'd be surprised how different the styles were, especially for brass playing. Like the Russians used to play with these big vibratos, the French horns would sound like saxophones. Today, you would be able to recognize those sounds, it's so different from the past. Now with communications and everybody exchanging ideas, it's beginning to blend all together, which takes the fun out of something. You can't really learn something from somebody when they play just like you do. You always want to look for new ideas. Even if you don't like them."

Having different ideas is a way of life with Jay Friedman. "I generally disagree with the majority of the opinion in the orchestra," he says. His disagreements range over everything from conductors and personalities—he liked John Weicher, for example, and Jean Martinon—to the suitability of Orchestra Hall. ("Most people say this hall is really bad; it's really hard to play in; and they hate it and this and that. But I'm so used to this place, I'm so at home here that I don't think of it as a bad hall to play. I'm so used to it that when something doesn't sound good, I blame myself; I don't say the hall is bad.")

None of these exceptions is demonstrated assertively. Friedman is a quiet, slender, gentle man who has, in his balding head and ascetic features and overall demeanor, something of the feeling of a Christ image. He became first trombone player at the age of twenty-four. He was the youngest principal trombone in the country and today, at thirty-four, he is still the youngest. But he got where he is through unpredictable means and improbable routes. His father was a dancer but he died when Jay was five years old. The child was then shuttled around with relatives for a long while before winding up going to a military school in Chicago. He started playing the baritone horn in school and continued playing it all through high school—eight years altogether. And at the same time, he developed an ambition to become a player in a symphony orchestra, never quite realizing that "you can't make a living playing the baritone. Nobody uses the baritone." He was studying the brass under Vincent Cichowicz, the second trumpet in the Chicago Symphony, and it was Cichowicz who suggested that Jay switch to the trombone. (*Trombone* is Italian for *big trumpet*.) Friedman agreed and Jay switched to the trombone. "So then for the next two to three years, I was practicing like eight hours a day. Just like a madman." The trombone is the oldest of the modern symphonic instruments—at least the oldest in the sense that it has pretty much retained its original characteristics. It was conceived in the early 1400s—before Columbus discovered America—and, though it is part of the brass, it functions on the theory often associated with woodwinds: on a the-longer-the-pipe, the-deeper-the-tone theory. The trombone spans more than three octaves, but it does not reach every note by a shift in the slide of the trombone. In fact, only seven of the thirty or so semitones available to the trombone are played by moving the slide of the trombone. The rest are produced by various manipulations of the breath supply and lips. Friedman had to learn all this and more in a stunningly brief time, for he reached the Chicago Symphony by the time he was twenty-two.

His route took him through the Chicago Civic Orchestra and the Florida Symphony. In the latter, he played under Henry Mazer, now associate conductor of the Chicago Symphony. In the former, he played under John Weicher. "I probably learned more from him than I did from anybody," he says. "He was a great guy. Really something." This was not a view held by everybody in the parent organization. "Funny thing," says Friedman, "when he used to lead the Civic, he was so jovial and he was laughing all the time. And then I talked to my teacher who was in the symphony then and I told him, 'Wow, Weicher is a lot of fun in the Civic—he's so nice and everything.' He said, 'Are you kidding? I've never seen that guy smile in my life.' And I know when I got in the orchestra, he was like that—very morose, just really very stern. But with the kids in Civic, he was jovial, he was a different person, and he was a very good conductor."

Weicher also was instrumental in bringing Friedman into the Chicago Symphony, though the method was hardly as regular as it is today.

"The assistant first trombone left and went to Los Angeles," recalls Friedman. "He got tired of the job because he never played. He never got to play—*period*." His job was simply to fill in if the first trombone player was absent, "which they never did back then," says Friedman. His teacher told Jay he'd get the job. Weicher told him the same thing—that they wouldn't have an audition because they didn't have the time to take before filling the opening. But he never got a call from the management of the symphony. "Months and months went on and they kept saying, 'Don't worry about it. You've got it.' Here I didn't have a job and I was married and my wife was going to have a baby, and they kept saying 'Don't worry.' " So he worried. He worried a lot. Just three days before the season was to begin, he got a phone call and was told to report for work.

His work was not to work. "The first year I was the typical assistant—I never got to play anything at all." Reiner was just easing out of total responsibilities for the symphony and no principal vacated his chair to let an assistant take over in those days. "You see the other guys all playing and you don't get to play," he says. He'd get paid for doing nothing but he didn't like it. "You get bugged after a while. You show up for concerts and rehearsals and you don't play." It happened that the first trombone player was, by that time, his teacher. One day in Friedman's second year in the symphony, he got a call from the first trombone that took the general lines: "Look, I'm having some problems. I'm not going to be able to play as much anymore. You're going to have to cover for me." Jay thought the man was going to vacate the first chair and give his duties to the natural alternative—to his assistant. That wasn't the way it went. "He really didn't want to lose his job. He wanted me to sit there beside him and play everything along with him, and he'd just sort of play as well as he could."

The problem, as Friedman understands it, was nerves. He's never shared the problem—"I've never had any problem with nerves or anything," he says. But he knows that the tensions do get to a lot of principal players. "It's just having to play by yourself. You know—knowing that you're playing first chair—you might have a solo or something and you're nervous as hell if you're not quite sure you can do it." Of his predecessor in the first chair, he says: "He just didn't have a heck of a lot of confidence. He should have. He was a very good player. But some people can do something great, and they're still nervous about it. No matter what, they're always nervous."

As Friedman remembers it, he covered for the first trombone for the full season. The conductor knew what was happening. "The conductor was nice. He didn't want to make a big scene, and the part was covered and he thought he'd give the guy a chance to straighten out and see what happens." The conductor? Jean Martinon.

"Martinon was very nice," says Friedman. "He never got anybody"—certainly not in this, his first year with the orchestra—"and he gave people a chance. So we spent the whole year doing that. Which was nerve-racking for me, but I didn't really care—I wanted to see him get straightened out. But he never did. It got worse and worse."

The first trombone player finally gave up under the strain. He left the symphony and he left music and he went to Colorado where he started to build a new life for himself.

But Friedman didn't know all this. He filled in for the man at the Ravinia season—"that was the first time I had actually played by myself"—but he thought the individual would return for the regular season. "I went to the first rehearsal and they had a real hard program for trombones. Really, *really* difficult things." He sat down in the assistant's chair and waited. The first trombone didn't show up. "So I thought, 'Well, he'll be here in a few minutes.' But he doesn't come and time is going by and finally they're tuning up and he's not there. And I'm thinking, 'Well, what should I do? Should I just stay here or should I sit in the first chair and just take over? Nobody has told me anything. Should I play or not play or what?' So finally the rehearsal starts and he's not there and I thought, 'Well, I better do something.' So I sat in the first chair and played the rehearsal." From that point on, he was the Chicago Symphony's first trombone.

Later he discovered that his predecessor had phoned the symphony office and told them that he wasn't going to be in until he felt better. "But they hadn't told me," he says. "They could have called and said, 'You're going to play first chair in the Chicago Symphony' because it's a very 'pressure' chair, especially when you don't know what's going to happen."

Nor did the symphony management formalize the shift in the customary way. "When it got to be later in the year, they knew he wasn't coming back," he says now. "So I felt, 'Well, they'll probably have some auditions for this chair, get some really big names in from New York and all over the country.' So I went up to the office one day and talked with the manager." It was then Silas Edman. "And I said, 'I was just wondering whether—since the vacancy is there—would I be considered for the first chair? I mean, would I have a chance to audition or anything—to try out?'

"He said, 'What do you mean by audition. From what Martinon tells me, you've got the job.'

"I said, 'I have the job?' I didn't expect to get the job. I thought they'd have a big audition, there would be 10,000 people who would give their left arm to be first trombone in the Chicago Symphony and here I am just a kid."

That was the first that Friedman learned how high he stood in the musical estimation of Jean Martinon. "He had liked the job I did in the first half of the year. We did a lot of hard things and apparently he was satisfied with the way I did it. So at the end of the year they made an announcement to everybody that I had gotten the first trombone position."

The breakdown in communications astonished him. But the method that sprang spontaneously out of it—letting a man play in the position—is, he feels now, "actually the best way to hire somebody. Not through an audition, because a guy could play real well by himself. We've had that happen. Many times somebody has played a fantastic audition and you put him in the orchestra and you find out that he can't play with other people. He can't really blend the instrument or just be part of the kind of sound that helps us get the style that we do. So actually, that's the best thing they could have done—was to have somebody try out on a long-term basis where they can see what he does under the conditions that he would be working with. That's why they were sure that I would work out, because I had actually done the job and not just played one audition."

He goes on about the long-term tryout versus the audition. "You have to be able to follow a conductor in a certain way, which has nothing to do with an audition. In an audition you play by yourself; it doesn't really mean that much. It means that you can play or can't play. But there's a lot more than that—following, blending, playing the right kind of dynamics, getting the type of sound that fits in with your section. Whether you come through in a pressure situation for a concert or something like that—that's a whole different thing."

Out of the whole experience, and of the experience of the next five years, Friedman came up with a different view of Martinon.

"I'm sure," he says, "you've gotten a lot of flack from people who say he was the worst conductor that ever will live. That's a bunch of baloney. I don't know if he was in over his head with a certain part of the repertoire, like the classical things, like Beethoven, Brahms, and things like that. He could do it but it just wasn't the way that people wanted to hear it around here. But for modern music—there were few people that were better than he was for modern music." He holds to the notion that Martinon came in trying to be a nice guy whereas Solti "doesn't give a damn what the orchestra thinks about him as long as we respect him. He knows he's great and that's all he has to worry about." But Martinon did not come to Chicago with a "fantastic reputation" and "he wasn't that secure in the world and maybe he felt he was lucky to be here. I don't know what it was." In any case, he says, Martinon "wasn't the best conductor that ever lived but he wasn't the worst, either." The problem was that the orchestra did not rise in reputation while he was in Chicago and the players felt that it may have been in decline. "They wanted a more famous conductor, I think. Somebody who would really help the orchestra. Because the orchestra was very good. It was just about as good then as it is now, I think. But nobody knew about it because we never went to Europe; we hardly made recordings or anything.

"It was like having the greatest thing in the world in a small box. If nobody sees it, who cares? It has to be displayed."

And the following, Friedman thinks, is the ultimate statement delivered on Jean Martinon. "My feeling is that maybe he wasn't the right man for the Chicago Symphony—okay, I'll say that: he was not the ideal conductor for us. But he was a very competent conductor. He was always prepared. He was easy to follow. He was generally very nice—he was never abusive with anybody.

"He just wasn't the guy to take us to the top, like Solti. Which we deserved, I think. He got some great performances but they were not consistent enough. There weren't enough of them."

Among his many apostasies—small and acute as the driving rods on an O-gauge railroad—are his views on the orchestra's competence to judge a conductor.

"I don't think that musicians who play in an orchestra are able to estimate the real greatness of a conductor," Friedman says. "*Because* they play in an orchestra. I think there's a lot of things that escape people while they're playing the notes, while they're involved in a performance. There's something they can't really hear because they're involved in it, and that is the actual music that the conductor projects.

"They're more likely to be impressed with somebody who has a very good ear, which, of course, all conductors should have. And a very good stick technique. Gets everybody to play together—all the technical things right, good sound and everything. But those are only tools. Like a painter has colors and his brush, he executes right, everything is in its place. That may be. Everything may be perfectly in place, his style may be flawless, his technique fantastic, but if the picture doesn't add up to anything . . .

"But the people that play in an orchestra really can only judge the technical things. They can't really tell whether the concept of the music is a great one. That can only be heard from out in the audience, or by listening to records, so that you're not involved in technical things. I include myself in that too. I try to listen to recordings at home, go to concerts. I have my favorite conductors"—and his nonfavorites.

James Gilbertsen (left), associate principal trombonist, and Jay Friedman, principal trombonist.

Among his favorites—outside the Chicago Symphony's own family—is Rafael Kubelik, who resigned in 1974 as music director of the Metropolitan Opera. "He has a terrible beat. He looks funny. He has a bald head—and he's not the glamour image at all. But the music that comes out—I didn't form this opinion by playing with him; I've listened to him make music for many, many years and over that time I came to esteem his musicianship. I mean his concept of music, his feeling for the architecture of music which to me is the most important thing. Maybe the technical things are not all there. But the music that comes out is something magical that happens—it has nothing to do with the technique. That's the indefinable thing about conducting. It's really hard to make that happen and when it does, you don't know why it happens. It has to be within the conductor, the concept, the musicianship, the sensitivity, the feeling, and everything. And many times it escapes the people that are working very close technically, reading the notes and everything. In one sense the guy playing triangle at the back of the stage can actually listen better than the concertmaster. The concertmaster is so involved in leading, he really can't comprehend. He really shouldn't have to. It's not our job to do that—that should be done by people who write and supposedly know. Not that we can't have our own opinion, but they should not only be based on what we do in the orchestra. It should be something you do as a music lover and not as a musician."

And among his other-than-favorites?

It leans to the hotshots. "Look at somebody like Ozawa, who I feel is totally overrated. Really, really overrated guy. . . . He's smart. . . . He's studied all the famous conductors. He's studied all the moves. All the techniques and everything. He's got all the moves down, the techniques for impressing an orchestra, impressing an audience. But when it comes to originality—I mean his personal concept—I don't even care whether or not it's a great concept as long as it's something that belongs to him. He doesn't have it. He's a sort of mishmash of things that he's studied because he wanted to make it big."

But he *has* made it big.

"People get fooled by that. Critics get fooled by that. Everybody gets fooled by that. That's my opinion. Who is to say I'm right?—but everybody should have their opinion. That's the way I feel about it. There's an example of somebody who's very studied. He studied with all the conductors. He has all the looks and everything. But as far as an original mind, and there has to be originality to conduct because it's re-creating. . . . You can fool people for a long time. Many people are fooling people. But if you really listen to his records, or the records he made with us, I think anybody who knows—not even knows but has a feeling for art, you can tell it's phony. It really is. It sounds like a compendium of standard interpretations. . . ."

His own life is a search for something that is beyond his own success. "I don't think I'm going to be happy doing this the rest of my life, just staying here, right at the top of my profession. I've got to do something else. I want to do other things."

So far, Friedman's "other things" have been on the level of spare-time activities. He began raising horses in the last few months. He finished remodeling the attic of the home he had in Wilmette so that he would have a studio, a practice room "and everything. I knocked down all the walls myself"—he seems far too much the aesthete to know how to do it—"and I put in insulation, put in windows all over the place. It took me a whole year to do the room but I finally finished it."

Musically, he's searched for other sounds within the symphony. When he was in Europe, he "picked up a couple of instruments"—German trombones that "are even more mellow-sounding and sort of Germanic-sounding for certain works like Brahms and Bruckner. That's the fun—to change instruments to get a different sound. You should try to change your style. I know the trumpet players do this, so that's what I've been trying to do, too—trying to change instruments, getting different sounds."

He has no compelling interest to become a conductor, but he would like to get some free time to devote to composing. "I have an idea to write a piece for the Chicago Symphony that I've been thinking about for years." It would be for the whole orchestra, not just the brass section—"I've done just a little, a little tinkering. Most of it has been in my mind."

In a corner of the players' quarters one day, Arnold Jacobs was tinkering with mouthpieces and tubas. "I own fourteen different tubas and forty different mouthpieces," he says. "In our trombone section"—which he sits next to—"and in our hall, we have quite a large range in our dynamics. So my choice of instruments and mouthpiece is equated together. It's based on whether I need a certain strength in the fundamental of the tone, because if I use a mouthpiece that makes a horn too bright, when the trombones intrude into the overtones, I'm not left with anything. I tend to disappear. So I have to find a mouthpiece that tends to bring out the fundamentals and lessen the overtones a little bit. Otherwise the balance in the sections would be lost." He slipped one mouthpiece into the tuba and said: "Light music. General work." He tried another: "Berlioz, any of the bright-sounding works. You'll hear a thinner sound. On the stage it would be close to the trombones and it would be more articulate." Then he tried still another: "This one is even lighter. On a wave anaylsis, you'd see very bright overtones and very small fundamentals." Still another: "This is for the larger, more massive tones." And still another: "This is rounded out a little more." He blew a few notes. "See, that changes the color." For Mahler. For Bruckner. "For organ sounds. The heavy sounds. If we went on the stage with that big ceiling, you would hear primarily fundamentals. In other words, you can vary the wave analysis by taking the same instrument and varying the mouthpiece. Or you can take the same mouthpiece and vary the instrument."

Whereas Jay Friedman might be called The Skeptic in the orchestra, Arnold Jacobs is The Scholar. He does not merely speak to a subject; he explores it like a speleologist, carefully probing its corners and deepest recesses—no matter how dark and unlikely—and developing coherent theories that apply to life as well as to music. He has never had any trouble wondering what else he might do with his life. Since 1945—"when I had some physical troubles"—he has been exploring the biological/physiological aspects of music. Today he is not only the world's foremost tuba player but the foremost "musical biologist," if you will. He has his own laboratory in a building near Orchestra Hall, and doctors and musicians from all over the world send him "cases"—students, patients—to analyze, discuss, help if he can.

He is, in a sense, his own best "case."

For in this season he was running a very subtle race against time—the time when his own career might end.

Part of it was because of a case of bronchial asthma. "Incapacitating," he says. "I've been on steroids for my third year now to control the symptoms. I have no air to work with"—he has, in fact, less air to blow into the tuba than do any of his students. "In other words, my vital capacity is down. When these attacks become incapacitating, playing the tuba—you can forget it." It is particularly bad when the skies lower over Chicago and the pollutants from autos and steel mills and the wretchedness of urban living concentrate in the air. "When you breathe massive volumes of air unfiltered in or out of our lungs, as we do in heavy playing, continuous blowing—well, I almost think they should pass a law prohibitive of playing, because you're taking unfiltered air and moving it in or out." Yet none of this inhibits him when he has to play something like the Mahler Sixth ("the most demanding of the season in terms of physical endurance"). But he is not about to give up. "I'm still competitive." He is more than that; he is one of the world's great virtuosos on the instrument. "But when I get ready for the performance now, I'll use bronchial dilation before I go on the stage."

There is another reason he feels in a race against time—which time will inevitably win.

"Usually the life of a brass player in the symphony orchestra is not as long as a string player," he says. Brass players tend to give out in their early or middle fifties, whereas string players can—and do—continue well into their sixties or until they're seventy. That may be the reason that there are younger men in the brass sections of the symphony than in the strings; there's greater turnover because age begins affecting the players of brass instruments earlier. "There's a deterioration that occurs in the aging process that affects the playing of the brass, even of the wind instruments," he says matter-of-factly. "There is a loss of elasticity in the lung tissue, and the flexibility of the function of the bellows system [in the body] begins to lessen." For the brass player is dealing with air and how much he can deliver at any one instant—what his capacity is for air flow, and what his habits are in delivering that capacity into the instrument. "The vital capacity lowers without the individual realizing it. If he's using limited amounts of fuel"—air—"say he's used to taking half a breath, the air that he may draw from that fuel supply may be adequate to play his instrument at the age of twenty, but not at forty-five or fifty or fifty-five. When the fuel supply lowers, the half that he gets is a smaller quantity than it was at twenty, and you can run into very severe problems of playing."

Arnold Jacobs's own vital capacity—his fuel supply, so to speak—is to draw on 3.7 liters of air every minute. He uses about 50 percent of that—say, 1.5 to 2.0 liters of air—in the first second of the actual playing of a phrase. And all that is a considerable drop from what it was at his peak. Then his vital capacity was at least 4.7 liters. He not only had more but he could use more of the air supply in the past; not every bit of air is expelled in playing the tuba—but Jacobs was able to use a surprisingly large amount—as much as 80 percent in the first second. The amount of air he is actually able to deliver at peak needs has been cut by almost 40 percent in recent years. "They used to have a pension arrangement in the Chicago Symphony where a brass player would be eligible for a pension at the age of fifty-five because so many brass players break down at that age." Jacobs is aware of the breakdown because of his age, but his playing doesn't reflect it. "I'm working quite hard," he says of his playing and practicing. "Nature's unkind in one way. And that is the skills that we have, if we don't keep them constantly used, are going to lessen and gradually disappear."

Few men in any field—much less men in a symphony orchestra—have had as dazzling or diversified a career as Arnold Jacobs. He's been scientist as well as aesthete; he's played jazz as well as classics; he's been accomplished in so many different forms of music that he won scholarships to the Curtis Institute of Music in Philadelphia in both tuba and in singing.

"I started out in a little town in California as a bugler," he says.

The town was Willowbrook, a hot dusty little place in the 1920s on the edge of the California desert. His father was an accountant; his mother had been a pianist in vaudeville—on the old Pantages Circuit—and later a pianist and organist providing background music in the silent film days. "She was involved in the pictures, in the atmosphere on the lots while filming," he says. And so it was natural that her children would be involved. His sister was offered a contract by a movie company, but his mother wouldn't let her take it ("they had this Fatty Arbuckle scandal"). Arnold himself remembers "getting paid $5 once to appear in a picture that Mary Pickford was doing. I remember I was eating an ice-cream cone in this scene. I was about five years old and it was the first money I ever earned."

When he was ten, his parents gave him a bugle and a book of instruction. He worked on it, and listened to his mother when she picked out the bugle call notes on the piano. "I won a silver bugle in Boy Scout competition even though I was not fully a Scout"—one had to be twelve years old to qualify for the Scouts. "They put me in a uniform anyway and I entered the contest and won the silver bugle," he remembers. Then his father bought him a trumpet but he forgot to get an instruction booklet. "So again I had to learn everything by ear." He won a school competition on the trumpet. But he got discouraged about it. "I was working on the *Carnival of Venice* at a very early age, and doing a fairly good job at it. But we had a record of Herbert Clark doing it. He was a marvelous cornet soloist, and my dad was always saying, 'You don't sound like he does. You're not doing so well.' He kind of put me down and it turned me off the trumpet." So Arnold scraped together $10 and bought an old trombone—"But I loved that instrument." He worked long and hard at it and perhaps he might still have been playing the trombone, except for the disappearance of that beloved old instrument. "One year we were touring Texas on a vacation in one of the old-time cars—they had running boards—and we had the trombone strapped on the side, and it disappeared." He was heartbroken.

When he got back to junior high school—"we were in Santa Monica by this time"—he hoped to get another one to use and play through the school band. "The bandmaster said that they didn't have a trombone, but they did have a tuba and they'd let me play the tuba." He didn't particularly care for the tuba. "There's relatively little motivation for anybody to play the tuba," he says candidly—even on the highest professional levels. The reason: "There's only one tuba in a major symphony orchestra"—so there's relatively little work to go around. Also, there are the size and grotesque shape of the instrument: if you could stretch out its metal coiling, it would come to a total of thirty-five feet. But in the hands of a virtuoso it can be used to make beautiful music, something much more facile and stirring than the classic "om-pah, om-pah" that many people associate with the instrument. When Jacobs teaches the instrument now, he focuses on the fact that his students are musicians. "I never let them dwell on the fact that they're playing the tuba," he says. "I always have them dwell on the fact that they're musicians. They're learning to make music and to interpret the music through the medium of the tuba. But the challenge is the music, not the instrument, and so they get into a more comprehensive development as a musician." For he knows and understands some of the reasons that people have for turning to the tuba. "Usually it would be like my case, where some trumpet player or trombone player somehow will be shanghaied and wind up playing the tuba. Rarely is it by choice."

His trouble was that he played the instrument too well. When he was fifteen, he won a scholarship for tuba at the Curtis Institute, and so his family moved to

Philadelphia so he could continue his studies. But he was still pulled in other directions and, in his second or third year in school, he'd spend his free time playing the trumpet or trombone in shows, theaters, parties, and dance bands. "Some of the faculty members were at a party that I was playing and they mentioned that around the school. Anyway, I was called in and told I had to specialize."

In symphony orchestras, unlike pop music groups, there is relatively little doubling—playing more than one musical instrument in the orchestra. "They told me all the virtues and values of staying on the tuba," he says. "That it pays more than a section instrument"—since the tuba *is* a principal player, he gets paid more than, say, the second trumpet or second horn. "In other words, you get sort of a bonus to play the instrument and you get lots of time off. Such as when there are Mozart or Beethoven programs—Haydn. In other words, music written before the middle 1800s would not include the tuba; about 1835, it came into being, so usually, prior to that period, composers didn't involve the tuba in their music. They painted a very rosy picture. They didn't tell me about the problems of it—carrying it and purchasing it and the huge volumes of air that an aged player would need to have to cope with it. Well, maybe they couldn't very well go into those topics. Anyway, I did enjoy the instrument and I have a nice career as a tuba player."

The restrictions imposed by Curtis Institute didn't totally inhibit Jacobs. "In those days"—the early 1930s—"they used tuba a great deal in Dixieland jazz," he says. "They weren't using string bass because the old carbon mikes wouldn't pick them up." So he went on working almost every night. "I'd do my Wagner and Brahms in the daytime and my Tiger Rag at night. It was a very rewarding experience for me."

It also made him one of the most articulate commentators on the difference between the symphony style of play and the jazz style. The music given one and the other will be exactly the same but the sound will be completely different. "When you listen to jazz interpretations and have it noted down on paper, and give it to a musician who does only the classics and have him interpret it—you'll hear the difference. It'll be a completely altered performance, a completely different type of interpretation." The people in the audience can hear the difference, he says, "but they wouldn't be able to define it—where the differences would lie." They lie in the subtleties of playing—"the pattern of rhythm, the duration of a sound, the attack and impact made on certain notes." For there is a different feeling, a different interpretation, on so meaningful a matter as how long a quarter note might be held—only if it's for the tiniest fraction of a second—where the emphasis on the note will come while it is being held. "Our quarter note has to have four-sixteenths; theirs may have five-sixteenths." The jazzman may attack the note much harder than the classical player; he may hold it not only longer but give it a different kind of coloring and tone while he holds it; then he leaves it in a different way to attack the next note—also in a different way." Nobody thinks about this in jazz; it is part of the culture of the music, the unspoken—and unnoted—interpretation that has helped create the sense of freedom within the idiom. Nor is there any sense of snobbishness about the difference within the Chicago Symphony in general or in Arnold Jacobs in particular. "Dixieland on tuba I'd be perfectly at home with," he says. He'd also be pretty much at home with it on the string bass, though he played that instrument most notably with society dance bands, "like Meyer Davis."

Of course he had to learn to play the string bass. But that wasn't hard once he was given the motivation. "About 1932, the dance band I was working with said they wanted me to take up string bass because of the new microphones that were coming in," he says. "They were using the string bass more and more, and they didn't want to let me go because I was a very good tuba player and there were some shows they still wanted the tuba in." So he got a fingering chart and an instrument at Curtis Institute and began teaching himself the fingering, enough so that he could play fairly easily in the band. "But then I started taking lessons on it and eventually I became quite a proficient player. I had another nice career on the string bass, all aside from the tuba. To the point that I became a staff bass player at CBS in Chicago."

The string bass almost led him off into another and separate career—in fact two or three of them. For it led him into playing commercial dates with a combo called the Three Blue Blazers—violin, guitar, and string bass. One of their regular dates was at WBEN in Philadelphia where they played in several variety shows a week before the radio microphones. "It was very similar to what you have today—the 'Tonight Show,' and so forth." Soon Jacobs was doubling again, this time on voice. For the program producer asked him to sing in a quartet on the show. He was pretty good at it. Indeed, his singing was so good that he was offered another scholarship at Curtis Institute to concentrate on vocal work. But he turned it down—"I figured it would mean another six years of study," he says. At the radio station, the management liked his voice so well that they gave him some lines to read as an announcer—"it was during the summer months and they needed somebody to read the lines." He was so spontaneously skilled in it that the station offered him a full-time job as an announcer. He was very much attracted by the offer. "It appealed to me very much, but of course this was in the days before they paid big money," he says. He thought it over carefully. "It was one of those crossroads in life"—could he give up his scholarship at Curtis, and the vocal studies on the side, and go into full-time announcing? He decided not. "With that scholarship at Curtis, I decided I didn't want to branch out."

The trouble was that his success in music with the tuba and the string bass was so marked that he couldn't afford to turn to talking for a living. Indeed, his all-around success was so great that, at first he couldn't afford to turn to a symphony orchestra for a living. When he was eighteen, and far from finished at Curtis Institute, Serge Koussevitzky heard him play and offered him a job with the Boston Symphony Orchestra. "At the time I was working a nightclub in Philadelphia and between salary and tips was making about $90 a week. He offered me $90 a week to go with the Boston Symphony." But at the time, the Boston Symphony Orchestra was a nonunion shop; its conversion to a union shop would become one of the traumatic moments in the orchestra's history. "I would have gone except that I heard how tough Koussevitzky was—that he was hard to please—and I was so afraid that if I didn't satisfy him, I'd be tossed out of the orchestra. And I would have been out of the union automatically for joining the Boston Symphony at that time. So I turned it down at that time." He also turned it down several times later, after he'd joined the Chicago Symphony. He also turned down bids from the Philadelphia Orchestra. Of course, all this didn't happen suddenly. He played in the Indianapolis Symphony and in the Pittsburgh Symphony, under Fritz Reiner, before coming to the Chicago Symphony Orchestra. That was thirty years ago, when he was only twenty-eight years old.

In the Chicago Symphony, he has won a unique stature not simply because he's a superbly talented musician—he's hardly alone in that—or because he's so cerebral a man—he's not alone in that either.

It's because he thinks about, and investigates, such remote, and yet musically pertinent, subjects that he possesses an esoteric and mind-blowing pragmatic fund of knowledge.

His charm is that he can speak, albeit in somewhat heavy academic terms, on matters light and heavy, personal or distant.

A light, personal, and pragmatic example is his explanation for the reason that tuba players are usually heavy. Jacobs himself is a burly man: he weighs 215 pounds, stands 5 feet, 10½ inches. But he was not always overweight: when he was young, he was quite slender—"skinny almost." And the tuba weighed as much then as it does today: the C-tuba he uses weighs twenty-two pounds. Nor does he think it's an advantage to be overweight. "In fact, it's very disadvantageous for a tuba player—terribly so. It affects our respiration. In other words, we're terribly crowded internally. It makes all our inner respiratory movement quite complicated. There's always some material that has to be pushed around to make space for air."

The reason for the heaviness is many-dimensioned. Part of it is in the life-style of the tuba player. Just as he has more time off to study—because he does not play the Beethoven, Bach, Haydn numbers—he also has, says Jacobs with a very small smile, "more time to spend in the coffee shop."

But there is another and more scientific reason. "The problem with playing the tuba is that there is a very moderate amount of hyperventilation associated with the instrument." The hyperventilation usually makes the player hungry. "I usually have a tremendous appetite after a taxing concert. I become very hungry and thirsty after extensive playing," he says. "I feel like I've played a football game, or created some large, manual labor project. But we don't use the big muscles of the body and so, though we do burn up a great deal of energy, it's not used up on exercising the proper musculatures." So the energy loss is not enough to make up for the food intake of the tuba player after he's played an arduous concert.

The hyperventilation has another effect. "When you hyperventilate a bit, you actually alter the pH of the body. In other words, the alkaline/acid relationships are affected, and a person is apt to feel a little bit peculiar with very moderate hyperventilation. Usually it will start out as dizziness. How will I say it—a little leaving of the ground—you begin to float a little bit."

Why is this?

"The symptoms of hyperventilation are due to a lack of carbon dioxide and its effect on the brain," he says. The carbon dioxide is washed out of the blood by the heavy pumping of the respiratory system—keeping the air flow into the tuba at the maximum—and the blood is soon carrying a higher percentage of oxygen to the brain, making the person feel dizzy." It's not a dramatic effect; it's quite moderate. "A little light in the head," he says.

But Jacobs made studies with research scientists at the Pulmonary Functions lab at the University of Chicago, and every indication was that he *should* have been suffering from something worse. "According to their tables, the volume of air that I was moving in and out of the lungs, I should have been in massive hyperventilation." The question was: Why wasn't he? Why don't tuba players, as a rule, suffer from massive hyperventilation, particularly after arduous numbers? They perceived, of course, that the breath expelled into the instrument contained carbon dioxide—the carbon dioxide that he was exhaling. When he took a breath to replenish his lung supply, he'd get fresh air in through the corners of his mouth—that's how tuba players learn to breathe—but he'd also be regulping some of the air he'd expelled into the instrument. That air contained an excess of carbon dioxide and, when he brought it back into his mouth, it created enough of an excess of carbon dioxide in the breath going into his lungs—and then to his brain—to mute the pure-oxygen effect on the brain. "Now when I get into these huge, massive blowing episodes, like what they have in 'The Great Gate of Kiev' at the end of *Pictures at an Exhibition*, I will deliberately take the air back through the instrument to forestall hyperventilation."

Jacobs's investigations into the body impact of playing or singing involve some of the most sophisticated and abstruse physiological and biological theories extant. "I prefer to teach music, by far," he says. But he went into biology as a hobby and his mental drive, and his curiosity, carried him deeper and deeper into it. He got started in the most casual of ways. Back in the middle 1940s, when he'd been in the symphony only a year or two, he began having some physical problems—nothing serious—and he phoned a doctor-friend and "told her I wanted to learn a little about the body and the senses. That was probably the motivating cause: I wanted to have a better understanding of what we're all about." He has a very ordered intellect and the doctor gave him a very ordered list of reading. "I started out with the skeletal structure and went right down through the muscles and the circulatory system. I made quite a fair study of anatomy and I found I enjoyed it, even though it's a dry subject." Then he plunged into physiology and other studies of man and his body. He went to summer school to audit classes; he worked at the University of Chicago labs; he opened his own lab to carry out investigations into the relationship between music and the body.

Those investigations have carried Jacobs into many exacting and improbable fields. The results have made him eminent in the field; he is now sought by medical men as well as musicians to explain certain phenomena. Just two of the facets he's studied are the flow rates of air demanded by the various instruments, and the capacity of the player—the vital capacity, as he puts it—to store and then produce that air.

Consider the tuba.

To play in the lower range, and play it at its loudest—"maximum fortis-simo"—would consume as much as 140 liters of air in one minute. That's the flow rate—140 liters per minute.

Now, of course, neither Jacobs nor anybody else can hold that note for a full minute. It's usually a matter of a second or so. For nobody has the breath for it: nobody can inhale 140 liters of air and then store it in the body's storage bins, to let it out on such a note.

In fact, nobody has anywhere near that capacity. In his younger days, Jacobs had a capacity of 4.7 liters of air. The highest figure he's ever recorded was 6.5 liters. It was for Bill Scarlett, a trumpet player in the Chicago Symphony. That was most interesting because Scarlett demonstrated that it clearly was not a matter of size: he is nowhere as big a man as is Jacobs. "It's a matter of body type," says Jacobs. "He has a long body and short legs. It's a matter of the torso's shape"—whether the lungs have the room and the capacity for accommodating large quantities of air.

In any case Jacobs has made a deep study of what it takes to play various instruments in various modalities. (See the section on Ray Still and the oboe, pages 167–78.) On the tuba, for example, Jacobs is not blowing all out all the time. He has found that "the average flow in mid-dynamic range"—just a broad average—"would run somewhere between 40 to 60 liters per minute." And at the lowest, softest range—"minimal pianissimo, as soft as I can play—the flow rate is 5 to 7 liters per minute.

"In an extreme pianissimo on a low C on a trumpet, with a fine player playing, you have a flow rate as low as 4 liters per minute," says Jacobs. "In loud playing, the flow rate might go up to maybe 15 liters per minute." At the "maximal fortissimo," he would expect the flow rate to be 40 to 48 liters per minute.

For the oboe, the range is much smaller because the flow rate is so snug, so small. "The flow rates in the oboe would average in pianissimo about 3 liters per minute and in fortissimo would go up to about 5 liters per minute."

From all this, it is apparent that a player with a vital capacity of more than 3 liters per minute could learn to play the oboe for a full minute without taking a breath—once he'd achieved breath control. Similarly, with the trumpet: a player with more than 4 liters of lung capacity could play certain pianissimo notes in the low register for a full minute—though he'd never be asked to do it.

Jacobs also went about measuring the vital capacity of a great number of players. There is no particular correlation, except the obvious ones: tiny women—without the huge lung capacity—are not often asked to play the tuba. "Some of these little ladies with extremely small lung capacity would be somewhat handicapped with a high flow rate instrument like the tuba or the bass trombone," says Jacobs.

The irony is that a good many women are given, unthinkingly, assignments on the other high flow rate instruments. "They will so frequently assign girls to play flute, which is a high flow rate instrument," says Arnold Jacobs. "It takes a fairly good lung capacity. But it's a small instrument, very petite, easy to carry, and so forth. But it presents a moderate handicap because so frequently the little ladies just do not have the lung volumes to complete the phrases, as you might say, that the flute traditionally calls for."

Arnold Jacobs, *principal tuba player.*

He's found the obvious: that women do not have the vital capacity for inhaling, storing, and using air that men do. "Their potential for moving air out rapidly from their lungs should be quite high," he says, "but they don't have the quantity"—it's quality without quantity. "Take, as an example, a man five feet, five inches and a girl five feet, five inches—most of the time you'll find that the girl will have quite a percentage less lung capacity due to the contouring of the ribs and the general smallness of their structure, compared to the male. You could express this maybe 20 percent less vital capacity for the persons of the same heights, age, and general body type, as far as we can equate the female and the male."

Thus there is some intelligence needed in picking a player—particularly a woman—for a particular instrument. "If they're using low flow rate instruments like the oboe, there's no harm done," says Jacobs. For most women will have a vital capacity that can accommodate the flow rate of the oboe. "Woodwind instruments in general, outside of the flute, have a low flow rate and not much harm is done. On trumpet there's usually adequate fuel supply. But when they get into trombone and tuba, the smaller girls can run into problems, particularly if they use limited respiratory activity."

One of the difficulties, with men as well as women, is that the player rarely, if ever, uses all the air in his lungs. He may have a vital capacity of 4.5 liters per minute: that's his *capacity*, but that's not what he literally uses. He uses only a fraction of that capacity. The person trained for this might use 75 or 80 percent of his vital capacity; others will use half of it or less. Of course, the time of using the air is also important; it is important to use as much as possible as soon as possible, and bring the other out in reserve.

"I can only get about 50 percent of my lung capacity out in one second," says Jacobs, now hobbled by asthma and age. "It takes me about nine seconds to remove the rest. In a normal set of lungs, you get about 80 percent in one second and in three or four seconds you've removed the rest."

So the trick is not simply in nature; it is not solely in having a large lung capacity. It is in using the lung capacity that's available. It is better to use 80 percent of a 4-liter vital capacity than 50 percent of a 6-liter vital capacity. But it is better to have the vital capacity to begin with.

"I had one of the fine players in the Philadelphia Orchestra come in to see me," says Jacobs. "He had emphysema." Jacobs made a test and found that "he was able to get about 40 percent of his lung capacity out in one second. Nineteen seconds later, he still hadn't emptied his lungs. Fortunately he had a very large vital capacity." So he undertook treatment for the emphysema and he understood instruction on how to increase his use of his lung capacity. "He's been able to keep the disease arrested, but he has to take in large volumes of air so that he can get into the position where air can be moved out rapidly." Not in nineteen seconds.

Not all of the cases he accepts are so readily diagnosed. Or aided. He spoke about one young lady—an oboe player who was a talented musician—who was having problems with her respiration. He found that she still had her tonsils; in Jacobs's own youth, the tonsils were often removed as a guard against infection, and that tended to open the air passage more. But her biggest problem was that she had an oversized tongue—"her tongue in repose was taking up too much room in terms of what you think of as a normal person's oral cavity," he says.

His method of dealing with the problem was not to lecture her about her tongue. There was nothing that he—or she—could do about its size. Instead he started by giving her speech exercises. "We had to do it by opening up the airway. You can't communicate with a tongue. It will just stiffen up on you and be very uncooperative. But you communicate beautifully with it through speech." He started by making the speech out of vowels. He also started by showing her how to compensate for an airway blocked by the tongue. "Take a drowning person, what do you do? He's choking on his tongue—you pull his chin forward and pull out his tongue. Just moving your chin forward will tend to open the pharynx." So she could see right away that there were ways she could compensate for her tongue by opening her airway more. He demonstrated how it is done reflexively in speech by the use of vowels. Then bit by bit he built on this insight so that she learned "over many, many months to tie into a vowel concept where her airway became subconsciously open."

He is just as analytical about his own work. "Most players, by the time they reach my age on my instrument have either left the business or deteriorated to such a point that they're no longer competitive," he says. The way he stays competitive is by a varied system of programs. "I usually keep three programs alive constantly," he says.

One is a constant conditioning program of scales and finger drills.

Another is a "long-term program of recital where I spend one to two years developing maybe five or six numbers." A recital for *tuba?* That is not improbable at all. He regards the instrument as a highly individualized force that can have the appeal, in a recital, of any of the brass instruments. In fact, he often practices études for trumpet in this period. Of the numbers in general, he says: "Usually you can read them, or they're developed after a few weeks. But you spend the time after that in refining them and interpreting them and tearing them apart and seeing if you can improve them. In other words, these studies refine all the neuromuscular patterns because of the connection between thought and physical response. You're going into a little detail. It becomes more and more a mentalization, which I think is very important."

His third program is a "short-term period of solo and orchestral work, involving maybe one to four weeks on specific studies and general reading, and so forth." In this period he prepares his parts for the upcoming programs if, indeed, that hasn't already been incorporated into his long-term program. The Mahler Sixth Symphony was, as we've seen, a test of physical endurance—something that Jacobs is quite sensitive to. "But it's not difficult to play," he says. "It demands a certain amount of interpretation and development as a musician but I would not say, by far, that it's the most difficult I've played this season."

Just as scrupulous—but far different—in his practice habits is Adolph "Bud" Herseth, the first trumpet player. "I practice every day," he says. But not the same amount every day. It's three hours on days when the work with the orchestra is light; it's one and a half hours when it's heavy. He also paces the practices to the style of music that's being played in the hall—by doing the opposite. When the week's work involves "heavy" music—"Mahler, Bruckner, Strauss, Wagner"—he spends his practice time on the light, highly refined works. When the week's program is light, he turns to the heavier works. "I just try to balance it out."

Thus he works on his articulation—in opposition. In weeks of work on pieces demanding heavy, almost percussive, articulation, he looks for "soft" works to practice on, so that he's always in shape for the music that's coming up. "I sometimes have to remind myself that, if we've played several weeks of 'hard' concerts—very aggressive, very hard playing—you tend to fall into the habit of using your articulation, your tongue, in a forceful way. And then you are playing nothing but delicate little things, like Mozart or something like that the next week." So his practice is not always aimed at what the work of the week is, but at what it is not. For he'll get seven and one-half to ten hours of rehearsal on the work of the week at Orchestra Hall, and he feels he needs to use his private practice time to balance it all out.

Nor does he practice on just one trumpet. At some point every week he'll practice with smaller trumpets. He's got a total of thirty-four different trumpets at home, most of them experimental in one form or another. ("We try a lot of different things—different shapes of the bell, different bore sizes, different tapers in the lead pipe—any changes that might make a big difference in the quality of sound in the instrument and in the gradation of volume that is available.") In particular, he'll work intensely in the extremely high ranges of the instruments. "Well beyond the range where I play," he says. "I practice so that the high C's are easy to reach—once you've played enough above them, you know that you can cope with them."

He augments all this quite religiously with a program of exercise patterned after the Canadian Air Force system. He got started on it as a way to avoid a recurrence of an attack of sciatica nine or ten years ago, and he continues it as a way of maintaining his endurance on the trumpet. "The trumpet is physically the most strenuous instrument in the orchestra," he says. "That is one reason why trumpeters do not play as continuously as violins, for instance. The violins' type of strenuous work comes from the continuity with which they have to play. But their actual effort is by far nothing—bar for bar—compared to playing the high registers in the trumpet."

The rewards of all this labor are many and varied.

Some of them come from particular performances. A season or so ago, Herseth was asked by Solti to play Bach's *Brandenburg* Concerto in F Major, no. 2. That, he says, "is the hardest single piece in the repertoire for the first trumpet. That is the most demanding of all. Nothing—nothing can be compared to the Brandenburg." For one thing, the range is extremely high, so high that many orchestras do not give it to the trumpet to play. Instead they'll turn to the soprano saxophone to take the trumpet part; in fact, the Chicago Symphony often had it played by an E-flat clarinet in the days before Herseth took over the first trumpet's chair.

Another problem is in the articulation. "Not only do you have to play some phrases hard, but you have to remember to play select phrases lightly because you are in a concert-type group, trying to balance with a flute, fiddle, and oboe and you do not want to be too predominant."

He was so stunningly successful at it that Solti asked him to repeat the last movement as an encore, in response to the storm of applause that the performance arouses. "I don't remember any other time that we did an encore on a Thursday night performance," he says—and he's been in the orchestra for twenty-five years. Solti himself was so moved by the work that he wanted to hear it again. ("He said to me, 'Can you do the last movement again?' And I said, 'Well, let's find out.' ") He did it again, to new and thunderous applause—and one suspects that Solti was barely restrained from doing it once more. Certainly the audience wanted it.

This acclaim comes not from audiences alone. His colleagues in the orchestra hold him in even higher regard. It is not just, as we've seen, that he's regarded as the finest trumpeter alive; it's that some of them regard him as the finest trumpeter who's *ever* lived. Yet Bud Herseth himself reflects none of this; there is no vanity or conceit or even self-awareness in him. He relaxes between rehearsals, or listens to the replays of tapes, in an old plaid shirt, puffing on a pipe, looking like nothing so much as a somewhat stout farmer, gray-haired and grandfatherly, who's stopped to listen, as if at an auction for some prize Herefords. He lives in a comfortable old house in Oak Park and he practices in the basement—"in a corner where all my son's mountain-climbing gear is." He has two sons, one working for the CIA—"he's an economic researcher, not a cloak-and-dagger type"—and the other teaching school in a far western suburb of Chicago and living at home ("he knows the basement refrigerator is always full of beer"). He *is* a grandfather—twice: he has a daughter who's married to a bandmaster in Wisconsin.

He's an equable man of equable habits. His preconcert meal invariably is a broiled chopped steak—"small is best." His most ardent enthusiasm is for golf and he bears its results cheerfully: he played at least nine holes every day last summer, eighteen holes on some days, while fitting in a full schedule at Ravinia and working an hour and a half of private practice into the schedule. ("The best round I had for eighteen holes was an 86, which is not all that great, but for me it was as good as I can do." He devotes his free time to his church, giving it some of the finest instrumental playing in its history—for free, of course—and he's even been known to conduct some numbers. But he's one of the few men in the Chicago Symphony who harbor absolutely no ambitions for conducting.

"If I would ever be a conductor," he says, "I would want my orchestra all composed of ex-conductors."

Why?

"So I could get even!" he says with a laugh.

He is perfectly happy being first trumpet and studying the techniques of the players—in discerning the difference between the way the same notation is played under different composers. For example: "You do not play a quarter note the same way in Wagner as you do in Mozart," he says. "You have to have that understanding. This is where you separate the simply adequate symphony players from the really good ones—the concept of the styles of the composer and of your instrument and of the instruments around you."

He even gave up a busy and prosperous career as a trumpeter in a dance band to concentrate solely on his symphonic work. "I enjoyed it immensely but once I got on the track of studying with symphonic trumpet players, I decided I was going to try to do it all in the classical sense. I really did not want to mix them." He greatly admires certain jazz trumpeters—Maynard Ferguson, for one. "A very exciting player. Enormously accomplished." And he encourages young people who want to know if they should go into rock groups to "go ahead and play. Enjoy it. Music is to enjoy and to communicate to others. I try to impress on them to play in as 'musical' a style as possible. And, of course, musical styles from one kind of group to another are quite different." The jazzman enjoys a freedom while the symphonic player endures a discipline, for example. The jazz player, he says, "is not bound by the discipline of matching intonation and attack and volume-level with a flute or a clarinet, and the different stylistic requirements of playing first Mozart and then Strauss and then Weber, and what have you." It's been a long time since he played jazz and dance music professionally, but he has always felt that he could "go back to it if I wanted to. You don't lose it that quickly. But there are a few aspects of that sort of playing that do not mix well with the disciplined style that goes with a symphony orchestra."

What are some of the differences?

"Well, for one thing, you play with a rather heavy, hard articulation in dance music. In other words, you strike the note pretty hard when you are doing dance work and you tend to lose the finesse of articulation if you play too much of that.

"Secondly, you play—in a normal situation—at full volume. You blow loud all the time. So you lose some of the delicacy you need in symphonic work. God! To try and sit down and play a Mozart symphony after you've been playing dance bands—you just cannot make it. So I decided to concentrate on just one area."

Normally he puts the blame for his plight, and his pleasure, on his father. For it was his father—who was a school superintendent in a tiny town in Minnesota called Bertha—who got Bud introduced to the trumpet. "A little threat here, a little threat there—that sort of thing, you know." Bud was thirteen or fourteen years old at the time; he'd gotten a trumpet when he was in second grade but he pretty much ignored it in the interim. Then his school got a new band director, his father got him a new book of instructions, and Bud developed a new interest. "I found that the more I practiced, the better I played and the better I played, the more I enjoyed it. Obviously. That's the way it always works." He began playing solos in high school and later at Luther College in Iowa.

He studied mathematics as a major in college but when he went into the service, it was as a member of the Iowa pre-flight school band. He was sent overseas and when he was on the troopship coming home after the war, he wrote letters of application to four schools—the New England Conservatory in Boston, Curtis Institute in Philadelphia, Eastman School of Music in Rochester, New York, and the Juilliard School of Music in New York City.

"I really did not have any intention of being a professional trumpet player," he says. "I wanted to get a master's degree for teaching purposes. I wanted to study with a high-class symphonic trumpet player because I found I enjoyed that kind of music and I enjoyed hearing those guys play."

The Curtis Institute never answered his letter. Juilliard and Eastman put him off for a year. But the New England Conservatory said they'd admit him at the next semester, in January 1946. He started his studies there and was still immersed in them—spending his free time hanging around the Boston Symphony Orchestra—when he got a telegram telling him that Maestro Artur Rodzinski would be pleased to audition him in his Fifth Avenue apartment in New York City. Herseth knew that Rodzinski was music director of the Chicago Symphony, but he'd never given much thought to playing in a symphony. He just figured that Rodzinski was between appearances in Chicago and was looking around for some reserves, perhaps "someone to play down at the end of the section." He adds, "I did not know how he got my name or anything else."

He went to New York and auditioned in Rodzinski's apartment for an hour and a half. When it was over, Rodzinski congratulated Herseth: "You are the new first trumpet player for the Chicago Symphony." Herseth was astounded. "I about went through the floor," he says. But he wasn't inclined to turn the job down.

Subsequently he discovered that he job had been offered to the first trumpet player of the Boston Symphony. He'd turned it down but, having heard Herseth play, he recommended him for the job. The irony was that Rodzinski left the Chicago Symphony after that and Herseth never played under him. "I often joke that they fired him as soon as they learned he'd hired me"—a twenty-four-year-old who hadn't finished his musical studies, as the first trumpet in the Chicago Symphony.

He knew very little of the repertoire or of the routine and specifications for the symphony. But he was fortunate on two counts. One was that the No. 2 trumpeter who was in the symphony decided to work with him instead of against him. "He told me he could really foul me up, give me wrong notations, wrong signals on where to enter—all those things. And he could have. But he didn't," says Herseth.

The other piece of good fortune was that, after Rodzinski left, the symphony had two seasons of guest conductors. They were all big-name conductors. They were all on their best behavior—that is, they were careful not to abuse the players —because they might be tapped for the job. And most of all, "they all came with 'big' programs." Every guest conductor came with his best possible repertoire, so that he could make the best possible appearance. "I probably got five or six years of repertoire experience in those two seasons," says Herseth.

Eventually, under Kubelik, the routine settled down. But for Herseth it was never a dull routine. One reason was the auto accident he suffered in 1952. It might have—indeed, it should have—ended his playing career. It didn't because of the personality of Herseth. "It never entered my mind that I wouldn't play again," he says.

He was the driver in a one-car accident—"I broke the steering wheel of the car off with my lower jaw," he says. He split his lower lip and had to have fifteen

Adolph Herseth, principal trumpet player.

stitches taken to close it. "It's still numb," he says. The two middle teeth in his lower jaw are gray and dead—"the nerves are gone." But they are his teeth; they were just raised vertically again after the crash laid them flat within his mouth. "All the bones around the roots of the teeth were crushed." The other teeth were sheared off at the gumline. So the teeth had to be rebuilt around pegs inserted in his jaw. "There are just white crowns set on pegs," he says.

Considering that nothing is more important to a trumpeter than his embouchure, it is astounding that Herseth ever tried to play again. For his embouchure—his lips, the meeting place of man and trumpet—was destroyed. But instead of playing out of the center of his lips—the classic placement for the trumpet against the lips—he angled the trumpet, moved it over to the left side of his mouth and learned to play it there. "I just fooled around with it until I found the way it worked best," he says. He's played it that way for twenty years, with increasing—not decreasing—skills. In recent years, some degree of sensation is returning to his lower lip and he's been readjusting the embouchure. "Gradually now, very gradually, I have been moving it back to where it was," he says. "The only time I can do that is between seasons, because then I have time to fool around with it."

There was no time to fool around with it now. For the rehearsal and recording pace was so urgent. Moreover, Solti was going back to the original score of Mahler instead of accepting the occasional, minor changes that had been inserted into the score over the years. (Mahler did not deny that others might tinker with his score as he tinkered with those of others. Otto Klemperer once quoted Mahler as saying that if Mahler's Eighth Symphony did not sound good, anybody could "with an easy conscience" make changes in it.) In the last movement of Mahler's Sixth, there are two resounding hammer blows that cry out for the symmetry of a third blow. The story is that Mahler himself had been made apprehensive about it, seeing it as an omen of his own doom and thus had edited it out of the score. But over the years, other conductors, including Solti, put it back into the score, presuming to maintain the symmetry of the moment. It can be heard in the recorded version of Mahler's Sixth Symphony that Solti did for London/Decca. But in this week's concert-hall version, he edited it out.

Nobody seemed to mind. For both audience and critics seemed to feel that composer and conductor had come together in celestial union in his work. "Brasses from tuba to trumpet are set off against one another in unbelievably delicate interplay," wrote Thomas Willis in the *Chicago Tribune*. "Solti conducted with rapt dignity," said Karen Monson in the *Chicago Daily News*. Said Roger Dettmer in *Chicago Today*: "To single out for special praise the horn solos of Dale Clevenger, the violin of Samuel Magad, the trumpet of Adolph Herseth, the tuba of Arnold Jacobs, the trombone of Jay Friedman, the oboe of Ray Still, the timpani of Donald Koss is an act of respect that must not, however, neglect an entire augmented congregation that honored Solti and thereby Mahler."

THIRD
MOVEMENT

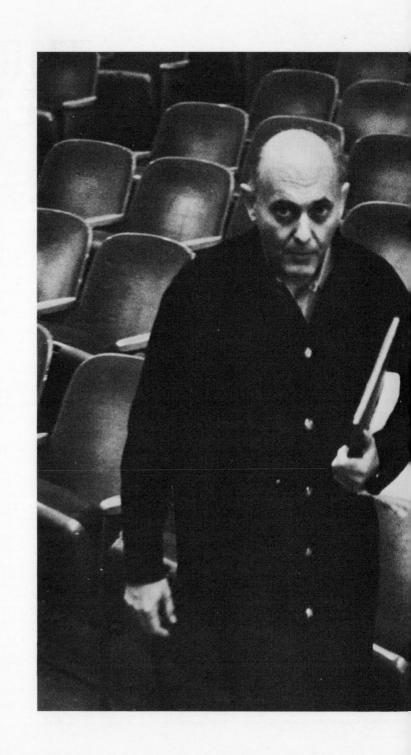

The Eastern Tour

By comparison, the week that followed *Missa* and Mahler was quiet.

It involved only four concerts in four cities in six days.

For this was tour week. It would begin with youth concerts in Chicago. There are two of these but they are short ones—usually two and one-half hours total. (A half hour of this is an intermission between concerts at Orchestra Hall, as the hall is cleared of one set of grade school students and a new set is admitted for the second concert.) This is considered to be one "service" by the members of the orchestra.

That was on a Tuesday morning. On Wednesday at noon, the orchestra would fly to New York and play a concert in Carnegie Hall that night.

On Thursday, the orchestra would fly to Connecticut to play a concert that night at the University of Connecticut in Storrs.

On Friday, the players would have a day off.

On Saturday, the orchestra would play another concert in Carnegie Hall.

And on Sunday, it would fly to Washington where it would play a concert in the Kennedy Center on Sunday afternoon. Then it would fly home.

To many members of the orchestra, it would seem like a vacation—or at least a diversion—because the work load, though heavy, would be less than in the previous two weeks.

And they knew they'd be going to an area where they are not merely accepted or tolerated but are rapturously acclaimed.

Most of all, they would be leaving the cold, blustery late-autumn-early-winter chill of Chicago to a Manhattan that was bathed in sunshine in temperatures in the middle seventies.

But, as with most "vacations"—working or otherwise—there were the moments of frantic preparation that occupied, or preoccupied, everybody.

Georg Solti and Lady Valerie were all ready for evacuation. The trunks were packed for storage. The suitcases were packed for travel. The lists were finished for reference. And the trip was started before anybody else's trip. The Soltis would be returning to Europe after this tour; they'd leave directly from New York instead of returning to Chicago with the orchestra. So they decided to send the children on ahead with their nanny. The family flew together to New York on Monday—Solti would not lead the youth concerts; that's the responsibility of his associate conductor, Henry Mazer. The children and Miss Ferguson flew on to London. And so he was free of any conducting responsiblities until Wednesday night. He decided to spend those extra days in New York. He had much to do in working with his record company, his management agent, his literary people, even his dentist. It is a mark of Solti that his closest friends in many cities are not in classical music: a dentist in New York, a doctor in Chicago, Bing Crosby's band leader in Los Angeles. He "saves up his pain" for them—particularly for his dentist. "I have no dentist in Rome or Paris. No dentist in London." He just takes the time in either coming to the United States, or leaving it, to stop off and see his dentist.

So two days before the rest of the orchestra he was in New York, relaxing and working at nonconducting diversions from a tenth-floor suite in a Fifth Avenue hotel.

In the basement of Orchestra Hall, stage manager Jim Palecek and his crew began making sure the fifty-five wardrobe trunks, and the instrument trunks, were filled. With exceptions, all instruments are shipped by truck. The players simply put their violins, for example, in specially designed packing cases that can be closed and sent as a unit. They put their formal wear and their dark suits—for afternoon concerts— in the wardrobe trunks. Some of them have an extra set of tails and carry them in their personal luggage, in case the trunks get lost. Nothing is done haphazardly; every trunk is splashed with color so that Palecek and the players can identify at a glance which trunks hold the clothes of what section players: green is for the woodwinds, blue is for the violas, orange is for the trumpets, and so forth. By Tuesday afternoon, only a few hours after the youth concert ended, the truck would be rumbling down the back alley behind Orchestra Hall, heading for the Dan Ryan Expressway, and from there to Indiana, Ohio, and Pennsylvania turnpikes. It would get to Carnegie Hall before the musicians would.

On the seventh floor, John Edwards and some of his assistants decided to leave early for New York. Carl Fasshauer, a youthful-looking gray-haired man—one of those men with a beckoning expression who can close down his face in a moment, like a door slamming shut—checked and rechecked the detail of the itinerary. The outline ran five pages and would start by providing for the pickup of players over much of Chicago. ("One bus leaves Orchestra Hall for O'Hare Field [via Oak Park Arms Hotel] . . . one bus leaves Howard Street station for O'Hare [via Touhy and Cicero"]. Some of the details would not be made apparent in the itinerary: three buses would meet the chartered plane at the landing ramp at Kennedy Airport in New York—and one would be a special bus for smokers. ("Usually it's the last one, or the outside bus, in line," says one player.) Some would be only half-apparent: the itinerary would specify that there would be 36 first-class seats and 123 seats filled in the tourist section, but it did not say who would fill them. This is just one of the small abrasive points that arise continually on a tour. At one time, it was assumed that management would get as many first-class seats as it wanted. But now, seat distribution is in the hands of the members' committee. "We have the privilege of saying who in management sits where and when"—that is, who gets the first-class seats. It is not really a difficult matter: John Edwards is given a first-class seat as a matter of courtesy (though he won't be on the outbound flight). Other management men, such as Carl Fasshauer, prefer to sit in the tourist section with the players; his grandfather had been eminent in the musical affairs of the Chicago Symphony, and Carl was as comfortable as a pair of slippers with the players.

Of course, that leaves the problem of assigning some players to first-class seats and the rest to tourist. This could get to be an anxious little race at the gate of every chartered flight ("We have one guy who makes sure he's on the plane first on every flight so he can grab a first-class seat," says Koss.) Actually, the members' committee also has control of that. Says Koss, like a good schoolteacher, "We devised a method of starting alphabetically in the beginning, middle, and the end." So every player who had first-class rights on the charter flight would know it before he got on the plane. The rest would occupy the tourist section.

Individually, every player had to make last-minute preparations.

Warren Benfield, the bass player, had to resolve a last-minute emergency: he woke up on Wednesday morning—the day the tour started—to find a tree had been blown over on his lot in Lombard, a suburb west of Chicago. He is an easy, urbane man who is not much thrown by such problems. "I just called one of my students and asked him to try and chop it up and clean it out while I was gone," he says.

Frank Brouk, the horn player, routed out a sewer in his home on the southwest side of Chicago just before he left. Norman Schweikert, the horn player, had to make emergency calls to relatives to take care of his children while he was gone. His father-in-law was undergoing sudden open-heart surgery and his wife had flown to be at her father's side during the crisis. Now Norman had to leave town with the orchestra—and relatives had to come to Chicago to get the children. "It's almost going to seem like a vacation," he said, as he escaped the pressures of home and the task of caring for the children.

Fred Spector, the first violinist, carefully packed his violin and carried it with him. He would not ship it by truck. Indeed, he would barely put it down all through the tour; he planned to carry it with him everywhere. "I can't leave it in the hotel room," he says. "The hotel won't take responsibility for it." He and Samuel Magad and Victory Aitay are among those similarly burdened—Magad and Aitay, because they have virtually priceless Stradivarii, Spector because his instrument has a price—but a high one. "A dealer told me that I might get $75,000 for it now," he says. Spector is, among other preoccupations, expert in the style, quality, and value of violins. Other players come to him to get advice on what's available and if their value meets the price. "Things are wild in the violin market," he says. The instrument has become wildly popular in improbable areas: Japan, for example, has not only exported the Suzuki system but has exported a great many string-instrument musicians who may soon be filling the gaps in the major orchestras in the world. But the Japanese enthusiasm for the violin—combined with a pre–oil-embargo prosperity in Japan—allowed the Japanese to seek out excellent instruments and push the price on them up and up. "I bought this instrument fourteen years ago for $14,000," says Spector of his violin. "It took me two or three years just to pay off the loan on it." Now its value has multiplied fivefold, and "I can't even begin to afford the insurance to cover it." And since New York hotels are constantly the target of thieves—Spector and Magad and Aitay didn't want to take the chance of losing their instruments, even to a thief who didn't know what he was getting.

Bud Herseth packed his golf clubs. So did Don Koss and Burl Lane. The fact that it was mid-November did not discourage them; they are golf nuts and they were perfectly confident that they would have time to get in one or two rounds. "Probably in Van Cortlandt Park, up in the Bronx," said Burl Lane.

He is, in a sense, the most notable member of the orchestra. For he is obviously the product of different cultures—of the athletic as well as the musical. He plays in the orchestra—the bassoon and the contrabassoon—but he lives in the lineaments of sports: he wears the taut sport shirts and the well-tailored square-shouldered jackets of the jock, he walks with the bouncy confidence—the hint of the strut—of the accomplished athlete.

He has been torn between the two cultures for much of his life. He grew up in a mining area of northeastern Oklahoma, near a little town called Picher. "Mickey Mantle and his family—his father's name, the only name we ever knew him by was 'Mutt'—lived on the farm adjacent to us. And long before Mickey was known to millions, his father would take all his boys—Mick and Ronnie and Rick—out to the field after the chores were done. An hour before sunset. They had a large field that was plowed up and they would practice hitting baseballs every evening until dark, every evening after they'd milked the cows. Mickey's father died almost broke"—he died of cancer before Mickey became an renowned player—"because he sold the farm, he sold everything to have money to send Mickey around to baseball camps. And he never knew that his son turned out to be one of the greatest baseball players of all time."

Burl Lane's own choice was more combative. "My bandmaster and my football coach had a knock-down-drag-out fight in the schoolyard over who'd get me when I was in junior high school," he says. He was then a guard on the football team and a saxophone player in the band. Who won the fight? "Well, the band director was pretty good at waving a baton, but not very good at waving his fists, I'm afraid. He came out on the bottom of the pile. Besides," he says, "the football coach was an enormous man who was slightly unbalanced mentally to start with, and it was a short-lived fight." The irony is that the coach won the fight and lost the player: Burl Lane eventually turned to the saxophone and won his scholarship to college in music, not in football.

His route to the Chicago Symphony Orchestra was not only improbable but almost spectacularly so. For it was locked in the culture of the Okies of the Depression, though not precisely as John Steinbeck wrote about them in *The Grapes of Wrath*.

"My father was in the water business in town," says Burl. Visions of utility magnates and millions of dollars go dancing through the mind—but they were only visions. "You might not understand about the water business in northeastern Oklahoma during the Depression," he says. "Until about 1940, the people in that part of the country didn't turn on a faucet and get water. You went out to a barrel and dipped a bucket in the barrel. My father was in the business of hauling water to everybody's house and putting water in their barrel. For a nickel a barrel."

About the only musical exposure the family had was in square dancing. "My father and mother still square-dance," says Lane. They weren't alone. Everybody in the family went square dancing. "During my early days, my childhood, living on the farm in Oklahoma, it was a family kind of thing: my brothers and sisters, all married with their families, all of us living on the farm, running the farm, and for a little bit of diversion in the evening my uncle had a violin." He'd gotten enthusiastic about the violin some years earlier when everybody would go off to barn dances. "So he sold scrap, bottles, and his Kansas salve and saved up enough money and went out and bought himself a little violin," says Lane. "Brought it home, and took it out and drew the bow across it like he saw when they played "Turkey in the Straw." Well, it wouldn't play "Turkey in the Straw" for him. So he got disgusted and he wouldn't have anything to do with it.

"Well, eventually he outgrew that and he actually tried to play the instrument a little. And in the process of listening to the violin, he got outside the barn dance and he began buying records and eventually he wound up with a large number of recordings of Leopold Stokowski and the Philadelphia Orchestra, during the time when Stokowski was *the* conductor in the United States. When the decor of the inside of the hall in Philadelphia had to be matched to the color of Stokowski's blazing blue eyes—he didn't want anything to clash with the color of his eyes." In this very quiet, most unlikely way, Burl Lane began to hear classical music—on a scrawny little farm in the parched Oklahoma mining lands. It was to change his life.

The change was moved forward by his father—in more obvious ways, though for down-to-earth reasons.

His father was caught by the sound and the looks of the saxophone. So when Burl was in about seventh grade, "he went out and paid $40 for an old silver saxophone. That's when I became a saxophone player."

He was pretty good at it. "I didn't really realize it but it seemed pretty easy to play." He began playing in a band and winning local solo contests and soon glamorous careers were dancing through his mind. "At the time, I anticipated being a saxophone player in the Glenn Miller band or some similar type of organization," he says. "The Benny Goodman story, the Glenn Miller story were showing at the local movies at that time and I'd sit through each one five or six times and see myself in the place of one of the fellows in the saxophone section."

He also played football and loved it. He was a guard—the classic watch-fob guard—and when the crisis between music and football came up, his first instinct was to stay with football. "The pressures from my friends on the football team were great enough to get me to play football," he says. "In my own mind, I felt that playing in the band was out of the question, because all the guys I ran around with were football players. And I just wouldn't be able to face them anymore if I quit playing football and wound up in the bandroom."

However, Lane was getting some pressure from his parents to take up music "because it was a little less hazardous than football." And he could keep up with his musical activities by playing in local combos and dance bands through high school. The real break—the division of the cultures—came when he prepared to go to college: he won a music scholarship to the University of Tulsa. That in turn led him to the bassoon—and it is a wry commentary that so many of the symphony players wind up playing not the instrument of choice but the one that's put off on them.

"I was enrolled in a music education course," he says. That would qualify him to teach school and be a bandmaster in Oklahoma. "During the course of study, you're required to take what they call 'minor instruments' so that when you become a band director, you can at least play "The Star-Spangled Banner" on all of the instruments," he says. "So I came to a particular part of the training where we were required to take a minor woodwind. The only instrument left after everyone had made their selection was an old army-issue bassoon, lying at the back of the bandroom. And I was forced to take that."

Again, it seemed to him to be an easy instrument to play. "Any instrument is easy to play up to a given point, then it gets to the point where you have to make the instrument do as you wish and not have the instrument playing you."

But the bassoon was not the center of his life. The saxophone was. So when he got out of college, he got a job with Fred Waring at Shawnee-on-Delaware in Pennsylvania. "I went to work playing poolside cocktail music and then inside the main lodge in the evenings," he says. When fall came, he got the news: there was no room for him in the orchestra on the fall tour. He was married. His wife was expecting. And he was out of a job.

Lane's wife suggested that "since we're so close to New York, why don't you see if you can get into Juilliard?" He was awestruck at the presumption of her suggestion. "Being from a very small town in Oklahoma, and having heard the name of Juilliard, I was completely intimidated by the notion of actually going to Juilliard School of Music. Of auditioning for admission to that school." But the way things were in Shawnee-on-Delaware, he figured he had nothing to lose. "But I was scared to death at the thought of approaching Juilliard."

He overcame his fears. He made the approach. He played the audition. He won admission to the school. And then he found out that he was all wrong.

"All of my training had been with the notion of becoming a solo saxophonist," he says. But this is not a "classical" or, normally, a symphony orchestra instrument. It had other drawbacks. "I soon became aware of the facts of life in New York City, a saxophone player must be a commercial player or he will not exist. He simply will not eat. And you also become what is known as a 'doubler'—one that plays more than one instrument—if you're a wind player. The only players that make a satisfactory living in the woodwind field are doublers, outside of people in the Philharmonic and the opera and so forth. I discovered this problem when I went to join Local 802 Musicians Union in New York City. I got a union book that listed all the names of all the people by instrument. I decided to see how many saxophone players there were in Local 802. Well, I began counting and there were no less than 5,000 saxophone players listed in Local 802. I thought immediately that my chances of getting work were pretty slim. So I decided I'd better do something to try to improve my chances of getting work. Whereupon I obtained a bassoon and started practicing and, before long, switched my major from saxophone to bassoon. And I graduated with a diploma in bassoon from Juilliard, a master of science degree from Juilliard, and went on to a year in the doctoral studies program at Columbia University in education prior to coming to Chicago."

In the years that Lane spent in New York, he had to make a living—for his family—as well as go to school. He remember that, even while he was with the Fred Waring organization, he'd made a trip with his parents to New York and had seen *The Unsinkable Molly Brown* at the Winter Garden Theatre. "I was all agog at the musicians in the pit and I was thinking how great it would be actually to work the pit in a Broadway show." He decided to try it. He could double on a lot of instruments—he plays the clarinet, the flute, and the piccolo as well as the bassoon and the tenor saxophone, the baritone saxophone, the alto saxophone, and the contrabassoon. Not all of them are "pit" instruments, but his flexibility was an asset. He played with the Radio City Music Hall Orchestra for a time and he played in the pit orchestra for *What Makes Sammy Run?* and the Steve Lawrence Show—"that played the 54th Street Theatre for some time"—and he substituted in *No Strings*. He also worked in a number of off-Broadway musicals. "One ill-fated show was called *King of the Whole Damned World*, which was a fairly decent show for off-Broadway. It ran for two whole months but we had the unfortunate problem of opening directly across the street from the *The Fantasticks*. We were hoping to get the leftovers—there was a lot of traffic on the streeet, of course, but nobody was coming through our doors."

That wasn't all he did. He played in nightclubs and bars—"rock, everything. I went through the whole Elvis Presley era with a saxophone in my hands," he says. At first he was absolutely enchanted by it all. "For a really green greenhorn coming to New York City and winding up playing in the pits of Broadway shows and so forth, it was, at first of course, an enormous thrill," he says. "The novelty wears off in a hurry, however, when you are continually bucking the competition, which is really fierce. Once you have successfully landed a job playing, your troubles are not over. You are still subject to the efforts by other people to get that job away from you through any means possible, and some of them are subtle and some are not quite so subtle. You will be called in, for example, to substitute for someone in a Broadway show or Radio City, or the ballet or whatever, and you are expected to go in and sight-read the part that this man's been playing, for however many weeks or months. And do the job equally as well as the guy that has been doing it all the time; otherwise, you're obviously just no good. In order to insure that a substitute will not come and play the part better than the regular, the regular guy will make alterations in his part, indicate cuts, indicate different notes, so that when the substitute comes in, he's going to make some pretty unbelievable mistakes—and quite obvious ones—to insure that he will not sound better than the guy he's replacing for that one occasion. This has happened to me, and it's happened to everybody that winds up as a sub. I did work the Radio City Music Hall, in the pit there, as a substitute and, as it turns out, they hire one substitute who will sort of make the rounds in the woodwind section. As a result, I think I worked more hours than the regulars there."

Eventually it began wearing on Lane. "After a while, this continual hassle of free-lancing, and doing everything you can to avoid making contractors mad at you, gets to be too much. The last thing in the world you could afford to do was make a contractor mad, because there were so many people looking for work that if he even called you once and you had to turn him down because you were already obligated, chances are very good he'd never call you back again. As a result, guys would accept multiple engagements on the same evening, then turn around and start subletting their work to other musicians. It was a wild business, and my particular temperament is not geared for that sort of life for very long and as soon as—I knew as soon as an opportunity came along—that I was going to leave New York City. It was an absolute madhouse. The opportunity came in the spring of 1965."

The opportunity came through classical music. For he was working as hard at his classical studies as he was on his commercial income. "I practiced—in addition to my school hours—I practiced eight hours a day. Which left very little time for sleeping," he says. In addition, he was playing in the American Symphony Orchestra, in the National Orchestral Association, and in the Juilliard symphony. In fact, it was the Juilliard experience that propelled him—without his knowledge or desire—into playing the contrabassoon.

One year he had to take a leave from the Juilliard orchestra for a week or so while his wife had a baby. While he was away, "a friend of mine went to the conductor behind my back and convinced him that I should be playing the contrabassoon and that he should be playing second bassoon. So I came back and found that I was no longer playing bassoon in the Juilliard orchestra. I was playing contrabassoon."

At the time he was quite upset. "I had a running fight with the orchestra conductor for the remaining two and a half years that I was at Juilliard."

There is a significant difference between the instruments. The usual bassoon is 109 inches long and has its bell sticking upward—it looks a little like a thin log with a twig (the crook with the reeds) sticking out of it. The contrabassoon is 192 inches long—16 feet in all—and it must be wrapped back on itself to accommodate the player. The bell points downward about midpoint on the instrument. It plays an octave lower than the bassoon and it has a sound that is more ominous and ponderous. Its rumbling tones can be heard deep down in the orchestra when John the Baptist's head is severed in *Salome*. Its subterranean notes are used to describe the hollowness of the dungeon in the prison scene of Beethoven's *Fidelio*. It provides an impression of almost unbearable weight when, in Haydn's *Creation*, it sounds the low note, at fortissimo, on the last word of the phrase "by heavy beasts the ground is trod."

The contrabassoon is not an easy instrument to handle or to master. It was one of the very few instruments that Burl Lane did not find easy to play. "It's a very unwieldy thing as far as being able to play it in tune and actually produce a discernible tune," he says. "And there are differences in the fingering problems on the instrument. The way it looks and the way it sounds, it's very difficult to play the thing in tune. To play it in tune, because these instruments are, by their very nature, built out of tune with themselves. In other words, playing a one-octave scale, you have to physically manipulate the pitch of each note to get the thing in tune; it's just built out of tune with itself. It's just the nature of the beast; the finest instrument made is still a long way from anything which would be considered perfection. The other big problem with it is producing a pitch that can actually be heard as a pitch. The frequency of sound that comes out of this instrument is such a low level, low number of vibrations per second, that you have to work quite hard in order to hear the pitch in the very bottom of the instrument. In fact, most conductors haven't the slightest idea of what pitch you're playing: you can play absolutely anything within half an octave and it sounds about the same to most conductors. It's a novelty instrument in many respects, but depending upon the way it's used in the orchestra, it can be really quite effective. The Brahms symphonies and Mahler, for example, have many large quasi solo parts for a contrabassoon."

Then there were the living conditions in New York. It is the usual story: people don't live in New York—they subsist. When Burl Lane moved to New York, he moved into a public housing project at 125th Street and Broadway some five blocks north of the Juilliard School. "It was quite inexpensive—$39 a month for a two-bedroom apartment." He and his family lived there until the summer of 1964, when the summertime riots and the random killing of people began. That was one of the summers that he was attending the Aspen Festival and playing in the Aspen Festival Orchestra in Colorado. "During an evening newscast on television, we saw a large riot in progress and squads of patrolmen firing at an apartment building. It turned out to be our apartment building. So the first thing we did when we returned to New York was to move. We moved across the river into New Jersey. I had to commute across the George Washington Bridge."

A year later, he had a chance to audition for a job in the Chicago Symphony. It was the result of all his trials with the contrabassoon. "It was a job basically for the contrabassoon. It is rather rare to find people that really play it," he says. Some forty persons showed up for the audition and he was the winner. He would have to play the bassoon also in the symphony, and he thinks his studies at Juilliard on the bassoon and contrabassoon won him the job.

Lane remembers cutting his ties in New York, in particular with the American Symphony Orchestra under Leopold Stokowski. For Stokowski was still one of his great heroes. "He has changed, mellowed considerably, of course, but for me . . . one of the greatest thrills I've ever had, knowing that there was a conductor named

Stokowski since I was very young—even though we lived in a quite primitive area as far as culture was concerned—was to wind up playing associate principal bassoon under Leopold Stokowski in New York City. That's possibly one of the biggest thrills I've ever had. . . . I'm just very thankful that I had the opportunity to work under that man—an absolute genius, in my estimation, in all musical respects." He feels that he learned a great deal in the American Symphony Orchestra. "The extent of my experience with symphonic orchestra playing was, for all purposes, nonexistent. I was learning on the job."

To go to Chicago for the auditions, he had to ask Stokowski's permission to skip a couple of rehearsals of the American Symphony Orchestra. He armed himself with every logical argument—"a wonderful opportunity . . . "How much I wanted the job"—and Stokowski simply looked him in the eye, without saying a word. When Burl Lane was finally done, he asked only one question: "How many wives do you have?" The answer was clear: he was married to a woman, not a symphony orchestra. So he went west and got the job.

There were several shocks associated with it. One was the pay: he thought it was more than anything he might have expected: "I had an income that I actually had to pay income tax on," he says—after years of having subsisted below tax level.

He also found the problems of Orchestra Hall taxing in their own right. For his instruments, the lack of humidity in the hall tends to dry out the reeds that he uses. "For this little piece of equipment"—the reed—"to function properly, there must be the right balance of moisture in the wood itself," he says. "Obviously you're blowing through this wood all the time, which tends to dry it out. And when you're playing in a hall where the humidity is often near to 5 or 10 percent, it's like playing in the middle of the Sahara Desert. When the cane dries out, then the reed tends to quit vibrating, and of course that's quite serious when you're depending on these vibrations to produce your sound. It has a detrimental effect on all of the instruments, including the strings. All of our string players use little humidifiers of sorts that they soak in water; they look like pieces of rope that they've soaked in water and placed in their cases so that when they leave their instrument in Orchestra Hall, there will be humidity in the thing. It is entirely possible that an instrument might come entirely unglued."

The bassoon and contrabassoon have problems of dryness that go beyond the reed. "We have to keep machine oil on our mechanisms about once a week because the oil evaporates at that rate. Also the dry air simply does not conduct sound waves as efficiently as a more properly balanced environment should."

Burl Lane has been playing in the Chicago Symphony since 1965. He learned fast—not only the repertory but the routine. "When I came to the orchestra, I didn't reveal to a living soul for two years that I played the saxophone or anything else because of the disdain which symphony musicians have for commercial doubling musicians. Because as a rule, doubling musicians play an instrument just well enough to get by."

But he admits now that he plays the sax. In fact, he plays it for commercials and jingles in Chicago, along with the flute and the clarinet. But now the orchestra has started to ask him to play the saxophone on some of the concert hall works that it tackles—"*Pictures at an Exhibition,* for example. And we're going to do the Rachmaninoff *Symphonic Dances,*" he says.

He has also bought a home in Chicago. He bought four of them, as a matter of fact. Consecutively, not concurrently. He went to Northwestern University night school and took a course in real estate law and decided to deal—on the side—in real estate. He buys a house, rents it for a while, then sells it at a profit. It's the pull toward the prosperous world outside the symphony. "From an investment standpoint," he says, "one can hardly do better than buy a house and rent it out and let somebody else pay for it for you. At the same time, you derive the same that the large real estate investors enjoy, in terms of depreciation and tax benefits."

He's just fascinated by finance and real estate and by the details of the deals that develop out of them. On the plane, somebody tore out the first page of an article in the airline magazine and handed it to him. It was nonverbal sarcasm. The article was about "Twentieth-century's horn of plenty . . . Investing in franchises." In fact, the bottom had already dropped out of many franchising deals, and Burl Lane and his family were among those who'd taken a bath in franchising deals.

That was a continuing problem, now more remote than other problems. For the plane had gone out to the runway, parked, and come back. The pilot got on the public address system to say something about shifting baggage because the plane was tail-heavy. "Just take off the golf clubs and leave 'em," cried out one player. Lane glanced uneasily out the window: they *were* taking off the golf clubs. He watched until he could see that they were restoring all the clubs in a forward cargo hatch.

The plane was half an hour late in taking off. This annoyed Koss and some of the other players who had hoped to get into New York before the traffic jams developed. As it happened, the buses were waiting on the tarmac at Kennedy —and they continued to wait as they inched slowly to New York through the late afternoon traffic jam. On the way, Vladimir Kalina, a bass player, avoided glancing out the bus windows. He had first come to New York in 1925, when he was a member of the Cincinnati Symphony, under Fritz Reiner. He didn't like New York then and he doesn't like New York now. He had no exotic plans for the stay in New York. He's past that stage. He's seventy-three years old and he's played bass in the Chicago Symphony for thirty-six years. His musical start was, as always, atypical. His father had a tavern on the west side of Chicago—this was before World War I—and "he had a player piano that worked for a nickel. On Saturday night I'd play the fiddle while the piano played." He shrugged. "It kept the nickels going into the piano." But now he'd had an operation on one eye and figured he'd have to have an operation on the other. But he was still hale and vigorous—he cut the lawn and shoveled the snow around his home—and only rarely did his mind wander into the future. When the work stoppage took place, for example, he laid out a deliberate program of keeping himself busy, perhaps around the house more than in music. "I kept trying to remember, 'This is how retirement feels.' "

There's always something that gets fouled up on every tour. The delay of the plane and the subsequent immersion—almost disappearance—in the New York

Bassoons (from left): Burl Lane, John Raitt, Wilbur Simpson, Willard Elliot, principal bassoonist. Lower right: Clark Brody, principal clarinetist. Violas (top center): Sheppard Lehnhoff (left) and Samuel Feinzimer.

traffic jams were only the openers. The worst was yet to come. For as the players got out of the bus and went into the New York Sheraton Hotel—diagonally across the street from Carnegie Hall—the word went through the lobby: "They don't have the rooms."

It was true. Reservations made months in advance and the hotel didn't have any rooms. Some 110 persons—105 players and a few hangers-on—descend on the New York Sheraton late in the afternoon and the hotel says they're filled up.

"Three people from management in the hotel since Monday," muttered Don Koss, and "none of them thought to check the room reservations."

Said John Edwards: "The morning of the arrival they had been called and they guaranteed there would be no problem."

With more than fivescore people storming around in a state just less than rage, the management made a search. There *were* some rooms but not enough to accommodate the whole orchestra. The hotel would book only those players who took double rooms. This is a matter of personal preference as well as money. The players pay for their own meals and hotel rooms while on tour (though the orchestra supplies the planes and buses). To be sure, the Orchestral Association pays a per diem rate to the players for their expenses on the tour. This season it would be $38 a day in the major cities. That sum is broken down into $16 for hotel rooms, $14 for food, and $8 for miscellaneous items. Now there is virtually no chance to get a hotel room for $16 in New York, but the New York Sheraton—as do many other hotels—would offer a special rate to the Chicago Symphony. Usually a single room would cost $16 to $20, a double room around $35. Naturally the hotel wanted to sell only doubles—not only to accommodate as many players as possible but to generate as much income as possible from the rooms they'd held back.

Many players had already agreed to double up. Now many others made instant deals in the lobby to share rooms. But still there weren't enough to go around. And some of the principals, who enjoy a greater income than the *tutti*, prefer to have single rooms: they can afford them and they like a certain solitude when they are preparing for a concert-on-tour. So it became a matter of finding other hotels that would take the overflow.

That wasn't easy. Earlier the same day, the Boston Symphony Orchestra had landed in New York and gone to the New York Sheraton and discovered that its reservations had not been made. (The Boston was scheduled to play in Lincoln Center; that location was shifted to Hunter College because the striking players from the New York Philharmonic were picketing Lincoln Center.) So the Boston had enterprisingly gone out and gotten many of the rooms that were available. Beyond that, the Leningrad Symphony had also come to New York that day and it had, logically, occupied many of the rooms in hotels close to Carnegie Hall. The Sheraton people wanted to help but, they said, all their other hotels in New York were also booked solidly. The trick was not only finding a hotel with rooms but one with the special low rates that the Chicago Symphony was guaranteed. So players like Don Koss and Radi Lah and Bud Herseth were left adrift—until word came that the Royal Manhattan Hotel would provide a few rooms.

The Royal Manhattan was a recently refurbished hotel but all of the refurbishing had gone into the lobby. Thus it was a Janus among hotels. The lobby was sleek and chrome and enormously exciting: the Royal Manhattan books a lot of tours from overseas and its clientele is a potpourri of Europeans visiting the United States. Jim Gilbertsen, a trombone player in his early thirties—an engaging man who is the orchestra's current barefoot-boy-without-cheek—had barely walked into the lobby before he'd gotten into a deep and prospective conversation with a Russian girl. ("She was a model, on 'To Tell the Truth.' She was telling me how plastic and phony that show business world is.") But the rooms themselves were out of the 1930s. The water pipes groaned when one turned on a faucet; the electrical lines snaked along the baseboard and around the doors; the windows looked out onto blank walls; the street was peppered with erotica. Nearby Times Square is more faithful a cultural center than most New Yorkers dare to believe—just a tiny slice barely visible around the sharpened angles of the view.

But it was only going to be for one night. The next day, all the players would check out and fly to Connecticut for a concert in Storrs. Moreover, it had the right rates, even if it was in the wrong location. The location was to provide a problem. Until now, both players and management had expected that the musicians could have an early dinner, a little rest, and then walk out of their hotel and stroll across the street to the stage entrance of Carnegie Hall whenever they chose. But now, dinner would be rushed. There would be no time for rest. And not all the players scattered around in different hotels could walk to Carnegie Hall: the Royal Manhattan is about a mile from the concert hall. So then management had to find buses to pick up the players and take them to Carnegie Hall. And they had to have buses come in shifts: some players like to get to the hall very early, others are content to be there an hour or forty-five minutes early.

It was all done. In fact, John Edwards himself was waiting to help the players on the bus. "The players," he said softly, "picked the Sheraton. We didn't." The mistake was not one of overbooking. John Edwards believes it was because of fewer checkouts than anticipated, but hotel employees told me that the hotel had reserved the entire block of rooms for Thursday instead of Wednesday.

The seven o'clock bus was virtually deserted. There were no more than a half-dozen players on it. As it ground into gear, some of them began talking about the wear and tear on Manhattan buses and on transmissions in general. That got Jim Gilbertsen to talking about "how they change the pitch of the blades inside the torque converter. Some models have a variable torque so you can get the most efficiency out of an engine. Because each engine has a torque curve and is probably more efficient at higher RPMs, which you don't often get in driving here. . . ."

The conversation was indicative of the unexpected scope of the players in the Chicago Symphony Orchestra. Grover Schiltz, the oboe and English horn player, raises dachshunds, collects oriental rugs, collects porcelain, has become an expert on wines—some say the finest in the orchestra—and collects bottle- and can-openers. Fred Spector, the violinist, collects violin mutes—he has thousands of them—beer mugs and steins, stained-glass windows, and guns (he has a pistol range in the basement of his home). Dick Graef has one of the most esoteric of hobbies: he collects carnival glass ("got that piece for $96, worth at least $200 today"). Gordon Peters collects precious amber glass: he also collects everything from old belt buckles—"this is a Coca-Cola nude from the last century"—to antiques, from sleigh bells to Vanity Fair prints. But Jim Gilbertsen is even more remarkable because his passions are almost totally scientific and technological, not aesthetic.

He studied engineering, as a matter of fact. He came out of a small town —Janesville, Wisconsin—and he went to the state university on a scholarship to major in electrical engineering. There were, to be sure, a few contradictions in this. He'd gotten the scholarship through the summer music program of the University of Wisconsin, for he seemed to be a "natural" as a trombonist. "I was very fortunate in that I had straight teeth. That is a very important consideration, although there are many fine trombonists who do not have straight teeth. The lucky thing it meant for me was that I was able to have a center embouchure right from the beginning." Even as he studied engineering, he played at music—in jazz groups, in classical ensembles for wind as well as for wind and brass. "Frankly, I didn't like sitting in a drawing board and drafting course," he says. Eventually he could see that "I wasn't doing academically what I should be doing. I was spending too much time sneaking out of chemistry to go play in the wind ensemble or the brass ensemble or the jazz workshop." So he switched to a music major and eventually worked out an almost celestial schedule: he'd go to Florida and play in the Florida Symphony—then under Henry Mazer—in the winter quarter, and he'd spend the fall and spring quarters at the Northwestern Music School. "Fun in the sun and practicing. It was really a super time. God, I really loved it." He did it for five years, until he got his master's degree from Northwestern. He'd be doing it today if it hadn't been apparent he could play on the level of the major symphony orchestras. He tried out for the Chicago Symphony at twenty-four and just missed. He tried out for first trombone at the Philadelphia Orchestra and finished third behind two of the more renowned orchestral trombone players in the country. One of them had to turn down the job; the other came from the Chicago Symphony. "So then I knew that Chicago was open and I auditioned and I got it."

He was twenty-seven at the time. But in all this time, he'd never quite given up his interest in the technological and scientific world. "I even enjoy chemistry now," he says. Not only does he grind telescope lenses but he feels that building electron microscopes is easy. "It is something you can make yourself, using available parts. You form a vacuum in a tube and you have a hot cathode that emits electrons. And then you have focusing magnets and your 'objective piece.' And then the electrons are focused on photographic papers, and you develop the film or paper and you get a picture of your specimen. It is fascinating."

Gilbertsen's interests are many and varied. He makes stained-glass windows in his apartment ("Very primitive, simple designs; I take small sections and solder them up") and steam engines in the basement ("I got some casting the last time we were in England"). He's making a sound level meter in his spare time ("it'll give me a sixty-decibel range; most of them are for twenty-five"), and he's been known to tear apart his car and rebuild the differential ("oil all over the garage"). He's done everything from build his own linear amplifier for his hi-fi set at home to building a little two-meter radio unit—he's a ham operator—to use when he's bicycling. ("I can carry it with me when I'm cycling, have a little transmission receiver, and talk around town or maybe up to a twenty-five-mile range.") In fact, this was his preoccupation of the tour: he was sitting in his seat in the plane, doing some soldering on his ham radio unit. ("I can carry it with me on the airplane. In fact, I did most of the work while I was on the plane. I had a little portable soldering iron and I was soldering little parts. It's nice when you're on tour. You have a little bag and your equipment and all the components are in it so you can work on it when you please.")

By the time Gilbertsen and his colleagues got to Carnegie Hall, half the orchestra was getting dressed or getting onstage. Don Koss was a little of each: he was onstage testing, working on, and practicing the timpani—in a sport coat. Upstairs, in the green room—the dressing room above and behind the stage—a score of players were changing into their formal wear. The wardrobe trunks were scattered around in clusters of blue and green and orange, and the bass fiddles lay long-edge-up on the floor, looking like a row of ocean liners at dock on the waterfront. (There was one exception. Wayne Balmer ships his bass in an aluminum case, not the fiber-and-fabric case customarily used for the stringed instruments. So he can set his metal case upright—some six feet high at the top—remove the bass more easily, and then use the empty case as his own private wardrobe closet, hanging his clothes in it so that they don't get wrinkled.) The players were grumbling about the snug quarters in the changing room. Actually, it's a lot roomier than it was in the past when the New York Philharmonic used to occupy the room and leave a good deal of their equipment there. And it would become roomier in the future as a nearby room was turned into a special changing room for the bass players—and storeroom for their instruments.

Some of the players were sweating lightly. Already the day had had its sweat-inducing excitement. Radi Lah had remembered he'd left a $700 camera on a bus; he rushed out into the night to retrieve it. Somebody had left a garment bag of clothes on the charter plane; Lah retrieved *that* as a matter of course. Beyond all this, the temperatures were summerlike in New York—the peak would be around 77 degrees—and Carnegie Hall was quite warm. The players and management of the Chicago Symphony suggested to the Carnegie Hall staff that the air conditioners be turned on, preferably long before the concert, so that the instruments as well as players would have time to adjust to the coolness. But nothing had been done: "It probably cost them $25 extra to turn on the air conditioner," grumbled one Chicago Symphony man.

The concert opened on Wednesday night in heat and expectation. Even as Solti stepped onto the podium—before a single note was played—the audience broke into loud applause and cries of "Bravo! Bravo Solti!" The program was to open with Weber's overture to *Oberon* and to close with Beethoven's Third Symphony. Both had been the focus of intense work the week before during the recording sessions. Sandwiched in between was Henze's *Heliogabalus Imperator*. The orchestra had played it a year or so earlier in Chicago but had spent considerable rehearsal time in the last week working over it. (One player said, "I've played some very strange sounds in the last few days, they were all by Henze.")

Two of the three numbers aroused pronounced reactions in the audience. One was, curiously, touched off by the way that Solti conducted Beethoven's Third Symphony. He conducted the second movement—the funeral march—slowly. Some players thought it was the slowest they'd ever heard it played. But Solti has the reputation for playing as he lives: brisk, even brusque. Indeed, he's been criticized by some for conducting the orchestra too fast and thus submerging the details of the repertory in its very movement. Now the pace of the second movement was quite slow.

Suddenly, somebody in the left rear of the main floor stood up and yelled, "Solti! Do better! Go faster, Solti! Finish!"

The orchestra didn't falter but a buzz went up in the audience until finally the vocalist was hustled out by ushers.

That was the most dramatic reaction of the night, but it wasn't the deepest or most controversial one.

For the playing of Henze's *Heliogabalus* aroused an antagonistic reaction. The first sound in the hall after the close was applause. Then boos began building —and building. The New York audience did not come to Carnegie Hall to hear Henze—they wanted Wagner and Mahler and Bruckner and Berlioz. Henze offers all kinds of strange sounds—birds and crickets, tom-toms and Japanese temple bells among them—and difficult rhythms. Henze is twentieth-century in tone, though not extremely so. ("I think it is not avant-garde," says Solti. "It is within the normal progressive line of music. There are much more crazy pieces written.") But the Chicago Symphony Orchestra has not heard boos in Carnegie Hall in many seasons and some of the players were taken aback. ("Why do we play this trash?" asked one principal the next day concerning the Henze.) Eventually the boos settled and the applause swelled again and Solti brought Henze onstage to take a personal bow.

Solti's personal response to the boos was not despairing. "I think this is good as I think this creates a lively interest," he says. "I did not know why the people got so excited. Probably it is that we have here an audience which is very conservatively oriented, a kind of anti-Philharmonic audience. Don't want to hear from me, probably, Henze. They want to hear from me—it was probably a reaction, 'Please don't play that, we want to hear from you nineteenth century. . . . But I enjoy it. I always enjoy it tremendously in Carnegie Hall."

He was more deeply concerned with the work itself rather than the response to the work. "It is fiendishly difficult conducting the piece," he says. "It is the most difficult piece that perhaps I have ever conducted. Fiendishly difficult. And only that sort of orchestra as my children can play it. Not very carefully played, the piece is just falling apart. Very, very difficult. There are rhythmical problems. Very serious problems, but in the first ten minutes. After that it is easier, but the first ten minutes are among the most hair-raising rhythmical problems. I am changing quick, quick bars, changing all the time, in a split second, and once you are out, you are not coming in anymore so it is a question of staying alive, don't make mistakes."

In their various ways, the critics seemed to agree with Solti.

"It's the kind of a piece that will probably disappear," wrote Speight Jenkins in the *New York Post*, "but it should be heard several times before a final verdict is given."

"This is not a piece that any orchestra can play," wrote Harold C. Schonberg in *The New York Times*. "It demands tremendous virtuosity and it needs a conductor who can handle the wildest melange of sound and the most complicated rhythms. Needless to say, Sir Georg and his players were always on top of their notes. The performance had sweep and assurance, polish and power."

The interesting thing about the reviews was that they were not the unrestrained raves that usually follow the Chicago Symphony's performances in Carnegie Hall. "Solti and the Chicagoans Not Exactly a Smash" said the headline in the New York *Daily News*.

In the *New York Post*, Jenkins observed the commitment to Beethoven and observed that the first movement of the Beethoven Third Symphony "sounded wildly aggressive, a real affirmation of life. But from then on, the general heaviness of what was played and the frequent distended phrases submerged the music in a high romantic sound not persuasive either as Beethoven or as a taut symphony composition."

Schonberg was notable for his probative neutrality. About the *Eroica*, he commented: "Sir Georg had his own ideas about the music. In the fugato of the 'Funeral March, for instance, he had the bass moving in slow but giant strides, and he voiced every entrance in the manner of a strict Bachian fugue. Nothing was taken for granted, and the interpretation had passion as well as control. In a way, it was a Klemperer-like performance, square in the Central European tradition. As Sir Georg went along, he convinced many there was no other way."

In the aftermath of the first concert, the players broke up and many went to eat. Burl Lane went out to have some cheesecake. "With what it takes to play that contrabassoon," said Don Koss, "if he ate dinner beforehand, it would be all over the walls before the night was over." Solti paused in the foyer to his dressing room, tieless, with a scotch and water in front of him, accepting—with evident embarrassment at the rapturous greetings—the congratulations of friends and admirers. Later he, too, would go out to a dinner arranged for him by Terry McEwen of London/Decca records, but just after midnight he would thank everybody very kindly and, with Lady Valerie, slip quietly away. To get his rest.

He'd have to be up early to make the trip to Connecticut. But nobody would have to be up quite as early as David Harvey, the assistant general manager. He was going to make sure that the hotel problems in Connecticut didn't develop as they had in New York. So he was up and on a 7:30 A.M. flight to the next stop on the tour.

There is something notable almost every time the Chicago Symphony Orchestra hits a college town.

Mostly it is financial: the fee for the orchestra for one night is $17,500. Interestingly, college communities are more than willing to come up with the fee—perhaps because the community has a cultural orientation—and Solti is more than willing to play for them: he feels it's a chance to exchange an interest with young people in traditional music of the classics.

Sometimes it's notable for its boyishness. One time when the orchestra was playing in a small college town in Michigan, Burl Lane and some of the other golf nuts were practicing their putts in the corridors when somebody bet Lane that he couldn't hit the door of Maestro Martinon's suite with a sixty-foot putt. "It was good on accuracy, long on distance," he says. "The ball hit the door with a very sharp smack." The smartness of the sound was like the signal of a conductor. "It was like little kids running—everybody was getting back into their rooms," says Lane with a laugh, "before Martinon came to the door."

Sometimes it's the unexpected: the Chicago Symphony produced a slow-moving streaker in Princeton the season before. The reason was the disgust of the players at the accommodations. The concert was to be played in the field house, explains one of the players, and there seemed to be no room for the wardrobe trunks and the 105 players or so to change their clothes. So the trunks were dumped on the main floor of the field house and and the players discovered, by searching for the alternatives, that there was no place else for them to change clothes. And so they changed right there, in full view of the early-comers. "I mean, it's not every day you get a chance to see the Chicago Symphony Orchestra undress in public," recalls one player. By way of making his comment on this, Richard Oldberg, the horn player, took off *all* his clothes and marched naked around the floor of the field house for a while—anticipating the "streaking" fad of the future—and giving the local folks a show before donning his formal wear.

In this case, the trip to Connecticut gave the musicians a good many options. Some of them stayed in Connecticut for a while: others drove back to Manhattan on Thursday night after the concert; most took the bus back to New York in midday Friday.

Bob Swan, a viola player, didn't come back right away. He went to visit relatives in the area—he'd long lived around here—and to give them their Christmas presents. His idea of relaxation is to wander the woods of the land north of New York City, doing a little fishing—in season—and hunting—in season. "My heart is in the wilds," he says. "If the Chicago Symphony Orchestra was playing in Butte, Montana, I'd be happy."

Frank Miller, the cellist, flew home on Friday morning. He would conduct the Evanston Symphony in one of its regular concerts on Friday night. Then he'd board a plane Saturday and fly back to New York to join the Chicago Symphony.

Gordon Peters, the principal percussionist, also would fly home on Friday. He would conduct a concert of the Chicago Civic Orchestra on Friday and then fly back to New York to join the Chicago Symphony.

Burl Lane would lead the golf nuts on Friday to the Hartford Country Club. He'd shoot an 83 on a rainy, chilly, gusty day. Bud Herseth would shoot 104. Both would think it was worth it. "Golf is like therapy to me," says Lane. "Sometimes I bring the golf clubs along—even if I can't play—just to be able to take them out and fondle them."

Fred Spector, the violinist, would go back to New York. He and the other members of the Contemporary Arts would gather in one room or another—now at the Sheraton New York—to work on the scores of their upcoming recitals. Spector had found release: he went to a violin dealer in mid-Manhattan who would take custody of his violin, and lock it in a vault while Spector went touring. He went, sans violin, to see a Broadway show starring Kaye Ballard—she had been top banana in a show that he was conductor for on the national tour nineteen years earlier. He went browsing in some bookstores on 57th Street and got $110 worth of books for him and his wife. Then he had second thoughts. His wife is head of the Department of Movement—of dance—at the Goodman Theatre in Chicago and he'd bought the books that he knew she wanted. But now he wondered if she wanted them that much—"$100 for books!" Even for Fred Spector, that's a little much for impulse buying.

Georg Solti went back to Manhattan. He had to resolve a problem because Thomas Schippers had to cancel his guest appearance with the Chicago Symphony because of drastic and imperative surgery. He had to find a replacement and someone—the feeling was that it was Solti's friend Terry McEwen—had suggested young John Nelson, who'd filled in for Rafael Kubelik in an emergency situation and conducted a brilliant performance of *Les Troyens*. Now he had to decide whether to hire Nelson as a replacement and how to adjust the program to the emergency.

Norman Schweikert, the horn player, went back to New York. On Saturday he would spend six hours going through the musty records in the New-York Historical Society. He'd be looking up the city directories for New York from 1883 to 1900 in an effort to trace the location and antecedents of the musicians who moved to Chicago, with Theodore Thomas, when the Chicago Symphony was started in 1891.

Arnold Jacobs, the tuba player, and Dale Clevenger, the first horn player, took out a close and mutual friend, Joe Singer. "Joe is Arnold's first cousin, so there's more than a musical relationship there," says Clevenger. "Twice a year we're together"—either dinner at Singer's or dinner out together. This time it was dinner at a French restaurant.

Willard Elliot, the principal bassoonist, headed north from Storrs, not south. He rented a car and drove north to Worcester, Massachusetts, where he began poking around "in the deeds in the courthouse." His ancestors had come from this town and he was looking now for deeds and papers that might extend the genealogy of his family.

His own history—particularly his musical history—is remarkable. For he fell in love with an instrument he'd never seen and couldn't really play. It was down in Fort Worth, Texas, where his father was working as a freight agent. His father was an opera buff. In the days after World War I, he was working on the reconstruction of French railroads and one day he happened to hear a record of *La Traviata*. That did it: "He became solidly hooked on opera." So there was music in the Elliot home all the time, and young Willard started out on the piano and then the clarinet. But he knew he was going to play the bassoon.

He had never seen one but he'd looked up pictures of the bassoon. He simply had fallen in love with the sound that he heard on the records. From the time he was seven or eight years old, he knew he was going to play the bassoon. But he couldn't even begin to play and practice it at that age. "It is not until one is about age twelve that your hands are large enough to accommodate the front holes, which are widely spaced on the bassoon."

Even then, he couldn't get a bassoon. They are expensive instruments: a first-class bassoon today would cost about $3,500. And there's a waiting list of two to three years to get them. When Willard Elliot was finally old enough to finger a bassoon, World War II had broken out and—though the United States was not yet involved in it—there was no chance to get a new bassoon out from the most prominent source: the bassoon-makers in Germany. So he was nineteen years old before he had a chance to buy one. And he was a little older before he could find a professional bassoon player to teach him.

He didn't spend these years waiting. From the time he was twelve, he played on borrowed bassoons and he studied under bandmasters and music teachers in school. It was not until he was out of college—North Texas State—and had decided to go to Eastman School of Music in Rochester to get his master's degree that he studied under a professional bassoon player. But once started, his studies and his skills proceeded apace: after Eastman, he played for three years in the Houston Symphony and for three years in the Dallas Symphony before coming to the Chicago Symphony ten years ago.

He never really stops practicing, if only because the fingering of the bassoon is so complicated. "With the bassoon, we have to use both our thumbs," points out Elliot (whereas the clarinet demands only one thumb for playing—manipulating one key—and the other thumb simply for supporting the instrument). "Our two thumbs operate more keys than the rest of the fingers put together," he explains. "For the left thumb alone, there are nine keys to be worked. The right thumb has four keys to operate."

That is only part of the problem. "I suppose that the hardest thing is to find a reed that you can play on," he says. "Especially for a student when you don't make your own reeds. You buy a reed at a store, when you've had no instruction about it. The reed either works or it doesn't work, and of course it never works like it should work and you can only experiment and then you get into a lot of bad habits, trying to make the reed work. Fooling around with reeds, and making them work, takes away from practice time—a brass player, a string player, even a flute are spending their time practicing while we are still trying to make a reed to practice on."

Elliot is a white-fringed man in his late forties, a man of very mild demeanor; his every step, his every gesture seems an exercise in humility. He is, as we've seen, a man of many hobbies—orchids, genealogy, the collecting of fossils. He has thousands of fossils, many of them hundreds of millions of years old. "I am a little bit partial to trilobites," he says. "They are very curious little animals which became extinct right around the time the dinosaurs appeared." They had a very small brain but a very large, even peculiar, asset: they could, in principle, see perfectly. It is a feat of evolution. No other animal known has developed such a perfect sense of vision. "It was once extremely numerous 400 million, 500 million years ago," says Elliot. "And then they just disappeared." He preserves the fossil specimens by coating them with clear nail polish. It must be done with extreme care, for Elliot has—from the disciplines of playing the bassoon—very strong fingers. "I'm afraid that they'd turn to dust in my fingers," he says.

It takes just as precise care to develop his reeds. For in the hands of Willard Elliot, the making of the reeds is virtually an art form. They have to be tailored to the temperature and humidity of the season. Elliot makes a different kind of reed for the hot humid summers at Ravinia than he does for the winter in Chicago. They have to be tailored to the hall. Elliot finds that Orchestra Hall is much drier, for example, than the concert hall he worked in when he was with the Houston Symphony. (It is, in fact, so dry that in busy weeks—such as those preceding the tour—he cannot control the cold sores that tend to break out on his lips.) They have to be tailored to the sound of the music. "When we are playing something of Bruckner, you need a quality of sound that is something like a French horn, a thicker quality than you would want if you were playing, for instance, a Haydn symphony, in which you'd want a lighter sound."

He makes his own reeds in a den of his home—he calls it his "torture chamber" because he must spend so many hours at exacting work in it every week. But the process actually starts in the canefields of Southern France—"the Var District between Marseilles and Nice." It is there that the cane is grown that he prefers for his reeds. It is not the only place such cane is grown: certain parts of Spain, Italy, Greece, and the United States have the same kind. ("It also grows in Texas," he says. "I grew up with it, not knowing what it was. In fact, it was growing in my grandfather's backyard in Waco. When I was a small child I used to cut stalks off it and make holes in it to make 'flutes.' It wasn't until much later that I found out it was the same thing we use for reeds." Why does he choose the French cane over that produced by other countries? "The Var District is supposed to be responsible for the superior quality of the cane," he says. "The climate, the soil, the cold, dry weather that comes down from the Alps." And, of course, in other countries, the cane is not always harvested and cured in a way to make it of maximum use to musicians.

Elliot buys it by the gunnysack-ful. "A sack about three feet high that's filled with tubes. They are a minimum of five inches long and they run about seven or eight inches long—sometimes they are long enough where you can cut them in half and get twice as many pieces of cane from them." He then chucks the gunnysack into his basement and waits. Sometimes for a year or so, sometimes for five, six, eight, or more years. "Whether it is ready to use or not depends on how well the cane is seasoned," he says. "Once in a while I get a batch of cane that I can start using right away. Usually it seems like I have to let it sit around for a few years to season." The reeds that he made for this season came out of a batch that he bought in 1971 and another batch that he bought in 1964. The latter "did not work right away but after about five or six years, it began working."

How can he tell when the cane is ready for work?

"The cane becomes much harder as it seasons. Very often the reeds do not work simply because the cane is too soft, or maybe a little green," he says. "Then there might have been a little too much tension in the cane and with additional seasoning, the cane shrinks and the tension is less."

To develop a reed out of the cane is a long and tedious process. Willard Elliot figures he invests a minimum of two hours on each reed, but not all at one time. For there are several different processes in making a reed—cutting the cane, gouging it, shaping the reed, then shaving it to the proper dimensions. What he does is take a batch of cane and, at one sitting, cut it into fifty or sixty pieces and start gouging them all. He does this "mostly in the summer because it is a very tedious, time-consuming process. But it's good for the muscles of the hand"—which is, of course, important in the playing of the bassoon. He usually brings each batch of cane to being "blank" or unfinished reeds. He's able to get this far only because he has air conditioning in his home. If he didn't, the "summer-made" reeds would change dramatically as the temperature and humidity begin falling in the autumn and winter.

He's already studied the program and much of the scores of the upcoming season so that he knows what general shape of reed he'll need for different works. "I use a wider reed for Bruckner, one that gives a thicker sound," he says. "It depends also on the instrumentation. In many of the Beethoven symphonies, for example, we need a very dark 'covered' sound but capable of a wide dynamic range. For Tchaikovsky, I like to have a fairly thick sound because of the nature of the writing of Tchaikovsky, especially when we are doing his Sixth Symphony, the *Pathétique*, which is so somber at the beginning. And also it depends on the range of writing for the bassoon because playing in the high register for the Stravinsky *Rite of Spring* will take a different kind of reed than playing the Tchaikovsky Sixth Symphony, or *Pathétique*.

He does not, at this stage, try to force the reed into a particular pattern. "I don't try to predetermine what the reed is going to be," he says, "because I think the cane dictates more what the reed is going to be than what you do with it. So in making up a lot of reeds, I make up a lot of blanks in different shapes. The different shapes will have different tendencies so I will start working with those shapes in regard to what is coming up, and then the cane will tell me what it is going to do—whether it is going to be deficient in the high register. And if it is, I try not to go too much against the natural tendencies of the cane because very often you will ruin the reed completely by trying to put something into it, something that is not there. Either that happens or you go so slowly on the reed that you never get it to work. This is something one of my teachers taught me, that it is a waste of time to piddle around with a reed for fear of ruining the sound, because the sound is in the cane. Go ahead and get that reed to working, take the wood off, and get it to vibrating. And if the sound is not good, you haven't wasted that much time. Just go on to another one."

Elliot spends his weekends doing the shaving and testing of the many reeds he's gotten to the "blank" stage. He may turn out a half-dozen reeds for one program:

he usually goes onstage with two or three times that number in a "ready reserve." On occasion, the weather will make obsolete all the reeds that he has in reserve. And then bring them back to life again. "I have a couple dozen reeds that were working at the start of the season that won't work now," he says—because he brought them to their final state when the early autumn weather was warm and sunny and then it had turned bitterly cold. "I have lots of reeds that were brand-new, were working beautifully, they are all ready to go—and then none of them work." They could be used this week in New York, however, simply because the weather was unusually warm and humid.

That's one of the reasons he never throws a reed away. "I have a whole shoe box full of them," he says. Normally a reed will last him as long as two weeks but he's gone through that shoe box and found five-year-old reeds that will serve to solve a special problem. One example was a reed that he'd used for very, very pianissimo low-register playing on pieces in the late 1960s. But he got it out, tested it, and found that it had a particular kind of life. "It would make a good special reed for something like the ending of the Tchaikovsky Fifth Symphony, in which you need a very, very low soft B to blend in with the double bass at the very end of the movement. Usually I need a special reed for that because the normal reed that will sing out on all the nice solos will be just too much sound for that final note—to fade it out. In the past, conductors used to cut that note out entirely from the bassoon and just divide the basses and have some of the basses play that note. But that was in the days before so much was expected of the bassoon. In some of the very old parts we come across from time to time this part is marked out. But that is never done anymore."

Not all reeds serve so special a function. Quite often Elliot must work on the reed so that it can serve a broad number of functions—the very function that the music demands.

For this tour week, for example, he'd been hoarding a particular reed to play during Beethoven's Third Symphony, the *Eroica*, in Carnegie Hall. He thought it was finished "but somehow it came back and I used it on our recording sessions for the Beethoven symphonies. Then I put the reed aside and saved it because I was going to use it for the Carnegie Hall performance." He did not use it in rehearsal, he did not use it in the Youth Concerts, he did not use it in the programs of the Mahler Sixth Symphony. ("I used another reed for that because the requirements for the Mahler Sixth are not quite so great.") The reasons he treasured this reed are embedded in the demands of the *Eroica* on the principal bassoon player.

"You just have a lot more solos to play in the *Eroica*, a lot more delicate playing. A lot more continuous, sustained, exposed playing plus a wider ranger of styles.

"In the second movement, you need a real singing reed which you can blow out on and sound just spills out. In the first movement and in the third movement you need one that has a light, crisp, staccato capability. Plus it has to have at the same time a very smooth legato for the trio of the scherzo, and in the last movement your lips start getting tired so the reed must not be too resistant—it must not take too much muscle with the lip to control. And when you get towards the end of the symphony, when the reed itself is most tired, then the most delicate part of all comes in—a little half-staccato passage with the flute—where it has to get so very soft at the end. Some very difficult notes to cover the sound on. So for this reason, you need to be very particular about the kind of reed you use on the *Eroica*.

"Now on the Mahler Sixth, which is much heavier, much louder. There are just a few, few little spots where you have to get so delicate. And it is not as difficult to get delicate on some short passages, as, say, in very long ones and with much more continuous playing, such as you have in Beethoven's *Eroica*. Beethoven is much more taxing to play with a bassoon than Mahler. Mahler gives enough rest to the bassoon player. But with Beethoven, and with Brahms, it is just a matter of continuous playing. Either you are playing solos or you're playing harmonies or you're playing bass lines or something. Always very, very continous and very often quite exposed. Plus you have to play soft enough to blend in when you're playing the harmonies."

No matter how scrupulously he prepares, Elliot can never design a reed ahead of time that will serve all his needs. "You can't select a reed far ahead because the reeds won't stay the same." It took him time to learn this. "I would select a reed and save it, thinking 'This is the perfect *Rite of Spring* reed.' And then when the time came, it did not work at all. In fact, some years ago, when we recorded the *Rite of Spring* with Ozawa, the reed I selected only two weeks ahead for the recording did not work when the time came. So the reed that I used was the reed I had played the *Rite of Spring* on a couple of summers before under Lukas Foss at Ravinia. And which did not work on anything after that. But just out of curiosity I got it out and it worked good."

It is not just the reed that governs the sound; another factor-of-wood is involved with the instrument itself. Willard Elliot has two instruments. One was made in the 1930s—though he didn't acquire it until after World War II—and another was made in the early 1950s. ("I got it in 1956.") Of the older bassoon, he says, "the wood has shrunk and there's a natural tendency of a woodwind instrument when it is played for a long time—the wood becomes thinner, the sound becomes lighter. Fortunately, in the case of a bassoon, they do not wear out, like oboes or clarinets do. An oboe or a clarinet will wear out in just a few years because they have such a strong tendency towards cracking, but the bassoon being made of maple, does not crack nearly as easily. And because of the lining that the manufacturer puts in the crucial parts of the instrument, the bore does not change through many many years. So we can keep playing our bassoons for literally a lifetime. Which is fortunate because of the price that bassoons are now."

The trouble is the time gap between deciding to get a new bassoon and actually getting it into operation in the orchestra. It may be two or three years. Part of the time is devoted to waiting—just to getting a new instrument. "And when you do get a new bassoon, it is not in playable condition," says Willard Elliot. "It has to be gone over—retuned, readjusted, and so forth. Partly because of the climate in Germany compared to here. They do not have the extremes that we have here. Partly because we use a little different type of reed. Partly because the pitch of the orchestra is a little differrent. And partly because we require more of our instruments."

The Eastern Tour

It is intriguing that the bassoon section of the Chicago Symphony has the extrovert in Burl Lane and the introvert in Willard Elliot. Elliot, for example, is one of those rare principals who has no ambition to conduct. He's tried conducting, largely in rehearsals for opera workshops that he's engaged in. "But it was always very frustrating to me to be waving my arms around and not be able to produce the music myself," he says. "I would much rather be playing my bassoon." He would, in fact, much prefer to spend his time composing. His *Elegy for Orchestra* was a co-winner of the Koussevitzky Foundation award in 1961, and he's had a concerto for bassoon played at Ravinia and a trio for oboe, clarinet, and bassoon played in the chamber music series of the Chicago Symphony Orchestra. "Unfortunately, I have not really had time recently—my composing in the past was always done during the off-season and now there is not much of any off-season." —particularly since he has to spend so much time gouging out cane, making blank reeds, and preparing his work for the future. That's why pursuing his family's genealogy in the archives of Worcester, Massachusetts, was—on this day in November—something of a lark for him.

This is one of the reasons that a tour—no matter how hard the schedule—seems like a vacation to some players. It's not just a change of scene and a change of audience —both stimulating to many musicians—but a release from the harsh disciplines of their work.

Willard Elliot, principal bassoonist.

Clark Brody, principal clarinetist.

Clark Brody, the principal clarinet player, had the time to go and see friends in New York City—he'd worked there for ten years, most of it with the CBS Symphony Orchestra. But it might have been the same anywhere, as long as he could get free of the tyranny of the reeds.

"I spend an hour and a half a day, maybe ten hours a week, on the reeds," says Brody. He doesn't have quite the problems of the oboe and the bassoon; the clarinet uses only a single reed while the other two instruments use double reeds. Moreover, Brody doesn't take the time to develop his reeds from the original cane. Not this season, he didn't. Instead, he bought blanks—reed forms that had the general outline of the reed—and he'd shape and shave them. And still it takes ninety minutes out of his day, every day. He's tried developing them from the original cane in the past—"I go from one to the other depending on what seems to work best at the time," he says.

He doesn't need as many reeds as does Willard Elliot. He can get by with one or two "actives"—"you always narrow it down to your best one or two reeds, and those are the ones that you play. Of course, sometimes you will take a lesser reed in rehearsal so you don't wear out your number one reed too soon."

A change in weather, of course, can affect the reed. But it is as likely to affect the entire instrument. The reason is that the wood expands and contracts at a different rate—under weather changes—than do the metal keys. In hot weather, he says, "a key sticks or binds and it has to be adjusted. In very cold weather, the wood shrinks and the metal ring at the top of a joint will come loose and *that* has to be adjusted." But these are minor problems compared to the endless demands for making reeds.

There is another type of player within the orchestra whose work does not ease, even on tour. These are the men who are, or wish to be, conductors. In this week, Frank Miller flew back to Chicago on Friday to conduct a performance of the Evanston Symphony Orchestra. Gordon Peters also flew back to conduct a rehearsal of the Chicago Civic Orchestra. Even if they didn't have performances scheduled they'd have to be spending their free time studying scores and perhaps marking them—amateurs and students do not have the savvy for marking scores that experienced symphonic musicians do.

Perhaps the most ambitious—and Herculean—schedule in this respect was undertaken a few years ago by Milton Preves, the principal violist. There was a time when he was conducting not just one . . . or two . . . or three symphony orchestras; he was conducting four of them while playing a principal part in a fifth.

Today he conducts only the North Side Symphony Orchestra. He's done it for twenty-six years. But in the past he also conducted symphony orchestras in Oak Park, a near west suburb, and in Wheaton, a far west suburb, and in Gary, Indiana, beyond the suburban line into the steel country of northern Indiana.

It was an astonishing effort that had him working seven nights a week. He'd play with the Chicago Symphony on at least two nights a week in Chicago; he'd also play with the symphony one night a week in Milwaukee. And on the other four nights each week he'd rehearse or conduct a different symphony orchestra.

It takes a certain dedication, and ingenuity, to stay with symphony orchestras that represent small communities. For the lessons of the great symphony orchestra are not always applicable to the community symphony orchestra.

"The real personnel headache in directing an amateur group is personality clashes," he says. "You have to be a Solomon to deal with section seating and the friction that comes out of that. They come to you saying, 'I play better than that guy, so why do I have to sit behind him?' So you better have an answer."

There is also a difference in programs. It is not simply what the players in the community orchestra can play; it is what they want to play. "I like to have a novelty on each program," says Preves. "But most of the members are cool to twentieth-century music. They find it difficult and unrewarding. But there are also problems with Haydn and Mozart because their orchestration does not provide opportunities for everyone to play. So we end up offering a lot of twentieth-century works."

There is another problem that Preves encountered in the early 1960s: music as a sociopolitical problem. He was, at the time, conducting the Oak Park/River Forest Symphony Orchestra and he made the classic move: he hired a soloist for her musical skills. It turned out that she was black and the good people of Oak Park and River Forest were not about to have *that* kind of talent unloaded on them. They knew what black talent would mean to the future of the suburb: some black people might actually want to *live* in Oak Park or River Forest. Preves refused to fire the soloist, cancel the performance, or change the program. "So there was quite a hassle in Oak Park. It really blew up."

It ended with the soloist performing as Preves knew she would.

It ended with his post-concert resignation as conductor of the Oak Park/River Forest Symphony.

It ended with the city officials in Oak Park adopting a nondiscrimination clause for the future.

So he won the battle though he lost the job.

Since then, he's moderated his conducting schedule—but not his busyness. For he not only conducts the North Side Symphony and plays in the Chicago Symphony, but he also plays in the North Shore piano quartet and the Chicago Symphony string quartet. In fact, on these days in New York, he would get together with the other members of the Chicago Symphony quartet and—even though Frank Miller was back in Chicago on *his* conducting assignment—they would practice in their hotel rooms.

Perhaps nobody in this genre—of the part-time conductors, full-time players—was busier this week than Gordon Peters, a conductor in three different orchestras, the administrator of the Chicago Civic Orchestra, and the principal percussionist in the Chicago Symphony. For one function he had to be in Chicago, conducting the rehearsal of the Chicago Civic Orchestra. For the other he had to be onstage in New York, Washington, and Storrs, Connecticut, to play some of the most arduous and important works of the season for the percussion—Mahler's Sixth Symphony and Henze's *Heliogabalus*. And to do the nonvisible work on each stage that is so vital a part of playing an important work.

Much of that work is simply arranging the instruments. For the percussion section has responsibility for a great variety of sounds and of instruments—gong, chimes, marimba, tambourine, tom-toms, cymbals, celesta, triangle, the glockenspiel, the xylophone, not to mention occasional needs for cowbells, thunder sheets, wind machines, and even sirens. All this is in addition to the kettledrums, the snare drums, the bass drums, the tenor drums. In fact, the responsibilities are so various that the Chicago Symphony, like most major symphony orchestras, has one man—Don Koss—working exclusively on the kettledrum and another separate group of men working on the rest of the instruments. Sam Denov is one of them and Gordon Peters is the leader, as "principal" among them.

It is one of the important responsibilities of Peters to see that the instruments are not only played well but placed well. The playing is demanding enough; it's not just a matter of hitting a drumhead. The important part, says Peters, is controlling the color by playing so many different instruments with precisely the right stick or mallet—by knowing exactly what sound will be elicited, depending on how limber the sticks or mallets are, how well-covered, how large, how seasoned they are. And then knowing precisely how hard to hit with them. "We don't have the violinistic problems of the transition, but we have to face the volume problem," says Peters. For only the expert ear can pick out a mistake by the violins but everybody in the hall knows if the percussionist hit his instrument too hard, too late, or too soon.

The placement problem is just as important. For the percussionist just doesn't walk onstage with his instrument and sit down, as do the violins and the flutes and most of the other instruments. "The percussion—you know the instruments are large and you have to be able to get to them," says Peters. "You have the different instruments and the music stands—you've got a part on one music stand here and you've got to be able to get over and pick up the part on another instrument reading off another music stand. I mean, in percussion, it is largely a logistical and administrative thing."

What he does is as carefully orchestrated as the music itself. "I go to the library and get the music in advance," he says. He then sits down and studies the score carefully—what it needs in the way of instruments, how much time is given by the composer to get from one instrument to another ("we do get a lot of rests"). Then he looks for the subtle traps in the score; he's got not only to be able to hear the music in his ear but to see the playing of it—at least by the percussionists —onstage. "If I discover a technical problem for any of us, I forewarn the players," he says. Then he maps out everything on paper. "I make charts out for each piece"—what instrument will be here, what instrument will be there, where the players' stools will be, where the stocks and mallets will be located, where the player will stand, where the music stands will be, what the paths will be to get between the music stands and instruments so the right player arrives at the right instruments at precisely the right time. And all this must be accomplished so there is no visible sense of rush onstage, a continuous blur of movement that might distract visually from the aural impact of the music. Then it has to be done all over again for the next piece. If there's an intermission between pieces, then there's plenty of time to make the placement changes; if there's not, then everything must be designed so that the changes can be made swiftly and quietly. "Then I put the charts in the locker of each player so that they can study them and compare them with the music," says Peters.

In time, everything becomes reflexive—as long as the stage is the same. Peters knows, for instance, how best to set up his instruments in Chicago and in

Milwaukee, where the Chicago Symphony plays ten times a year. The tour demands special thought for each hall. Carnegie Hall is not a problem but the one-night stands in college towns sometimes offer problems and so do some of the new halls that are springing up around the country. Then the charts he's made for the pieces as they are to be played at home have no relevance to the new hall. "You lay it out in what you consider to be the most efficient posture, and then you get to a place where the floor plan is different and everything is up for grabs." He remembers a season or so earlier when the Chicago Symphony played the Henze *Heliogabalus* in the John F. Kennedy Center for the Performing Arts in Washington. The stage there does not have a single flat floor; it has several different levels on which the players take their positions. That introduced the problem of going up and down steps to get from one instrument to another while keeping the available pathways clear. "So you no longer had the possibility of having your instruments where you wanted them in playing the work on earlier programs," he says. The *Heliogabalus*, as we've seen, is a complicated work with many different and demanding rhythms, most of which are pronounced by percussion. And Solti has an inclination to play it briskly. "He was pushing the tempo at times," says Peters. "I can't put him down for that—it's what makes the piece a bit of a challenge." But in Washington, the challenge got a little unrealistic. "I confess to you, I missed an awful lot of my entrances that day because I simply couldn't get to my instruments," he says.

Peters always seems to move briskly, onstage and off. He is a slender man with suppressed energies. He is also highly articulate and inquiring and he has the ability to organize his work and himself most efficiently. He needs to, because he is working at writing books, teaching, composing (one of his works is the fourth most played composition for percussionists), organizing (he was first president of the Percussive Arts Society ("It started with eighteen members and now it has three thousand") and conducting three different orchestras. His conducting is in the forefront of his mind and his ambitions. He studied for many years in the summer workshop for young conductors that Pierre Monteux ran in Maine and he thinks of it in terms that are fresh, original, and untarnished. One example: "I feel there are horizontal conductors and vertical conductors and if you are one or the other you must be aware of it and try to balance it out." It is not hard, he says, to identify the horizontal or vertical conductors. The horizontal conductor is "more the legato conductor, the sonority conductor who makes beautiful smears on the canvas." In other words: a Giulini. "Then the vertical conductor is the one with the sharp stroke, the percussion, the wrist, the beat, the timing, the clarity ensemble approach." Or a Georg Solti.

The place he puts into practice his thoughts and experience about conducting is in his work with the Elmhurst Symphony Orchestra, the Youth Symphony Orchestra of Greater Chicago, and the Chicago Civic Orchestra. The Civic is, perhaps, the most demanding. He is administrator as well as co-conductor (with Margaret Hillis) of the Civic and its reponsibilities are heavy ones. For it is the training orchestra for the Chicago Symphony: it provides a platform for learning for young people who might one day become accomplished enough for the

Chicago Symphony Orchestra. It is the only training orchestra directly affiliated with a major symphony orchestra. Though it is supported out of special endowment funds, it is administered by the Orchestral Association and has its offices and holds its rehearsals and performances in Orchestra Hall (though it pays rent for the privilege). At the moment, says Peters, some 60 percent of the Chicago Symphony Orchestra is made up of players who once performed with the Chicago Civic Orchestra.

The Civic actually got its start in the hatred and prejudice fanned by the belligerent feelings of World War I. Until that time, the Chicago Symphony Orchestra got its musicians mainly from Europe—from Germany and the neighboring areas where the musical products were most closely attuned to the Teutonic sound of the Chicago Symphony. But World War I inhibited the importation of such musicians. When the United States got into the war, there was a pronounced reaction against the Germanic nature of the symphony. Indeed, conductor Frederick Stock, who had continued in the tradition of recruiting German-born personnel, was forced to take a leave of absence in 1918 because of the anti-German feeling of the time. (He'd also neglected to complete taking out his citizenship papers, though he'd been in the United States since 1895. When criticism of Stock in the press became intense, he stepped down from the podium and returned later in 1918—after getting his final naturalization papers.) That impressed on him the need for finding American-born musicians of a caliber needed for his symphony orchestra. There were plenty of musicians in those days. "Every restaurant had an orchestra or a string ensemble. You had orchestras in the pits of the theater—vaudeville and even the movie theaters—playing background music for the silent films," says Gordon Peters. There were bands for Sunday afternoons in the parks and bands for parades and schools and the military services. So there were plenty of American-born musicians—"but they couldn't play Wagner and Beethoven and Ravel and all the things of the symphonic repertoire," he says. So Stock suggested that a training orchestra be formed in which American musicians could be taught symphonic music and its needs; it would be from that orchestra that he could begin taking the musicians he'd need in the future. And so the Chicago Civic was founded in 1919. (One of the youngsters in the violin section, John Weicher, rose—as we've seen—to become concertmaster of the Chicago Symphony, conductor of the Chicago Civic, and personnel manager for the Orchestral Association). Over the years, the Civic has funneled literally hundreds of players into the Chicago Symphony Orchestra. Though Peters estimates that 60 percent of the players currently in the Chicago Symphony played originally in the Chicago Civic Orchestra, the Civic players are not required to go into the Chicago Symphony: many of them help fill symphony openings all around the world. Just in the last year or so, one product of the Civic, Lynn Marcell, left the Civic to become the principal oboe in the university symphonic orchestra of Mexico City (under Eduardo Mata), another—Tim Kent—was named principal trumpet in the orchestra of Trier, Germany, and still another —Dwight Decker—was named principal trombone in the Florida Gulf Coast Symphony in St. Petersburg/Tampa. Other Civic products of the last year went to the Rochester Philharmonic, the National Symphony Orchestra of Washington, and the Florida Symphony Orchestra in Orlando and the Tulsa Philharmonic in Oklahoma.

They are not only children in the orchestra. Only 8 of the 110 players in the Civic are sixteen or under; the median age, says Peters, is twenty-one. (On one occasion a few years ago, he says, "we had an eleven-year-old boy who was bordering on the genius. Why deprive him because of some arbitrary rule?" The youth is now studying at the Curtis Institute in Philadelphia.) There is a tendency to halt recruiting among people twenty-eight to thirty or over but exceptions are often made. One is when the applicant has been in the service and thus may qualify for late training; the other is when the orchestra needs a particular position filled—let's say, in the strings, perhaps even as concertmaster—and a teen-age player may not be able to do the job. '(But there are, in fact, only eight players who are thirty or over.)

Auditions for the Civic are held every spring and every autumn. They are not just to fill seats in the Civic. They are to reconstitute the orchestra: everybody in the orchestra has to reaudition to prove that he or she deserves the seat more than somebody coming in from the outside who's auditioning for the first time. "No one is 'in.' There's no politics. There's no insurance except your own ability," says Peters. "If you can't compete—if you can't play well enough to get into and continue in the Civic, then you're fooling yourself. You'd certainly never be able to get into a professional orchestra because the competition is enormous."

Though many of the players come to the Civic as longtime students, and perhaps even skilled musicians, they do not often know much about life and playing in a symphony orchestra. Indeed, tuning forks are handed out to some of them so that they'll capture the sound of the A in order to bring the instrument closer to orchestral tuning—before they get onstage. "About 90 to 95 percent of the players who come in here haven't the slightest notion of style or orchestral interpretation, and you just can't be a professional musician without that." The reason is that private teachers are concerned with teaching fundamentals and basic technique, and the music schools don't have enough good students to make up a symphony orchestra. So that is why the best of the incoming students have little experience in playing in an orchestra; they know nothing about ensemble playing and two of the most important specifications of symphonic playing—sight-reading ("this takes 60 percent of our time") and knowing the repertory. "I'd say at least 80 percent of them are doing these works for the first time," Peters says. So he and Miss Hillis have to teach them as well as conduct them. "It's an arduous task but ultimately there's a—oh, let's call it a certain rawness. The orchestra is untarnished. It's a jewel, a diamond just out of the ground." He gives it a quick polish and the kids respond to his efforts: one Chicago critic listened to the Civic and pronounced it "Chicago's third orchestra of note"—after the Chicago Symphony Orchestra and the Grant Park Symphony Orchestra. "I think our orchestra plays with a fair degree of refinement," says Peters. "Certainly not something like the Chicago Symphony Orchestra. But it has an emotionalism. It's a spark, a charge, it's a thrill. And you can't get that from any older orchestra."

Gordon Peters, principal percussionist.

The only compromise he makes in a choice of programs is to avoid what the Chicago Symphony is doing in any one season. And to try to get works which represent the whole span of classical works, from the earliest effort to up-to-date compositions. "But we don't hedge on the difficulties of the work," says Peters. "There isn't anything here that is in any way watered down. If anything, there are a couple of programs here that are harder than the average professional orchestra program. It gives incentive. And if it isn't perfect in the performance, it really means nothing in the end if there's an occasional wrong note because our first criterion is to teach the orchestra."

He involves the conductors of the Chicago Symphony—both guests and principals—in the teaching experience. "We've had Giulini and Leinsdorf and Steinberg—many of the big names in conducting," he says. "And they come very willingly, I must say. And with no fee. And many of them—Boulez spent two hours with them. This was before he had the New York Philharmonic post. He related beautifully to them—he has a fantastic ear. Abbado who is coming soon will spend two hours with them. It's a remarkable thing, expecially when you get an international conductor. The orchestra is so pent up they really sound extraordinary. The adrenalin is something extraordinary. I couldn't believe Solti's rehearsal with them last year. He did two hours of *Eroica* with them. It was incredible."

The teaching of the guest conductors is augmented by the day-to-day, week-to-week instruction of the principals from the Chicago Symphony. For they spend, as individuals, two to four hours every week with the youngsters who are learning the orchestral use of their instruments. Thus they get an angle of vision, through instruction as a section, that they could never get through instruction as individuals.

In his own instruction of the Civic, Gordon Peters finds an area between the technique of the principals and those of the Great Conductors with their own orchestras.

"Silly! Silly! Silly cellos! Can't you hear that the clarinets have the melody here? You have pianissimo and you just play away so loudly 'woo-o-o, woo-o-o woo-o-o." Or to the concertmaster: "Don't you have double stops there? Why do you play a single line of notes?" Or to the orchestra in general: "I hear an A from someone. Nobody should be playing an A at this point." From time to time he calls out—in the appropriate moment—"*Subitement, moins animé*" which translates as "Put on the brakes, kids."

This is far more chatter than most conductors would dare unload on the Chicago Symphony. But, says Peters, "There are times when you must talk. Sure, there are those people who talk too much in the professional situation. In the student situation, you stop for what has to be done and told. And what cannot be told with the stick has to be told with the mouth. That has to be the priority. So that as time goes on in a rehearsal period for a particular performance, there's less talk and more playing, as you approach the degree of refinement that you're seeking."

The Civic runs two rehearsals every week, on Tuesdays and Fridays from 5 P.M. to 7 P.M. "Which is the low point of the day, dietetically and psychologically," says Peters. The rehearsals are conducted usually after the players have put in a full day's labor elsewhere, either in school or at work. And the rehearsals sometimes take place under conditions more difficult than that experienced by the parent Chicago Symphony Orchestra. "Sometimes," says Peters, "a guest conductor won't come in until Wednesday to start rehearsing with the Chicago Symphony Orchestra for a Thursday program. You can put these things together that fast with a professional orchestra." But not, he thinks, with a student orchestra.

Even so, the Chicago Civic Orchestra is a coveted target of a good many conductors and soloists. The Civic needs them. It puts on about a dozen programs a year including a summer music program and a chamber music series. Gordon Peters will conduct some of them. Margaret Hillis will conduct others. They get guest conductors for the others and soloists from outside for some of them. In this season, for example, the soloists for five of the first six programs would be players who rose out of the Chicago Civic Orchestra and its soloist contests; the other was placed by a New York management agency which sought to give one of its clients exposure with a Chicago orchestra before a Chicago audience before he made a formal debut with the Philadelphia Orchestra. The guest conductors also seek a certain exposure: management agents come to Chicago to see them, the press comes to review them, the hierarchy of American music—obviously including those in control of the Chicago Symphony and the Ravinia festival—come to examine them. This year, the guest conductors would include men who run the BBC Orchestra of Wales, and the Symphony Orchestra in Hamilton, Ontario, Canada, and the St. Louis Symphony—the last-named conductor was guest with the Vienna Symphony, the orchestra run by Carlo Maria Giulini. The men who've conducted the Civic in the past have gone on to such posts as conductor of the Milwaukee Symphony and the Kansas City Philharmonic, and resident conductor of the Cincinnati Symphony.

The program and the import of guest conductors are difficult for the eyes and the ears of the young and inexperienced symphony players. For them, Peters has one word of advice: "try to keep going and don't get lost."

The rehearsal that Peters was conducting back in Chicago during tour week was for a program a month distant. It embraced Bach's Symphony no. 4, a Sibelius violin concerto, and a Bartók concerto for orchestra. By the time he got back, the weather had changed. On the day that he and the Chicago Symphony had landed in New York, the temperature was on its way to the upper 70s. "What is this?" asked Pete Hamill in the *New York Post*. "Where is the snow? Why doesn't the wind blow off the North River, icing the streets, freezing the bones? No matter. Forget Nixon. Forget criminals. Forget the end of America. Maybe it's time to tend private gardens." But by the time that Peters got back to New York, the weather had settled into a deep winter chill though New Yorkers, beguiled by the occasional sight of the sun, still wandered in Central Park, dodging the bicycles and the muggers.

In a suite whose bedroom overlooked Central Park, Georg Solti was wrestling this day with the wake of a week-long problem: he had to find a replacement for guest conductor Thomas Schippers. Schippers, music director of the Cincinnati Symphony, was to have conducted the Chicago Symphony in mid-December. Suddenly he underwent a chest operation for surgical repair of esophageal constrictions and a hiatus hernia. John Edwards learned of the surgery only just before the New York tour opened. He was called by Columbia Artists, the management-agents for Schippers, and was told that Schippers would be out of action for at least two months. "They started right off by saying they do not have anybody else to suggest," says Edwards. That struck some as strange, for Columbia manages a name familiar to many Chicago concertgoers: James Levine, the principal conductor of the Metropolitan Opera and the music director of the Ravinia Festival near Chicago. It just happened that Levine would be on vacation in the week that Schippers was to play—yet there was no mention by Columbia of Levine or his availability. There was, to be sure, some question whether the Chicago Symphony could or would bring him in, given the symphony's policy of not treading on Ravinia's conductorial grounds. But the important thing was that Columbia management did not venture to mention his vacation of that week; there were some people in Chicago inclined to remember that reserve. To replace Schippers, Solti had been advised—as we've seen—to turn instead to young John Nelson. ("My manager called me up and said, 'How would you like to guest with the Chicago Symphony?' " says Nelson. "Of course, I had heart failure.") The question then was what he would develop for a program. The scheduled program was specially designed and built for Schippers. It consisted of Cherubini's Symphony in D, Shostakovich's Symphony no. 5, and Barber's *Medea's Meditation and Dance of Vengeance*. This week Nelson would talk with Solti and Edwards about the program. "They said I didn't have to take his program—I said I *could* take it if you wish," says Nelson. "His program was one that I was basically unfamiliar with. I could have learned it if I had to, but I preferred to do my own program. They said, 'It is absolutely your show.' So I submitted a program to them, and Mr. Solti said, 'With one exception we will accept it.' " He suggested that Nelson—as a young American conductor—would want to play a work by an American composer. Nelson took the suggestion. He named one piece that would exploit the Chicago brass; as it turned out the scores would come late and the principals felt they had no time to learn the solos in it. It is the fate of the guest conductor, particularly the one who is spontanteously summoned: he can have his choice of programs, subject to the desires of the music director and the inclination of the principals. In any case, in his conversations with Solti, he laid out a program of Dvořák's Symphony no. 6 and Stravinsky's *Petrouchka*, and—after the first proposal for an American work foundered—he elected to play Ives's *The Unanswered Question*.

Solti's own skills in building a program were reflected in the Saturday night program in Carnegie Hall. He'd played the Mahler Sixth Symphony alone —nothing else on the program—in Chicago. Now he paired it with the Bach Suite no. 3. Thus the one program in Carnegie Hall would reflect the skills of the Chicago Symphony in presenting the small, precise genius of Bach—the chamber music skills—against the huge, crashing sonorities of Mahler.

The technique fed the appetites of his New York audience. There were no boos this time, no raucous voices of criticism. After the Bach suite he was called back for ten bows. After the Mahler symphony he was called back for ten bows. Wave after wave of applause swept through Carnegie Hall and the pounding—à la Paris —cries of "Sol-TI! Sol-TI!" welled up from the audience. For fifteen minutes, it seemed that the galleries would never move. Then slowly people began filing out. One player looked up quizzically. "After the Mahler Eighth in Chicago," he said, "he took nineteen bows."

The New York appearances ended in precisely the way that Solti and the Chicago Symphony hoped they would.

Desmond Shawe-Taylor, writing in *The New Yorker*, reflected the view by describing the Mahler performance as being "of such blazing power, precision, and beauty of detail that it will long remain in the memory of those present. . . . It is hard to believe that the most dedicated Mahlerian could have resisted this Carnegie Hall performance. Every page of the huge work demonstrated the unanimity, brilliance, and musicality of the Chicago players, and the performance had also the special character of complete conviction from first to last. It was all meaningful. The hard grinding sonorities of the first movement; the idyllic nature of the Andante; the grotesque, almost gruesome black humor of the Scherzo—all these were stated by conductor and orchestra with the certainty that admits of no doubt. As for the vast Finale, it swung between aspiration and bottomless despair, until the famous third hammer blow brought the tragic but not pathetic, end."

There was to be yet one more effort in this season with Solti. It would be in Washington. It would be a relaxing counterpoint to the past two weeks.

One reason was that all the players had gotten together at the New York Sheraton when the symphony came back from Connecticut. Thus there was no strain in getting to and from Carnegie Hall on Saturday night, there was no strain in getting picked up by the bus on Sunday morning—all those who were going to go would find the buses leaving from the New York Sheraton at 10:15 on a Sunday morning. Time enough for breakfast and church—for those who were interested in either.

Another reason is that not all were going. The orchestra would play Beethoven's Third Symphony and Beethoven's Eighth Symphony in Washington. Not all the brass were needed—roughly half the horns and trumpets would make the trip —and not all the percussion. They would fly home via commercial airliner from New York on Sunday afternoon.

The orchestra itself would also go by commercial airliner. For this leg of the trip would be made by scheduled airline flights—from La Guardia to Washington, then after the concert, from Washington to Chicago. (The itinerary read: "24 first class, 96 tourist.") There would be no meals served on the plane: the airline was unaccustomed to having 120 passengers in one group on a one-hour-plus flight on a Sunday noon. But there would be box lunches, especially ordered and placed in each seat by the tour committee and by management. So the players could eat lightly three hours before the concert.

At La Guardia, the routine was changed ever so slightly. The players had to show special tabs and be checked in at the gate. There they encountered a rare specimen: a woman who was a True Passenger, not part of the tour. Moreover, she was a True Passenger in the first-class section. Except there was no room for her in the first-class section. The airline had neglected to tell her this small detail when it had accepted her reservation for the first-class section. It neglected again to mention this small detail when she confirmed the reservation on Saturday. So she'd been sold a first-class ticket with room only in tourist. "Ah have *nevah*," she said in Scarlett O'Hara overtones, "*evah* ridden in a seat in an airplane that wasn't in the first-class section." Today she would ride tourist, if she would ride at all. With this many people occupying the plane, the airline didn't much care what she did.

The bus had gotten everybody to the gate a good forty-five minutes ahead of time. Victor Aitay was in the swirl, carrying his violin as a protection against thieves. "Only in America. Not in Europe," he said. "Somehow I feel more secure in Europe." Frank Miller and Milton Preves were talking about the next performance of the Chicago Symphony String Quartet—"in the Public Library," said Preves, "next Sunday." The bridge players were at it again: any time they had more than thirty seconds of waiting time, they got the game going again—on overturned luggage, on the seat cushions, on the edges of desks.

All are equal in their enthusiasms for the game but the most equal of all was Joe Galon. He is a dark-visaged, highly verbal man of forty-three who makes his own yogurt in the morning, swims up to half a mile in the apartment-building pool every night, was one of the precocious youngsters of the late 1940s (he graduated from the University of Chicago at the age of nineteen), and who survived the multiple ambitions of his youth. ("I was determined that I was going to be a professional violinist and a professional baseball player and then I got interested in acting—I figured I would play violin during the winter season, I would play baseball during the summer season, and at night I would be on the stage acting.)"

He turned out to be neither actor nor ballplayer, but instead became a professional violinist. He is, today, the first chair man among the second violins and, as such, a symbol of the care and authority that the Chicago Symphony invests in the often forgotten dimension of symphonic care. For Joe Golan was once one of the smothered prodigies of symphonic music: he was twenty-two years old when he joined the orchestra, and then, under the system of the time, he put his time in among the second violins—eleven years altogether. He won a change—in those days it was considered a promotion—to the first violins. Then, after six years with the first, he sought an audition to go back to the second violins. As first chair man, of course—as successor to John Weicher.

That was more than four years ago and he can still remember the trial and the reaction. He was one of eight members of the Chicago Symphony to get first crack at the job ("which is something that we achieved in our contracts, instead of always bringing in somebody from the outside"). He was the third man of the eight to play the first round of the auditions. He was one of the two men asked to go into the finals. But by that time, he'd cooled off; there'd been a wait of several hours. Now he encountered a curious personal reaction. He is not normally nervous, no matter how tough the test in performing. But in auditioning, things are different: "I have a reaction which is very damaging," he says. "My hands become very cold and sticky. Of course, for a violinist this is a terrible plague. It cuts down my efficiency considerably. When I play solo in an audition-type situation, I really am playing at about 42 percent efficiency. I would have to work twice as hard as normal to get half as far ahead. My hands become just like ice. They are just freezing and very sticky. I fight it by warming up—it is not cured, but at least I put a blanket on it and it helps me through the period somewhat. I am still somewhat handicapped but I sweat through it."

So, faced with sticky, ice-cold hands, he asked his colleague and competitor to take the first tryout in the final round so that he, Golan, could get warmed up. The competitor declined; he'd just performed and he was warmed up and he wanted to see how Golan would do, particularly without a warm-up. They finally flipped a coin and the competitor won. "You go first," he told Golan. "My hands were cold and getting colder by the moment. From nerves," says Golan. "So what I did—and this was totally spontaneous . . ."

What he did was go out and play jazz for the opening of the audition. He likes jazz and he likes improvising—in contrast to the symphonic discipline—and he thought that if he could so some jazz improvisations he might get his fingers unglued. "I thought I'd be most at ease under this," he says. Solti had no objection—"I was prepared for him, for any conductor, to say, 'Let's not play games; let's play Bach or Beethoven and get down to business.' " After listening to ten or fifteen minutes of Golan's jazz improvisations, Solti said, "All right, Mr. Golan. You have established yourself in the key of D minor. Now how about the key of D major—the concerto of Beethoven?" By that time, Golan was warmed up—and he played the requested symphonic repertory well enough to win the audition. "But I always felt that this business of improvisation, which was totally foreign to the orchestral situation, helped me get the job."

He is not only a leader of the second violins but an outstanding interpreter of the role of the second violins. For in the Chicago Symphony, the second violins are different from but equal to the first violins; they are not stigmatized—as in many orchestras—as being poorer players than the first violins. "In an orchestra as great as the Chicago Symphony, where you get the best players in the world to fill the chairs for first or second violin," he says, "You need not worry about having weak sisters that you so often see elsewhere in the second violins. So that is not as real a difference as it is a psychological difference in the audience."

The way that Solti and the Chicago Symphony members look at it is that the second violin is not an inferior player but a different instrument. Says Golan: "You can think of it as a different instrument just as you would think of the bass and cello and violas as being a different instrument," says Golan. "The orchestral composer calls upon a depth to the string section which includes a number of strata; to that extent the second violins fill the role between the violas and the first violins. It is just like color in a spectrum; it is not necessarily better or worse, as far as skills are concerned."

The musical material is different, but not always. "There are many times when the first and second violins are doing exactly the same thing," says Golan. "I mean truly identical, as if it was one big violin section. There are many times when the first and second violins are playing practically the same thing except that they are in harmony. Usually the first violins being higher pitched than the second violins, such as the first and second sopranos in a chorus. Many times the first and second violins are in octaves, but otherwise doing the same thing—the first violins an octave above the second violins. On rare occasions, the roles will be reversed, with the first violins playing under the second violins in pitch and even dynamically. A frequent device is to have the first and second violins playing countermelodies against each other—they intertwine or answer one another: the first violins play a musical statement and they are answered by the second violins, either identically or as an echo or maybe in a different key. There are times when the second violins

Joseph Golan, principal second violinist.

will accompany either the first violins or another section of the orchestra. I mean they are in a secondary or supportive role, such as a singer accompanying himself on a guitar, you know, playing chords and rhythm."

All this is not generally perceptible to the audience unless it is following a score. What are perceptible are the demands on the skill of the first violins. "The first violins are more likely to get up and play a solo, play a concerto," says Joe Golan. But the sound of the string section, leading up to and leading out of the solo would never be the same—without the second violins.

There is no ego-diminution for Joe Golan in being a second violin. Like many of the other first chair men, he plays in smaller ensembles, including a rock group—The Chicago Current—which he formed under the aegis of the Chicago Symphony. ("I like to improvise because it gives me a chance for personal expression.") He was concertmaster, under the conducting of Dale Clevenger, on a Sea World sound track during the work stoppage. He is a contractor on a great many of the jingles and commercials that the members of the symphony play —that is, he is the man contacted by the producers to line up the musical talent for the sound track. He is a section coach for the Chicago Civic Orchestra, working with both the first and second violins. And he is king of the bridge play-ers—"eighteen consecutive years with the same four guys," he says.

When the gates to the plane opened, the bridge game was closed. It would be resumed seconds later, on board. The flight itself was brief and uneventful —except for those nonorchestra persons on board. They couldn't comprehend just what kind of "tour" was made up mostly of men in their middle or advanced years—men who were not boisterous, bothersome, who were so obviously quite self-possessed. And yet men who acted like men anywhere: some of the players set about making sure that all the other passengers on the plane got box lunches since the airline itself wasn't serving a meal. And so a massive trading and giveaway program began, somewhat spontaneously, on the plane.

When the orchestra got to the Kennedy Center, they found their trunks awaiting them and their equipment already set up onstage. For the stagehands had had, if anything, a more difficult time of it than the players in the late stages of this tour. They got into Manhattan at noon Saturday—on the return from Connecticut —and immediately made the setup for the orchestra in Carnegie Hall. After the Saturday night performance, they worked until 1:30 in the morning, striking the set and loading everything back on the trucks. The trucks began the rush via highway down to Washington while the stagehands caught a little sleep. Then they were up at 5:30 A.M. to catch a train to Washington so that they could get into Kennedy Center in plenty of time to unload the trucks and set up the equipment onstage one last time.

It was cloudy and cold in Washington but the reception to the music of the Chicago Symphony Orchestra was warm and easy. The fiery edge of the orchestra seemed somewhat muted, perhaps from the calisthenics of the tour or, indeed, of the last three weeks. ("The orchestra's vast reservoir of power was leashed all afternoon," wrote critic Paul Hume in *The Washington Post*, "expressing itself rather in restraint and balance appropriate to the music.") The liveliest moment came in the second movement of the *Eroica*. Conductor Solti got so exercised that he lost his baton and it went flying off among the second violins. But the stage manager had carefully placed an extra one on his music stand so—after conducting a few moments with his hands—he was able to reach down, pick up the reserve, and continue as before.

In the intermission, he called the players together in the corridor. He would not see them again in this season; he was flying back to New York while the orchestra was flying on to Chicago. "I want to thank you very much," he said of the season that was closing. "It has been much hard work, very much hard work." There were the moments when the sense of last things was appearing. He talked for a few more minutes. Then with a last good-bye, he said "Thank you" once more and disappeared into his dressing room.

There were a few minutes more of work. The last of the Beethoven—until spring. When it was over, Solti took five bows and walked offstage. "Too much music!" he said, almost to himself. "Too much misic!"

His listeners didn't think so. In his last paragraph—the final punctuation mark on this season with Solti—Paul Hume wrote of Solti and the Chicago Symphony: "The nobility of his reading placed Solti in the direct line of greatness that has led this orchestra in this same music from Theodore Thomas through Frederick Stock and Fritz Reiner to today's singular pinnacle."

The Weeks of Giulini

The next morning, Georg Solti flew back to London. His season in Chicago —the autumn season—was ended. He went as he came: worrying about a cold. ("I got it back again—I am hoarse, as you can hear. . . . Everybody in my family has had colds. My wife had a cold, my two daughters had a cold, housekeeper had a cold, Eileen the secretary had a cold, only Jill the nanny did not have a cold.") In London he would rest for a few days. Then he would go to Paris to take up his duties with L'Orchestre de Paris. He would take it on a tour to Switzerland; the later tour in China would be canceled—"political problems," Solti explained —and the orchestra would go instead to Spain and Portugal. Later in the musical year, he would quietly give up his post as music director of L'Orchestre de Paris. He could not, he felt, carry the load of running two orchestras on two continents. He would, of course, fulfill his years-long commitment in Paris: Daniel Barenboim would succeed him in September 1975.

Thus the season in Chicago was over for Solti.

But it was not over for the Chicago Symphony Orchestra. There was a month left of the autumn—a month of winter storms and guest conductors.

On the very day that Solti left for Europe, Giulini flew into Chicago from Europe. He would conduct the Chicago Symphony Orchestra for two weeks—"two golden weeks," in the words of one player. For the appearance of Giulini after the appearance of Solti is, for the Chicago Symphony Orchestra, literally a crème de la crème. "When you speak of Solti, you speak of respect, of admiration," says one violinist. "When you speak of Giulini, you speak of love."

The love is found not only in the graceful flow of Giulini's music but in the warm affection of his personality. In his first few days in Chicago, he would make sure that he saw and personally spoke to every player in the orchestra, exploring their families and their feelings since last he saw them; to Solti, many of the players are faces that he connects to sound—"we got a new young cello player; good, she is very good"—but not to feelings. At least not so obviously as does Giulini.

"I have a great human contact with this orchestra—everything is a great affection with these people," he explained in his gentle Latin accents. He said that he did not feel he is making music as a conductor when he is with them; it is more intimate and spontaneous, as if he were playing with them in a chamber music group. "And I think this orchestra is the most intelligent of all," he went on. "The intelligence of this orchestra is something that always surprised me. Because they have such quick reactions and they act so fast in getting the point. You really need only to say in a small gesture, a movement of the baton, the hand; they are very immediate to understand what you mean. The time between asking for something and getting it is perfect."

There is an intellectual process as well as an emotional one to the music that Giulini evokes. It is not all spontaneous and lacking analysis. Donald Peck, the flutist, knows exactly what he does to produce the Giulini sound, and the Solti sound—as do most of the other members of the orchestra. "For Solti," he says, "you play the flute with tighter lips, with a smaller lip opening. Or you may curl in the flute so that the embouchure opening is smaller. And then when Giulini comes, and you want to sound deeper and darker, you roll out the embouchure and open your throat more. If you open the throat at the back, it darkens the sound and makes it fuller. If you close it up, it thins the sound out. It is a matter of syllables in your throat. If you say 'e' you have a different opening in your throat, and of course you get a different sound, than if you were saying 'ah' or 'uh-h-h.' This is something the Giulinis, the Soltis, the good conductors evoke from you—the quality of their sound."

The two weeks of Giulini would be transcendent in their music. And when it was over, he would go as he came—gentle, grave, affectionate, elegant. "I am at an age now where I have no ambition at all. Just to make good music. Nothing for myself. Nothing as a conductor. Only as a musician. If I can do good music, I am happy."

The Season of the Guests

The weeks that followed were filled by other guest conductors—Michael Gielen, John Nelson, Henry Mazer. They would also be filled with the controversy and contradictions that follow in the wake of great music.

The most dramatic example was the week in which John Nelson filled in for the stricken Thomas Schippers.

When the morning papers appeared, the critics took totally opposite views.

"The most significant happening of the fall music season," wrote Thomas Willis in the *Chicago Tribune*. "Not since Seiji Ozawa's Ravinia substitution for Georges Prêtre has there been a first appearance of like magnitude."

"He was plainly out of his depth," wrote Robert C. Marsh in the Chicago Sun-Times. *". . . has no business being before an orchestra of the rank of ours."*

"We have been introduced to an American conductor of major stature, more immediately persuasive than James Levine or Michael Tilson Thomas," wrote Willis.

"For a start, he has the manner and temperament of a reference librarian, and he leads the musicians with prim baton patterns that might serve as textbook illustrations but in fact do not produce firm orchestral control or provide the basis for genuinely exciting interchanges between the performers and their leader," wrote Marsh.

"On the basis of this performance, I can say without fear of contradiction that Nelson is as skillful and exciting a musician in this repertory as he is reputed to be in operatic and choral literature," wrote Willis. "Everything he did Thursday crackled with a rarely encountered high voltage combination of intellect, technical proficiency, and contagious regard for the potential of each melody."

"As a whole, the major shortcoming of this performance was simply dullness," wrote Marsh. "As Nelson was busily counting beats, he seemed to forget that he should also be shaping phrases, marking accents, and making use of the wide

range of color Stravinsky suggests and the musicians were ready to provide."

"In Stravinsky's *Petrouchka*, he matched a dry wine selection of tonal balances with a comprehensive undertaking of the ballet's exquisite interlocking rhythmic relationships," wrote Willis. "The basic fast tempo was a little rushed, to be sure, but the whole performance—complete, 1974 version—was as metrically clear and well-knit as any I have heard."

"To close the evening he chose the Symphony No. 6 of Dvořák, warm, flowing lyric music that he projected successfully as long as he was able to keep it moving," wrote Marsh. "Unfortunately, in the development of the first move-ment, and some later moments, the lyric energy of the performance seemed to run out. In the final two movements, when a firm sense of pulse and drive was called for, they were never fully developed, although the work was sustained reasonably well."

"It was Dvořák's D Major Symphony—Opus 60, now labeled as his Sixth—that provided proof positive of his talent," wrote Willis. "A melodious work which juxtaposes Beethoven heroics, Brahms counterpoint, and folk-like songs of sur-passing sweetness, the Sixth is for good reason only seldom played. Only a gifted conductor can make it hang together. Playing safe simply doesn't work. Nelson took the risks, turning phrase endings in the Adagio with subtlety, providing delicately articulated contrasts in the Scherzo, and searching out just the right tempo for the heroic finale."

The orchestra itself was just as divided. In the evaluation sheets that the orchestra makes up on every guest conductor, twenty-six players gave him above average to excellent marks on his knowledge of the score (out of the forty-seven players who made out an evaluation sheet). But only five gave him similarly high marks for his "Knowledge of the Orchestra," and only four gave him high marks for his rehearsal technique. The feeling was that Nelson had stopped the orchestra a little too often and talked to it a little too much. After the soaring musical eloquence of Solti and Giulini, the Chicago Symphony was not prepared for being talked to by a relatively young and inexperienced conductor. "He needs to learn some humility when conducting a great orchestra," wrote one player in the comment section of the evaluation sheet.

Meanwhile, life went on in all its dimensions—earthy and otherwise—for the members of the orchestra.

Gordon Peters went on working on the revision of his college thesis, "Treatise on Percussion." He'd revised 159 pages and when it was done, he would print it and publish it himself. He felt there was a market of several thousand copies for the book. "There's more I would like to do . . . Two and a half years I spent on this project. But one thing I feel happy about: it has some validity."

Fred Spector, the violinist, figured out how to use the ten-foot-high stained-glass windows leaning against the stairway of his home. A friend had saved them for him from a church that was being torn down in Tipton, Iowa, and he drove to Tipton, jammed the two huge frames into a Volkswagen station wagon, and drove back to Glencoe with them. Then he discovered he had a problem. "They are exactly ten feet, two inches high," he says, "and our ceilings are ten feet high."

But now he knew how he'd fit the extra large into a "large": he'd cut the bottom plate of the frame off, have an iron foundry make two steel bases for the window—"which I'll install"—and with two inches of metal, not glass, eliminated, "I'll be able to fit them right in here."

Jimmy Vrhel, the bass player, was planning his annual Christmas trip down to the family citrus fruit property near Brownsville, Texas. "One-third of the crop has been picked now," he says. "The rest will be in during the next few months." He and his family would market the fruit—principally a grapefruit called "ruby red blush"—in gift packages for the Christmas trade. So there'd be a lot of shipping out of grapefruit just before Christmas. "Get $150 a ton for grapefruit when you sell it as gift packages," he says.

Burl Lane, the contrabassoonist, had decided to explore a change in career: during the winter season, he'd start studying law—though he'd continue to play in the orchestra. There were many reasons for it. "Accidents can happen to you. —you know, losing the use of one finger, having teeth knocked out accidentally, or a combination of these things spells the end." Or: "I have accomplished what I wanted to accomplish and now I want to accomplish something else." Or: "To tell the truth, I am just getting tired of making reeds."

Sam Denov almost missed entering law school this next semester. He'd been bothered with abdominal pains, off and on, for several years and now they became serious enough to cause him to miss two weeks of the season and enter the hospital for observation. The doctors found a singular problem: "I have an extra foot of the large intestine that's curled back in the abdomen," he says. Some day, perhaps, he may undergo surgery to correct the problem. In the meantime, he's taking a vegetable bulk-producing agent—and going about his life as always. He entered John Marshall Law School with Burl Lane—"we sit next to each other in class"—and he is spending three nights a week and Saturday afternoons there, in addition to his work with the orchestra. "It'll probably take me four years to finish," he says.

Not everybody was so fortunate.

David Greenbaum, the little Scots-born cellist with a vast gift for humor and for imitation, fell seriously ill with a cardiac condition. He was in intensive care in the hospital for many weeks and, when he was released, he could no longer continue with the orchestra. And so he retired to California, where he died shortly thereafter.

Paul Kahn, a first violinist who'd been tutor and teacher to concertmasters in the Chicago Symphony and many other major orchestras—and who'd just married a beautiful young girl this season—came to a concert on Saturday night complaining of pain in his left arm. He left at the intermission and went to a hospital. There it was discovered that he was suffering from a heart attack. He felt better on Monday but was persuaded not to leave the hospital. On Tuesday, he suffered a massive cardiac incident and died. He was fifty-seven years old.

The cadence quieted now. But the measureless beat of time—of the minutiae of men and their music—went on. Solti would return in the winter and again in the spring. But there would be a difference. A maturity. A coming of age. He had been called in years past to preside over a crisis to which no answers were clear. He had resolved the crisis of the Chicago Symphony Orchestra and he had brought it to greatness. He did not do it alone. He could not do it alone. But he had set out on his course believing that he understood the forces shaping music and the men who made it, and that he could influence, and even compel the partnership of the men who spoke to those forces. He was right. He had opened up new visions and vast miracles for the Chicago Symphony Orchestra, and—in the details of their day-to-day lives—summoned them to the glory that is their music—as it is known around the world.

INDEX